HD60 .E587 2006

Entrepreneurship as
 social change
    c2006.

MW01120482

2009 03 13

Humber College Library
3199 Lakeshore Blvd. West
Toronto, ON   M8V 1K8

Entrepreneurship as Social Change

165101

Entrepreneurship as Social Change

A Third Movements in Entrepreneurship Book

Edited by

Chris Steyaert

University of St Gallen, Switzerland

and

Daniel Hjorth

Copenhagen Business School, Denmark, and ESBRI and Växjö University, Sweden

esbri

In association with ESBRI

Edward Elgar

Cheltenham, UK • Northampton, MA, USA

© Chris Steyaert and Daniel Hjorth 2006

All rights reserved. No part of this publication may be reproduced, stored in a retrieval system or transmitted in any form or by any means, electronic, mechanical or photocopying, recording, or otherwise without the prior permission of the publisher.

Published by
Edward Elgar Publishing Limited
Glensanda House
Montpellier Parade
Cheltenham
Glos GL50 1UA
UK

Edward Elgar Publishing, Inc.
William Pratt House
9 Dewey Court
Northampton
Massachusetts 01060
USA

A catalogue record for this book
is available from the British Library

Library of Congress Cataloging in Publication Data
   Entrepreneurship as social change : a third new movements in
   entrepreneurship book / edited by Chris Steyaert, Daniel Hjorth.
       p. cm.
   Includes bibliographical references and index.
   1. Social entrepreneurship. 2. Social change. I. Steyaert, Chris. II.
   Hjorth, Daniel.

   HD60.E587 2006
   338'.04—dc22   2006011134

ISBN-13: 978 1 84542 366 7
ISBN-10: 1 84542 366 6

Typeset by Cambrian Typesetters, Camberley, Surrey
Printed and bound in Great Britain by MPG Books Ltd, Bodmin, Cornwall

Contents

List of figures   vii
List of tables   viii
List of contributors   ix
Foreword and acknowledgements   xi

Introduction: what is social in social entrepreneurship?   1
Chris Steyaert and Daniel Hjorth

PART ONE: CONCEPTS OF SOCIAL ENTREPRENEURSHIP

1. Social entrepreneurship: the view of the young Schumpeter   21
   Richard Swedberg
2. The practice of social entrepreneurship: notes toward a
   resource-perspective   35
   Yohanan Stryjan
3. Communities in the global economy: where social and
   indigenous entrepreneurship meet   56
   Robert B. Anderson, Benson Honig and Ana Maria Peredo
4. Location and relocation, visions and revisions: opportunities
   for social entrepreneurship   79
   Ellen S. O'Connor
5. Public entrepreneurship: moving from social/consumer to
   public/citizen   97
   Daniel Hjorth and Björn Bjerke
6. The rhetoric of social entrepreneurship: paralogy and new
   language games in academic discourse   121
   Pascal Dey

PART TWO: CONTEXTS OF SOCIAL CHANGE

7. Entrepreneurship, shifting life orientations and social change
   in the countryside   145
   Denise Fletcher and Tony Watson
8. Women, Mother Earth and the business of living   165
   Kathryn Campbell

9. The dynamics of community identity making in an industrial
district: the spirit of Gnosjö revisited 188
Bengt Johannisson and Caroline Wigren

10. Entrepreneurship as boundary work: deviating from and
belonging to community 210
Monica Lindgren and Johann Packendorff

11. Discursive diversity in fashioning entrepreneurial identity 231
Karin Berglund

12. City of enterprise, city as prey? On urban entrepreneurial spaces 251
Timon Beyes

Notes 271
References 277
Index 317

List of figures

1.1   Economic change and social entrepreneurship, according to
      the young Schumpeter   34
2.1   Modes of conversion and reproduction   54
3.1   The global economy, after Anderson et al. (2003)   73
5.1   From social/consumer to public/citizen   102
7.1   The relationship between social change and entrepreneurs and
      their clients 'becoming other'   152

List of tables

1.1 The Man of Action and the Non-Entrepreneurial Person,
    according to the young Schumpeter   29
2.1 The enterprises: activity and resource mix   47
2.2 The team: members and strategies   50
3.1 The characteristics of aboriginal economic development,
    adapted from Anderson and Giberson (2004, p. 142)   57
9.1 Participants in social worlds – a typology   195
9.2 The outsider as an insurgent   203

List of contributors

Robert B. Anderson, University of Regina, robert.anderson@uregina.ca

Karin Berglund, Mälardalen University, karin.berglund@mdh.se

Timon Beyes, University of St Gallen, timon.beyes@unisg.ch

Björn Bjerke, Malmö University, bjorn.bjerke@ts.mah.se

Kathryn Campbell, Trent University, kcampbell@trentu.ca

Pascal Dey, University of St Gallen, pascal.dey@unisg.ch

Denise Fletcher, University of Sheffield, denise.fletcher@sheffield.ac.uk

Daniel Hjorth, Copenhagen Business School & Växjö University, dhj.lpf@cbs.dk

Benson Honig, Wilfrid Laurier University, bhonig@wlu.ca

Bengt Johannisson, Växjö University, bengt.johannisson@vxu.se

Monica Lindgren, KTH – Royal Institute of Technology, monica.lindgren@indek.kth.se

Ellen S. O'Connor, University of Paris Dauphine, o_connor_ellen@hotmail.com

Johann Packendorff, KTH – Royal Institute of Technology, johann.packendorff@indek.kth.se

Ana Maria Peredo, University of Victoria, aperedo@uvic.ca

Chris Steyaert, University of St Gallen, chris.steyaert@unisg.ch

Yohanan Stryjan, Södertörns högskola (Södertörn University College), yohanan.stryjan@sh.se

Richard Swedberg, Cornell University, rs328@cornell.edu

Tony Watson, Nottingham University Business School, tony.watson@nottingham.ac.uk

Caroline Wigren, Jönköping International Business School, caroline.wigren@ihh.hj.se

Foreword and acknowledgements

Entrepreneurship as Social Change is the third book in a miniseries of four publications called *Movements in Entrepreneurship*. The journey from a so-called writers' workshop to a publishable manuscript is a collective process wherein the quality of dialogue and conversation needs to develop into a focused and enriched book. A new movement in the field of entrepreneurship – in this case social entrepreneurship – is taken up for the purpose of a critical and crucial discussion that does not reproduce just more of the same (entrepreneurship), but rather creates a chance to change our understanding of entrepreneurship itself. Whether this book succeeds in accomplishing such a movement, we will leave up to the interested and critical readers. This cannot prevent us from acknowledging the committed efforts of many direct and indirect contributors that have made the transition from workshop to book a smooth and worthwhile endeavour.

With the theme of the 'earth' – after the ones of water (see *New Movements in Entrepreneurship*, Steyaert and Hjorth, 2003) and air (see *Narrative and Discursive Approaches in Entrepreneurship*, Hjorth and Steyaert, 2004) – we entered the site of the small and beautiful village of Tällberg, Sweden. The village resides on a slope looking down on Lake Siljan. Lake Siljan is one reminder of the third largest meteorite impact in our planet's history. Around 360 million years ago, a 4-km large meteor fell from space and had an enormous impact on the Earth here, making it a worthy place to explore the groundings of entrepreneurship. Close to Tällberg, we visited the extraordinary festival stage of Dalhalla, a former limestone quarry. The open mining in this area has created a natural amphitheatre – 400 m long, 175 m wide and 60 m deep. How this performance arena came about offers an excellent illustration of cultural entrepreneurship as social change, which was shared with the workshop participants through the intriguing story told by Per Frankelius (University of Örebro). We are grateful for his contribution. Furthermore, Ellen O'Connor (University of Paris Dauphine) and Tor Hernes (Norwegian School of Management BI) gave excellent keynotes to stimulate discussions. We would also like to thank all participants in the workshop including those whose contributions did not make it into the book. Many of the participants acted also as valuable reviewers for the papers of other authors during and after the workshop. We also acknowledge the valuable contribution of the external (anonymous) reviewers who helped us in sharpening the arguments of the different chapters. In particular, we would like to thank Magnus Aronsson who, as director of ESBRI, organized a flawless workshop event that made the whole experience pleasant and socially stimulating. The publisher Edward Elgar – especially Francine O'Sullivan and Jo Betteridge – have responded with patience and enthusiasm, two rare qualities that we value considerably in this cooperation. Finally, the editors' special 'thanks' go to Pascal Dey, whose intellectual and practical support in preparing the final manuscript has been invaluable.

Keep looking at the 'Movements', *Chris and Daniel*

Introduction: what is social in social entrepreneurship?

Chris Steyaert and Daniel Hjorth

This book investigates the social of social entrepreneurship: what is meant by connecting entrepreneurship with the social? How does the social make social entrepreneurship different from entrepreneurship, if at all? Is social entrepreneurship a new field within entrepreneurship research that needs its own theories and concepts? Or is it just an *epitheton ornans* and is it better to question any distinction between entrepreneurship and social entrepreneurship? Or, yet again, does the social appellation create new chances to probe into the sociality of entrepreneurship and into a (new) entrepreneuriality of society?

The title of this third *Movements in Entrepreneurship* book – *Entrepreneurship as Social Change* – suggests a probing answer in the form of claiming a double sociality for entrepreneurship. Firstly, the title indicates that entrepreneurship is connected to social change and societal transformation. This is an observation, belief and concept that has become popular in the recent rise in interest in social entrepreneurship, which we take up to inspect critically, yet affirmatively: how is social change understood, imagined and practiced? By connecting entrepreneurship with social change, we believe the platform or the 'space' of entrepreneurship becomes disclosed as part of society (Steyaert and Katz, 2004; Hjorth and Steyaert, 2003) and we can grasp the chance to look into the multidiscursive construction of entrepreneurship beyond any economic or progress-instrumentalist reductionism. However, some contend that the emergence of social entrepreneurship brings along rather a return to economic and economizing discourse and an intensification of managerial logic. This book examines this claim more closely, asks whether this is an inevitable evolution and inquires what alternative turns or twists can be formulated and tried out: this book asks what people to come, what society to come is unimagined in this dominant approach to 'social entrepreneurship', and brings such examples to our readers.

Secondly, the title puts forward a concept of entrepreneurship that says that entrepreneurship is a process based on the course of social change. By conceiving entrepreneurship as social change, we believe a possibility is created to inquire into the social nature of entrepreneurship and to switch the all-too-familiar inclination of the field of entrepreneurship to return to a possessive individualism for a broader social science view (Swedberg, 1999) that conceives entrepreneurship through concepts of sociality such as relation, community, social cauldron, legitimacy, spatiality, resistance, citizenship and the public. Also an opportunity exists here to alter the disciplinary hierarchy that has favoured theories from economics and (individualist) psychology and to connect with concepts and notions of less frequently visited disciplines and theoretical domains (Steyaert, 2005). This book then combines and inter-weaves two beliefs we think the rise in interest in social entrepreneurship enables us to explore, which can help to move the entire field of entrepreneurship: entrepreneurship is a complex social-creative process that influences, multiplies, transforms, re-imagines and alters the outlook of the space of society in which it is at once grounded and contextualized.

As a work in the series *Movements in Entrepreneurship*, this book hopes to create some movement itself. At a moment when the interest in social entrepreneurship booms in media, education and politics and is well on its way to becoming the next fad in entrepreneurship studies and business schools, we believe it well timed to engage with an in-depth inquiry into the social aspects of entrepreneurship and the surprisingly entrepreneurial aspects of society, and well placed to make possible a movement that brings social entrepreneurship out of its endangered position of fashionable topic for philanthropists, pensioned CEOs equipped with problem-fixing managerial tools, education programmers and social change engineers. The movement that might become possible is one that makes entrepreneurship social: that is, one that enables us to imagine and invent new possibilities, to contribute to its heterogeneity and democratic spread in society, and to reach out for the well-being of all on this earth. The movement from 'social entrepreneurship' to 'making entrepreneurship social' requires us to leave fixed understandings of entrepreneurship behind and to release its multiple versions: the becoming social of entrepreneurship and the becoming entrepreneurial of the social. As social entrepreneurship is not yet a solidified signifier, it might be possible to rescue and make public some of the less evident meanings that otherwise might remain at the margins of the currently academic and popular discourse of social entrepreneurship. In that sense, we hope the book to be programmatic, not as a definite plan with distinctive steps, but in the etymological sense of the Greek *programma*, meaning 'a written public notice', stemming from *prographein*, 'to write publicly'. In that sense, with this book, social entrepreneurship becomes written in the public domain (see the contributions of O'Connor and Hjorth and Bjerke below) and can become envisioned as a 'public matter'.

The argument of this introductory chapter evolves as follows. First, we will situate the thematics of this book on entrepreneurship as social change in the light of the recent rise of the phenomenon of social entrepreneurship and the increased attention being given to it. We summarize the types of interventions this book aims for, which we find important to secure some of the promises at the margins of the current discourse of social entrepreneurship. The goal is to indicate how entrepreneurship might become social. Second, we will relate the social of entrepreneurship to the metaphor and idea of the earth as the space where the social is not only grounded and contextualized but also changed and transformed. We find the idea of the earth pertinent as it does not carve out the social as disconnected from nature and can allow us to conceive new – read entrepreneurial – versions and understandings of the social. Third, we will give a commentated overview of the first section of this book that comprises the range of conceptual explorations in relation to the emergence of interest in social entrepreneurship. We will travel – move – between a refreshing reading of the early Schumpeter and a rhetorical analysis of the current academic literature on social entrepreneurship, exploring in between four empirical studies that question narrow conceptions of social entrepreneurship and try to engage with new theoretical formulations. Fourth, we will introduce the second section of this book that presents several contextual examples of how entrepreneurship can create and shape social change, which illustrate that the richness of empirical research opens up our understanding of the sociality of entrepreneurship rather than keeping it limited or frozen. We will travel – move – here between the countryside and nature, small towns and industrial districts and large cities and virtual spaces, indicating how social change has become initiated in various social settings, relationships and communities.

SURPRISING THE ACADEMIC FIELD OF ENTREPRENEURSHIP?

This book connects to the recent movement where social entrepreneurship has taken centre stage at a moment that the academic field of entrepreneurship is trying to emerge: as a distinctive field of research (Shane and Venkataraman, 2000), as a field that copes with its adolescence (Low, 2001), as a mature discipline that exploits its many years of exploratory research (Welsch and Liao, 2003) and as a field establishing a self-limiting discourse (Steyaert, 2005). There can be no sharper contrast than the one between the field of entrepreneurship contemplating how to limit and restrain itself and the unreserved and unrestrained enthusiasm for the phenomenon of social entrepreneurship that reminds one of the fervour and keenness of the newly arrived entrepreneurship scholars in the 1980s (Steyaert, 2005).

The 'rise' of the social entrepreneur (Leadbeater, 1997) and the 'spring' of social entrepreneurship seems unstoppable in academic attention, in practice and in policy-making. For instance, Gentile (2002) has pointed out in a review of the literature centred on the notion of 'social entrepreneur' that 75 per cent of those articles had been published in the last three years of a period of fifteen. Also social entrepreneurship should be more frequent than mainstream entrepreneurial activity, based on comparisons of socially entrepreneurial activity and total entrepreneurial activity presented in a UK-GEM study (Harding, 2004). In the US, non-profit organizations are the fastest-growing category of organizations (O'Connor, this volume). In policy-making and in political circles, social and civic entrepreneurs get central attention in those discussions on how to rebalance the role of government, businesses and civil society known as the so-called 'third way' (Giddens, 2000) and in discussions of welfare reform (Leadbeater, 1997).

This interest in social entrepreneurship seems to arrive simultaneously from very different corners of society with partly overlapping, partly different and even contradictory agendas: initiative-takers from voluntary, public and non-profit organizations look into methods and approaches that are mainstream in management and business life, while people from entrepreneurship and business life understand their (possible) impact on social welfare and civil society and take along their management experience and business methods and engage with philanthropic and social venturing or enter typically non-profit areas, such as health and education. 'Social entrepreneurship', then, forms the 'hybrid' signifier and 'oxymoron' that can cover many diverse initiatives, oriented as an approach that can change welfare and social problems in the interfaces of the non-profit, public, voluntary, philanthropic and private sectors. Many initiatives have recently been rephrased as forms of social entrepreneurship (Thompson et al., 2000; Wallace, 1999) that previously were not seen as such and where the key actors have 'trouble' seeing themselves as 'entrepreneurs'.

Social entrepreneurship has had offspring in such diverse areas as the health sector (De Leeuw, 1999), the informal sector in the Third World (Morris, Pitt and Berton, 1996), ecology (Pastakia, 1998; Albrecht, 2002), non-governmental development organizations (Fowler, 2000), and various other cultural and social domains (Borzaga and Defourny, 2000; Dees, 1998). Both Borzaga and Defourny (2000) and Fowler (2000) suggest that these new forms of social entrepreneurship go beyond the current concept of the non-profit sector and the social economy and recommend examining them as a new kind of social entrepreneurship and civic innovation. Such new initiatives can be seen as a form of R&D in the welfare system as Leadbeater (1997, pp. 9–10) argued, since social enterprises 'operate as a kind of research and development wing of the welfare system, innovating new solutions to intractable social problems. [. . .] Most importantly they set in motion a virtuous circle of social capital accumulation. They help communities to build up social capital which gives them a better chance of standing on their own two feet'. As a consequence the concept of social entrepreneurship figures in such non-traditional outlets of entrepreneurship research as: *New Directions for Philanthropic Fundraising* (Reis and Clohesy, 2001), the *International Journal of Public Sector Management* (Thompson, 2002), *Public Administration Review* (Eikenberry and Kluver, 2004), the *International Journal of Nonprofit and Voluntary Sector Marketing* (Mort, Weerawardena and Carnegie, 2003) and the *Journal of Third World Studies* (Najafizadeh and Mennerick, 2003).

Many questions emerge, when analyzing the upcoming social entrepreneurship movement, around how the field of entrepreneurship is currently considering it 'now a part of the mainstream' (Stevenson, 2004, p. 11). Has the academy of entrepreneurship slightly been surprised by this emergent interest? Can we assume this is rather and just a trend that will as quickly pass as it came along or at least quickly settle itself in the comfortable home of the maturing entrepreneurship field without asking too many disruptive questions? Or should we believe that the attention that social entrepreneurship provokes can form a line of flight that can destabilize this urge for established maturity and even pose new questions to the field of entrepreneurship that it is otherwise likely to exclude from its agenda, in its desperation to become that distinctive field? There are indeed some signs that indicate that the interest and activity around social entrepreneurship in many ways has taken the academy of entrepreneurship by surprise.

A first sign is that the academic entrepreneurship literature had been rather silent on social entrepreneurship for quite some time. Social entrepreneurship has never been a thematic section or even a chapter in the edited review books that regularly probe the 'state of the art' of the field (see Kent et al., 1982; Sexton and Smilor, 1986; Sexton and Kasarda, 1992; Sexton and Smilor, 1997; Sexton and Landström, 2000; Acs and Audretsch, 2003), and it has hardly been mentioned as a 'theme to watch out for' in the numerous review articles that look into future trends of the entrepreneurship field (see for example, Davidsson, Low and Wright, 2001; Grant and Perren, 2002; Busenitz et al., 2003). It is not an exaggeration to say that social entrepreneurship has been mostly neglected in the literature on entrepreneurship and has mainly been given the attention by scholars that typically do not belong to the core contributors of this field. For instance, Defourny (2000, p. 11) suggested that social enterprises might be seen 'as the expression of a new entrepreneurship', which is a claim well worth looking at more closely, but it is only slowly taken up by entrepreneurship scholars. That entrepreneurship scholars have started to follow this trend is illustrated by two special issues on social entrepreneurship, one published in the *International Journal of Entrepreneurship Education* (edited by Kourilsky and Walstad, 2004) and one on in the *Journal of World Business* (edited by Christie and Honig, 2006). Also an edited volume on 'The Way Ahead' for entrepreneurship by Welsch (2004) contains a small section on 'social entrepreneurship' (besides the usual themes of processes, technology, types, education), with two articles on community-based enterprises (Kuhns, 2004) and distressed inner cities (Fairchild and Greene, 2004). Social entrepreneurship is considered a new branch in the early stage of its development, figuring next to other branches such as family business, corporate entrepreneurship and entrepreneurship in the arts. As the definitions, associations, and academic treatments of social entrepreneurship are in their early stages, it is considered 'a cluster', characterized by its ideas 'being few in number, disorganized, ill-defined, and without significant academic theory' (Welsch and Maltarich, 2004, p. 60).

A second sign is that the entrance of social entrepreneurship is not announced with a little, modest knock on the door of the entrepreneurship field, asking permission for some empirical attention. The arrival of social entrepreneurship on the academic scene is rather loud and seems to be about big money. For instance, benevolent donations of entrepreneurs like Jeff Skoll to set up a social entrepreneurship research centre in the range of 4.4 million pounds to the Said Business School of Oxford University, did not go unenvied (and without resistance behind the scenes) by other business schools. Social entrepreneurship seems to come with large ambitions and heroism (see O'Connor, this volume). With unprecedented speed, social entrepreneurship courses have entered the programmes of top-tier business schools in the US (such as Harvard, Duke, Columbia and so on) and Europe (London and Said Business School).

Third, given the considerable disconnect between the 'core establishment' of entrepreneurship scholars and the 'new scholarship' of social entrepreneurship, social entrepreneurship might evolve relatively independently of the ongoing developments in the 'main' field of entrepreneurship or even try to establish itself as a 'separate' domain. In such a scenario, it is not unlikely that the scholarly coverage of social entrepreneurship might repeat the history of the academic entrepreneurship literature. For instance, there is a considerable concurrence between the emphasis on case studies, short stories and best practices examples of social entrepreneurship and their widespread use in the early entrepreneurship literature of the 1980s. One can notice a similar lamenting on the lack of clear definitions, generalizable models and theories. For instance, Thompson (2002, p. 412) observes with regard to the increasing use of the term social entrepreneurship that 'its meaning is not widely understood'. Another example is that the tendency to individualize the process of entrepreneurship, which was strongly rejected in entrepreneurship studies (see Gartner, 1988), reappears, and entrepreneurship becomes reduced to the study of the lone social entrepreneur. For instance, Drayton (2002) revisits the question 'who is the social entrepreneur?' and many of his illustrations of social entrepreneurship are stories of persons highlighting their skills and motivation

(Roberts and Woods, 2005). Another parallel is that by placing it in the business schools, the 'ownership' of entrepreneurship is emphasized as falling to management. Students trained as managers are the ones supposed to 'enter into society' and apply their concepts and methods in order to fix what's wrong. This inevitably contributes to the re-description of the social as a form of the economic, whereby the managerial tools become much more applicable and the managerial role correspondingly more central, something which has similarly happened with entrepreneurship in general (see Hjorth, 2003).

But maybe – we would like to suggest – social entrepreneurship can surprise the field of entrepreneurship when the latter moves into that delightful position of 'letting itself be surprised'. By turning to unknown territories and groundings and by embracing the indefiniteness of social entrepreneurship, the field of entrepreneurship can open itself to new and innovative questions and angles – in short to the entrepreneurial. In this sense we would like to point to Michel de Certeau's (1984) ideas of tactics and tacticians as describing well how the field of entrepreneurship might move: always by creating surprising uses of the dominant conceptions of society and by not hanging on to what it wins, by not being defined by its trophies but rather, precisely to the contrary, by being perenially changed by the latest chapter in its emerging story. This book thus lets itself be seduced by 'the other' of social entrepreneurship and seeks to take its chances to redirect and sculpt the current attention being paid to social entrepreneurship in a direction where 'the social' of social entrepreneurship is the 'strange attractor' and the 'virtuality to be actualized' that focuses and innovates our thinking. Especially, with this book, we want to accentuate the point that the whole connection between entrepreneurship and social change needs to be seen in a broader and more critical light. Entrepreneurship joins here a complex discussion on welfare, social justice, civic society and the role of government that has been taking place for a longer time than the current hype indicates, that is, it doesn't start with management awaiting the economization of society that allows for the subsequent managerialization of solutions instrumental to the 'enterprising' new way forward. We believe this requires a little reservation to claim the main seat at the table of social welfare and civil society discussions. That social entrepreneurship is seen as the newest option does not come at all as surprise (see Dey in this volume), since it coincides with, and is an exponent of, the rise of the enterprise discourse (Hjorth, 2003). However, the current literature on social entrepreneurship has neglected any discussion of enterprising discourse and instead proposed social entrepreneurship as an all-encompassing solution at a moment where faith in the more traditional models of non-profit, governmental and voluntary solutions is waning (see Dey, 2006). The chapters in the first part of this book will try to examine social entrepreneurship in a critical light and stretch the discussion into its societal and political parameters, going beyond the alignment of social values with: (the recognition of) entrepreneurial opportunities (Dees, 1998), the making of the citizen sector as competitive as business (Drayton, 2002), and the marketization of the non-profit sector (Eikenberry and Kluver, 2004). Rather than turning to a business framework, social entrepreneurship offers a chance to also theoretically innovate the concept of entrepreneurship by examining its own sociality and starting to explore the various social theories that the metaphor of earth instigates us to.

THE EARTH AND (UN)GROUNDING ENTREPRENEURSHIP

Let us think entrepreneurship through the image of a machine, trusting that, in doing so we are aided in bringing entrepreneurship beyond subjectivity or any organizing centre (for example, an institutionally fixed empirical 'foundation'). Imagine that entrepreneurship *is* nothing more than the connections and productions it makes; it is what it does (Colebrook, 2002, p. 55). Deleuze's use of the concept of machine, towards which we now are leaning, is unconventional. Take the bicycle. It has no end or intention. It works only when connected to another machine, such as the human body. The production of these two machines can only be achieved through connection: the human body becomes a cyclist and the bicycle becomes a vehicle. However, Deleuze extends this understanding to all life: 'there is no aspect of life that is not machinic; all life only works and *is* insofar as it connects with some other machine' (Colebrook, 2002, p. 56). A machine has no home or ground, but is in a constant process of deterritorialization – or, in other words, it is constantly becoming other than itself, brought beyond the limits of what it presently is taken to be.

This book tries to deterritorialize social entrepreneurship to show how it is first of all free from any single origin and that it is performed by a plurality of collective assemblages, temporarily ordered in social institutions, but always transformable in forming new 'social machines'. Such machines continuously extend experience through imagination. A social territory can be seen as a set of social and cultural presuppositions operating as contexts for statements and practices. A thought's territory is expressed by conceptual personae – the figures presupposed by the concept. In the case of 'social entrepreneurship', the conceptual personae are the vaguely defined figures of managerialist thinking, philanthropist-CEOs reflecting upon 'what's wrong with society?' One would find an analogy in Descartes as the conceptual persona of the *cogito*, a concept whose territory is expressed by the figure of the solitary and doubting Descartes. This book would like to destabilize the seeming monopoly of this persona of social entrepreneurship. The empirical studies brought to you in this volume instead make the entrepreneur – as a figure of a desire to create sociality, as a productive connectivity inventing practices beyond the limits of present experience to enhance the possibilities for living for citizens – into the conceptual persona of social entrepreneurship. This becomes part of our attempt to affirmatively express what the social in social entrepreneurship is.

The creation of sociality, which is also the transformation of society, is of course not presocial. Rather, it is open-endedly social: 'it is social in a manner prior to the separating out of individuals and the identifiable groupings that they end up boxing themselves into (positions in gridlock). A sociality without determinate borders: "pure" sociality' (Massumi, 2002, p. 9). This sociality is before any form of interaction and before any model that we (social scientists) might use to order it. One of those forms and models launched as an ordering tool for certain forms of interaction represented as 'problem solving' by entrepreneurial means is now popularized as 'social entrepreneurship'. The characteristics of this form are what our book is about. Such characteristics are socially and culturally negotiated in different contexts. Herein lies the point of stressing contextualization. We need local images of such determination of various forms of social entrepreneurship. This should happen differently in US culture when compared to European or Swedish culture. It should happen differently within Europe as well – within specific countries, regions, cities or communities. This heterogeneity is battled in this book. We try to rescue social entrepreneurship from being incorporated in any such context-dominant determination.

If we do not assume the model of one dominant discourse to be in place, our task is instead to precisely describe and narrate contextualized concepts for this interaction-in-the-making, this relation, through which it gets socially determined. Heterogeneity in terms of descriptions and variations of contexts would therefore be a qualitative criterion of any attempt to bring studies of social entrepreneurship together in one volume.

We believe it is not farfetched to describe these various contextualizations of social entrepreneurship as expressed in the chapters of this book. This also illustrates how the emphasis on grounding and the 'earthly' in our call for the book has increased authors' sensitivity, confronted by peoples' practices of living, the mundane, the relational. Our images of entrepreneurship are here produced in a higher resolution. The belongingness of entrepreneurship to life is made more evident. Possibly as a consequence of this, even in those cases where this is not an explicit purpose of authors, the usual 'grand narratives' of entrepreneurship research (the singular, alert individual; opportunity recognition; start-up and growth models) are simply not put to use with the usual frequency. The earthly, in effect, has made authors performatively question these models or grand narratives in favour of more contextualized and practice-oriented descriptions. We are brought closer to life/ground, to relations, to the social of entrepreneurship and to the entrepreneurial of the social.

Most often, this grounding, this sociality-focusing effect from the 'gravity' of the earthly, does not appear as a break or a revolutionary disruption of entrepreneurship as such. Rather, these new groundings are brought about as contextualizations of entrepreneurship in processes and practices previously excluded from studies of entrepreneurship (see especially part II of the present volume). There is a double movement here: firstly, there is a continuity in terms of entrepreneurship multiplying in different contexts and connections – with other disciplines and other practices; and secondly, there is, in this multiplication, also a disruption of the continuity of the history of entrepreneurship. The promise of one paradigm or of stabilized definitions is not nurtured by these studies. Rather the book affects us as an event in the sense of 'something that allows time to take off on a new path' (Colebrook, 2002, p. 57). It provides new lines of flight for entrepreneurship, new ways in which it is brought beyond its present limits. Again we might describe this freeing of the event of entrepreneurship from its actual origins as a 'deterritorialization' of entrepreneurship. This book brings us examples in which the becoming of entrepreneurship 'escapes or detaches from its original territory' (Colebrook, 2002, p. 59). The academic discourse on entrepreneurship is thus multiplied and deterritorialized/ungrounded in this book, especially so in part I.

We have, however, also presented – especially in part II – examples of how the becoming of entrepreneurship is re-territorialized. Bodies of thought and practice are brought together (such as when Kathryn Campbell makes entrepreneurship meet discourses on sustainability and care-of-the-self practices in Chapter 8) and create events beyond those bodies. Entrepreneurship is re-territorialized in new languages, new cultures, new practices and new socialities. These re-territorializations of entrepreneurship produce novel ways of making sense of the entrepreneurial: Fletcher and Watson (Chapter 7) bring us inside a community-building work, an urban-rural movement forming the context of entrepreneurial possibilities with consequences for how people organise their daily lives both as entrepreneurs and as inhabitants of rural areas. Campbell's chapter shows us how self- and world-making go together in the invention of everyday practices in their minute details, just as these are related to global issues of immense importance. She indicates how the personal and the global are already first social through friendships, family and community. Johannisson and Wigren, in Chapter 9, tell us about an ungrounding-in-the-making, namely the story of how the self-reviewing capacity of the community of Gnosjö is about to lose its local force and escape into a master narrative. Grounding this again seems to require a living story of the present rather than a grand narrative of the past – a collective identity grounded in action and not simply carried as a brand. Lindgren and Packendorff, in

Chapter 10, show how grounding locally is a highly political process of seek-ing legitimacy while still maintaining one's flexibility. In a way they bring us the story of a small rural town being deterritorialized by a group of rock enthu-siasts and re-territorialized as a Rock-City. Berglund further describes how the gap between productive discourses and what one can do in one's local commu-nity is handled in the self-forming practices of her entrepreneurs. From Beyes, finally, we learn how art can deterritorialize what we took for granted and re-territorialize this in surprising ways. This creates effects and this in turn takes us back and allows us to start thinking from a new ground.

In effect, this multiplying of entrepreneurship and contexts for entrepre-neurship, which is one important contribution of this book, democratizes entrepreneurship by multiplying the practices through which becoming-entrepreneurship happens in society. We believe that it is in this sense that we could claim that this book is also entrepreneurial, in that it manifests an active thinking that affirms the de- and re-territorializations of entrepreneurship and, by doing this, prepares both the study of entrepreneurship and the study of society to become affected by entrepreneurship, something necessarily related to society's capacity to act entrepreneurially.

CONCEPTUALIZING SOCIAL ENTREPRENEURSHIP

The first section of this book – entitled *Concepts of Social Entrepreneurship* – starts with a chapter by Richard Swedberg that encourages us to *reculer pour mieux sauter* and to avoid the idea that social entrepreneurship develops itself without any historical notion of the development of the thinking on entrepre-neurship, so as not to reinvent the wheel. Swedberg joins the current interest in some writings of Schumpeter that have been translated from German only recently, which allow us to speak of a 'young' Schumpeter as some of his more radical ideas in Chapters 2 and 7 of the 1911 edition of his book *Theorie der wirtschaftlichen Entwicklung* had been heavily reduced and rewritten if not totally omitted from the later English edition of 1934 entitled *The Theory of Economic Development*. Swedberg undertakes a close reading of both chapters to trace what Schumpeter has to say on the relationship between entrepre-neurship and both economic and social change.

The consequence of Swedberg's undertaking is twofold. Firstly, he stimu-lates those who participate in the study of social entrepreneurship to connect their interests to a general theory of entrepreneurship, which centers on the notion of change as a form of development 'from within' in contrast to change as adaptation 'from the outside'. These qualitatively new changes have ambiva-lent social consequences as they are only temporary for the entrepreneur and might be contested and envied by others. Secondly, especially the reading of the seventh chapter makes it clear that Schumpeter extended his dynamic understanding of change and creative destruction to society, in light of which social entrepreneurship can be understood as a form of dynamic behaviour in one of the non-economic areas of society. The current need for more elaborated theoretical developments of social entrepreneurship can thus be addressed within Schumpeter's general theory of entrepreneurship. However, Schumpeter's view on entrepreneurship emphasizes predominantly the individual role of the (social) entrepreneur instead of taking a social view on entrepreneurial processes.

To conceive of the social of entrepreneurship, Yohanan Stryjan proposes in Chapter 2 to reframe social entrepreneurship by shifting the focus from the social objectives of social enterprises to their modes of action. Using a resource perspective, he suggests focusing on the mobilization of and investment in resources over time and on defining and mustering the support of an emerging community. Looking for quasi-anthropological manifestations of entrepreneurship beyond the usual high-profile 'suspects', he illustrates the practices of cooperative enterprises in the Swedish context since the 1970s that range between welfare, social and community cooperatives. Social entrepreneurship involves the mobilizing of socially embedded resources and their conversion into (market-) convertible resources, and vice versa. The conversion, re-conversion and reproduction of resources are the practices that enact and maintain these social enterprises and show how their social elements both precede and create the social communities in which they are embedded.

Robert B. Anderson, Benson Honig and Ana Maria Peredo (Chapter 3) aim to introduce indigenous entrepreneurship as a promising research domain for the study of social entrepreneurship. They investigate the specificities of social entrepreneurship as it relates to indigenous people in a global economy, extending the (complex) interdisciplinary context of social entrepreneurship with literature on socio-economic, indigenous and community development. The life situations of indigenous people and their communities, often characterized by social disintegration, poverty and poor health, require us to investigate 'how development can be understood' and 'what the role of community can be in this'. Indigenous people, dominated and often mistreated in a geographical, political and economical sense by later inhabitants and maintaining a distinctive socio-cultural identity, see entrepreneurial activities as important vehicles to 'develop' and change their socio-economic situations and to rebuild their communities. The authors investigate three perspectives on development to see whether they are compatible with the hope and ambition of indigenous people to plan and control their own development and to 'negotiate' a constructive participation for themselves in the global economy. Besides the assimilation and dependency models, the authors argue that the contingency models represented by regulation theory can be best aligned with the context of indigenous peoples, as it enables an understanding of other people and cultures. This is because its central focus is on processes of social regulation which can make the role of communities and their counter-hegemonic potential in the context of alliances and relational contracts clear, as the global economy is created and sustained through localized processes where community-based entrepreneurial activities can take shape.

In Chapter 4, Ellen O'Connor focuses on what she calls 'high-profile social entrepreneurship', which represents a particular interpretation of social entrepreneurship: framed in a distinct way by elite business schools and their stakeholders, social entrepreneurship brings a market-orientation to social issues and promotes the professionalization of the non-profit and public sectors. Instead of such high-profile social entrepreneurship with its simultaneous global scope and narrow vision, O'Connor suggests a different articulation of social entrepreneurship that focuses on the local, mundane, accidental, informal and modest, which relocates and extends this discourse from business schools and elites to communities, grass-roots organizing and local problem-solving. This opening up of the participatory platform of social entrepreneurship is illustrated in three compelling stories related to research work Ellen O'Connor did on homelessness and management history and which interweave the political, social and historical dimensions of each entrepreneurial story of social change. These stories thus expand social entrepreneurship in two directions – as social activity that is entrepreneurial in nature and as enterprise that is social in nature. This forms the social cauldron of entrepreneurship – the minutiae of persistent and emergent interactions among a multitude of players, played out through elusive social processes and social scenes. The first story looks at the so-called 'homelessness industry', which forms a complex social network with its government agencies, professional and policy-making institutions and NPO and local communities, and which was once initiated 'entrepreneurially' through social actions like activism and hunger strikes. The second case tells the story of Jane Addams and how she established – an entrepreneurial endeavour by itself – Hull House, a well known settlement house in Chicago for young female students at the beginning of the twentieth century, from which one of the greatest social movements would follow. The third case tells of the emergence of academic entrepreneurship in a broadly social light, entangled in the complexities of history between the two world wars.

In Chapter 5, Daniel Hjorth and Björn Bjerke question whether we can hold on to the overcodified term social entrepreneurship and inquire into the possibilities of the notion of public entrepreneurship both empirically and conceptually. They depart from the experiences they have had in a Swedish learning arena, where participants in different kinds of entrepreneurial projects were sharing experiences and reflecting on their own self-understandings and practices of how they were creating new social contexts for themselves and other citizens. These experiences of everyday entrepreneurial practices are set apart from the more general observation that the social more and more becomes an epiphenomenon of the market, turning citizens into consumers. Hjorth and Bjerke resist such consumerist understandings of these entrepreneurial initiatives. To safeguard the space of sociality and citizenship, they undertake a genealogy of the social and the citizen. On such an account, they indicate how the constitution of society and the social has targeted the conscious consumer as a member of an enterprising society, and look for alternative routes for conceiving the social. To inscribe (social) entrepreneurship into a process of social change, a move from the social to the public, and from the consumer to the citizen, is suggested. Interpreting the learning arena experiences of the participants within this new framework, they point out that these initiatives can be conceptualized as citizen-driven, where the creation of the social outside an economic logic is what makes a difference for the participants' everyday practices. Hjorth and Bjerke propose to affirm the political and ethical possibilities of social entrepreneurship where the social becomes shaped in new ways through these intensive and collective forms of public entrepreneurship. Where people are invited to practice creative citizenship and to bring collectivity into the public space, the social is understood as collective investments in desiring images that are transformed in public spaces where creating and experimenting – and learning and resisting – can take place. Social entrepreneurship conceived in and through public spaces might be seen as a form of 'citizenship-becoming-public-entrepreneurship' that can emphasize the ethical and political effects of social change brought about by social – read public – entrepreneurs.

Pascal Dey, in Chapter 6, wonders why the academic literature creates a univocally positive image of social entrepreneurship. Taking a rhetorical view on social science, he looks into how the scholarly community has appropriated the term 'social entrepreneurship', how certain constructions become favoured while others are elided. Reading how social entrepreneurship is constructed in academic texts, Dey brings forward traces of a multiplicity of discourses, such as the ones of 'medical treatment' making 'patients' at once dependent and accountable, of 'progressive development' rejecting the status quo and reifying external pressures, of an 'economy' that is at once global, anti-bureacratic and universal, of 'technical rationality' that privileges measurement, scientific method and the normal and of 'individualism' that makes social entrepreneurs at once morally superior, supernatural individuals and male. Taking social entrepreneurship as an indeterminate sign, core tensions and power struggles can be located and new language games might be imagined. Dey's deconstructive reading shows how the writing on social entrepreneurship favours an economic calculus and technical rationality, medical dependency and 'progressive' development; in short it follows the 'programme' of entrepreneurship research in general. This becomes interpreted in relation to what Lyotard has called the principle of performativity, keeping social entrepreneurship measurable, programmable, predictable and instrumental. Returning to an open meaning of the social and thinking of an ethics of social entrepreneurship, Dey argues that there is no a priori judgment of social entrepreneurship as socially and morally possible; rather it appears vital to imagine social entrepreneurship as an act that is addressed unconditionally to the genuine other. As part of a prospective agenda of social entrepreneurship, Dey suggests (in Spivak's terms) a 'practical politics of the open end', where small narratives evoke the multiple possibilities of the undecidable and open other avenues of social entrepreneurship. A series of such stories that attempt this follows in the second section bringing various contexts of social change.

CONTEXTUALIZING SOCIAL CHANGE

The second section of this book – *Contexts of Social Change* – takes us to the not-so-obvious places of entrepreneurship. Bound together by their attention to – and sensitivity before – shifting locations, places and the spatiality of entrepreneurial processes, these chapters contextualize entrepreneurship through their relational–societal constitution in various collective bodies as social change.

The section opens with a chapter by Denise Fletcher and Tony Watson. They bring us stories of urban–rural shifters, people who, for a variety of reasons, move from their urban homes to settle in rural areas and do so through different ways of living. In studying people developing rural areas (the community of Kerston, UK) into attractive places for living and those making the urban–rural shift, Fletcher and Watson are interested in the meanings that these people attach to their lives and the moves they have made. They concentrate on how such an urban–rural move facilitates market opportunities in rural communities and how such opportunities, when actualized, open new lines of flight through which social change takes place. Following an entrepreneur-developer (Eddie Newhall), we learn from Fletcher and Watson's conceptualization of the entrepreneur–client relationality how social change processes transform the Kerston district as well as the people involved in this social becoming. Using the concept of (shifting) life orientations, the authors thicken their story of the interrelated nature of social change and entrepreneurship.

In Chapter 8, Kathryn Campbell argues for the expansion of the entrepreneurial debate to contemplate the merits of localized, small-scale, non-heroic enterprise which she studies in Africa as much as in rural Canada, in our times as much as in the early nineteenth century. Her text assembles or – in her own words – 'quilts' together three stories, differently told, of women who invent the 'business' of living through gardening – a healing process that connects their selves, their work lives and the communities they take part in. Interweaving ecofeminism, bioregionalism and the survival subsistence perspective, the concept of social change she envisions is what is called 'grounded entrepreneurship' that aims at a sustainable entrepreneurial ethic and that recognizes a life-sustaining dependence on 'Mother Earth'. Campbell's stories manifest how change starts at home and how women gardeners – living from and with the land – become expert guides for grounded entrepreneurship.

Bengt Johannisson and Caroline Wigren set out to 'rock' the stable story of an entrepreneurial local community – Gnosjö, Sweden – known for its historically (re)produced hotbed of entrepreneurship. Their sociality in focus is the interrelated individual and collective identity constructions in the context of a local community – a community dominated by multi-generational family businesses with modest growth ambitions (as Johannisson and Wigren put it). Approaching this industrial district as one always celebrating the 'good old times' (in the authors' words, an imprisoning curse) rather than self-reflexively developing alternative futures, the authors are concerned with the need for a remaking of the community's identity. Revisiting Gnosjö as ethnographers and readers of their own previous texts, Johannisson and Wigren trace forces that would counteract their initial description of an industrial district trapped in its historically mediated and outdated self-image as successful, and thereby provide seeds for reconstructing entrepreneurship and social change. They bring us stories of 'participants' in 'social worlds', and through putting these concepts to use, make it possible to connect the future story of Gnosjö with forces guiding a way out of the present 'social prison', typified in the complexities of the 'master narrative' of the 'spirit of Gnosjö'. 'Outsiders' to the dominant social world of Gnosjö provide challenges to the 'normal' by thriving on ambiguity, and Johannisson and Wigren show how the tension this generates for 'insiders' can be creative in crafting an alternative collective identity.

Monica Lindgren and Johann Packendorff intensify our relationship (from Chapter 10) with boundary work in relation to the local-cultural context. The story of the small town of Hultsfred, Sweden, and the Rock Festival is one of deviating and belonging, a story of people constructing boundaries in order to stretch and test them, a story of entrepreneurship from a relational–constructionist viewpoint. The authors bring us narratives of punk-rebels-becoming-entrepreneurs and rock-festival-becoming-town-development centered on a national music centre, business incubators, university education in music management and so on. Lindgren and Packendorff, while telling the story of Hultsfred, do not leave out the stories of organizers-becoming-parents and informal-networking-becoming-professional-board: processes that enrich the thick description of this case of entrepreneurship as social change. Struggling with the tensions between a nonconformist rock music lifestyle and the need for belonging to local, regional, national and international communities, change is propelled by boundary work resulting in a continued responsibility and desire for developing Hultsfred as town, region, national centre and rock festival. This boundary-work shares similarities with Johannisson and Wigren's story in that the rock festival people continuously need to work on changing the way the citizens of Hultsfred view themselves and their community in order to develop the festival. Lindgren and Packendorff do not leave us with a model or some packaged solutions, but, on the contrary, show how entrepreneurship as boundary work is a continuous, slow, and ongoing endeavour of (in the authors' words) balancing sensibility and belonging for the sake of changing practices against strangeness and deviation for the sake of redefining how the world is seen and handled.

Karin Berglund discusses in Chapter 11 how two entrepreneurs draw on discourses in order to make space for their entrepreneurial identities. She provides us with close-up stories of becoming-entrepreneur. In the context of a local 'catastrophe' – 1,500 people made redundant entering into the state of 'job-seekers' – timed with a large EU-project promoting entrepreneurship in minority groups, we get to follow Lena and Sara who are about to start their own businesses. Berglund's two-year ethnographic study of these women develops into a journey where the women relate to the equality and enterprise discourses prevalent in the region in quite different ways, while simultaneously changing their lives and identities in the processes of becoming entrepreneurs. In this interplay between identity and discourse, the different stories of these two entrepreneurs and their fashioning of entrepreneurial identities unfold. In the context of identity formation, the process of becoming-entrepreneur, Berglund concludes, should be seen as a complex collection of processes taking place in different arenas of life. Social change is here the result both of discourses affecting a community and its self-descriptions as well as how these two women fashion their identities as entrepreneurs. But the possibilities of these discourses (equality and enterprise) are also shaped by the social change described locally as 'the catastrophe' (large-scale sudden unemployment). Berglund's case brings to the fore how entrepreneurship is made visible in society, and she asks us to consider the relationship between these forms of visibility and the ways in which entrepreneurship is practiced.

Entrepreneurial discourse has entered city life and requires a critical analysis of its effects: what spaces are produced and excluded? What social realities created? To make such a critical analysis, Timon Beyes enters a small theater in Berlin and watches a play by the German playwright Pollesch, entitled *City as Prey* that forms its own entrepreneurial genre of theater discourse.

Watching and reading this play allows him simultaneously to point at the dominant discourse of enterprise that literally encloses the life of citizens and to look for alternative spaces. In a first, apocalyptic, reading of the play, it seems there is no escaping the hegemonic reign of enterprise discourse as city space is produced and controlled through this master discourse. A second, exemplary, reading attempts to provide a social and political critique, pointing out that the reproduction of grand narratives can become interwoven with alternatives developed through heterotopic spaces. Not in the least the artistic space itself can form a heterotopia that intervenes and might alter dominant conceptions of the so-called entrepreneurial city, suggesting how entrepreneurship in a different mode can bring vitality and creativity to cities: urban spaces may then be regarded as potential 'lived spaces' or as heterotopias. Heterotopic sites and spaces are where social change and transformation are constituted through entrepreneurial activities. This double reading of Beyes, creating a presence of difference, implies also an aesthetic form of writing that at once makes visible and complex the things that might 'escape' the attention of the audience of Pollesch's play in the theater or that might be taken for granted in the play of urban entrepreneurialism we all take part in.

PART ONE

Concepts of social entrepreneurship

1. Social entrepreneurship: the view of the young Schumpeter

Richard Swedberg

One of the most interesting advances in recent entrepreneurial thought is the idea that the notion of innovative or entrepreneurial behavior, which was originally invented to deal exclusively with economic phenomena, is today also used to explain what happens in social or non-economic areas of society. As examples of this one can mention expressions such as moral entrepreneur, political entrepreneur, organizational entrepreneur and so on. There is also the increasingly popular phrase social entrepreneurship, which is traveling around the world and traces its origin to the United States in the 1990s.

One of the difficulties with the notion of social entrepreneurship (which I shall use in this article to represent the general trend of analyzing social change with the help of the economic theory of entrepreneurship) is that it is not connected to a general theory of entrepreneurship, but is usually used as a slogan or inspiring phrase. It is true that sometimes in the literature on social entrepreneurship one can find references to theories of entrepreneurship. David Bornstein, for example, refers both to Schumpeter and Peter Drucker in his excellent *How to Change the World: Social Entrepreneurs and the Power of New Ideas* (Bornstein, 2004). But even in a case like this, a sustained theoretical attempt fails to accompany the references. The result is that the current literature on social entrepreneurship is richer on inspiring examples and anecdotes than it is on theoretical insights and analytical power.

Is it then possible to develop a theory of social entrepreneurship that is linked to our current theories and knowledge of entrepreneurship? This remains to be seen. In the meantime, and as a modest effort in this direction, I will use this article to explore what Joseph Schumpeter had to say on entrepreneurship and social change. I shall begin by presenting and explicating his most famous attempt to capture this phenomenon, namely his idea of creative destruction. I shall then proceed to his general theory of entrepreneurship, as outlined in his most important work on entrepreneurship, *Theorie der Wirtschaftlichen Entwicklung* (1911, 1926; trans. 1934).

The term 'creative destruction' is typically used in a loose sense, roughly meaning that wherever there is entrepreneurship, there will also be social change. Sometimes there is an aggressive undertone to the use of the term along the lines that if there is to be an omelette, you will have to break some eggs.

What Schumpeter actually says about creative destruction is somewhat different from this, and one reason is that his notion of creative destruction is closely related to his general theory of entrepreneurship. To show that this is the case, one only needs to take a closer look at the way that Schumpeter uses the idea of creative destruction in his work. The notion of creative destruction was introduced in a short chapter in *Capitalism, Socialism and Democracy* (1942), entitled 'The Process of Creative Destruction' (Schumpeter, 1994, pp. 81–86). Schumpeter refers explicitly to 'creative destruction' twice in this chapter. The central passage reads as follows:

> The opening up of new markets, foreign or domestic, and the organizational development from the craft shop and factory to such concerns as US Steel illustrate the same process of industrial mutation – if I may use that biological term – that incessantly revolutionizes the economic structure *from within*, incessantly destroying the old one, incessantly creating a new one. This process of Creative Destruction is the essential fact about capitalism. It is what capitalism consists in and what every capitalist concern has got to live in (Schumpeter, 1994, p. 83).

A little later Schumpeter also refers to 'the perennial gale of creative destruction' that can be found in capitalism. He adds that 'capitalism, then, is by nature a form or method of economic change and not only never is but never can be stationary' (Schumpeter, 1998, p. 84).

If one takes a close look at these statements one quickly notices that Schumpeter has a special type of change in mind when he talks of creative destruction. He specifies that this type of change has to come *'from within'*, and he uses italics to draw attention to this qualification. Can change then also come from the outside, and, if so, what would this type of change be like? Furthermore, how would this latter type of change be related to entrepreneurship and creative destruction?

From Schumpeter's way of expressing himself in the section on creative destruction in *Capitalism, Socialism and Democracy*, it is clear that he is referring to a set of ideas that he expects the reader to be familiar with. It is, however, my sense that many of the readers of *Capitalism, Socialism and Democracy* may not be acquainted with Schumpeter's ideas on change; and I shall therefore take this opportunity to present and discuss them. In doing so – and this is what constitutes the *raison d'être* and novelty of this article – I will exclusively draw on Schumpeter's *original and most radical formulation* of his ideas. This is to be found in the first edition from 1911 of *Theorie der wirtschaftlichen Entwicklung*, an edition that is still untranslated and which Schumpeter rarely referred to during his career. Schumpeterian scholars (as well as Schumpeter himself) instead usually cite the second edition of this work, which was translated in 1934 into English as *The Theory of Economic Development*. The first edition, however, is much more original than the one from 1934 and also breaks in a much more decisive fashion with mainstream economics.

In the following, in brief, I shall focus on what to my mind represents Schumpeter's most creative attempt to address the issue of entrepreneurship and social change. By drawing attention to the first version of Schumpeter's theory of entrepreneurship, it should also be added, I join a recent trend in Schumpeterian research that argues that we know very little about the young Schumpeter (see Shionoya, 1990; Swedberg, 1991, Ch. 2; Becker and Knudsen, 2002; Backhaus, 2003; Koppl, 2003).

The first edition of *Theorie der wirtschaftlichen Entwicklung* is a large book of more than 500 pages, of which huge parts are devoted to a technical attempt to work out the economic theory of entrepreneurship. In two of the chapters – Chapters 2 and 7 – Schumpeter addresses the more general issue of how to define entrepreneurship and how it is related to different forms of economic as well as social change. Chapter 2 is entitled 'The Fundamental Phenomenon of Economic Development' and was reduced by some 50 per cent in the second edition that appeared in 1934. Chapter 7 ('The View of the Economy as a Whole'), which is 86 pages long in the original edition from 1911, was totally eliminated from the 1934 edition.

Important theoretical changes were also introduced by Schumpeter in the 1934 edition, in an effort to make this work easier to appreciate for mainstream economists of the time. These changes no doubt also reflect the fact that Schumpeter by the early 1930s was some twenty years older than when he published the first edition. In 1934 Schumpeter was an established scholar at a well known mainstream university (Harvard University in the United States), as opposed to the days when the first edition of *Theorie der wirtschaftlichen Entwicklung* was conceived and Schumpeter was an unknown scholar at a provincial university (the University of Czernowitz in the Austro-Hungarian Empire).

While small parts of Chapter 2 have recently been translated as well as the whole of Chapter 7, these two important texts are still not widely known in English-speaking academia and have not been properly assimilated either in entrepreneurial or in Schumpeterian scholarship (for the translated parts of Chapter 2, see Schumpeter, 2002; and for the translation of Chapter 7, see Schumpeter, 2003). One purpose of this article is to help this process of assimilation along, and also to add to the discussion of the early Schumpeter by taking a close look at these two chapters. I will especially try to show that the early Schumpeter, who wrote *Theorie der wirtschaftlichen Entwicklung* (henceforth *Theorie* in 1911) is much more interesting and relevant for today's discussion of entrepreneurship in general than the later Schumpeter, who was not as radical and also concerned with integrating his work into mainstream American economics. Schumpeter, as I see it, also has an important contribution to make to any contemporary discussion of the relationship between entrepreneurship and social change.

CHAPTER 2 IN *THEORIE DER WIRTSCHAFTLICHEN ENTWICKLUNG*: DIFFERENT TYPES OF CHANGE AND WHAT AN ENTREPRENEUR IS

Chapter 2 in *Theorie* deals only with what happens in the economic sphere of society, while the rest of society is held constant (politics, population, and so on). Chapter 7, which will be discussed later in this article, deals in contrast with the situation when the economic sphere is in interaction with the rest of society. From this statement, a reader who is unfamiliar with Schumpeter might conclude that he only deals with economic changes in Chapter 2, and with the interaction of economic and social changes in Chapter 7. This, however, is not the case. Schumpeter deals with economic as well as social change in both Chapter 2 and Chapter 7 – but he does it in different ways.

While Schumpeter's theory of entrepreneurship, which is famously presented in Chapter 2, is centered around what we today would call change, the terminology that Schumpeter uses is distinctly his own. The key term is 'development' (more so than 'entrepreneurship'), and it covers a very special kind of change, namely the type of change that can only arise *from within* the economic sphere.

But there also exist different types of changes in the economic sphere, namely those that originate in response to processes *outside* this sphere, and Schumpeter refers to these as 'adaptation'. 'Development' and 'adaptation' have nothing in common, and Schumpeter's whole theory of entrepreneurship, as well as his attempt to develop a new type of economic theory, is centered around the distinction between these very different types of change.

The definition of development that Schumpeter provides in Chapter 2 reads as follows: 'By "development" we shall understand only such changes in economic life that are not forced upon it from without, but arise by its own initiative from within' (Schumpeter, 2002, p. 405). No definition is given of 'adaptation', but it is described as economic changes that are not 'qualitatively new' and emerge in response to forces from outside the economy (Schumpeter, 2002, p. 406). This type of change, Schumpeter says, is simply 'dragged along', and as examples he mentions 'mere growth' in population or wealth (Schumpeter, 2002, p. 405).

Ordinary economic theory (what we today would call neoclassical econom-ics) only deals with static phenomena, while there does not yet exist a theory that is capable of explaining development. Schumpeter's purpose in Chapter 2, and in *Theorie* more generally, is precisely to complement existing economic (or neoclassical) theory with one that can deal with development. Later in the chapter Schumpeter will introduce the term 'entrepreneur' for the economic actor who causes development.

Schumpeter uses the terms 'development' and 'static' not only as concep-tual tools in his attempt to construct a new approach to economic theory, but also to denote concrete economic phenomena that exist in the world. While we may think that most of the economy around us today in the industrial world is dynamic and in a state of development, he says, this is actually not the case. Nearly everywhere economic reality is static. This also goes for the most dynamic part of economic reality, namely industry. When something qualita-tively new happens in industry – say, that Carnegie decides to get rid of some perfectly good machines because he has found some better machines – every-body is surprised. What we should wonder at instead, Schumpeter says, is why development takes place in the first place.

Statics – defined as no change or automatic change in response to outside forces – is 'the general rule throughout the history of mankind' (Schumpeter, 2002, p. 111). Statics is, for example, the norm among artisans and peasants. While these are always very eager to make extra money and work very hard in what they do, they only act within given limits. The artisan does not want to change the way that he produces his goods, and the peasant is at the most ready to switch from one type of crop to another in an effort to make more money. But they never do anything radically new, and in this they are similar to people in countries like India and China as well as in primitive societies. People in all of these societies, Schumpeter says, are wed to the old, and if they ever make any changes, it is only because something happens outside the economy, and they are forced to adapt.

What then accounts for the nearly universal existence of 'non-develop-ment', as Schumpeter calls it? Do people in static economies not have to satisfy their material needs, and does this not lead to change and development? Not at all, Schumpeter says; most people only try to satisfy their needs within given circumstances. What accounts for the prevalence of static economic behavior, he argues, are instead two very distinct factors. One of these is soci-ological in nature, and the other psychological. Together they effectively block development from taking place.

The sociological factor that prevents development from taking place is *other people* or rather other people who are static. When you try to do some-thing new, other people tend to react negatively. Deviance is something that evokes this reaction in all societies, according to Schumpeter. 'Each act of deviant behavior on the part of a member of a community meets with disapproval from the other members' (Schumpeter, 1911, p. 118). People react negatively to deviance because they feel psychologically threatened; they are used to doing things in a familiar and 'safe' way. If Sartre says that 'hell is other people', Schumpeter might have said that 'what kills entrepreneurship is other people'.

But there is also a psychological factor involved, and that is the resistance to doing something new that each economic actor feels within himself or herself. While doing what is familiar, Schumpeter says, is always easy, doing what is new is not. 'The whole difference between swimming with the stream and against the stream is to be found here' (Schumpeter, 1911, p. 121). To do the right thing presents few problems as long as everything is known, but it is very different when you find yourself in a new situation. In a static economy 'the principle of rational behavior' (read: rational choice) works perfectly well – but not when it is a case of economic development (Schumpeter, 1911, p. 123). When you have to do something new, there is no logical or correct answer.

In order for something radically new to emerge, the economic actor has to be bold and willing to fight against the old. Obstacles have to be overcome. In brief, if there is to be any economic development, there have to be *leaders* – those very special people who display energy to act in new ways and are also motivated to do so. Schumpeter repeatedly refers to this type of person or leader as 'Man of Action' (*Mann der Tat*), and he describes him as someone who does not accept reality as it is. If there exists no demand for a good, for example, the Man of Action will create one: he will *make* people demand it. He (and the Man of Action is always a 'he' for Schumpeter) is full of energy and leaps at the obstacles. Schumpeter writes: 'The Man of Action acts in the same decisive manner inside as well as outside the usual tracks in the economy. He does not feel the restrictions that block the actions of the other economic actors' (Schumpeter, 1911, p. 132). The Man of Action, in brief, does not have the same inner obstacles to change as static people or people who avoid doing what is new. But what then drives the Man of Action? As opposed to the static person, who goes about his business because he wants to satisfy his needs and stops when his goal has been accomplished, the leader has other sources of motivation. He charges ahead because he wants power and because he loves to accomplish things. In Schumpeter's formulation: 'he takes pleasure in a social power position and in creating' (Schumpeter, 1911, p. 138). The leader has no equilibrium point at which the energy expanded equals the satisfaction received, but keeps fighting till he is too old or otherwise defeated by the forces that the static person does not even think of confronting.

At this point of his argument Schumpeter raises the question: can one not say that the static person as well as the Man of Action are quite similar in that both of them want to be satisfied, albeit in different ways? Viewed from this perspective, do they not have quite a bit in common, and can they not therefore be analyzed using the same analytical tools? To my mind, Schumpeter here raises a very interesting question that is similar to the one that economists often raise today, when they argue that egoism and altruism (or whatever gives a person satisfaction) are basically one and the same thing, since both of them represent a distinct value to the actor. And since this is the case, there is no need to develop a new type of approach when we deal with something like altruism in economic life; the existing one, based on egoism, does very well.

How does Schumpeter respond to this type of argument? The answer is that he violently rejects it and says that it is nothing but a play with words. Development *is* very different from adaptation, and you *do* need a new type of economic theory to handle it: 'The fact that we have to do with two fundamentally different types of behavior, which lead to diametrically opposed results, must not be formulated away' (Schumpeter, 1911, p. 149). Schumpeter also notes that the qualitatively new phenomenon that the Man of Action brings about does not come out of nowhere; it already exists in embryonic form in reality. The Man of Action can only bring about 'something whose time has come' (Schumpeter, 1911, p. 152). You cannot force what is new out of nothing; it has to be there in some form, ready to be seized on and developed.

As opposed to the situation in static theory, however, this potential for coming into being and what the Man of Action does with it, cannot be easily measured and translated into ordinary science. Development therefore represents an enormous challenge to economic theory; and the researcher has to proceed in ways that are fundamentally different from the ones that are used in static theory. The idea of equilibrium, for example, does not work when it comes to entrepreneurial behavior, and neither do the ideas of marginal utility and rational choice.

How is one then to proceed, in order to account for development? Schumpeter's answer to this question represents what we today know as his theory of entrepreneurship; and it is first at this stage of the argument that he introduces the term 'entrepreneur' (*Unternehmer*; Schumpeter, 1911, p. 171). Schumpeter explains: 'The entrepreneur is our Man of Action in the area of the economy. He is an economic leader, a real and not only an apparent leader as the static leader' (Schumpeter, 1911, p. 172).

What is characteristic of the entrepreneur is that he does something qualitatively new; and in the area of the economy this means that he recombines or makes a new combination of already existing resources. The entrepreneur is not an inventor; instead he introduces 'new ways of using existing means' or 'factors of production' (Schumpeter, 2002, p. 409; 1911, p. 175). Schumpeter sums up: 'Our assumption is that he who makes new combinations is an entrepreneur' (Schumpeter, 1911, p. 172).

Schumpeter also notes that the number of possible combinations is nearly infinite and that the entrepreneur cannot possibly go through all of them in some rational manner. His talent consists instead of being able to intuitively pick a few of the ones that are possible and decide to go with one of these. The entrepreneur does not make a rational choice, but an intuitive one; and it is the capacity to make the right intuitive choice that separates a good entrepreneur apart from a bad entrepreneur.

Schumpeter gives several examples of what he means by a new combination in the area of the economy: 'the introduction of a new quality of a good, or a new use of an already existing good . . . a new production method . . . the opening up of a new market (and) the change of economic organization, e.g., in founding a trust, establishing a large corporation, etc.' (Schumpeter, 2002, p. 410). He also importantly states that the most common form of entrepreneurship is to create a new firm: 'the most typical case representing all the different possibilities and all the different sides of the matter, the organizational, commercial, technical side, etc. *is the founding of a new enterprise*' (*Unternehmung*; Schumpeter, 2002, p. 410).

What is absolutely crucial for the entrepreneur is to be able to envision some new combination; and as opposed to the static person, this is something that comes very easily to him. While the universe of the static person is limited to the combinations that already exist, the entrepreneur wants to break the old mold and create a new one. Where the static person sees nothing but routine, the entrepreneur knows that there exists a nearly limitless number of new ways of doing things.

But knowing that there exist different ways of doing things is not enough to turn someone into an entrepreneur, according to Schumpeter. 'There always and everywhere is a richness of ideas and plans' (Schumpeter, 1911, p. 177). It is true, he says, that only a minority of people have the capacity to envision that things can be done differently. But only a minority of *this* minority has also the capacity to transform one of these new combinations into reality. Ideas are cheap, Schumpeter says, and what is truly difficult is to face the risk and uncertainty that comes with doing something in reality, not just in your mind. Schumpeter makes this point with so much force that one must conclude that he prioritizes doing over thinking in *Theorie*.

In order to successfully carry out an entrepreneurial enterprise, the leader needs the help and cooperation of other people. The problem with this is that other people are typically static and do not want to take the risk of doing something new. 'The disposition of the mass of people is static and hedonistic', while 'new enterprises mean new dangers that may cost you your existence' (Schumpeter, 1911, p. 183). The way out of this dilemma for the entrepreneur, according to Schumpeter, is to buy the labor power of other people and order them to do what is new.

To be in a position to buy the cooperation of workers and employees, the entrepreneur needs money; and this is where the banker or the capitalist enters into Schumpeter's theory. The entrepreneur borrows money that has been created by the banks, and in this manner finances his enterprise: 'The principle is this: the entrepreneur buys productive labor and thereby removes it from its ordinary static use; he makes use of it without asking its owners for permission; and in this way he forces the economy into new directions' (Schumpeter, 1911, p. 189). Schumpeter sums up the argument in Chapter 2 of *Theorie* as follows: '*Like the carrying out of new combinations is the form and content of development, the activity of the leader is the driving form*' (Schumpeter, 2002, p. 434). Entrepreneurship, in brief, represents a very special type of economic change – a type of change that consists of a new combination that is translated into reality by a leader. All other changes in the economy lack a dynamic element and are fundamentally passive (see Table 1.1).

Table 1.1   *The Man of Action and the Non-Entrepreneurial Person, according to the young Schumpeter*

The Man of Action	The Non-Entrepreneurial Person
dynamic	static
breaks out of equilibrium	seeks equilibrium
does what is new	repeats what has already been done
active, energetic	passive, low energy
leader	follower
puts together new combinations	accepts existing ways of doing things
feels no inner resistance to change	feels strong inner resistance to change
battles resistance to his actions	feels hostility to new actions of others
makes an intuitive choice among a multitude of new alternatives	makes a rational choice among existing multitude of new alternatives
motivated by power and joy in creation	motivated exclusively by needs and stops when these are satisfied
commands no resources but borrows from a bank	commands no resources and has no use for new resources

Note: In *Theorie der wirtschaftlichen Entwicklung* (1911) Schumpeter draws a sharp line between the entrepreneurial and the non-entreprenurial person. He refers repeatedly to the former as Man of Action (*Mann der Tat*) and the latter as static.

CHAPTER 7 IN *THEORIE DER WIRTSCHAFTLICHEN ENTWICKLUNG*: CHANGE AND ENTREPRENEURSHIP IN SOCIETY AT LARGE

In the chapter of *Theorie* that has just been presented, Schumpeter only looks at entrepreneurship and change within the economic sphere itself, while the rest of society is kept constant. This restriction is removed in the last chapter in Schumpeter's book which is entitled 'The View of the Economy as a Whole'. While Schumpeter rewrote, compressed and on a few crucial points also changed the chapter on economic development for the 1934 translation, the reader should be reminded once more of the fact that he totally eliminated this last chapter.

In approaching the topic of the economy as a whole, Schumpeter says, you may either use economic theory or economic history. While these two approaches ultimately complement one another, Schumpeter says that he prefers to deal only with economic theory in *Theorie*. The reason for this is that economic theory is more theoretical in nature than economic history in that it attempts to conceptualize reality in terms of regularities and processes. Economic theory allows you, as Schumpeter later would phrase it, to lay bare 'the *mechanism of change*' (Schumpeter, 1934, p. 61).

Schumpeter then moves on to the classics of economics, by which he roughly means the economists from Adam Smith to Alfred Marshall. While static theory views economic change exclusively as a response to forces outside of the economy, and dynamic theory as a response generated from within the economy, the classics take what may be termed an intermediary position. They also single out five factors as central to economic development: an increase in population, a rise in capital, new technology, new forms of organization and new consumer wants. Each of these factors is seen as capable of moving the economy forward, and not just to a new equilibrium, as in static economic theory.

According to Schumpeter, this rejection of a stable equilibrium represents a definite advance over static theory, but it is also clear that Schumpeter finds the approach of the classics wanting in some important respects. There is one particular problem with their way of conceptualizing development, he says, and this is that economic progress is ultimately seen as happening by itself. It is, for example, implied that better technology automatically leads to progress. But Schumpeter is not willing to accept a type of analysis in which the entrepreneur has for all practical purposes been eliminated: 'The economy does not grow into higher forms by itself', as he puts it (Schumpeter, 2003, p. 75).

In the last chapter of *Theorie* Schumpeter also insists on another crucial feature of dynamic theory, and this is that it can *never* lead to an equilibrium.

This is one of the most radical ideas in *Theorie* and a full quote is therefore in order:

> There is no such thing as a dynamic equilibrium. Development, in its deepest character, constitutes a disturbance of the existing static equilibrium and shows no tendency at all to strive again for that or any other form of equilibrium . . . If the economy does reach a new state of equilibrium then this is achieved not by the motive forces of development, but rather by a reaction against it. Other forces bring development to an end, and by so doing create the first precondition regaining a new equilibrium (Schumpeter, 2003, p. 76).

Just as Schumpeter removed all of Chapter 7 from the 1934 edition, he also eliminated this very radical emphasis on dynamics and the idea that entrepreneurial change can *never* be at rest or reach an equilibrium. He now chose instead to emphasize what he termed the discontinuous nature of economic reality and that it moved from one equilibrium to another – a formulation that is quite similar to the one that he earlier had used to characterize static theory (Schumpeter, 1934, p. 64). Again, he presumably did this in order to not situate himself too far outside mainstream economics.

In trying to fully understand the economy of a concrete country from the perspective of economic theory, Schumpeter continues in *Theorie*, you have to take a number of different forces into account. There is, first of all, static and dynamic economic behavior, and the way that these two types of behavior interact and influence one another. To this must also be added other causes, some of which are closer to the economic core of society (such as population, technology and capital), and others that are more distant (such as war, chance events and political interventions).

The result of all these forces acting and interacting together is an uneven type of economic development, according to Schumpeter. The economy moves forward through a series of partial advances and setbacks, rather than through a continuous movement. It essentially goes up when entrepreneurship flowers, and down when it declines. Workers mainly benefit from entrepreneurship, but there is also temporary unemployment because of the downward movements. Regardless of the positive impact of entrepreneurship on the economic situation of the workers in the long run, they are hostile to the entrepreneur. The average worker, Schumpeter says, 'considers the profit of the entrepreneur as being robbed from him' (Schumpeter, 2003, p. 105).

In mentioning the opinions of the workers, a non-economic element is introduced into the analysis of the economy, and according to Schumpeter it is absolutely essential to also take the non-economic areas into account when you produce a picture of the economy as a whole. When entrepreneurs move ahead, for example, static businesses will soon begin to experience problems. They will begin to dry up and eventually they will disappear, a process that is very painful for the individuals involved. While it is true that this is all for the good in the long run, this is of little consolation for 'those about to be crushed, when the wheels of the new era roll over them' (Schumpeter, 2003, p. 85).

In his attempt to analyze the interaction between the economy and the social, Schumpeter points out that the economic success of the entrepreneur deeply influences his social position or his position outside the economy. But even if successful entrepreneurs rise in society and join the upper class, a group of entrepreneurs is not the same as a social class, according to Schumpeter. A number of entrepreneurs is just a collection of individuals, while a class is a distinct social group. An entrepreneur is also only an entrepreneur as long as he does something new; and he cannot bequeath his entrepreneurial talent to his son:

> His position as entrepreneur is tied to his performance and does not survive his energetic ability to succeed. His position as entrepreneur is essentially only a temporary one, namely, it cannot also be transmitted by inheritance: a successor will be unable to hold on to that social position, unless he inherits the lion's claw along with the prey (Schumpeter, 2003, p. 101).

In discussing the different areas that together make up society, Schumpeter points out that these are all relatively autonomous. He also proposes that the prevalent behavior in all of them is either static or dynamic, precisely as in the economy. Schumpeter considers this last idea as absolutely fundamental to a future theory of social behavior. It constitutes, he says, '*the dawn of the scientific understanding of human affairs*' (Schumpeter, 2003, p. 106; emphasis added). He also notes that while the analysis of static behavior has advanced very far in economics, it is still very much wanting in areas such as politics and art.

Schumpeter ends *Theorie* with a brief discussion of a country's general culture. While in most of the book he presents himself as an advocate of methodological individualism, in approaching this particular topic he takes the stance of methodological holism. There is a totality to a country's culture that simply goes beyond its individual parts, he says. As one would guess, Schumpeter also suggests that there are static as well as dynamic elements to the culture of a country. But in the last hand – and this is how *Theorie* ends – little is known about the forces that ultimately shape the culture of a country.

CONCLUDING REMARKS ON ENTREPRENEURSHIP AND SOCIAL CHANGE

By way of summarizing Schumpeter's position on the issue of entrepreneurship and social change, the following may be said. Schumpeter makes a very sharp distinction between economic changes that are caused by entrepreneurship and those that are not. The former means economic progress for the entrepreneur and in the long run also economic change in a positive direction for the rest of the population – but not for everybody.

Schumpeter also suggests that economic change of the entrepreneurial kind has distinct social effects. The successful entrepreneur will not only make money (entrepreneurial profit), but also rise in the social hierarchy of status and class. For all of this he will be resented, especially by the workers. They will draw economic benefits from his work, but will nonetheless view him as a profiteer and a bit of a thief. Owners of static businesses will slowly go under, suffering not only from economic decline but also from a painful decline in social position.

Is anything of what Schumpeter says in his work from 1911 relevant for today's debate about entrepreneurship and social change? As I see it, the answer is a clear 'yes'; and I would especially like to point to what Schumpeter says in the last chapter of *Theorie*. We can here read that in other areas of society than the economy also, people can be divided into those who are dynamic and do what is new, and those who are static and only repeat what has already been done. Social entrepreneurship, to use a term that is popular today, can be translated into Schumpeterian terminology as *a form of dynamic behavior in one of the non-economic areas of society*.

Does it really help us to know that the term social entrepreneurship can be translated into Schumpeterian language in this way? Again the answer is 'yes', as I see it, and the reason for this is that Schumpeter, in contrast to many of those who discuss social entrepreneurship today, had worked through what a general theory of entrepreneurship should look like *before* he approached the phenomenon of social entrepreneurship. The advantage of proceeding in this way is that you can then single out what factors social entrepreneurship has in common with entrepreneurship in general and ignore the rest. In brief, it helps to have a general theory of some phenomenon before you begin to analyze a sub-phenomenon of that phenomenon (see Figure 1.1).

Does the fact that Schumpeter's theory is so strongly centered around an individual – a nearly heroic individual – detract from the value of his ideas on entrepreneurship? My answer would be yes and no. Entrepreneurship is indeed a social process, and Schumpeter no doubt has a tendency to hero worship. On the other hand, one of the many interesting things about both economic and social entrepreneurship is precisely that a single individual can make an enormous difference (for social entrepreneurship in this respect, see e.g. Bornstein, 2004). There is also the fact that Schumpeter himself suggested a few times that one may want to conceptualize the entrepreneur as a group or some other collective. As I see it, the most valuable insight in Schumpeter is his notion of entrepreneurship as the putting together of new combinations, not that it is an individual who does it.

	Economy	**Society**
Dynamic or entrepreneurial change	Development	Social entrepreneurship
Static or non-entrepreneurial change	Adaptation	Social evolution

Note: In *Theorie der wirtschaftlichen Entwicklung* (1911) Schumpeter presented his most radical and original theory of entrepreneurship, which encompasses not only economic but also social change. In the last chapter, for example, he suggested that his argument about dynamic and static elements in economic life is also applicable to what happens in the non-economic areas of society. He argued as well – but this is not captured by the figure above – that dynamic economic change ('development') typically entails a series of social changes.

Figure 1.1   Economic change and social entrepreneurship, according to the young Schumpeter

What do Schumpeter's ideas tell us about the agenda today for social entrepreneurship? The main answer to this question, I believe, is that students of social entrepreneurship can draw quite a bit insight and inspiration from what has already been accomplished in the study of economic entrepreneurship along Schumpeterian lines. We would, for example, expect that there will be quite a bit of *resistance* to social entrepreneurship, and that this needs to be studied. It would probably also be useful to explore the distinction between *inventions* and *innovations* when it comes to social entrepreneurship. And there is finally also Schumpeter's idea of business cycles, which should lead us to ask ourselves if there are similar ups and downs – caused by the rise and fall of social profit? – in social entrepreneurship.

Let us now sum up the argument of this article. Through his work from the 1910s to the 1940s, Schumpeter worked out what I consider to be the most important and creative theory of entrepreneurship that is currently in existence. Being an entrepreneur means to do something new and to break the mould. More precisely, being an entrepreneur, Schumpeter suggests, means (1) to seize on *a new combination*, (2) *push it through* in reality (3) and to do this *through sheer willpower and energy*. Finally, it is an unfortunate sign of the lack of interest in Schumpeter's work that the first and most radical version of his theory of entrepreneurship is still so little known. But since it also so happens that the young Schumpeter explicitly tried to extend his theory of entrepreneurship to non-economic areas of society, or to what today is called social entrepreneurship, there now exists one more reason why we should pay attention to his ideas.

2. The practice of social entrepreneurship: notes toward a resource-perspective

Yohanan Stryjan[1]

> If the economist is to understand the behaviour of firms, he must make some assumptions on why they do what they do, . . . (Penrose, 1959/1995, p. 26).

REFRAMING SOCIAL ENTREPRENEURSHIP

The notion of social entrepreneurship and the manifest linkage between social entrepreneurship, social change and economic development are attracting increasing attention from scholars and policy-makers alike. A generally accepted definition of the concept and a conceptual framework in which it could be integrated are, however, still lacking. The approach proposed in this paper focuses on social entrepreneurs' *mode of action* rather than this action's objective, motive or social justification as is often the case in current approaches to social entrepreneurship (Alvord et al., 2004; Thompson et al., 2000). It follows a Schumpeterian line of reasoning that centers on the creation of new combinations of resources by discrete actors (Schumpeter, 1934). An enterprise is primarily a combination of resources, or, more precisely, of the 'services' that can be extracted from those resources (Penrose, 1959/1995). Identifying these 'extraction' possibilities, and (re)combining them in new configurations is the central function of the entrepreneur. It is suggested, accordingly, that a search for a definition ought to focus on *the constitution of the actors that engage in the pursuit, the nature of resources mobilized, and the practices pursued over time in extracting them.* Social entrepreneurship is here not defined by its 'usefulness' to others (see Baumol, 1990), nor constrained to any one particularly 'social' form of enterprise (such as non-profits, charities or social enterprises). Nor is it restricted to a narrow range of activity. Any undertaking called into being by an act of social entrepreneurship has to meet the key requirements of: (a) being core activity for target populations; (b) maintaining financing/resource mobilization *over time* (sustainability); and this second requirement presupposes (c) mustering the support of a community, however defined.

In handling these issues, the entrepreneurship literature tends to be drawn towards the spectacular, the successful and the highly visible. This bias towards high-profile achievement sways the choice of cases studied. Rather than exploring the spectacular, the path chosen here is, in a quasi-anthropological manner, nearly the reverse (Steyaert and Katz, 2004), namely exploring manifestations and problems of entrepreneurship in some of the arenas and actors *least* commonly associated with entrepreneurship. An example is the public provision of welfare, focusing on actors that normally are found at the receiving end of entrepreneurial initiatives rather than at their creative center: parents, the gravely handicapped, mental patients, the permanently unemployed and the marginalized. Such ordinary endeavours can provide an illustration of entrepreneurship stripped to its essentials. Innovation, a central element of entrepreneurship (see Schumpeter, 1951/1989), manifests itself in our cases primarily through ingenious ways of assembling and utilizing available resources to form enterprises – from unlikely elements and against all institutional odds.

The article is organized as follows: some initial considerations on social capital and its relationship to social enterprising are presented in the next section. Practical applications of a resource-based approach to the study of grass-roots enterprising in Sweden will be presented in the section that follows; the study object and arenas were deliberately chosen to highlight aspects of social entrepreneurship that otherwise tend to be obscured by high-profile fundraising and practices of conspicuous distribution. The presentation proceeds from rudimentary cases that are organized around a single process of resource conversion to more complex ones. The themes highlighted in this section are subsequently integrated into a tentative model that re-examines the relationship between social structure, entrepreneurship and resources, which is presented in the closing section.

A FIRST LOOK AT SOCIAL ENTREPRENEURSHIP AND SOCIAL CAPITAL

The ability of actors to mobilize resources by virtue of their social affiliations is often referred to as social capital (Portes, 1998, p. 6). Coleman (1987, 1988) suggested that a high level of reciprocal ties between members of a community and the presence of social norms facilitate action, and thus are conductive to higher economic achievement. This generally positive ambience is labeled 'social capital' by Coleman (1987). Later works by Bourdieu (Bourdieu and Wacquant, 1992) and Portes and Sensenbrenner (1993) link social capital to individual and household achievement but elaborate the concept in divergent directions. Bourdieu (ibid, p. 119) speaks about 'a durable network of more or less institutionalised relationships of mutual acquaintance and recognition' and the ways in which these are appropriated and drawn upon by individuals and groups in pursuit of their own ends, while Portes (1998), and Portes and Sensenbrenner (1993) address the social control aspect (through norms and configurations of social ties) of social capital, and the mechanisms through which it is attained.[2] Though Bourdieu emphasizes competition and Coleman, Portes and Sensenbrenner consider social capital to be a public good, all authors focus on its role in facilitating individual or sub-group achievement within the context of a given community. Simplifying the issue somewhat: while Bourdieu's question is why some in a given community achieves more than others, the aim of Coleman and of Portes and Sensenbrenner is to provide an explanation of why certain communities appear to be more conductive to achievement than others. The possibility of aggregating individual achievement into community welfare is indirectly allowed for by both Coleman and Portes' approaches, and hinted at in the illustrations they provide.

Putnam's (1993a) seminal work *Making Democracy Work* played an important role in spreading the concept into the domain of policy formation and implementation.[3] Putnam's approach broadly follows Coleman's rather than Bourdieu's, though the focus of research is shifted from diffuse 'features of social organization, such as trust, norms and networks' to their formal and, thus more readily measurable manifestations, such as associations and voluntary organizations. The level of social capital in a given community is generally seen as enhancing economic welfare and civic governance. A claim is made to the effect that such findings may be generalizable across entire nations and regions (Putnam, 1993).

A basic weakness, as pointed out by Portes (1998), is the arbitrary fashion in which a 'community' whose social capital is being mobilized and the social contexts that facilitate social action, are defined. While we may accept the fuzziness of 'neighbourhoods', or even nations, the conceptual difficulty becomes evident in cases in which social action precedes and triggers the emergence of a supporting community that, once created, spans or splits previous boundaries or asserts identities that previously were denied.

Quite in keeping with the tendency of treating the 'community' as a predefined given that is 'mobilized' by the focal actor, social capital is seemingly drawn upon at will from this source, to facilitate action and/or pave the way to economic resources. Its reproduction is seen as a (largely unintended) sideeffect of the ensuing economic or social activities (Coleman, 1988). The reverse pattern of purposive formation and maintenance of social links, and the investment of physical resources in such pursuits remains largely unexplored.

Entrepreneurship evidently spans the conceptual gap between the domain of social capital and the domains of economic performance and 'conventional' capital. The paper explores the relevance of this positioning for the practice of social entrepreneurship, and does not venture to trace or resolve the definition and measurement problems that the 'social capital' concept gives rise to. I resort to the concept of social capital, somewhat in Coleman's (1988) spirit, as a convenient shorthand label for the stock of social ties that make up a community, and as 'an aid towards making the micro-to-macro transition without elaborating the social structural details through which it occurs' (1988, p. 101). The focus, however, is on the purposeful action rather than on the structure surrounding it. In a reversal of Portes and Sensenbrenner's stated goal of exploring 'how structure constrains, supports individual goal-seeking behaviour' (1993, p. 1321), the ambition here is to explore 'how agents (individual or collective) purposively attempt to generate, and avail themselves of social structural features in order to further their own pursuits, and how resources are both mobilized and invested in this pursuit'. Different aspects of this practice will be presented in a review of various forms of welfare service cooperatives and social enterprises in Sweden in the next section.

SOCIAL ENTERPRISING IN SWEDEN: SOME EXAMPLES

The examples to be discussed below are Swedish welfare service cooperatives, social cooperatives, and community development enterprises. They illustrate practices developed by social enterprises in dealing with the Swedish welfare system and local society. Though none of the organization forms is unique to Sweden (indeed, some of the cases related below were inspired by American or UK examples) their entrepreneurial features are set in relief by the Swedish context. The Swedish welfare state's institutional set-up and organizational tradition differ significantly from both the American one and from those of most European countries. Consequently, organizational forms and practices within welfare and social entrepreneurship differ from the mainstream, to the extent that claims were raised (James, 1989; Boli, 1991) that 'there is no third sector in Sweden'. Some of the Swedish model's central features (Stryjan, 1994b) directly impacted our field of study, such as: an acknowledged primacy of public solutions within the provision of health education and welfare services, a public monopoly over the financing of welfare services, and an ingrained negative attitude towards charity – a term that has clearly derisive connotations in Swedish usage.[4] The resulting composition of the organizational population, the fields of activity chosen, the range of resources available, and the practices developed in Sweden can hardly be considered typical or representative of social entrepreneurship at large. The prime advantage of this research setting lies precisely in its 'otherness'. In something of a figure–ground reversal of the field, fundraising and conspicuous redistribution play a subordinate role in the Swedish case. Associations (voluntary and for-profit) maintain a higher profile than foundations, mutuality is preferred to charity, and public money is perceived as more legitimate than private donations by the organizations concerned and by the broad public alike. Lastly, the (re)allocation of resources accomplished by the mechanisms of the welfare state also places the practice of entrepreneurship within the reach of groups that would otherwise be found more at the demand rather than at the supply end of social services. The cases that follow, illustrate how the key requirements of social entrepreneurship – pursuing a chosen core activity, mobilizing and converting resources, and handling the enterprise's relationships with the community – may be met and integrated under the institutional regime of the Swedish welfare state.

Welfare-service cooperatives are alternative providers of mandatory social services. Kindergartens and assistance to the gravely handicapped are delivered by two such groups. Both groups, consisting of organizations started by service-recipients, played an important role in redefining the interface between social initiatives and the former public monopoly, and rely on similar public financing mechanisms, though their mode of operation and relations with the surrounding society are highly different. Social cooperatives are also constituted by their would-be users, namely persons excluded from the labour-market that attempt to create a workplace for themselves. However, they operate in a field in which institutionalized public financing mechanisms do not exist and private ones are not socially endorsed. Their survival hinges on business revenues and on goodwill from the public sector and the surrounding community. Finally, community enterprises are local development associations whose agendas also include the integration of marginalized groups. Community enterprises operate in roughly the same field as social cooperatives, but are started by considerably better endowed actors, and can therefore engage in high-profile business activity and a more active and multifaceted relationship with the local community and with the authorities. All descriptions are primarily based on material collected in a number of research projects conducted or led by myself.[5]

Welfare Cooperatives: Pooling and Conversion of Entitlements

Welfare service cooperatives illustrate some of the central features of the Swedish welfare state's institutions, and the way these were taken advantage of by social entrepreneurs. The Swedish tradition of solving social problems and answering needs through public (rather than private) intervention eventually led to a virtual public monopoly over welfare, education, and employment services, safeguarded by regulations that prohibited private financing for those services that are provided by the public sector (fees, where allowed, were

regulated at *below* own cost level) and by norms that strongly inhibit donations to those services that are not. This combination effectively hindered the
emergence of non-public initiatives within health education and welfare until
the 1980s (Stryjan and Wijkström, 1996). The emergence of parent-cooperatives played an important role in breaking this trend and in opening the field
for new social initiatives. The basic model of parent-cooperatives is relatively
simple, both conceptually and resource-wise: parents' statutory entitlement to
daycare for their children (that should otherwise be met by municipal units) is
converted into a public subsidy for a childcare place. A group of parents forms
an association that pools these (otherwise inconvertible) entitlements, creates
the appropriate governance structure, establishes a kindergarten for the
members' children, and recruits the professional staff (Pestoff, 1998).

At the core of this arrangement stands, on the one hand, the conversion of
a statutory obligation to provide daycare into a welfare entitlement that is, in
turn, convertible into funding, and on the other, the welding together of the
entitlement holders into a functioning social and organizational entity.

The rule-modification that made such transactions possible was accomplished by 'wild' initiatives, the first of which started as early as 1974
(Engström and Engström, 1982). The form's institutional breakthrough came
first in 1985. The first parent-cooperatives operated in an institutional limbo,
surviving through shrewd manoeuvring between the national and municipal
financing systems, significant material concessions,[6] advocacy, and sheer
persistence. Participants' commitment and the undertakings' entrepreneurial
dimension were crucial in that stage, but gradually waned in concert with the
organizational population's rapid expansion throughout the 1980s to nearly a
thousand by 1992 (Normark et al., 1993, p. 200), and the ensuing institution-
alization of the form.

The merit of the model lies in its simplicity and replicability. A single
mechanism of resource-conversion, whereby parents that join the cooperative
bestow on it entitlements that are disbursed by the public sector, constitutes the
model's backbone. Maintaining the group (a task that naturally includes
recruiting new parents and eliciting their outlays in fees, voluntary time and
competence) is the one necessary *and sufficient* condition for continued
financing. Local community support (beyond the highly formalized approval
by the municipality) needs not be sought and networking with similar cooperatives is limited.

The principle of *financing by affiliation* introduced by parents' cooperatives also stands at the core of *Independent Living* cooperatives that adminis-
ter around-the-clock assistance for gravely physically handicapped persons.
In this case too, welfare entitlements are converted into a source of financing
by a group of potential beneficiaries that pool these resources and create an
enterprise. The nature of the user/member group, and the organizational solu-

tion created to meet these members' objectives are substantially different, though.

STIL (*Stockholm Independent Living*), initiated in 1984[7] by a group of gravely handicapped activists from The National Union of Handicapped Persons, champions a consciously militant empowerment strategy, inspired by the American Centers for Independent Living (CIL) model (Gough, 1989). To let the gravely handicapped control the assistance that they are daily dependent on was seen as a key step in their attaining control over their own life-situations. After three years of negotiations a financing formula that decouples entitlements from public care-providers and adapts the CIL model to Swedish conditions was devised. At present, the model is anchored in legislation and works as follows: members recruit and coordinate their respective groups of personal assistants; the cooperative (whose administration is run by members) provides the administrative infrastructure. The administrative fee imposed on each member's entitlement-based account is the association's business revenue, to be used as it sees fit.

Besides improved service, the cooperative effects an important symbolic transformation of its members, from passive recipients of help to coordinators and employers (some members could, in fact, take well paid professional jobs). STIL's policy of employing a large number of unprofessional part-time assistants (rather than a handful of full-time professionals) can be seen as part of its members' quest to avoid binding dependence relations, and to follow their own personal inclinations and sustain broader contact networks. This policy places extremely high demands both on the individual members (indeed, some second-movers into the field adopted less ambitious formulas) and on the association's administrative capacity, and would have been quite impossible to sustain within a public sector organization. The cooperative, which is run by the handicapped themselves, provides the administrative infrastructure that handles personnel administration and budget negotiations with the social authorities, training for new members, and propagation of the Independent Living concept.

Structurally, the STIL organization is a network in which each member constitutes a node, and the network infrastructure and maintenance are indirectly supported by public funds. The stability of the basic financing arrangement provides the nexus organization with a platform for innovative administration practices and for active and expansive network management. Finally, through the organization of each member's circle of assistants, the construction of members' social networks is effectively underwritten by public funding.

Social Cooperatives: A Low-key Labour-Market Integration Strategy[8]

Social cooperatives are worker-cooperatives formed by individuals that were classed as permanently disabled (physically or mentally) by the social insurance and labor market authorities. Prospective founders of such cooperatives are entitled to housing and a subsistence pension – but are disqualified from seeking entry into the labour market.[9] While the two examples of welfare cooperatives dealt with (re)organizing delivery of mainstream statutory services by their prospective recipients and with the restructuring of recognized entitlements, social cooperatives aspire to create a workplace for a group that is statutorily deprived of the right to work. To circumvent the trap created by regulations, an 'employer entity' is created by those involved, that offers work (ideally, but not exclusively through a formal employment contract) to its members.

The first cooperatives of this type emerged in the late 1980s, as the traditional mental institutions were wound down, and were started by discharged former inmates. One of the pioneers of this first wave, the ICS cooperative was founded by a group of seven former inmates of the Kristinehamn mental hospital and two ward orderlies that stayed with the group (formally, as 'outstationed' public employees) as non-member tutors. The former mental hospital's carpentry shop became the cooperative's permanent premises, and defined its field of operation. Similar cooperatives were also started by and with groups of mentally handicapped, drug addicts and marginalized immigrants. Though the formal model closely reminds one of 'job-creation cooperatives' elsewhere (see Hirschman, 1980; Oakeshott, 1978; Pattiniämi, 2001), it differs on two important counts: (a) the presence of tutors in most of the cooperatives, made necessary by limitations on members' capacity, and (b) the cooperative is not a 'breadwinner-cooperative' in the strict sense of the term. Indeed, the direct economic benefit to members from obtaining a formal employment contract is marginal,[10] and members' alternative to participation is not economic misery but idleness. The enterprises' declared prime objective is personal rehabilitation and improving the life-quality of its members, through the creation of a positive (work) environment. Objectives such as labour-market integration or expansion are considered secondary to this task.

It is difficult to present a consistent general model of social cooperatives' resource-flows. The basic pattern of individuals coming together and pooling their resources, familiar from the illustrations of the welfare cooperatives, is repeated in this case as well. The tasks of keeping the group together and keeping the enterprise afloat merge in a single core task. However, the founders in this case are extremely low on personal resources and social contacts compared to better-endowed persons. Nor can they draw on clear-cut welfare entitlements that could be directly converted and pooled into a stable source of baseline funding. Thus, social cooperatives are immediately dependent for their day-to-day survival on their own business revenues and on the better-endowed actors in their environment. The resources that the participants can pool together and recombine in order to construct their enterprises include their time and effort (this 'sweat equity' is de facto underwritten by social transfers), and vaguely defined non-pecuniary welfare entitlements such as a statutory right for 'meaningful occupation', whose conversion into municipal support has to be negotiated on a case-by-case basis. Two categories of invariable production costs have to be met by the enterprise to stay afloat: (a) premises (and equipment) that may be rented or obtained free of charge, and (b) tutors' wages. In keeping with the Swedish normative makeup, tutors are considered a part of the production infrastructure and receive wages as a rule. Member-users' contributions, on the other hand, may be (and often is) voluntary.[11] Business revenues, augmented by external voluntary inputs, make up the balance. The eventual surplus determines the extent to which the enterprise can formally employ any of its members. The continuous resource hunting and gathering process (Stryjan, 1989a), involves exchanges with the public sector, and with local society and business partners. The tutors often carry the chief burden of providing the cooperative with a vital contact network.

The authorities participate in the enterprise's invariable costs in the form of a loan 'in kind' or a contractual obligation. Depending on the municipality's goodwill and the cooperative's negotiating skills, agreements regarding the purchase of services or the granting of subsidies may also be negotiated. Significantly, though many of the social cooperatives deliver rehabilitation services and provide occupation places to others than their members, this activity is seldom acknowledged as a professional service (and thus, a source of revenue for the enterprise) by the authorities. It would seem that social enterprises are more readily accepted as contractors for low-qualified tasks and recipients of subsidies than as business partners in the field of integration.

Social co-operatives' business activities tend to concentrate on services to the local population or to other SMEs in the immediate surroundings. They are seldom aimed at large corporations and only to a limited degree towards the public sector. Whether deliberately or by default, the activities chosen often facilitate a tighter social enmeshment for the cooperative and for its members, such as running a workplace canteen, a cafeteria in an industrial park, a day care dog-kennel, a second-hand bookstore, a pet shop, gardening and maintenance in a housing project, and so on (Bartilsson et al., 2000). Relations to customers are clearly personalized, and the duality of social and economic objectives is evident in this case: social links between the enterprise and its social environment meet members' needs, but may also be converted into new commercial contracts, or be instrumental in the pursuit of (economic) capital.

Though all social cooperatives do trade some output through market relations, their principal output is symbolic in its character (Stryjan and Wijkström, 1996). Their chief performance consists of transforming their members, and bestowing on them a status that has been denied them by society: that of having work, an enterprise to run, and a community of peers. In this respect, the enterprise is its own central product, and it is difficult to determine whether business dealings are due to the enterprise's business skills, or an expression of community support. This ambiguity is at times maintained in business to business relations as well. Thus, though ICS's relation to its corporate customers was ostensibly businesslike, there was (according to the manager) a tacit acceptance from these that ICS cannot handle short orders and rapid deliveries, a weakness that would probably have disqualified it in most ordinary business dealings. Keeping in mind the highly ambivalent attitude to charity in Swedish society, the ambiguity may well be deliberately maintained by all parts in the relationship, so as to convey the symbolical status of an 'ordinary' business enterprise on the entire undertaking (Stryjan, 2002).

Community Enterprises: an Integrated High-Profile Approach

The Community Enterprise model was directly inspired by UK experiences, and is the least specifically Swedish of the organization forms discussed in this article. Community enterprises (Stryjan, 2003/5) share most of the goals and values of social cooperatives, but integrate these within a larger agenda of community development. They generally start from a considerably stronger resource endowment, opt for high visibility, engage to a higher degree in transactions with corporate customers, and often link to (or incorporate) key individuals and organizations in the community. Environmental linkages would often be encoded into the enterprise's board, and most community enterprises studied have externally recruited board members (Levin, 2005). The illustrations in this section are taken from a case-study of *Medvind*, a community enterprise in southeastern Sweden that concentrates on integration of mentally handicapped. This enterprise, started as an offshoot of a grassroots development project, incorporates two local businessmen and the local bank director in its governance structure, and is chaired by a senior corporate executive.

These linkages are instrumental in mobilizing credits and business partners. The managing director's past experiences as a municipal officer, local politician, and activist in the national association for the mentally handicapped open a variety of channels to public authorities at local and national levels. The enterprise's manager neatly summarizes the approach: '[without] local support/embeddedness,[12] I could not run any activity whatsoever. If I do not have the bank then I cannot run any project here, and so on. Trust is enormously important to cultivate'. Cultivation of trust is an ongoing achievement that is attained through a flow of reiterative exchange transactions, in which the enterprise is not merely a client and a grateful recipient of assistance, but also an active participant that is called upon to reciprocate and prove his suitability and reliability. The public sector is met on several planes: as an authority, as important customer (of rehabilitation services), and sometimes as a partner in joint projects (Stryjan, 2003/5). Thus, the different interfaces to community, business and the public sector cannot be analytically separated as in the case of social cooperatives. The relation is perceived as a partnership between equals, rather than in terms of subsidiarity or subservience. 'The advantage is that we are free: we are not recipients of grants, we supply and sell services'. Public trainee placements are a central part of the enterprise's mission and a source of up to 25 per cent of its business revenue. Trainees may be directed and financed by *any* of the authorities within health, labour and welfare. There is a continuous, ongoing negotiation: about financing levels and financing forms, the employment status of participants and their grant-eligibility – but also about participants' housing situations and social services they receive – issues that lie outside the business relation proper. In parallel with cultivating business contacts, *Medvind* also actively seeks – and often obtains – financing from the selfsame public organs, for development projects and community initiatives.

Medvind's prime source of revenue is business-to-business services. The enterprise is highly aware of the importance of networking for *all* its commercial operations, and is active in the regional chamber of commerce and in local business events. A degree of strain exists between the commercially justified ambition to project a hard-nosed businesslike image, and the threat that this may generate among peers. Active involvement in projects that are oriented to common goals, such as enhancing the entire region's competitiveness, is one way of coping with this situation. At the same time, in a rare show of vulnerability, *Medvind* declined to pursue an ISO certification, which was judged 'too expensive' by the manager and board. That large multinationals are nonetheless willing to contract services from it may attest to the goodwill and good standing the enterprise enjoys.

The role of close ties, and the trust (and, whenever necessary, resources) they generate, is put to visible test in cases of crisis. *Medvind* did, in fact, recently weather a serious crisis: the withdrawal of a major client that stood, at the time, for 66 per cent of the enterprise's turnover, shortly after the enterprise took a major loan. Recovery was largely made possible thanks to contacts in the local business community, which aided a quick recruitment of new customers, to social authorities' willingness to increase orders, and to the bank's patient attitude. The considerable *sang froid* demonstrated by *Medvind*'s customers, creditors and business partners was proven justified in the long run.

OVERVIEW OF THE PRESENTED ENTERPRISES

Each of the enterprise types was started and is run by a group that is held together by a common need/life situation and a shared idea of how this need should be met or resolved. The activities initiated are self-centered, as their initiators either are identical with or included in the target population. In the first two cases they also are the customers. The four enterprise types are summarized in Table 2.1.

The resource mix mobilized by each of the four enterprise types varies considerably. This difference can be traced back to the rule regimes that govern their respective fields of operation, but also to the involved persons' endowments and life situations. All enterprises reviewed in this paper are organized along cooperative principles. This choice, though strongly swayed by the Swedish organizational tradition, also reflects the enterprises' economic rationale, which involves the pooling of resources that members can access, and applying them to a collective pursuit of common goals. These property-rights and collective action aspects of social entrepreneurship will be discussed in the next section.

DISCUSSION

Embeddedness Revisited: Institutions, Resources and the Social Context

Resource-wise, the entrepreneur's field of action is defined by the existing societal distributions of entitlements (Sen, 1981) and the available (in the sense of not being barred by accepted norms) modes of extraction in a given society. Understanding these rules and procedures is pivotal for understanding the practices resorted to by social entrepreneurs in handling socially embedded resources. While the concept of embedded transactions is widely accepted, the notion of *resources* being embedded may merit some discussion. Whether a resource that an individual is entitled to is alienable (may be freely contributed or traded by its holder) or not, and what conversion rules or limitations apply, would vary from one social context to another (Eggertson, 1991). The complex, ambiguous and culture-dependent character of such property rights and rule regimes is most evident at the interface between social entrepreneurship and business activity. Quite obviously, some assets held individually may not be transferred. Others may be transferred by way of gift, but not sold/exchanged (Titmuss, 1977; Geertz, 1973); the circle of potential transaction parts it may be transferred to may be open or restricted. Just as 'ownership' over a resource is not necessarily tantamount to control over it (Stryjan, 1989b), the *right to allocate resources* is not invariably linked to the right to use or appropriate them; the right to use an asset may or may not be transferable, and so on.

This complexity contrasts with the dominant market model, within which resources are normatively expected to be fully separable from their 'owner' if

Table 2.1   The enterprises: activity and resource mix

Enterprise type/ Actor/carrier	Need/key idea	Core service/ product	Target group	Resource mix
Parents' co-ops/ Group of parents	Involvement in own childrens' upbringing	Child care	Own	Affiliation/conversion, entitlements, fees and own voluntary work
STIL/ Group of gravely handicapped	Independent living	Administration of assistance	Own	Affiliation/conversion, entitlements and own voluntary administrative work
Social Co-ops/ Handicapped/ marginalized	Sense of own worth; Creation of work-place	Assorted products, proximity services	Own	Own (and committed others') voluntary work, business revenues, contributions (primarily public)
Community enterprises/ Key community members	Integration as community development	B2B services, trainee places for authorities	Entire community	Business revenues, project financing, some quality voluntary work on board

he or she so desires. Strings tied onto the free movement of assets so as to make them less alienable are perceived as market imperfections. Polanyi (1944/2001) suggested that mobility/alienability on the one hand, and the restrictions on it on the other, represent, in fact, separate normative orders. The ascendance of the market leads in this view to commodification, through which social ties and 'traditional' forms of property rights are displaced by impersonal market rules. Polanyi's vision, in which the economic market order is progressively dis-embedding itself from the social orders, and achieving domination over them is echoed (in an already victorious market-order) nearly sixty years later, by de Soto's (2001) 'bell jar' concept. The approach advocated (primarily as regards property rights to real-estate) is something of a conceptual mirror-image of Polanyi's. Inasmuch the ascendance of market institutions leads to a declassification of resources held through traditional rights of possession, and the exclusion from the market of those whose assets no longer are legitimately tradable, the path to empowerment leads through the market, by way of an institutional reclassification of held assets.

Non-market property regimes need not, however, be 'traditional'. A different set of 'non-market' property-rights and entitlement packages is defined, in advanced welfare societies, by the institutions of the welfare state. The rules that regulate transfer and (eventual) exchange in this case differ from those that would apply either in the economy or in civil society. The entitlements dealt with are, as said earlier, economic by their nature (either immediately, as in the case of transfer payments, or indirectly, when disbursed as publicly-financed transfer services), and social in their content. The drive to convert these entitlements into assets may, in fact, be considered as application of de Soto's reasoning to the welfare and labour spheres.

Common to the spheres of reciprocity and social relations and of welfare/statutory redistribution is the fact that assets are wholly or partly withheld from the market exchange mechanism, and linked to physical persons instead of being freely alienable. As a matter of common sense, the most feasible way of accessing resources that are embedded in such a fashion in social or institutional systems is through directly linking to these individuals that *can* access them. Simply put: wherever individuals and resources are bound together by formal or informal rules, the formation of an enterprise requires *assembling together actual human beings*, and not merely accumulation of impersonal physical (or financial) resources.

Actors and Resources: A Community of Action

Cooperative enterprise, the incorporation form resorted to in all the cases studied, is the traditional mode of linking individually held non-market resources. Historically, it was employed in integrating unlikely (and, at the time, seemingly non-marketable) resources into unified economic instruments: the purchasing power of the poor, the creditworthiness of smallholders (see Bonus and Schmidt, 1990; Yunus and Jolis, 2003; Bernasek and Stanfield, 1997), or the labor of the unemployable (Hirschman, 1980). Indeed, it is *the act of pooling* that renders such resources marketable, and provides a potential platform for entrepreneurial action. Though collective entrepreneurial action need not confine itself to institutionalized channels (Hirschman, 1981, 1984; Tetzschner, 1998), or specialized incorporation forms (Reich, 1987; Vyakarnam, Jacobs and Handelberg, 1999), cooperative governance structures can fulfill the twin tasks of safeguarding the resource-holders' rights and of facilitating joint action to advance their interests.

Entrepreneurial features are most manifest in a cooperative enterprise's founding years, during which a common unit is forged, members are motivated/mobilized to join it, and institutions are shaped. Studying new cooperatives' founding years (Stryjan, 1994a), we find that the crystallization of a core group that progressively links in additional participants, resources and fields of activity often proceeds in a non-linear, open fashion, seizing opportunities, as these present themselves. Prospective members' relation to their organization, and the possibilities open for collective action in the four enterprise types are presented in Table 2.2 below.

All organizations reviewed are created by volition, (though social cooperatives' members lack other realistic alternatives), and have shared perceptions of the enterprise's goal and activity. However, members' circumstances, and the available options and motivations for entrepreneurial action, differ considerably. Parent-cooperatives prime objective is to provide a stable environment for members' children, while independent living-cooperatives are created to promote members' individual development. Enterprise development is accorded a low priority on the organizations' and their members' agendas, and entrepreneurial action would be resorted to in managing crises and introducing improvements. By comparison, both social cooperatives and community enterprises are naturally oriented towards collective action. Both are conceived as open-ended projects, and both are committed to the advancement of their target community, though the perceptions of community and the orientation towards growth may differ somewhat between, as well as within, the two groups. The capacity for concerted collective action presupposes a shared conception of 'actorhood' and of the joint undertaking's intrinsic worth. To the extent that members are expected to commit personally linked resources (including intangible ones, as contacts and reputation) to the joint activity, transactions would follow, and aim to uphold, two basic assumptions (Stryjan, 1989b), namely those of mutual dependence and of permanence (see Uzzi, 1997). In parallel with forming the enterprise proper, the founder(s) often invest(s) in assembling a network of supporting individuals and organizations

Table 2.2 The team: members and strategies

Type	Alternatives available	Level of inclusion	Time-horizon	Strategy range	Supporting network/community	Resource mobilization mode
Parents' co-ops	Yes	Partial	Limited	Regulated	No	Affiliation/conversion
Independent Living (STIL)	Yes	Total/fragmented	Open	Partly regulated	No	Affiliation/conversion
Social co-ops	(No)	High	Open	Circumscribed by own limitations	Weak	Hunting and gathering
Community enterprises	(Yes)	High	Open	Open	Yes	Business, networking

in the enterprise's environment, which are essential to the enterprise's resource procurement. The boundaries between these 'outreaches' of the enterprise and the focal organization proper are often held vague, and intentionally so.

Converting Capital: Social Entrepreneurship and Social Capital Revisited

'Social capital stands for the ability of actors to secure benefits by virtue of membership in social networks or other social structures' (Portes, 1998, p. 6). So perceived, social capital may be seen as a tapestry of potential access paths, to be used by prospective organization-builders. The ties that link individuals' potential also link the resources that those individuals can access, mobilize (through his/her contacts) or allocate (through his/her position in other organizations/enterprises). Social entrepreneurship is thus largely a matter of connecting such nodes into networks so as to provide the desired resource-mix (Penrose, 1959/1995), effectively converting social capital into economic resources, and a set of nodes into an enterprise *in spe*. Rules of generalised equity (Ouchi, 1980) apply in such constellations, in the sense that members/participants in a supporting network expect that their contributions will be reciprocated *in the long run*, though not necessarily in the same currency. As different parts/nodes of an enterprise's support network may be located in different property-rights regimes, the nature of contributions and of reciprocation would vary, depending on the context and the giver/receiver. Ties, obligations, and exchanges are thus not exclusively bound to a single 'purely social' or 'economy only' sphere. On the contrary, material resources would often be reciprocated for by symbolic or social ones, and vice versa. The main types of such transactions will be reviewed in the sections below.

Contributions: Exchanges from Social to Economic Capital

The simplest traditional form of nearly linear conversion is that of volunteering (see Quarter et al., 2004). Credit cooperatives and associations are the best known institutionalized forms of direct conversion of individual pledges into (access to) capital (Bonus and Schmidt, 1990; Yunus and Jolis, 2003; Bernasek and Standfield, 1997). Welfare cooperatives convert social capital into affiliation in a similar manner, and the pooled welfare entitlements so gained into public financing. The full range of procurement and contribution strategies forms a complex and highly heterogeneous mix: donations in kind within the 'gift economy' circuit intertwine with highly sophisticated symbolic contributions, such as recommending an enterprise to another prospective customer, a credit assessment or (for officials) a liberal attitude in applying existing regulations and eligibility requirements. 'Good standing' in institutionalized welfare settings affects approval of projects, interpretation of entitlements, and allocation of contracts contingent on the applicants' perceived good faith and reliability. Important favors may be extended also by default (as demonstrated in the case of *Medvind*. The decision of the local bank director to let confidence win over prudence, and neither terminate *Medvind's* credit-line once its order-book problems became known nor move in to foreclose on the enterprise's considerable mortgage is a prime example of such restraint. In acting in this fashion, the director willingly exposed himself and the bank to risk, in a manner that can hardly be understood in pure business terms. His (in)action, in turn, put an obligation on the enterprise's management to refrain from filing in for a bankruptcy and to do its utmost in effecting a turnaround. This, in turn, enhanced the trust relationships that the enterprise evidently managed to build up, and the efficacy of its social strategy.

Reproduction: from Social Capital to Social Capital

All cases discussed illustrate a consistent strategy of construction and reproduction of supporting networks in the relevant environment. Nourishing a supportive relationship is, to an extent, a matter of promoting the intrinsic worth of the joint enterprise's operation, but reciprocity and utility that should be reinforced by deed, not by word alone, also play an important role. To put it bluntly, in order to enjoy continuing support, the social entrepreneur has to *repeatedly* prove the enterprise's actual or potential usefulness to partners and members. Such reiterative exchanges are self evident in customer and partner relations with households and local business. In all these, a viable exit option exists, and may be utilized by those dissatisfied. In formal settings, public or corporate, in which all parts are sensitive to allegations of favoritism, exchanges may be highly intricate and implicit. Some may involve contribution to a partners' standing in *other* networks that they participate in. Community enterprises such as *Medvind*, may provide additional indirect benefits to their partners through the extensive contact networks that they maintain. To an extent trust bestowed is reciprocated by facilitating contacts *between* partners and backers (that constitute nodes in the enterprise's network) and by making its own network accessible for the launching of new initiatives by other network members (see Badelt, 2003, p. 149).

Investment/Reconversion: from Economic to Social Capital

Donations and sponsoring are the traditional clear-cut examples of exchange situations in which economic resources are 'traded' by the giver for social or symbolic returns. Depending on the norms that apply in a given society, and the parties' respective standing, such transactions may be initiated by either party in the exchange and would enhance the standing of either of these or of both. For social enterprises that would normally stand at the recipient end of the gift relationship promotion and fundraising, rather than donations are likely principal modes of investment. This is, however, only a part of the picture: just as in the case of conversion, important reconversion decisions are often taken by default, most typically by declining to pursue an opportunistic course of action. The opportunity cost incurred when an enterprise chooses to follow the norms endorsed by its supporting network, instead of opting for swift returns, is in fact an investment. Viewed in this light, Coleman's contention that social capital is created 'mainly as a by-product of other activities' (1988, p. 118) seems quite inappropriate. Indeed, entrepreneurs that are dependent on goodwill, can be expected to consciously engage in activities that enhance their standing, and refrain from those who might jeopardize it.

Business venture as the reproduction of economic capital is amply described in the mainstream economic literature. Though economic activity can be, and at times is, pursued in utter disregard of its social context, it is socially embedded to some extent in most cases. Conversely, social undertakings would normally include an economic component, and have to meet some sort of economic boundary conditions vested in nurturing the relationships that provide it, both by deed and by default.

An Ongoing Reiterative Process

Conceptually, the four elements outlined above add up to a reproduction circuit that encompasses both economic and social relations in an ongoing reiterative process. Some of the typical modes of conversion and reproduction are schematically charted in Figure 2.1 below.

Each of the four elements can be practiced and observed largely independently of the others, either in isolation, or within a subset of the four.[13] Optimally, we should expect these elements to be congruent with, or content-wise supportive of each other. The enterprise's economic performance and the nature of its business activity should enhance its good standing and be partly directed towards reproducing its support base. The conversion practices engaged in to mobilize support should be congruent with its values and goals, and conductive to its business performance, and so on. To attain such congruity, the four fields of activity (or their target groups) should be embedded in, or linked by a common social context. While it is possible to envisage situations (as in the cases of classical philanthropy or exploitation) in which the target population of a service and its financing sources are fully separated from each other, these should rather be considered cases of windfall financing that remain viable as long as the benefactor's motivation lasts.

Thus, social entrepreneurs identify and *define a community* rather than

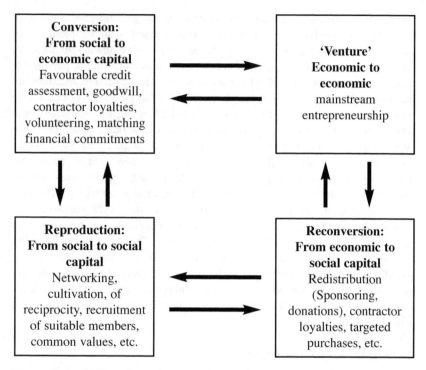

Figure 2.1　Modes of conversion and reproduction

merely contributing to a predefined one. The model outlined here goes well beyond the two simplistic assertions: that social capital is mainly a by-product of other activities (Coleman, 1988), and that 'social enterprises contribute to/produce social capital' (Evers and Schultze-Böing, 2001, p. 123; Evans CONSCISE, 2003). The boundaries of such provisional communities need not follow historically, geographically or politically predefined (for example local, national, regional) 'communities'. Only one of the cases discussed in this paper, *Medvind* and its supporting network, purposefully aspires to address (and to a degree, encompass) its entire local community. Even in this case, the boundaries are left intentionally vague, and advocacy shifts focus between home locality, the municipality and the broader region.

The links constructed by enterprises in our sample address, define, and bind together a *subset within a community*. The scope and structure of such a provisional community linking primary users/members and prospective partners is closely coupled to the enterprise's strategy and mode of operation. Cross-contacts *between* actors increase network closure (Portes, 1998). This in itself may be a source both of strength and of weakness (see Burt, 2001), depending on the range that is encompassed. Obviously, each enterprise defines and maintains the scope and level of closure it considers appropriate. Both parent-cooperative kindergartens and social cooperatives act in a highly circumscribed social space that is restricted to their own members/users; parents' cooperatives choose to conduct most of their social activities in other arenas, whereas for members of a social cooperative, the enterprise often is the only community available. Business activity is for them an effort to break the circle of isolation and become a part of a broader context. Finally, STIL, despite its historical Stockholm label, strives to create a decisional community of the likeminded wherever in Sweden these are located. STIL's social scope is deliberately limited to contacts *between* members, while closure through cross-contacts between subsidiary networks is discouraged.

The task of defining, crafting and maintaining/modifying (a) community through the 'mechanisms of coupling and decoupling that define the boundaries of trust and social affiliation' (Granovetter, 1992) lies at the core of social entrepreneurship. Whether the goals and values championed and the boundaries of affiliation thus (re)drawn follow those endorsed by society is a matter to be resolved by policy-makers and administrators, rather than by entrepreneurship theory. An approach that strives to present the practice of social entrepreneurship in economic terms, with a focus on mobilization rather than on the utilization of resources, increases the practice's relevance to the understanding of 'mainstream' entrepreneurship. It may also prove to be the best way to counter attempts to reduce the field of social policy to matters of redistribution or social engineering.

3. Communities in the global economy: where social and indigenous entrepreneurship meet

Robert B. Anderson, Benson Honig and Ana Maria Peredo

With the advent of industrialization, indigenous people around the world have suffered greatly as a result of shifting economic forces, advancing technologies, encroaching population centres, social acculturation, and colonial expansion (Cardoso, 2001). Once self-reliant and socially cohesive, indigenous communities have suffered, to varying degrees, both geographical and population dislocations (World Bank, 2001). What receives less attention, but is also important, is the degree of cohesion that remains and the desire among many indigenous people to rebuild their communities on a traditional and culturally grounded foundation while simultaneously improving their social and economic circumstances (Harvey, 1996; Lurie, 1986; Vinje, 1996). Many indigenous people see entrepreneurial activity as a central element in support of this multi-objective endeavour, clearly aligning themselves with the purposes of both social and economic entrepreneurship, all in a context in which particular histories, cultures and values play a prominent role.

The efforts to harness entrepreneurship toward both social and economic ends is certainly true of the Aboriginal Peoples of Canada, the First Nations, Métis and Inuit; the Maori in New Zealand; the Quechuas and Aymaras in Perú; and many other indigenous groups. Among these peoples, entrepreneurship and business development are widely accepted as the key to building a more vibrant economy leading to nation rebuilding (Anderson & Giberson, 2004; Peredo, 2001). This involvement in the global economy through entrepreneurial activity has been called the 'second wave' of indigenous economic development, with the 'first wave' being direct economic assistance (Stevens, 2001). Table 3.1 summarizes the characteristics of this second wave among Aboriginal people in Canada, also found representative of the Maori in New Zealand by Buckingham and Dana (2005) and Frederick and Henry (2004).

We do not claim that all indigenous communities exhibit the same degree of collectivity and mix of social/community and economic objectives in their

Table 3.1   The characteristics of aboriginal economic development, adapted from Anderson and Giberson (2004, p. 142)

The Aboriginal approach to economic development is:
1. A predominantly collective one centered on the community or 'nation'.
For the purposes of:
2. Ending dependency through economic self-sufficiency.
3. Controlling activities on traditional lands.
4. Improving the socioeconomic circumstances of Aboriginal people.
5. Strengthening traditional culture, values and languages (and the reflecting the same in development activities).
Involving the following processes:
6. Creating and operating businesses that can compete profitably over the long run in the global economy to
   (i) Exercise the control over activities on traditional lands
   (ii) End dependency through economic self-sufficiency.
7. Forming alliances and joint ventures among themselves and with non-Aboriginal partners to create businesses that can compete profitably in the global economy.
8. Building capacity for economic development through:
   (i) education, training and institution building and
   (ii) the realization of the treaty and Aboriginal rights to land and resources.

---

approach to entrepreneurship. The actual approach varies considerably, ranging from the primarily collective efforts of the Maori in New Zealand (Frederick & Henry, 2004) and the Aboriginal people in Canada (Anderson et al., 2005), to the predominantly individual entrepreneurial spin-offs from tribal casino gaming of the Kumeyaay bands in California, although it has been argued that gaming itself is a manifestation of a collective 'right' (Galbraith & Stiles, 2003). We do, however, argue that by their very nature, the characteristics that make a group indigenous (as described in the next section) favor a somewhat collective approach to entrepreneurship involving a mingling of social, cultural and economic objectives. We thus believe that the enterprise-related activities of Indigenous people in pursuit of their social/cultural self-determination and economic goals exemplifies a distinctive activity that can be called 'indigenous entrepreneurship', which operates at the intersection of social and economic entrepreneurship, perhaps even calling into question the distinction between the two. In the next section, we endeavour to address the question – who are the Indigenous? In answering this question, we offer some insights into both who and how they are shaping conventional notions of entrepreneurship.

WHO ARE THE INDIGENOUS

Depending on the definition employed, estimates of the indigenous world population vary. At the high end, it is estimated that the total population identified as indigenous ranges from 300 million to 500 million individuals worldwide, and that the population represents as much as 80 per cent of the cultural diversity on this planet (Indigenous Peoples' Human Rights Project, 2003). The UN estimates the figure to be approximately 250 to 300 million individuals, with approximately 5,000 different groups fitting its definition of indigenous. Overall, because of differences in definitions, the quality of population censuses between countries, and the self-reporting aspects of population estimates, it is difficult to obtain a more accurate estimate.

Regardless of the definition or estimates of size, one must begin by acknowledging the remarkable diversity of the world's indigenous peoples. Their communities are distributed throughout every continent of the earth, and their members range from traditional hunter-gatherers and subsistence farmers to expert professionals in industrialized nations. Some indigenous populations have remained essentially the same for hundreds of years, even into the modern era, while others have been highly integrated into the dominant cultural and economic society. In some countries, such as Bolivia, the indigenous population is a majority, but in most countries they are minorities of varying size.

One indisputable feature that sharpens the dilemma of economic development is the widespread and chronic poverty of almost all indigenous people. The World Bank, for example, prefaces its Operational Policy on Indigenous People with the declaration that 'indigenous peoples are commonly among the poorest and most vulnerable segments of society' (World Bank, 2001). Confronted with these depressing economic statistics, many, but certainly not all, modern nation-states have recognized the plight of their indigenous communities. For this reason, indigenous people, along with other poor populations of the world, have long been the target of a wide range of initiatives, efforts and programs to assist in economic development.

We now turn to definitions of indigenous peoples. A useful definition is that framed by the General Council of the International Labour Organisation in 1989. According to their convention, formally 'entered into force' in 1991, indigenous people are

> . . . peoples in independent countries who are regarded as indigenous on account of their descent from the populations which inhabited the country, or a geographical region to which the country belongs, at the time of conquest or colonisation or the establishment of present State boundaries and who, irrespective of their legal status, retain some or all of their own social, economic, cultural and political institutions (International Labour Organisation, 1991).

The United Nations employs a similar definition, omitting references to maintaining social, economic, cultural and political institutions. A 1995 resolution, for instance, states that

> indigenous or aboriginal peoples are so-called because they were living on their lands before settlers came from elsewhere; they are the descendants . . . of those who inhabited a country or a geographical region at the time when people of different cultures or ethnic origins arrived, the new arrivals later becoming dominant through conquest, occupation, settlement or other means (General Assembly of The United Nations, 1995).

Mme Erica-Irene Daes, former Chairperson of the UN Working Group on Indigenous Populations, provides another widely used definition. She designates certain peoples as indigenous on the grounds that: (1) they are descendants of groups which were in the territory of the country at the time when other groups of different cultures or ethnic origins arrived there; (2) because of their isolation from other segments of the country's population they have preserved almost intact the customs and traditions of their ancestors; and (3) they are, even if only formally, placed under a State structure which incorporates national, social and cultural characteristics alien to theirs.

Beyond the matter of definition lies a richer characterization of the real-life conditions of indigenous people. In identifying the target group for its policies on indigenous people, the World Bank declines to adopt a formal definition, choosing instead to specify a number of typical characteristics which are relevant when considering if a particular group is indigenous. Some of these echo elements in the above definitions, but others extend to a fuller account of indigenous circumstances. The Bank identifies indigenous peoples by their possession in some degree or other of many or most of the following (World Bank, 2001):

1. A close attachment to ancestral territories and the natural resources in them;
2. The presence of customary social and political institutions;
3. Economic systems primarily oriented to subsistence production;
4. An indigenous language, often different from the predominant language; and
5. Self-identification and identification by others as members of a distinct cultural group

The Asian Development Bank takes a similar approach in their Policy Statement for Indigenous People, stating that

> a starting point would be to define indigenous peoples on the basis of characteristics they display. Two significant characteristics would be (i) descent from population

groups present in a given area, most often before modern states or territories were created and before modern borders were defined, and (ii) maintenance of cultural and social identities, and social, economic, cultural, and political institutions separate from mainstream or dominant societies and cultures (Asian Development Bank, 2000).

While definitions of 'indigenous' may vary from institution to institution, and from researcher to researcher, they generally contain three core elements that we utilize for our operational definition of indigenous: (a) descent from populations inhabiting a region prior to later inhabitants; (b) geographical, political, and/or economic domination by later inhabitants or immigrants; and (c) maintenance of some distinctive social-cultural norms and institutions (Peredo et al., 2004). Attachment to ancestral lands and their resources, modern subsistence economic arrangements and distinctive languages help fill out the picture without suggesting that all indigenous peoples display all these characteristics. In spite of these commonalities, and given the particularities of indigenous cultures and their history, there is substantial debate regarding the causes of the current generally disadvantaged situation of Indigenous people. Among scholars and others, there is also a variety of opinions regarding the collective/individualist orientation of indigenous cultures with most emphasizing a collective tendency but some an individualistic heritage. There is also disagreement about the historical, current and future relationship between indigenous societies and their dominant counterparts with respect to land and other rights, and the degree to which they possess nationhood within, or distinction from, the country in which they find themselves. Some states, Canada and New Zealand among them, recognize a considerable degree of indigenous nationhood, other recognize less and some none at all. In the 1993 Draft Declaration on the Rights of Indigenous Peoples, the United Nations captures a sense of this separateness that is felt and sought by most indigenous groups. Article 21 recognizes

> the urgent need to respect and promote the inherent rights and characteristics of indigenous peoples, especially their rights to their lands, territories and resources, which derive from their political, economic and social structures and from their cultures, spiritual traditions, histories and philosophies.

The Declaration goes on to say

> Indigenous peoples have the right to maintain and develop their political, economic and social systems, to be secure in the enjoyment of their own means of subsistence and development, and to engage freely in all their traditional and other economic activities. Indigenous peoples who have been deprived of their means of subsistence and development are entitled to just and fair compensation (Economic and Social Council Commission on Human Rights, 1993).

This is certainly the expressed opinion of the vast majority of Indigenous communities. Indeed it is their sustained pressure over decades that resulted in the declaration. Their goal is not economic development alone, but economic development as part of the larger agenda of rebuilding their communities and nations and reasserting their control over their traditional territories. And in pursuit of this broader agenda, we see an increasing inclination on the part of many indigenous communities to engage in economic development activities 'on their own terms' (Peredo & Chrisman, 2005; Anderson et al., 2005; Anderson, Dana & Dana, 2006), often as set out in Figure 1.

Part of understanding the position of indigenous peoples, and the potential use of entrepreneurial activity to reinforce and support cultural, social, as well as economic activities, is understanding the underlying approaches using which modern economic development efforts for indigenous peoples have been, and are currently being, framed. It is also within this critical role of economic development that indigenous entrepreneurship research can be understood. However, the concept eclipses that of development, and also includes issues related to community identity and reconstruction. We turn now to this challenging subject. We begin by defining our terminology, followed by a discussion of three different theoretical approaches, and provide a clarification regarding the importance of focusing on indigenous social entrepreneurship, as opposed to 'ethnic' entrepreneurship.

SOCIAL ENTREPRENEURSHIP

The neo-liberal paradigm, as currently disseminated worldwide, focuses on the role of self-regulating markets in providing not only increased individual wealth, but also general improvements in society. For-profit firms and entrepreneurs are increasingly regarded as the potential source of societal advancement, reducing the role of the state and local and traditional community groups, and enlarging the role of corporations, especially trans-nationals, in enhancing social well-being. Part of this trend is the observable movement from inward-oriented cultures (Migdal, 1975) and import substitution (Cardoso, 2001) toward integration with the global economy, including outsourcing, strategic alliances, regional trading blocks, and the emergence of small, global firms (McDougall & Oviatt, 2000). From this vantage point, entrepreneurship is seen as an equalizer in a meritocratic universe, where the promotion, creation, nurturing, and encouragement of private sector firms is seen as providing wealth, a boon which it is assumed will 'trickle down' to all (Rostow, 1960). As a result, entrepreneurship has become a recognized and established field in what is called 'development studies' as well as in the discipline of business management. This view is certainly not inconsistent with the approach of many indigenous groups as they pursue their cultural, social and economic objectives.

Over the past two decades, there has been a proliferation of research investigating entrepreneurial behaviours in both Western and non-Western industrialized economies. Much of this research is premised on the belief that individual action, through entrepreneurship, brings about economic development, and that individual actors are better suited to make micro-economic decisions than the state. These beliefs, coupled with the assumption that the production and distribution of many important social goods is best allocated to actors in the market economy, has resulted in expectations that the private sector perform a dual role both as a source of trickle-down wealth, and as a supplier of the social services once provided by governments and/or community agencies. Thus, we see private sector entrepreneurial involvement in everything from penal institutions to primary education and from health care to security. This activity is also nurtured at the corporate and organizational levels (intrapraneurship), and is actively promoted everywhere from Tel-Aviv to Timbuktu. But need it be individual and 'private'? The approach emerging among many indigenous groups is community-based on the foundation of commonly-held assets and rights.

The retreat in many places of the 'welfare state' arguably contributes to this global entrepreneurship promotion trend, maintaining the notion that social benefits, including social goals such as poverty reduction, environmental protection, health care and meaningful employment, are best produced by a kind of market activity. This private-firm activity is increasingly seen as a crucial element of what has come to be known as 'social entrepreneurship' (Alvord et al., 2004). While definitions vary, we define social entrepreneurship as 'organizations combining resources toward the delivery of goods and services that provide social improvements and change.' These organizations include for-profit business, as well as governmental and non-governmental organizations, with the later including cooperatives, NGOs, community and indigenously owned organizations, as well as other organizations subject to regulatory control. This definition includes activities conducted by for-profit firms, including corporations that engage in support activities in the social entrepreneurial domain (Sagawa & Segal, 2000). While Alvord et al. (2004) provide one example among many of the intense current interest in social entrepreneurship, we contend that there is another form of entrepreneurship, one we call 'indigenous entrepreneurship,' which deserves study in its own right, but also as an important extension of this concept of social entrepreneurship.

We see a distinction between indigenous entrepreneurship and social entrepreneurship in at least two areas. First, the nation building or re-building aspects bring the state back in. For many indigenous groups entrepreneurial activities are undertaken by the group's governing body (i.e. their state) with the express purpose of strengthening the group's nationhood and self-determination. Second, we see a much stronger economic element in indigenous entrepreneurial activity. The focus is very often on enterprise development and profitable competition in the global economy, as critical to the achievement of not just economic but also cultural and social objectives. The comments below, from Chief Clarence Louie of the Osoyoos Indian Band and Chief Harry Cook of the Lac La Ronge Indian Band, capture a senses of this intermingling of indigenous state, for profit enterprise, and economic/ social/cultural objectives. Clarence Louie (Anderson et al. 2003, p. 10) says

> The Desert and Heritage Centre is probably going to be our biggest business venture, and it's going to combine all of those things that you see in a first class desert interpretive centre–the educational stuff, the scientific stuff, the desert trails, the walks, the scientific interpretive stuff . . . the other major component of it, which is really special, is the uniqueness of the Okanagan First Nations, with the language and the heritage and the cultural component to it.

While Chief Cook (Hindle et al., 2005, p. 6) says

> Because unemployment is so high in our community, it is a necessity that we continue to create jobs and training opportunities here at Kitsaki. One great way to do that is by selling our goods and services to people outside our community.

General manager Terry Helary of Kitsaki Meats echoes Chief Cook's sentiments saying

> The people we hire are taught a trade here, as well as life skills. For many, this is their first job, so it is very important . . . as we enter into other markets globally, Kitsaki Meats will also be improving life locally.

Social entrepreneurship is, first of all, entrepreneurship. As Dees puts it, 'Social entrepreneurs are one species in the genus entrepreneur' (1998, p. 3). It must be recognized that there is no clear consensus on what it is to be an entrepreneur (Brazeal & Herbert, 1999; Venkataraman, 1997). Nevertheless, there is a discernible core in scholarly commentary on the concept. Beyond the 'minimalist' sense of 'entrepreneurship' (e.g. Barber, 1998, p. 67) according to which entrepreneurship is just the launch of a commercial venture, there lies a more nuanced understanding drawing on the history of the concept. It is important to recognize, especially for purposes of this paper, that entrepreneurship is frequently an extended activity: it may well be carried out by a team or a group of people, as it is in many indigenous communities. The characteristics listed above could be thought of as roles in a performance; roles which may be split and/or shared. Others have pointed out that entrepreneurship may find a place in cultural settings where collective, rather than individualistic, thinking prevails (Peterson, 1988). Peredo (2003; Peredo & Chrisman, 2005) actually describes a situation in which it is plausible to speak of a community acting collectively to exercise entrepreneurship that is plainly social in many of its aspects.

But what makes social entrepreneurship social? It seems clear that what distinguishes social entrepreneurs is their aim to produce social value. As Dees states: 'Adopting a mission to create and sustain social value: this is the core of what distinguishes social entrepreneurs from business entrepreneurs even from socially responsible businesses' (Dees, 1998, p. 4). We take the term 'social value' to refer to a multitude of public goods that constitute the general welfare of a society, including everything from the fundamentals for subsistence, such as food, clothing and shelter, through employment and health care, to recreation and the arts. What makes social entrepreneurship social is that these are the intended outcomes of the activity and not merely the fortuitous by-products. There has been some tendency in the popular press to confine the concept to the endeavours of not-for-profit organizations (Taylor et al., 2000). In this paper, however, we follow the practice of business publications (Taylor et al., 2000) in extending the term to for-profit organizations with a 'social mission'. But how dominant must the social mission be? Must social goals be the only aims of the operation, or can some intention to make profits be admitted as well? If profits are accepted in the definition, must they be subordinated to social aims, or is the only requirement that social goals be somewhere in the organization's mix of objectives? We use the term inclusively, applying it to profit-making as well as not-for-profit organizations, as long as the provision of social outcomes is one of the explicit intentions of the operation, again clearly the case in many instances for indigenous people. This includes activities conducted by for-profit firms, as well as corporations, undertaken in support activities in the social entrepreneurial domain (Sagawa & Segal, 2000).

Our particular interest is the nexus of social entrepreneurship and indigenous entrepreneurship. To what extent can the neo-liberal policies ascribed to Western economies or even those of developing countries transfer to indigenous populations? While we now have some generalized understanding of certain aspects of the motivations and strategies of entrepreneurs, and their important contributions to economic development, there remains a question whether these generalizations are, in fact, applicable to indigenous peoples. The purpose of this paper is to introduce indigenous entrepreneurship as a promising research domain for the study of entrepreneurship, both social and economic; one deserving of further scholarly research activity. We further identify some of the more pressing questions that arise within this relatively unstudied area, in particular, how indigenous entrepreneurship relates to corporate intrapraneurship and corporate capitalism.

DEVELOPMENT AND INDIGENOUS PEOPLE

Over the years there have been numerous indigenous uprisings and protests, not unlike those experienced in England with the advent of the industrial revolution (Polyani, 1944). A common theme surrounding these debates has been the indigenous right at various levels to plan and control their own development. It should be noted that their insistence has not been so much on integration or isolation – issues which often seem to monopolize the debate – as it has been on the right to self-development (Peredo, 2001). Much like the battle for labour rights fought in the nineteenth and early twentieth centuries, indigenous peoples worldwide are actively asserting their rights in a variety of ways. The short story is that there is more than one way of 'framing' the processes that have been undertaken by 'developed' nations in order to benefit those who are 'undeveloped', including indigenous populations.

The desire of indigenous peoples to rebuild their communities raises two fundamental questions. Can indigenous people participate in the expanding global economy and its rapidly advancing socio-technological changes with a degree of self-determination; and, if so, how can this be done? The answer to the latter part of the question depends on the answer to the first, and the answer to the first depends on what we can learn from different perspectives regarding how we define and evaluate development. For the purposes of this paper, we consider three broad perspectives: modernization theory, the radical perspectives represented by dependency theory, and the emerging contingent perspectives represented by regulation theory.

Our aim in this section is not to recommend one particular framework for understanding the efforts and effects of socioeconomic development. Rather, we highlight some of the perceived deficiencies – related to cultural as well as social and economic issues – in all three, and discuss our preferred perspective in somewhat greater depth than the others. Our overall objective is to capture what we can from each of the perspectives, and by implication, to issue an invitation to continue this search for still better ways of understanding the wide variety of efforts often termed 'development'. Our very specific objective in this enquiry is to discover whether there may be a way of negotiating a constructive participation of indigenous people in the global economy in a way that allows them to preserve what is important to them as indigenous peoples.

Modernization or 'Assimilation' Models

Modernization theory has been the dominant development paradigm and has driven practice since the 1950s (Inkles, 1974; Cardoso, 2001). A number of notions contribute to this theory. First, it sees development as a process involving passage through various stages. Modernization theory implies that in order to progress and develop, traditional societies have to move toward modernity (Crewe & Harrison, 1998; Rostow, 1960). 'Modernization' and 'development' came to be used as synonymous terms. Secondly, monetary income, and therefore economic growth, are regarded as key elements in measuring the development. Thirdly, humans are or should be motivated by self-interest and rational economic behaviour (Burkey, 1993; Crewe & Harrison, 1998). From this point of view, development is measured in economic terms, with the expectation that the 'underdeveloped' will over time assume the qualities of already developed First World (Burkey, 1993). One of the underlying assumptions of modernization is that traditional culture, social structures, and differing languages are barriers to progress, as the following quotation illustrates:

> Pre-existing social relations . . . family, kinship and community, constitute obstacles to business enterprises and achievement. . . . Successful capitalism involves some rupturing of existing social relations and possibly the diminution of affective relations to leave more space to impersonal, calculating forms of social interaction believed to characterize the market economy (Moore, 1997, p. 289).

This general orientation has led to several neo-classical economic approaches to economic development; approaches that inevitably reside in some notion of assimilation. Modernization or 'assimilation models' essentially argue that cultural divisions and differences ultimately interfere with efficient economic production and the differential advantages that individual nations might enjoy. Attempts to apply this framework for economic development, however, have not led across the board to the accelerating spirals of development as expected. Broad based assimilation has not occurred with any great frequency – at least in the short-term. The complexities of the poverty dynamic in different settings, and need to respect local cultures and knowledge increasingly created dissonance for modernization scholars and practitioners. The 'green revolution' of the 1970s was a striking example of the way that growth could be produced while development lagged and poverty even increased. The negative growth and debt crises that ensued in some countries toward the end of the century called into question the simple implementation of modernization programs (George, 1988; Cardoso, 2001).

However, many developmental economists still argue for broad-based modernization programs with an underlying belief that past barriers to economic growth have been primarily politically motivated, to the overall detriment of indigenous populations. To some extent, the move toward economic globalization via institutions such as the World Trade Organization (WTO) and regional trade agreements, such as NAFTA is ultimately grounded upon a modernization or assimilation foundation. Whether the modernization movements represent opportunity or threat to indigenous people is still open to debate and discussion, but regardless of one's political, social, or economic orientation, the modernization framework should not be discounted from academic discussion. Perhaps, for certain indigenous people, some components of modernization (such as those essential for effective participation in the global economy) are sought after in order to rebuild their communities and strengthen those aspects of their culture and way of life that are most important to their Indigenous identity.

Dependency Models

In a historical sense, dependency models of economic development emerged not only as a critique of the failure of the modernization agenda to deliver the anticipated development outcomes, but even more fundamentally to draw attention to what is seen by some as a new form of colonization. In this analysis, the multinational corporation, the developed industrialized nation states and the global institutions such as the World Bank, IMF, GATT and later the WTO are cast as the villains (Hancock, 1989; Klitgaard, 1990). Rather than leading the 'underdeveloped' to a 'developed' state, through the lens of dependency models the actions of the developed world are seen as the basic (through conquest and colonialism) and continuing (through economic exploitation) cause of underdevelopment. According to the dependency critiques, participation by the underdeveloped in the global capitalist economy as it is currently constructed can only exacerbate their circumstances, not improve them. The evidence since the Second World War certainly offers some support for this view. While the reasons are debatable, the gap between the rich and the poor within and among some states, particularly in Africa, has widened, not closed, in spite of six decades of development efforts of various types (United Nations Development Programme, 2001), while other countries, such as India, have fared well, and still others regions, such as Latin America, have remained essentially unchanged.

The application of dependency models have led to programs such as import substitution, aimed at pursuing growth by developing internal resources without reliance on unbalanced trade with large and powerful outside nations. These programs, however, have also proved largely unsuccessful. It has been argued that part of the problem with dependency based models of economic development is that the theory is oriented more toward a critique of modernisation than developing a theoretically sound approach to development of its own. Indeed, according to Hettne (1982), the development perspective arising from dependency theory appears to be little more than modernisation theory applied to the locus of a nation state. Even adherents call for a redefinition (Cardoso, 2001, p. 278).

Despite modification in recent years (So, 1990), some argue that the modernization and dependency perspectives present incompatible views of the relationship between a 'developing' people/region and the 'developed' world. In a particular circumstance, one or the other of these approaches can often adequately explain what happened. However, when applied in any particular circumstance to offer insight into what might happen, the two produce conflicting answers, thus providing contradictory guidance to groups searching for a path to development, as they perceive it.

Contingency Models

In the closing three decades of the twentieth century, the conflict between the modernization and dependency perspectives led many to conclude that both are incomplete (as distinct from mistaken), with each describing a possible but not inevitable outcome of interaction between local regions seeking what they regard as a better form of life, and the global economy. This has resulted in what Corbridge (1989) describes as a powerful trend towards 'theories of capitalist development which emphasize contingency ... a new emphasis on human agency and the provisional and highly skilled task of reproducing social relations' (Corbridge, 1989, p. 633). As Tucker (1999) notes, this allows 'for the possibility of incorporating the experience of other peoples, other perspectives and other cultures into the development discourse' (Tucker, 1999, p. 16). Development need not be as defined by the 'developed world' and the interaction between a particular people and the global economy need not be as envisaged by the modernization or dependency perspectives; it can be something else entirely. Why not that which is being sought by indigenous people – development as they define it?

There has been substantial discussion about the increasing flexibility in modern economic production and consumption, and its impact on the strategies of the modern firm (Boyer, 1999; Galbraith & DeNoble, 2002; Harmon & Peterson, 1990). From a broader perspective, Toffler (1980) labelled this phenomenon the 'third wave' as contrasted with the industrial 'second wave' and the agricultural 'first wave'. Toffler and other economic futurists of the modern era have noted that new technological developments such as computers, robotics, biotechnology, global communication, and nanotechnologies are forcing a much more decentralized, demassified, and non-synchronized post-industrial society; a system that is fundamentally different from nineteenth and twentieth century industrial economies. The hope, it is argued, is that this process will open the way for economically efficient development that is more sensitive to intra-state differences, including those of the indigenous populations. In other words, they highlight the 'electronic cottage' or efficiently flexible micro-economies that are now possible for historically underdeveloped populations. Within this framework several different economic development approaches that attempt to accommodate the nature of increasing contingency and human agency have been suggested. We discuss one of these models, 'regulation theory,' to illustrate its potential to help us understand indigenous entrepreneurship and its role in development. We particularly like the regulation framework because it directs one toward considering and analyzing without prescribing any normative conditions about what is good or bad, expectations about what will work or won't work, and so on. When using it as an analytical approach, one can still find room to accommodate the very real forces of modernization, the unquestioned outcomes of unequal exchange (dependency), the reality of the articulation of modes of production, the enduring and not recent nature of the global economy (world systems perspective), and so on.

According to Hirst and Zeitlin (1992), the regulation approach executes, 'a slalom between the orthodoxies of neo-classical equilibrium theory and classical Marxism to produce a rigorous but non-deterministic account of the phases of capitalist development that leaves considerable scope for historical variation and national diversity' (Hirst & Zeitlin, 1992, p. 84). Expanding on this notion of variation and diversity, Elam (1994) says that on one hand, national and regional units are constantly in a state of flux as they adjust to the influences of the global economy. All must accommodate themselves at least to some extent to its hegemony. At the same time, these broader global influences 'are seen as having essentially local origins' (Elam, 1994, p. 66). This translates into a counter-hegemonic potential in terms of the activities actually undertaken by people as they negotiate their way locally through the global economy. It is not simply a case of conform or fail. Indigenous people and others may thus be able to move from a primarily inward orientation towards an outward oriented approach (Migdal, 1975).

Recognizing the increasing flexibility of modern economic systems, regulation theory analyses the global economy 'in terms of a series of modes of development based on combinations of the currently ascendant regime of accumulation and a variety of modes of social regulation' (Hirst & Zeitlin, 1992, pp. 84–85). The regime of accumulation determines the general possibilities for the economy. Scott (1988) says it 'can be rather simply defined as a historically specific production apparatus ... through which surplus is generated, appropriated, and redeployed' (Scott, 1988, p. 8). Importantly, with respect to geographic scale, the regime of accumulation is a 'relationship between production and consumption defined at the level of the international economy as a whole' (Hirst & Zeitlin, 1992, p. 85); it is what most refer to as the 'global economy'.

Regulation theory argues that stability in the global economic system is dependent on the emergence of a further set of social relations that preserve it, for a time at least, from catastrophic internal collisions and breakdowns. These relations constitute a mode of social regulation. They are made up of a series of formal and informal structures of governance and stabilization, ranging from the state through business and labour associations, to modes of social-ization which create ingrained habits of behaviour (Scott 1988, p. 9). In many ways, this governance is similar to the type of social democracy advocated by Polanyi (1944) but brought into a modern context, complete with the implica-tions of mass communication and technological enhancement that accelerates the flow of capital and ideas. Polanyi was impressed with the Owenite move-ment, particularly its ambition to harness the market and favour the human spirit, while bypassing some of the worst exigencies of capitalism. He consid-ered it a practical combination of individual freedom and dignity, social soli-darity, and acceptance of what we would now call 'globalization' (commonly referred to as industrialization, machinery). Hirst and Zeitlin (1992) seem to share a similar perspective, stating that a mode of social regulation (MSR), 'is a complex of institutions and norms which secure, at least for a certain period, the adjustment of individual agents and social groups to the over arching prin-ciple of the accumulation regime' (p. 85).

While regulation theory does not prescribe the exact nature of a particular mode of social regulation, it is generally agreed that a regime of accumulation does not create or require a particular mode of social regulation: 'each regime, in short, may be regulated in a multiplicity of ways' (Scott, 1988, p. 9). Because modes of social regulation are based on such things as 'habits and customs, social norms, enforceable laws and state forms' (Peck & Tickell, 1992, p. 349), unique modes 'can exist at virtually any territorial level – local, regional, national, global' (Storper & Walker, 1989, p. 215).

Another aspect of regulation theory – its historicity – adds further strength to the argument that modes of social regulation, and therefore modes of devel-opment differing considerably one from another, can and do emerge at every geographic scale, says Corbridge (1989), echoing the 'cyclical' or 'wave' arguments of Toffler (1980) and other historically based economic futurists. Regulation theory indicates that the global economic system has gone through four stages in the twentieth century. In stage one, the system was in equilib-rium. Stage two was a period of crisis or disequilibrium resulting from a shift from the extensive to the Fordist regime of accumulation. Equilibrium returned in stage three when suitable modes of social regulation emerged. The fourth (current) stage is also one of crisis caused by a failure of the monopo-listic mode of social regulation (in all its variants) to accommodate a 'selec-tive move from mass production [the Fordist regime accumulation] to various forms of flexible production' (Norcliffe, 1994, p. 2).

Forces responsible for in the shift to the new flexible regime of accumula-tion include: (i) technical limits to rigid fixed capital production techniques,

(ii) working class resistance to Taylorist and Fordist forms of work organization (Jessop, 1989), (iii) a change in consumption patterns 'toward a greater variety of use values . . . [that] cannot be easily satisfied through mass production' (Amin & Malmberg, 1994, p. 12), (iv) the increasing mobility of capital and the resulting ability of transnational corporations (TNCs) to move among spatially-bounded regulatory jurisdictions in the pursuit of greater profits (Leyshon, 1989), and (v) in the face of this internationalization of capital, the inability of national Keynesian policies [all variants of the monopolistic mode of social regulation] to avert crisis (Komninos, 1989).

What are the characteristics of this emerging flexible regime? Goldman (1995), for example, writes that the flexible regime exhibits 'a distinct set of relationships, interdependencies, and forms of interaction among suppliers, producers, distributors, and customers. It demands new approaches to organizing, operating, and measuring the performance of both individual companies and clusters of cooperating companies' (p. 1). Thus the theory of the firm radically changes from a hierarchical transactional process described by Williamson (1975), to one of varying modes of alliances and relational contracts (Galbraith & Kay, 1986; Kay, 1997; Teece, 1980). Goldman (1995) again notes that in 'a competitive environment of continuous and unanticipated change' companies are finding it 'advantageous on the grounds of cost, speed, or market penetration, to utilize only some company-owned resources, combining them with others available in other companies' (pp. 6–7). Similarly Dunning (2003) writes:

> We are moving out of an age of hierarchical capitalism and into an age of alliance capitalism. This is placing a premium on the virtues needed for fruitful and sustainable coalitions and partnerships (be they within or among institutions), such as trust, reciprocity, and due diligence (p. 24).

Everywhere and at every geographic scale – community, subnational region, national, supranational regions and globally – indigenous or not, people are struggling to develop modes of social regulation that will allow them to interact with emerging flexible regime of accumulation. Several authors have noted a shift in the locus of regulation from the nation state in two directions – to the supranational and the local (Amin & Malmberg, 1994; Scott, 1988). Dicken (1992, p. 307), for example, emphasizes that successful participation in the global economic system 'is created and sustained through a highly localized process' and that 'economic structures, values, cultures, institutions and histories contribute profoundly to that success'.

Under regulation theory, the firm appears to open a number of opportunities for indigenous enterprises and entrepreneurial efforts. This is due both to the changing regimes of accumulation arising from the increasing flexibility and decentralization in production and consumption activities, as well as to the changing models of social regulation, as hierarchical models of the firm evolve into alliance and relation based organizations.

INDIGENOUS PEOPLE AND MODERN INSTITUTIONAL FORCES

It is important to emphasize that in this discussion of social and indigenous entrepreneurship we are considering the entrepreneurial activities of indigenous people in their indigenous setting. They may or may not be located in native homelands – many have been displaced or relocated. But they are situated in communities of indigenous people with the shared social, economic and cultural patterns that qualify them as indigenous populations. The characteristics of entrepreneurship among indigenous people who migrate individually or in relatively small groups, especially to urban areas, may well be different from the populations we propose to study. It is tempting to suppose that their behaviour may more closely resemble that of ethnic enclaves (see below) but this represents a distinctive area that merits its own study (Peredo et al., 2004).

Given the well-recognized increasing flexibility of modern production systems and consumption behaviours, indigenous populations, as defined above, appear to now have a greater opportunity to efficiently and effectively participate in the modern economy while still maintaining those unique cultural characteristics they self-define as their indigenous culture. As a group, indigenous people in a particular community are likely to adopt their perspective on the global economy as a response to their direct experience with actors in the global economic system. Thus, they may form new types of indigenous enclaves, reminiscent of ethnic enclaves, but perhaps differentiated by their willingness to participate outside their group, in the wider economic environment.

The four groups of actors with whom indigenous peoples are probably most familiar (and therefore those that constitute the face of the global economy from their perspective) are (i) the exogenous economic entities such as corporations with which they interact as suppliers, customers, partners, antagonists and/or employees; (ii) the 'state' at local, sub-national, national and international levels; (iii) a myriad groups of the civil sector including non-government agencies (NGOs) of all types and special interest groups such as Amnesty International, the World Council of Indigenous People, the Sierra Club, and so on; and (iv) global and supranational bodies, such as the WTO, the UN, the World Bank, the European Economic Union and NAFTA. Figure 3.1 attempts to capture this complex and dynamic relationship.

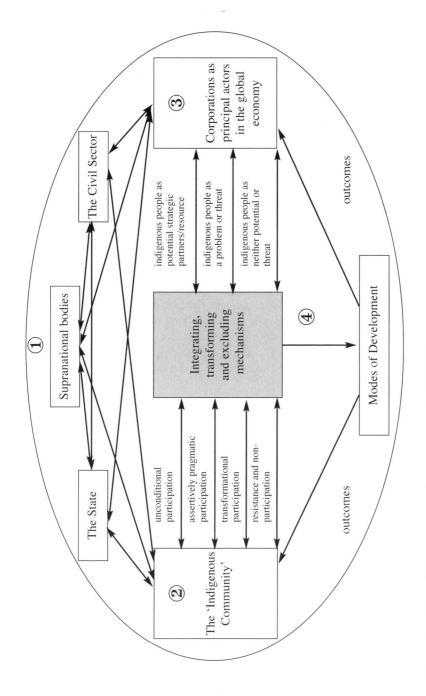

Figure 3.1 The global economy, after Anderson et al. (2003)

Corporations as principal actors in the global economy ③

The Civil Sector

Supranational bodies

①

The State

indigenous people as potential strategic partners/resource

indigenous people as a problem or threat

indigenous people as neither potential or threat

Integrating, transforming and excluding mechanisms

④

Modes of Development

outcomes

outcomes

unconditional participation

assertively pragmatic participation

transformational participation

resistance and non-participation

②

The 'Indigenous Community'

Corporations are most closely associated with the regime of accumulation; indeed for many indigenous groups they are the face of the regime of accumulation. That it is not to say that corporations are not influenced by and do not influence the mode of social regulation; of course they are, and they do. The state at all its levels is most closely tied to modes of social regulation. Indeed, the sum of the actions of the state at all levels constitutes the bulk of the overlapping modes of social regulation; the bulk but not the entirety. The organizations of the civil sector also play an important role directly and through their influence on the state and on corporations. Increasingly supranational bodies are taking on a powerful role in the economy that is more than the expression of the collective voice of member states. They are becoming a regulatory force unto themselves, with considerable impact on states, corporations and communities. For example, according to Szablowski (2002) the World Bank, through its policy on loans associated with the mining industry, is having considerable impact on the relationships that are emerging among mining corporations, local groups (often indigenous) and nation states. If we take a liberal view, we can consider World Bank efforts to partner with local groups to be a new trend (Dimaggio & Powell, 1983) although coercive aspects of World Bank policies may, in fact, be dominant (Klitgaard, 1990; Hancock, 1989). However, while acknowledging rejection of the world polity on the part of certain indigenous or traditional societies, institutional theorists highlight the supremacy of political-technological organization, including rational accounting systems, world trade, and modern bureaucratic organization (Thomas, 1987).

Indigenous communities may be either engaged or disengaged in economic activity, and their involvement may extend to either local or global interactions. It follows that the mix of integrating, transforming and excluding mechanisms adopted by a particular community in its approach to the global economy, and therefore the mode of development that emerges, is heavily influenced by the particular face of the state, global and supranational bodies (for example, indigenous peoples in Mexico have been able to appeal to a NAFTA panel on genetically-modified corn), and the civil sector and corporations that a community sees now and has seen in the past. This 'face to face' meeting, while heavily influenced by local circumstance, occurs within the context of the dominant global regime of accumulation and multiple, overlapping and often conflicting modes of social regulation. Further, communities may transform the local or global economic structures so as to enhance the social impact of economic activities. Such transformations may include substitutions involving tradeoffs of profit for other social benefits, such as job creation, health, and community welfare. Indigenous groups that choose to engage with the global economy are not at the end of the process – they are at the beginning. To successfully engage they must transform economic actors on their own terms. They do this by identifying business opportunities and marshalling resources, and develop organizations to realize the potential that these opportunities offer to satisfy their economic and other development objectives. This is the process of social entrepreneurship for indigenous communities. It combines elements of both the creation and sustaining power of small business with the desire for broader development within the community. It eclipses entrepreneurship exclusively conceived of as an economy-building, Schumpeterian process. Morris (1998) captures some aspects of this process by stating, 'entrepreneurship is a universal construct that is applicable to any person, organization (private or public, large or small), or nation' and that 'an entrepreneurial orientation is critical for the survival and growth of companies as well as the economic prosperity of nations' (p. 2). Expressing a similar view, Raymond Kao et al. (2002) define entrepreneurship as, 'not just a way of conducting business; it is an ideology originating from basic human needs and desires . . . [that] entails discovering the new, while changing, adapting and preserving the best of the old' (p. 44). Other authors, such as Blawatt (1998), Drucker (1985), Fiet (2002), and Moran and Ghoshal (1999) express similar views. In short, indigenous social entrepreneurship consists not only of economic prosperity, but also includes collective cultural and social identity and well-being.

INDIGENOUS ENTREPRENEURSHIP VERSUS ETHNIC ENTREPRENEURSHIP

How is indigenous entrepreneurship different from the more commonly discussed 'ethnic' entrepreneurship – and do either differ with from social entrepreneurship? And if there are differences, are they fundamental, or are they a matter of academic semantics? These are reasonable questions. It is our argument that while there are certainly some areas of theoretical overlap between ethnic and indigenous entrepreneurship, such as co-members sharing a common language, cultural identity or even a sense of historical domination, there are also fundamental differences.

First, ethnic entrepreneurship almost always addresses the issues of immigrant populations and the situation of relatively newcomers to a particular region or nation (Portes & Bach, 1985). In addition, ethnic entrepreneurship typically examines the economic interactions within a particular area of relatively new settlement, and the forces, such as social capital, that are brought into an area by the immigrants (Light, 2004). In contrast, indigenous groups, as discussed previously, almost always involve individuals that have a close attachment to ancestral territories and the natural resources in them. And while the topics of social capital and relational networks are important to understanding indigenous entrepreneurship, the historical context and sources of such capital and network links may be quite different.

Second, indigenous entrepreneurship is often connected with the notions of community-based economic development, whereas ethnic entrepreneurship typically involves enterprise development at the individual or family level. And while this certainly does not preclude individual entrepreneurial behaviour within indigenous communities, it is usually viewed by leaders and governments as a component of economic development, rather than a strictly individual initiative.

And third, since in many countries indigenous people have obtained quasi-governmental or 'nation' status, the economic factors of business enterprise are much more formally linked to, and perhaps indivisible from broader cultural and political factors. Certainly, these differences do not imply that the study of indigenous entrepreneurship stands in isolation from the study of ethnic business enterprise, or even from the general field of entrepreneurship. For example, the topics of social capital, networks, cognitive styles, technology adoption, competitive positioning, and entrepreneurial incentives are universal concepts in the field of entrepreneurship, but they must be carefully analysed and properly understood within the basic historical differences between immigrant co-ethnic populations and indigenous populations.

INDIGENOUS ENTREPRENEURSHIP AND SOCIAL ENTREPRENEURSHIP

The track record for external actors in the social entrepreneurship field is quite mixed. This is certainly true for the top-down externally driven attempts (whether by state or non-state organizations) to improve the circumstances of Indigenous people that dominated practice until recently. Honig (1998, 2000) points out the problem of both institutional forces and agency in biasing external NGOs and advocates in their attempts to promote social entrepreneurship. Well intentioned efforts may fail to yield effective results, in part due to the considerable social and cultural gap between providers and receivers of assistance.

More recently and in response to the failure of these top-down, externally imposed efforts, Indigenous people in increasing numbers are engaging in entrepreneurial activities with a social purpose beyond, and often only attainable as a result of, the creation and operation of profitable business enterprises. These activities fit our definition of social entrepreneurship – private and government and non-government public organizations combining resources toward the delivery of goods and services that provide social improvements and change.

Anderson (1999), for example, points out that the Canadian aboriginal approach to economic development is predominantly collective, centred on the community or 'nation' for the purposes of ending dependency through economic self-sufficiency, controlling activities on traditional lands, improving existing socio-economic circumstances, strengthening traditional culture, values and languages (and the reflecting the same in development activities). He maintains that these objectives are obtained by means of entrepreneurship – creating and operating businesses that can compete profitably over the long run in the global economy – often by forming alliances and joint ventures among themselves and with non-Aboriginal partners; and by building capacity for economic development through: (i) education, training and institution building; and (ii) the realization of the treaty and Aboriginal rights to land and resources. Similarly, Peredo (2001) reporting on indigenous peoples in three Andean countries discusses the desire of Andean indigenous peoples to pursue their own development based on collective activity, traditional lands, traditional values (especially respect for the common patrimony and common good) and pursuing multiple goals in order to reach the common good. Within the Andean community this is obtained by means of 'Community-Based Enterprise' (CBE), defined as a community acting corporately as both entrepreneur and enterprise in pursuit of the common good. CBE is therefore the result of a process in which the community acts entrepreneurially, to create and operate a new enterprise embedded in its existing social structure. Furthermore, CBEs are managed and governed to pursue the goals of a community in a manner that is meant to yield sustainable individual and group benefits over the short- and long-term. In the Canadian and Andean contexts, this is surely social entrepreneurship from within the indigenous community, as opposed to exogenously provided. These are but two illustrative examples from among many; including the Maori in New Zealand, the Aborigines in Australia, the Sami in Northern Scandinavia, the circumpolar Inuit people and Indigenous people in Asia and Oceania.

We believe that the study of Indigenous populations, including their efforts at social entrepreneurship, is not simply an exercise in analysing outliers in the global world-system. Rather, it provides a source for theoretical and empirical analyses of social entrepreneurship relevant to the development of generalizable theory applicable in many environments including, but by no means exclusive to, indigenous communities. Research in this area should provide insights into the impact of globalization forces on communities (indigenous or not), and the possible responses of individuals and communities that can balance the needs of individuals, communities, and economic institutions. From a theoretical perspective, this research is relevant to virtually every nation-state, ranging from classic notions of indigenous peoples in impoverished industrialized economies to communities such as the Basques, the Welsh, the Chechnians and the Scots.

From a purely instrumental point of view, global actors, including trans-national corporations, are recognizing the necessity of ensuring shareholder value in terms of ethical and social development towards long-term sustainability. All nodes that interact with market forces, including the state, the civil sector, and corporate entities, have an interest in promoting community development that leads to long-term economic development of markets, including the provision of jobs, the sharing of resources, and the support of relevant and situated communities.

4. Location and relocation, visions and revisions: opportunities for social entrepreneurship

Ellen S. O'Connor*

This chapter focuses on high-profile social entrepreneurship (HPSE) and ways to expand it. HPSE represents a particular interpretation of social entrepreneurship (SE) that attracts considerable attention and support but is narrow in its location and scope. SE has the potential to address vital relationships across entrepreneurship and society (Steyaert and Katz, 2004). This chapter pursues that potential. First, it seeks to explain HPSE's narrowness by locating it within specific historical, economic, and social contexts (limited to the US). Then it pursues an expanded SE through three cases. The cases portray social action observed through an entrepreneurial lens and entrepreneurship through a social lens. Doing so illuminates three aspects of entrepreneurship that HPSE excludes: society as a field where entrepreneurial action occurs, social processes and entrepreneurial action as interdependent, and entrepreneurship as emergent in this field through these processes. These ideas extend Kaufman's (1985) cauldron metaphor of entrepreneurship, which is reframed as the social cauldron.

HIGH-PROFILE SOCIAL ENTREPRENEURSHIP (HPSE)

More and more business schools have begun offering SE courses. Harvard, Duke, and Oxford, among others, have established SE centers and achieved high visibility as key players. Their work has accelerated material support such as enrollments and donations, leading to even stronger reputations. Once established, these reputations become self reinforcing. Harvard, for example, received $10 million in May 2005 from the Catherine B. Reynolds Foundation

* The author thanks Magnus Aronsson and ESBRI for the opportunity to participate in the conference that gave occasion to this chapter. She is grateful to Daniel Hjorth and Chris Steyaert for organizing creative conversations about entrepreneurship and for the invitations to be a part of them.

to fund 'students pursuing a businesslike approach to social science fields' (*Wall Street Journal*, 13 May 2005, p. D2). Certain individuals, foundations, and nonprofit organizations (NPOs) have secured status as thought leaders in SE. Gregory Dees (Duke University) has published extensively on the topic, as has Jed Emerson (who helped start the Roberts Enterprise Development Fund [REDF] – George R. Roberts being of Kohlberg, Kravis and Roberts, one of the best known private equity firms in the US). REDF, which calls its approach SE, is known for employing, training, and retaining employees that for-profit companies do not typically hire. Jeff Skoll, a Stanford MBA and the first president of eBay, gave $7.5 million to Oxford to establish the Skoll Centre for SE; and his Skoll Foundation has developed an online SE network, 'Social Edge,' with global reach. Skoll has partnered with Bill Drayton and his organization, Ashoka, offering a mentoring approach to SE and a model whereby funds go to individuals rather than to organizations. The approach focuses on 'systemic social change' by rewarding and cultivating 'social heroes'. The Skoll Foundation offers a checklist that applicants may use to determine if they are new heroes or not (www.skollfoundation.org/newheroes/index.asp). Sharing stories of social heroes is a means to cultivate more social heroes. To this end, Skoll has partnered with Robert Redford. Skoll funds Sundance, Redford's company; and Redford funds and makes films about social heroes for Skoll's foundation – 'documentaries that make a difference' (Antonucci, 2005).

HPSE resides in business schools, particularly the elite schools, who must lead and certainly keep up with the latest trends. It emerges out of entrepreneurship studies, itself a relatively new field in business schools – endowed chairs, for example, only having been established in the last generation. Economically and socially, it arises out of high technology and venture capital. It grew out of the 'new economy' of the 1990s in that wealthy entrepreneurs, particularly in Silicon Valley, began to apply their business acumen and networks to social issues in three ways: (1) Prominent venture capitalists (such as John Doerr), high-tech CEOs (such as Bill Gates, Larry Ellison, Ross Perot), and philanthropists intervened in the public school reform movement through political (lobbying) and charitable (donations, alliances) means as well as through for-profit educational enterprises (for example Leapfrog, owned by Ellison); (2) a new generation of young but wealthy entrepreneurs launched philanthropic efforts noted for a hands-on approach called 'venture philanthropy' (started family foundations, donated start-up stock to charities, funded and/or advised new NPOs); and (3) salons were convened, like the one in Silicon Valley by Laura Arrillaga, a lecturer in philanthropy at Stanford Business School (and daughter of a real estate tycoon and long-term Stanford benefactor), where young philanthropists discussed social investing and established 'social venture' portfolios. These networks are constructed and reconstructed through events such as social venture competitions at business schools, where venture capitalists, CEOs, new-generation entrepreneurs and philanthropists, MBA students, and others convene.

HPSE also represents the latest form of an ongoing engagement of business and businesspeople in society. Going back to colonial life, philanthropy arose locally and from the ground up, in schools and churches, and through network, neighborhood, and family ties, especially among the elite (Hall, 1992). Galaskiewicz (1997) emphasizes the role of peer pressure as elites build reputations and community ties by circulating across the three sectors. Corporations have maintained ties to their local communities long before the current 'strategic philanthropy' or 'corporate social responsibility' developments. 'Cause-related marketing' is hailed in the mainstream management literature as a pioneering development, with American Express's Statue of Liberty restoration campaign credited as 'the mother of all cause marketing campaigns' (Gourville and Rangan, 2004, p. 40). However, unnoticed by social marketing experts is the fact that in 1885, Macy's sponsored a sale of miniature copies of the Statue to raise funds for the pedestal of the original (Heald, 1970, p. 7). '[T]he firm's records show enough cases of assistance rendered to social agencies to indicate a sense of relationship to the community beyond the walls and hours of the business itself' (Heald, 1970, p. 7).

HPSE is of course managerialist, and that is one explanation for its narrowness. Baritz (1965) argued that management is only concerned with advancing its own agenda and cannot possibly address broad social issues. Collins (1998, p. 6) argued that such narrowness is characteristic of the US context. HPSE clearly brings a market orientation to social issues, and it originates in the US. However, business efforts to 'fix' society have a long history, perhaps the most noteworthy being Taylor's offer of scientific management as a way to solve social problems ranging from drunkenness and laziness to government waste (Taylor, 1911). At the same time, though, these moves represent business's own struggle to fix, or perhaps redeem, itself – to show that, despite size and power and their uses and abuses, business is a legitimate institution and management is a profession. In this way, HPSE responds morally to the latest round of scandals, including the Internet bust, eroding public confidence in business as an institution, businesspeople as citizens, and – particularly in light of external threats such as globalization, multilateralism, and Islam – US capitalism and capitalists.

Yet HPSE also comes with its unique contribution: an emphasis on vision and scale. The rhetoric of Silicon Valley, particularly in high-tech entrepreneurship, is about changing the world (O'Connor, 2000). It appeals to large-scale ambition and heroism (Collins, 1998, pp. 36–38 describes the figure of the 'hero-manager'). The high-tech industry (Apple, perhaps), was the first to establish formal job titles such as 'Evangelist'. Vision is a rhetorical and strategic statement in the appeal for moral and material support (O'Connor, 2002). Scale refers to the replication of one's vision and methods on a national or global level. Impact is dramatic and transformational: systemic change, global change.

TOWARDS A MORE COMPREHENSIVE VIEW: INTRODUCING THREE CASES

Steyaert and Katz (2004) focused on entrepreneurship as occurring in multiple social spaces (i.e., not only businesses but also neighborhoods, communities, and circles) and as conducted daily by ordinary people, considering 'social processes in the broadest sense' (p. 180). HPSE focuses on professional communities and elites. It adheres to formality in the Weberian sense (incorporation, contracts, business plans, and ownership). It has a high-tech twist through vision that is rhetorically dramatic and ideologically expansive. This narrow articulation naturally suggests its opposite: SE that is local, mundane, amateur, informal, accidental, modest, and/or random – or mixtures, such as a combination across elite and amateur. For example, John Doerr, an accomplished venture capitalist, upon first venturing into public education reform, was defeated. Although a member of the elite, he was an outsider to important communities of educators and voters. In hindsight, was there any aspect of his background or network that would have gained him a foothold with these constituencies? This question remains salient as corporate CEOs and interests move increasingly into education. Leapfrog Enterprises, the third largest toy company in the world after Hasbro and Mattel, is owned by KnowledgeUniverse, a partnership between Larry Ellison and Michael Milken. Leapfrog became profitable by selling an electronic phonics-teaching tool for young children, and now it is the only branded product in the US school system. Last year, the company formed a partnership with Wal-Mart wherein it uses the tool as part of a tutoring service for low-income children. Is this social entrepreneurship? Is it strategic philanthropy? Is it a youth program competing with public-school tutoring or even counseling? Leapfrog has a multi-million dollar contract with the US government to use the tool to teach illiterate women in Afghanistan about health and other topics. All these developments may be seen as blending social and strategic, and helping and money-making, activity.

Business and businesspeople must account for increasingly complex social forces (Yaziji, 2004); social and community actors must account for the increasingly complex activity of corporations (Thornton, 2005). SE, or a reframed HPSE, has the potential to do this. The cases pursue this opportunity. They model an approach to SE, and examples of SE, transcending the boundaries of HPSE. They extend HPSE out of business schools and elites to broader society and to specific local communities (including thought communities, Fleck, 1979). They move it away from the ownership of a thing (the company), formal practices executing the thing (contracts, business plans), and the quest to preserve the thing (management). Instead they align entrepreneurship with advocacy, activism, conscience, awareness, causes, problem-solving, and everyday living – including the basic problem of what to do in life or how to get a job. They expand the notion of the business field to include the social field or fields. They acknowledge legitimacy, a social process, as a moral currency that is more important than economic currency. Together, these ideas advance a new metaphor for the places and processes of entrepreneurship: the social cauldron.

Case 1: The Homelessness Industry

My brother telling me that he was at risk of losing his home and becoming homeless, and aware of the increasing homelessness in my neighborhood, I decided to learn more about this problem. I offered my services to the CEO of the largest homeless services agency in Santa Clara County. He stated that his Board of Directors had asked for a trends analysis in the field of homelessness – a document for strategic planning and decision making. I accepted the task. For several months, I reviewed academic literature, interviewed local individuals (activists, advocates, bureaucrats, NPO executive directors), and researched historical and real-time developments via the Internet, producing a final document (O'Connor, 2004). One part of the document represented an attempt to identify the key players and events in the homelessness field dating back to the late 1970s and early 1980s – which virtually every source I consulted, with the exception of one that took a historical approach (Hopper, 1990), identified as the beginning of what some sources explicitly called and many implicitly related to as 'the homeless industry'. In retrospect, two years later, I better appreciate the entrée to this study having been this particular agency and CEO. His agency was known for its competitive nature and he had a strong and controversial reputation. Yet I depended on him for introductions and he was indirectly present in every interview. Having my own firm motives and stakes in the matter facilitated more openness, though, especially for the non-interview-based research.

Alongside many social movements, the 1960s activists focused on a War on Poverty. During these years, John Kennedy launched the Peace Corps. Lyndon Johnson initiated a set of programs called the Great Society. Activists couldn't solve poverty, so they pursued more tangible agendas (Stern, 1984; Hopper and Baumohl, 1994); homelessness became one of them. One activist, Mitch Snyder, is retroactively given credit for his role in the Community for Creative

Non-Violence (CCNV) and for leading a national social movement to end homelessness (Baumohl, 1996). However, the same source states that this homelessness movement 'began locally, often in college towns, where pools of unemployed, ill-educated, and often homeless young adults – mostly White – had formed by the deep "stagflation" recession that began in the mid-1970s' (Baumohl, 1996, p. xiv). The CCNV was unique in its ability to 'demand that the public face up to the shame of homelessness' (Baumohl, 1996, p. xv). Local coalitions formed throughout the US. The Coalition for the Homeless formed in New York City in 1980, and in the next few years similar organizations formed in Boston, Atlanta, San Francisco, Phoenix, Minneapolis/St. Paul, Chicago, Columbus, Denver, Los Angeles, Richmond, Seattle, and Tucson. After taking the US presidency in 1980, Ronald Reagan cut social services significantly. For the first time (according to the accounts I obtained), people noticed women and children among the homeless. In downtown San Jose, a priest worked with local city officials to establish an emergency housing shelter. One Christmas Eve in the early 1980s, he welcomed a couple named Joseph and Mary to the shelter. He either made contact with or was contacted by a reporter at the *San Jose Mercury News*, who came to the shelter, interviewed the couple and the priest, and published a front-page story about homelessness at Christmas.

In the fall of 1984, Mitch Snyder chained himself to the White House gates and began fasting. The weather turned cold, and he attracted media and other attention. Celebrities began to join him for hours and nights at a time, which attracted more attention. An attorney who had been doing pro bono work on poverty proposed to Snyder that they work together to lobby for the homeless. In her account, she recalled being laughed at by staffers on Capitol Hill who 'could not imagine that homelessness could be taken seriously as a "legitimate" legislative issue' (Foscarinis, 1993, p. 45). But Snyder's strike 'galvanized the national public'. As no Congressional staffers had been designated to work on the 'issue', 'there was simply no one to talk to'. (However, Foscarinis notes that the CCNV had operated in Washington for years prior to 1984 and acknowledges its groundwork.) Draft legislation contained three main parts: emergency relief, preventive measures, and long-term solutions. Although an election was coming up, homeless people didn't vote. Foscarinis credits Mickey Leland of the House of Representatives and then-Senator Al Gore (via his wife, Tipper) for supporting the bill. In 1986, Congress passed the Homeless Eligibility Clarification Act. It removed permanent address and other requirements preventing the homeless from obtaining subsidized health care, food, and job training. A noteworthy point in the campaign was that 'the federal agencies took the position that no significant numbers of homeless people were being denied access to these benefits, so the Congressional Budget Office estimated the cost of these measures as zero. Given that estimate, bipartisan support was ensured' (Foscarinis, 1993, p. 48). Snyder disapproved of this deception and the advocates' having taken advantage of it. Instead, Snyder lobbied for more substantial funding, $500 million, called 'emergency aid'. 'Our strategy played directly into the desire of the political community to view homelessness superficially, and as amenable to emergency fixes' (Foscarinis, 1993, p. 50). Furthermore, the campaign capitalized on the emergency aspect of the issue as Snyder and other CCNV members spent the winter on a heat grate outside the Capitol. 'When he and I went on lobbying visits, I was a lawyer in a suit; he was an activist in an army jacket. We brought the sense of emergency, as well as the aura of legitimacy, into the congressional offices. . . . Congress expedited the legislative process and passed the bill by Spring'. Reagan signed the bill but did so in the evening to register his reluctance.

The McKinney Act, the name of this legislation, has been renewed regularly ever since, with increasing dollars appropriated, primarily to provide emergency housing for the homeless. Increasing numbers of NPOs apply and compete for this funding. What was once a dialogue about ending homelessness became one about lobbying, staffing, and getting government funds. The organization for which I did my pro bono consulting was considered by the local Housing and Urban Development officer (the agency of the US government that administers McKinney Act funds) as the most skilled at this activity.

Foscarinis regrets that some former advocates in NPOs who now receive federal funds may hesitate or even be tacitly prohibited from criticizing government policies. 'The price of moral consensus may have been the creation of a new lowest common denominator, a lowering of what is the minimum acceptable standard to meet basic needs: shelters and soup kitchens'. The movement 'lost its potency' at this point. While the original plan had three parts including a long-term solution, only one part was adopted. 'We had no . . . plan for a shift in gears once our strategy had served its purpose . . . we became victims of our own success' (Foscarinis, 1993, p. 58). The emergency approach (used in other social scenarios, see Lipsky and Smith, 1989) permits policymakers and the public to see the problem as solved (Foscarinis, 2000, p. 329). Shelters may even worsen the problem: amid a lack of permanent housing, they tend to become permanent, and those living in them, 'institutionalized'. They become legitimized as a solution. Then, as the problem remains unsolved, it appears unsolvable.

The phrase 'homelessness industry' came from one of my informants, an advocate in San Francisco, founder of one of the national coalition offices referred to earlier. When I described my research for 'the largest homelessness service provider in Santa Clara County' (with perhaps a tinge of self-importance), he replied, 'That is nothing to be proud of'. When I had introduced myself to my sponsoring organization's Board of Directors, one of them

commented that my work would position this already leading agency still
further as a leader in the field. I gained an appreciation for the phrase 'homelessness industry'. The passage of federal laws and the growth of federal funding means more and more NPOs in the homelessness 'business'.

   Public opinion and policy has often split in two directions, one viewing the
problem as having to do with defective persons needing rehabilitation, the
other deriving homelessness from economic and political policies (Marcuse,
2001). The former approach emphasizes social services; the other, housing.
Backing these viewpoints, thought leaders and decision makers line up in
government agencies, research and policymaking institutions, NPOs, professional associations and institutions, and local communities. What is now an
industry began humbly – with activists and hunger strikes, and with the poor,
who are still among us.

Case 2: Jane Addams and Hull House

Jane Addams (1860–1935) is often associated with the Progressive era, and/or
the Progressive era is used to explain her life (e.g., Davis, 1967). She achieved
fame for establishing Hull House, perhaps the best-known settlement house
(so called because 'the workers settled there'; Polikoff, 1999, p. 54) of the
settlement house movement (Carson, 1990), often situated in the context of
massive immigration to the US in the mid-nineteenth century (Lissak, 1989),
social reform movements, (Davis, 1967) and nineteenth-century utopian
movements.

   At least one source identifies the first settlement house as Toynbee Hall,
established by Arnold Toynbee in the mid-1880s (uncle of the historian of the
same name), 'a zealous young social reformer . . . who died at age 31, extending himself beyond his capacity to help the desperate poor' (Polikoff, 1999, p.
53). Somewhat similar places existed in London, such as 'People's Palace', an
institution inspired by Walter Besant's book, *All Sorts and Conditions of Men*
(Polikoff, 1999, p. 53). They provided places where workers pursued education, recreation, and social life. Addams found Toynbee Hall of great interest.
Its 'spiritual leader', Canon Barnett, provided a home for fifteen Oxford grad-
uates 'who carried out the Canon's belief that to help the poor you must live
with them and be available for all manner of daily needs and weekly crises'
(Polikoff, 1999, pp. 53–54). Addams spent several days at Toynbee Hall,
where she was exposed to its philosophy as well as operations. Nothing of
significance could occur between people, Barnett contended, unless a spirit of
friendship existed. To that end he counseled that their Whitechapel [local
community] neighbors be helped 'one by one'. The fifteen residents 'became
actively engaged in the life of the community, conducting a wide variety of
evening classes, aiding teachers in the overcrowded elementary schools, and

serving on committees of local charity organizations' (Polikoff, 1999, p. 55). Addams described Toynbee Hall in a letter to a friend: 'It is a community of university men who live there, have their recreating clubs and society all among the poor people yet in the same style they would in their own circle. It is so far from professional "doing good", so unaffectedly sincere and so productive of good results in its classes and libraries that it seems perfectly ideal' (cited in Polikoff, 1999, p. 55).

Addams did not, however, stumble blindly to Toynbee House nor did she do so as an empty slate. An especially influential event on the European trip was a bullfight in Madrid. Addams's correspondence indicates that she was struck by this experience. While her two friends could not witness the event and left the arena, she herself remained for six kills. This shocked Addams's friends and subsequently Addams herself. Reflecting on the event, Addams 'concluded that she had been so caught up recalling the great amphitheater in ancient Rome where Christian gladiators gallantly faced martyrdom, that she had not registered the utter cruelty of inciting a bull to anger and then slaughtering it' (Polikoff, 1999, p. 52). 'The natural and inevitable reaction came . . . and in the deep chagrin I felt myself tried and condemned, not only by the disgusting experience but by the entire moral situation which it revealed' (Addams, 1910, p. 86). During this trip, Addams 'gradually reached the conviction that the first generation of college women had developed too exclusively the power of acquiring knowledge and of merely receiving impressions, that somewhere in the process of being educated they had lost that simple and almost automatic response to the human appeal, that old healthful reaction resulting in activity from the mere presence of suffering or of helplessness' (Addams, 1910, p. 71). She attacked the assumption that

> the sheltered, educated girl has nothing to do with the bitter poverty and the social maladjustment which is all about her, and . . . breaks through poetry and literature in a burning tide which overwhelms her; it peers at her in the form of heavy-laden market women and underpaid street laborers, gibing her with a sense of her uselessness (Addams, 1910, p. 71).

Referencing her own upbringing, Addams wrote:

> Well-meaning parents set their daughters up to feel this disharmony by teaching them . . . to be self-forgetting and self-sacrificing, deliberately exposing them to the misery in the world by accompanying them to lectures on famines in India and China . . . But when the daughter graduated from college and attempted to do work to alleviate the suffering of the 'submerged tenth' the family claim is strenuously asserted; she is told that her efforts are 'unjustified and ill-advised' (Addams, cited in Polikoff, 1999, p. 91).

Addams explained her idea to found Hull House:

It is hard to tell when the very simple plan which afterward developed into the Settlement began to form itself in my mind . . . I gradually became convinced that it would be a good thing to rent a house in the part of the city where many primitive and actual needs are found, in which young women who had been given over too exclusively to study, might restore a balance of activity along traditional lines and learn of life from life itself, where they might try out some of the things they had been taught and put truth to 'the ultimate test of the conduct it dictates or inspires' (Addams, 1910, p. 85).

Addams selected Chicago as the site for her 'scheme', as she called it. The writer, Lincoln Steffens, described the city as 'first in violence, deepest in dirt, loud, lawless, unlovely, ill smelling, criminally wide open, commercially brazen, socially thoughtless and raw' (cited in Polikoff, 1999, p. 57). Irish immigrants fled the famine, German men and families fled the military, political exiles fled Russia. Looking for a better life in the US, many found barely subsistent wages if not unemployment, dangerous workplaces, tenement housing, poor or nonexistent sanitation, and disease. Addams's search for moral and financial support resembles the stereotypical entrepreneurial pursuit; for example, she won the backing of Julius Rosenwald, head of Sears Roebuck. Once a house was found and established, there was

> nothing dramatic about the opening of Hull House yet it was an historic event, for here was the beginning of what was to be one of the greatest social movements in modern America – the Settlement House movement (Henry Steele Commager, writing the introduction to the first edition of Addams's book [1990]).

There is, however, one interesting departure from the stereotype: 'Jane had no set plan for what she . . . would do on a day-to-day basis. Like an author who discovers what her book is about as she writes it, Jane discovered what Hull House was about by opening its doors and inviting her neighbors in. This lack of any planned program was deliberate. Following Toynbee Hall's model, she wanted Hull House to be 'flexible and able to respond to neighbors' needs as they arose' (Polikoff, 1999, p. 69). Addams's partner, Ellen Gates Starr, wrote to Jane concerning the readiness of several local girls who were

> glad to come and stay awhile and learn to know the people and understand them and their ways of life; to give out of their culture and leisure and over-indulgence and to receive the culture that comes of self-denial and poverty and failure which these people have always known (Polikoff, 1999, pp. 69–70).

Perhaps most extraordinary of all, she wrote: 'There is to be no organization and no institution about it. The world is overstocked with institutions and organizations'.

Three years later, speaking about Hull House to academic and professional audiences, Addams divided the activities of the House into four areas: social, educational, and humanitarian, and civic. 'They are not formally or consciously thus divided . . . but broadly separate according to the receptivity of the neighbors' (cited in Polikoff, 1999, p. 90). (Addams evidently made the distinction for the benefit of her audience – it was not an operational distinction she used to 'manage' the settlement house.) When asked if Hull House was a philanthropic endeavor, Addams said that it was

> unfair to apply the word philanthropic to Hull House as a whole . . . Working people live in the same streets with those in need of charity, but they themselves, so long as they have health and good wages, require none of it. As one of their numbers has said, they require only that their aspirations be recognized and stimulated, and the means of attaining them put at their disposal. Hull House makes a constant effort to secure these means for its neighbors, but to call that effort philanthropy is to use the word unfairly and to underestimate the duties of good citizenship (Addams cited in Polikoff, 1999, p. 91).

Also, as noted above, Addams saw Hull House as an opportunity for overly indulged local girls to 'give out of their culture and leisure'. She made no distinction between the provider and the user; they were one and the same.

As cited earlier, at least one prominent historian asserted that Hull House launched the larger social movement of settlement houses. In 1891, there were six settlement houses in the US; by 1900, there were over a hundred (Polikoff, 1999, p. 89). Addams did identify herself with, and was held by others to be a leader of, this movement (Polikoff, 1999, p. 92). Her work continues, although reshaped, to our day (Trolander, 1987).

Case 3: Academic Entrepreneurship

Elsewhere (O'Connor, 1999) I studied three great historical figures: the head of a fledgling Harvard Business School (HBS), Wallace B. Donham, who established financial and moral security for the School; Elton Mayo, who combined political theory and psychological practices to mount an argument for solving social problems (Trahair, 1984); and John D. Rockefeller, who, along with many other CEOs, sought solutions to labor problems, including violence, without admitting unions.

A conventional story of entrepreneurship might focus on Donham, who undertook the building of a new professional school. This was a serious financial challenge. A key reason for Donham's appointment as Dean in 1919 was his success at fundraising for Harvard College (O'Connor, 1999, p. 121). However, other concerns had to do with legitimacy. At Donham's hire, HBS had on its faculty Harvard's first professor to be hired without possessing a Bachelor's degree (Cruikshank, 1987, p. 42). It also held the distinction of issuing the first degree not conferred in Latin (Cruikshank, 1987, p. 50). A thought leader in the academic field, Abraham Flexner (Director of the Institute for Advanced Study in New York) targeted business schools, which he called 'a malign influence in American life', in attacking the falling standards of higher education (O'Connor, 1999, p. 121). In particular, he singled out HBS: 'Reference to researches carried on by HBS, to which no genuine scientist would give the name of "research" . . . Attention called to researches in advertising: "What Effect does the Summer Time have on Listening In", "How Long can a Radio Campaign be Run Before it Begins to Wear Out", which received Award' (O'Connor, 1999, p. 121).

Donham's responses to this challenge included hiring a historian, purchasing documents of the Medici family, inviting Alfred North Whitehead to lecture at HBS, and recruiting Whitehead's son to join Mayo's research agenda at HBS. In addition, Donham cultivated relationships with leading CEOs. He worked closely with Howard Eliott, a Harvard alum and business executive, to obtain a donation providing for the physical construction of HBS. Eliott, too, was concerned about Harvard's reputation – but in a very different sense. 'Those of us who are away from Cambridge hear a great deal of talk about the alleged radicalism and socialism of the atmosphere at Harvard'. Eliott wrote of a luncheon in New York with 'important and unbiased men' who criticized Harvard for its 'reputation for Socialism, Bolshevism, etc.' owing to the presence of Laski and Frankfurter, among others, on its faculty. He also singled out Robert Fechner, an HBS lecturer who served as an officer of a machinists' union, stating that he was a Socialist. Eliott suggested that having 'a man like Mr. Fechner' on HBS's faculty would make it more difficult to raise money. When Fechner's three-year appointment came up for renewal, he was not reappointed (O'Connor, 1999, p. 122). Donham, unable to get funding from Harvard's president, built alliances with CEOs, particularly to hire Mayo and to fund Mayo's research at Western Electric. This research gained support for HBS that enabled the institution to survive, develop and prosper. Donham not only accumulated the monetary but also the moral currency that founded the school as an institution and as the economic, social and political agenda that Donham called leadership (Donham, 1936). Donham's tenure at HBS ended with his retirement in 1942. Needless to say, by this time HBS was no longer a fledgling institution.

Equally, a conventional story of entrepreneurship might focus on Mayo, who struggled to gain a foothold – and a job, as he was virtually broke – in the US academic community (Trahair, 1984). Leaving his home in Australia and having abandoned medical school as a career path, Mayo took his unique blend of political and psychological theories on a speaking tour of US cities. At one of these talks, he captured the attention of Lawrence Henderson, leader of the Harvard 'Pareto Circle' (Keller, 1984). Henderson had been working with Elmer Southard, a specialist in neuropathology, to study social disorder, particularly 'industrial discontent'. This work was cut short by Southard's death in 1920. Mayo was favorably compared to Southard (Trahair, 1984, p. 150) and attracted Henderson's interest. On this basis, Donham, it is speculated (Cruikshank, 1987, p. 163), read Mayo's essay in the popular Harper's magazine, prefaced by the editor's praise for Mayo's casting 'fresh light on an ever-pressing problem of business and of society' and calling for a 'new study of the human mind' that would lead to 'industrial peace and a happier social order' (Mayo, 1924, p. 590). Donham shared Mayo's writings with Owen Young, the CEO of General Electric, who assured Donham that he would 'secure all the support needed' from other CEOs for Mayo, starting with his hiring by HBS in 1925 (O'Connor, 1999, p. 123). Mayo's research enjoyed remarkable professional success. Scholars have assessed Mayo's contribution as central to the formation of organizational behavior (Roethlisberger, 1977; Wrege, 1979), organizational development (Woodworth et al., 1982), and personnel policies and practices (Whitsett and Yorks, 1983, pp. 165–185).

Finally, a conventional story of entrepreneurship might focus on John D. Rockefeller, whose interests turned from oil to industrial relations after the Ludlow massacre (Rockefeller, 1917), a seven-month-long strike (1914–1915) at one of his mines in Colorado. (The years 1910–1915 have been periodized as the 'age of industrial violence', Adams, 1966.) The strike culminated in the deaths of ten men, two women, and twelve children. Helen Keller, herself having been aided by Rockefeller's philanthropy, called him a 'monster of capitalism' after Ludlow: 'He gives charity and in the same breath he permits the helpless workmen, their wives and children to be shot,' she said (quoted in Chernow, 1998, p. 579). Rockefeller was adamantly anti-union. He was also a Baptist and attended church services regularly. He was a philanthropist, having established the University of Chicago, a medical research institute that eventually became Rockefeller University, and charitable foundations. He approached Beardsley Ruml, the head of one of his foundations, the Laura Spelman Rockefeller Fund (LSRM), about supporting Mayo. The LSRM money was given to Mayo; and his research remains one of the most generously funded programs in the history of social science research (Gillespie, 1991). The CEOs successfully kept unions away until a Supreme Court decision in 1937 (O'Connor, 2001).

SYNTHESIZING THE CASES: OPPORTUNITIES FOR SE

These cases expand the construction of HPSE significantly from its current formulation as managerial, elite, professional, formal, scaled, and dramatic. They suggest relocations and revisions that expand both the social aspects of entrepreneurial activity and the entrepreneurial aspects of social action.

The cases suggest a domain one could call the social sphere or field as a site of entrepreneurship. (The term 'public sphere' could also be used, but in the US context this term is associated with government and citizenship; additionally, it fails to capture the private aspects of social life; for example, Addams established a house and built on the metaphor of home.) This refers to broad expanses of social action, with many players, and including complex phenomena such as currents of thought and processes of consensus. Blumer (1971) suggests that we focus not on actors or organizations but on social problems and on how they become collectively framed as such. He describes the 'career of a social problem': emergence (through agitation, advocacy, activism, violence, and so forth), legitimation (consensus as to explanation for problem), 'official solution', and implementation of 'solution'. This move shifts attention from individual social actors to vast scenes and highly inclusive processes. For example, Addams's work interacts with a progressive (lower case 'p') or social-reform-minded community as well as with a particular context of social class and its reproduction. Individual conscience is a factor, the derivation of which is problematic but must connect to social phenomena (Addams's father was a devout Quaker, the only identity he chose when introducing himself (Addams, 1910, p. 16); Addams also participated in the Social Gospel movement (Handy, 1966, pp. 118, 166, 183–184). Addams blamed her education, finding that intellectual pursuits blunted moral development (Addams, 1910, p. 77). She felt shame that her education had 'immunized' her against 'the automatic response to the human appeal'. Addams also takes her place with the many women leaders of the Progressive era (Muncy, 1991). Similarly, the founding of the homelessness industry may be situated in the context of social protest and activism. The cases of Mayo, Donham and Rockefeller illustrate complex social and ideological agendas at play. Businessmen wanted business to be a respected profession in the same way as law or medicine. The institution of the business school was struggling to become established. The schools needed acceptable research and content – advertising jingles would not pass muster. Science in the model of medicine and history in the model of the humanities were needed. The content was weighed relative to the loss of Latin, Greek, and according to some, even proper English. Appropriate faculty had to be recruited, satisfying education experts as well as the CEOs funding the enterprise. Socialists were said to be on the faculty at Harvard. Businessmen had made available the sums of money necessary to accomplish their agendas amid threats from education experts, humanists, socialists, workers, agitators, politicians, social workers, and regulators. Following common-sense depictions of entrepreneurship, one might say that Mayo sold an idea. But he was also broke and desperate to get a job, and his story is about getting work. He had dropped out of medical school, with a loss of economic and social status. But he creatively combined psychology, politics, and industry; and he walked into the opportunity of Southard's death and the larger opportunity of the struggle between industrial democracy and corporate autonomy (O'Connor, 2001). One might say that Donham built a business. But he also built an institution that is almost taken for granted in social and academic status today, starting from dire financial and moral straits.

Analogue terms moving from for-profit to nonprofit contexts are often proposed: 'donations' become 'investments', 'giving' becomes 'partnering'. Letts et al. (1997) translated venturing to philanthropy; Kanter (1999) repotted the corporate R&D function into philanthropy; Porter and Kramer (1999) adapted corporate strategy to large nonprofit foundations and their stakeholders. One value-laden term is claimed to carry over smoothly to another, but some nonprofit leaders dispute this (Sievers, 2001). In the social realm, alongside economic currency is moral currency. Legitimacy building draws from and traffics in this currency (Suchman, 1995). Legitimacy has a moral aspect, in which an institution meets social criteria as to what is expected and judgments as to whether its activities are 'the right thing to do' (Suchman, 1995, p. 579). It also has a hidden aspect in that it becomes taken for granted through repetition over time (Berger and Luckmann, 1966), that is, actions simply 'make sense' (Suchman, 1995, p. 575).

The cases support legitimacy as an analogue to monetary currency in conventional entrepreneurship, with one important qualification: legitimacy is arbitrated at the broadly social, local community, and individual moral levels. It does not require or lead to economic wealth, although it may. Legitimacy building depends on access to information and individuals being able to interact with others. It also depends on communities that tolerate or even welcome such an exercise. In the case of homelessness, public shame was mentioned as a moral currency. Winning the public sentiment was a goal and milestone, moving shame from an individual matter of defective persons to a social matter reflecting on the moral poverty of a community that tolerates homelessness. However, what complications ensue when public opinion, through Blumer's processes of collective definition, converges around the belief that, having granted money to a cause, this cause should be considered solved or should have been solved? Blumer notes that the career of a social problem includes dissolution: the problem becomes part of the order of things. Is the homelessness industry part of the solution or the problem? For the activist I interviewed, entrepreneurial action in homelessness still means ending homelessness. To allocate more dollars only further fuels the industry that needs homelessness in order to act in the accustomed ways. Here, the quest to understand legitimacy reverts to the original formulation of reciprocated typification (Berger and Luckmann, 1966). The power of repetition and the force of habit are deeply social processes, and entrepreneurship theory has not taken them seriously into account. Blumer's idea of the career of a social problem also shifts attention from the entrepreneur to the problem and to the social processes that fix a problem as such. The entrepreneur is not only not a hero but also is not even a main character. Whether or not SE could accommodate such a radical move is hard to say; however, this perspective significantly expands the view of the social.

Relocating entrepreneurship to social fields and acknowledging legitimacy building and dissolution as complex social processes greatly expands and deepens SE. Combining insights from the cases – the idea of a vast social sphere or scene and complex social processes of consensus building, moral currency, accumulation, consensus, and legitimacy building – opens a new metaphor for SE. As Kaufman (1985) proposed the 'bubbling cauldron of organizational soup' to capture entrepreneurial action, and as Aldrich and Martinez (2001) associated entrepreneurial action with turbulence, so does the metaphor of a social cauldron capture SE spaces and processes. It captures both the idea of a place (social spheres) and process (interaction, interdependence). It suggests the use of 'new combinations' and 'new organizations of industry' (Schumpeter, 2000) while challenging narrowly conceived notions of these constructs and their workings. Might one approach the case of Jane Addams as recombining a proper young girl's nineteenth-century education and upbringing, including the requisite European trip, with inspiration from utopian movements and the Quaker religion? She used Toynbee as a model – but she modified it too, and Hull House not only became better known that its model but also earned credit as founding the settlement house movement.

Could threats to the legitimacy of business and capitalism be viewed as inputs that Mayo and others recombined to develop services such as company unions or psychological counseling, and the foundational skills for personnel management? Could the CEOs who funded Mayo's research be considered co-founders or co-authors as well as consumers of Mayo's products, his ideas and counseling practices? Although entrepreneurship is usually approached as a planned process, the cases suggest a different view. Mayo did not see himself as constructing organizational behavior or personnel management. This is only seen in retrospect. Mayo needed a job. He pursued a relatively new field (psychology) in a relatively new place (industry). He benefited greatly from happenstance; Southard's death had left a void that Henderson wanted filled. Addams spoke of her 'scheme' and explicitly rejected the idea of building a thing – especially an organization. Conventional wisdom says that entrepreneurs create companies that they in turn own. However, these cases suggest different forms of and relationships to entrepreneurship. Instead of companies, we have campaigns, causes, and schemes. We have entrepreneurship with no owner and no main character. We have multitudes of bit players, minute but persistent and emergent interactions, defining moments of 'official' definitions, playing out through complex, interdependent social processes. What counts are the interactions and the intertwinings: who/what joins forces with who else/what else, how, where, to what ends, with what consequences.

Finally, SE is also a domain of knowledge. To the extent that we, as researchers, consultants, teachers, and practitioners, ignore or blindly adhere to disciplinary boundaries and the confines of our departmental, institutional, and patronage-based affiliations, our knowledge and practices will stay within these confines. Our work will replicate the logic and structures that enable them. 'Organizational analysis is an organized and an organizing institution' (Ackroyd, 1993, p. 104). As Ackroyd notes, this is a matter of linkage within the academic community as well as to 'the community more generally conceived' (Ackroyd, 1993, p. 113). What are our links to this more generally conceived community? So much of academic life disrupts links to communities, particularly local communities. We go away to graduate school, we are encouraged to move elsewhere for our first job, and then frustrated tenure-seeking often takes us elsewhere. Our legitimized research paradigms emphasize objectivity and underemphasize the role of local context in pursuit of generalizability. The business school dilemmas confronted by Mayo and Donham continue to this day. Striving to legitimize ourselves vis-à-vis the other professions, we have tended to adopt and reify the interpretations that they initiated, but other possibilities for legitimacy building exist as sketched in this chapter.

Twenty years ago, Peter Dobkin Hall called for studies of 'relationships among firms, government, and nonprofits within local, regional, and industry-wide contexts' (Hall, 1985, p. 66). He was not including still broader social concepts formulated here, such as the social cauldron, legitimacy, and consensus processes. Today he reports little advance, as such work requires 'Chandlerian breadth and Parsonian depth of theoretical vision' (Hall, 2005) – not the routine fodder of organizational studies.

SE offers the potential to pursue the theory and practice of creative action within and for society. Many avenues are open. For example, as Hall suggests, one might envision collaborations that cross domains of knowledge (disciplines) and practice (the three sectors). Promising directions are offered in sociology, specifically the social movement literature (McAdam et al., 1996) and in institutional and neo-institutional theory (Hwang and Powell, 2005). In addition, one might envision community-crossing collaborations focusing on the careers of social problems, this time including people who suffer from those problems (as co-authors, not subjects) and the broader stakeholder of society itself. This raises the question as to how to articulate the 'point of view' of society as a social actor. How do we articulate the point of view of this 'subject' from a methodological and ethical standpoint? This question has important political implications too, of far greater consequence to society than to organizational research per se. This chapter has drawn extensively on historical accounts. Indeed, history is much neglected as a research enterprise and as a data source. Using biographies, correspondence, and archives, social-entrepreneurial histories such as those sketched here offer rich examples to inform social action as well as organization studies. Finally, one could envision collaborations with contemporary social entrepreneurs working in social cauldrons and living out the ideas discussed here with practical consequences for business and society. Regardless of the path, SE presents wide openings and big opportunities – for us all.

5. Public entrepreneurship: moving from social/consumer to public/citizen

Daniel Hjorth and Björn Bjerke

Public: relating to, or affecting all the people or the whole area of a nation or state **b** : relating to a government **c** : relating to, or being in the service of the community or nation devoted to the general or national welfare : HUMANITARIAN
(Merriam Webster Collegiate Dictionary, 10th Ed.)

INTRODUCTION

Starting from a conviction that entrepreneurship belongs primarily to society rather than to the economy (Hjorth and Steyaert, 2003), and that we need to go after life rather than simply business to understand entrepreneurial processes (Hjorth, 2004a) we suggest locating entrepreneurship in the public. Let us contextualise our problem/focus.

The traditional division of society into two sectors, one called public and one called private, today seems less adequate. Traditionally public duties like schooling, sanitation and official transportation are in many countries often taken care of by private enterprises, and various traditionally private businesses are often run by governments, nationally or locally. But above all, a third sector has emerged as an important alternative in today's societies in the past decade or so. It has come to be called the *social sector*. We suggest, however, that it would be more appropriate to conceive of today's society as consisting of three sectors: one common sector (the traditional public sector, financed by taxes); one business sector driven by market forces; and one public, rather than social sector (the new 'public' sector in the original Greek meaning of the word 'public'), where community goals are achieved by creating sociality, including 'public businesses'.

We will present six cases, all from Sweden, which illustrate the point with thinking and practicing sociality-creating processes that enhance citizens' possibilities for living as 'public entrepreneurship'. The cases were part of a learning arena, organised by (amongst others) the authors, in which these different projects cross-fertilised through sharing experiences and dialogued with each other and us (as organisers of the learning arena) in order to develop

97

a language, approach to and understanding of what they did. The cases, with one starting question attached to each, are the following:

1. *Aluma.* This is about publishing a regular journal about homeless people, sold only by homeless people. The idea is to provide some finances as well as some decency to them. We can ask one starting question about this case, in the spirit of what this chapter is all about: Is there a 'public-entrepreneurial' possibility to help homeless people to help themselves to a more decent living?
2. *The old shipyard park.* The vision is here to build a huge outdoor skateboard arena on part of the ground of an old (closed) shipyard, in Malmö south of Sweden. We can ask the following question: Can the building of a large outdoor skateboard arena for young people to get together, making it possible for them to practise their lifestyle, be understood as entrepreneurship?
3. *The Brewery.* Some youngsters cannot make it in the official school, nor do they feel comfortable with traditional pedagogic ways. The Brewery provides them with an alternative. Question: Is it an entrepreneurial achievement to provide reasonable education also to people that do not fit into schools, which most young people attend without having a problem?
4. *Home Service.* Sweden is becoming more and more a country of immigrants. Along with this development come challenges of providing possibilities for a new life for these 'new-Swedes'. There is a growing home service black market where lots of 'new-Swedes' earn their income. The 'Home Service' project seeks to transform unemployment and social security money to start-up money for prospective home service entrepreneurs in this group of 'new-Swedes'. Question: Is it of public interest to create room for a heterogeneity of 'new-' and 'old-Swedes', to fit the former group better into their new society by, for instance, make them interested in working publicly as consultants in servicing homes and institutional buildings?
5. *The Green Room.* This is a cooperative effort among researchers, society and artists to build a place for recreation, therapy and relaxation in a horticultural setting. Question: How could such a project be described as entrepreneurship?
6. *Fair Play.* By setting up a training program for a soccer team, a problem that has been built to truly take care of the hopes and dreams of the team (consisting of young boys that have just become teenagers). Creating an arena to support sports in the broad sense rather than only encouraging elites requires resistance against dominant forces determining what sport is. It demands organisational skills to legitimise sports as exercise rather than competition. Is this also entrepreneurship?

This project has been truly built on giving and taking. The learning settings (what are later referred to as the workshops) have never been classrooms and the generation of a common language has opened a partly new world to all participants, project leaders as well as case participants. The cases will be described in more detail below.

We will argue that even if possibilities like the ones above have been actualised through significantly hard-working and idea-driven people that we could call entrepreneurs, we cannot, at the same time, make them resonate with either traditional business entrepreneurship (which is too common in the mainstream discourse on social entrepreneurship), or with 'new public management's' framing of such entrepreneurship in terms of economic efficiency, that is, in terms of management (as by Osborne and Gaebler, 1992). 'Public entrepreneurship' instead allows a novel discussion (and frees 'a people') that up until now has been missing in discussions of entrepreneurship as a societal force. We believe that the questions asked (along with the short initiation to the cases above) all call upon citizens to act, rather than upon consumers to buy. In this chapter we want to substantiate this characteristic of what we call 'public entrepreneurship': in order to create sociality that enhances life for people, it produces a public space in which citizens can act.

Public, Social, Consumer and Citizen

Public, in 'public entrepreneurship', is by no means a self-evident choice. What we want to say is related to a broad set of terms – perhaps more often collected under the 'brand' of social entrepreneurship. Public here stands in relation to private and as such forms a piece of history in itself. The Latin *privatus* functions in the context of law and describes that (often a right) which belongs to a particular person, group or class, as opposed to the public. Importantly it describes what cuts you off from the public, whereas the social – from *socius* – describes the bond. The Roman virtues of *abundantia* (the ideal of there being enough food and prosperity for all segments of society) and *aequitas* (fair dealing both within government and among the people) indicates how the discourse on the public was inaugurated. It seems to us, from our experiences of the workshops, that people engaged in public entrepreneurship have rescued the qualities and vitalities of these virtues from being marginalised in a Western history of gradual individualisation and subsequent privatisation of ethics (Bauman, 1993). Bauman would say that this (postmodern) ethics, resisting the privatised ethics of modernism, would be relational, based on a responsibility for the other. By public we are not referring to a 'public sector'. We use the term in a much broader, historically contingent, sense.

To contextualise our use of 'public' we need to relate it to 'the social', to the development of the early nation states' economic government and the subsequent establishment of modern capitalism:

> Ever since the end of the Middle Ages, and particularly as a result of the increasing frequency of war and civil war in the seventeenth and eighteenth centuries, the search was on for a behavioural equivalent for religious precept, for new rules of conduct and devices that would impose much needed discipline and constraints on both rulers and ruled, and the expansion of commerce and industry was thought to hold much promise in this regard (Hirschman, 1977, p. 129).

A certain form of governmental rationality – governmentality – more consciously debated after Machiavelli's *Prince* (1513), subsequently made the expression 'economic government' into a tautology, 'given that the art of government is just the art of exercising power in the form and according to the model of the economy' (Foucault, 1991a, p. 92). Between the sixteenth and the eighteenth centuries, the word 'economy' is in the process of acquiring its modern meaning. During this time it is also

> becoming apparent that the very essence of government – that is, the art of exercising power in the form of economy – is to have as its main objective that which we are today accustomed to call 'the economy'. The word 'economy', which in the sixteenth century signified a form of government, comes in the eighteenth century to designate a level of reality, a field of intervention, through a series of complex processes that I regard as absolutely fundamental to our history (ibid., pp. 92–93).

Within such a reality one could then describe the broader system of institutional and juridical forms that try to secure 'free, open market competition' as capitalism. It is in this context that contemporary uses of the terms 'private' and 'public' can be understood.

Through the emergence of the modern state, the private is by no means an autonomous sphere but rather a bundle of rights and guarantees mediated by the state. The social – a field of policies, institutions and scientific disciplines, in place sometime in the mid nineteenth century – can be seen as an invention (originating in post-revolutionary France) meant to make visible the specific problems related to inequality and poverty in a society founded on civil and political inequality (Dean, 1999).

We use the concept 'public' to think our way back from 'social and society'. We do this, as will be clarified throughout this chapter, as a reaction against how managerial economic rationality has come to define and refer to 'the social' while being called upon to provide expert knowledge in the recent urge for 're-inventing government' (Osborne and Gaebler, 1993). This move from social to public, however, necessitates a second move – from consumer to citizen. How come?

Being subject to governmental exercise of power in the form of the economy (Foucault, 1991a), the social has gradually been re-described as a form of the economic. This has happened through a 'progressive enlargement of the territory of the market – the realm of private enterprise and economic rationality – by a series of redefinitions of its objects' (Gordon, 1991, p. 43). Among these objects we here focus on how citizen has become redefined more and more as consumer. The social is today becoming an epiphenomenon of the market, and therefore represented as populated with consumers. Management knowledge – which is the provider of 'Social Entrepreneurship' and 'New Public Management' discussions – has thus found new areas for its expertise serving/staging 'social entrepreneurs' to this bundle of markets represented as 'society', where they act responsibly to meet the demands of *consumers*.

When we advocate a move from social to public we need to replace the role of consumer with a role as open and generative as we find 'public' to be. We have opted for the role of citizen and try to affirm the political and ethical possibilities this role brings. From there we imagine that the social again can become shaped in new ways through forms of public entrepreneurship. Later, we clarify the two moves our chapter seek to argue for in discussing entrepreneurship and social change, as described in Figure 5.1 on page 102.

Purpose and Structure

How can we understand entrepreneurship as social change if we want to avoid starting out from a composite concept (social) which is already ordering and limiting our possible imaginings of entrepreneurship? We are looking for a more raw point of departure, one that opens up the process of creating sociality as an entrepreneurial force and achievement in public space. In order for us to understand entrepreneurship as a force creating social change today, we have found it necessary to disassociate 'the social' from the market. Doing so we move the social away from being 'swallowed' by the market (particularly in neoliberal discourse) towards the public. The noun *public*, far from representing something unproblematic or good (vis-à-vis the social, which would then be the bad), describes the people as a whole (populace). As such it is more open and less composite. In public space sociality can be created and transformed. *Sociality* is understood as collective investments in a desired image, investments which produce an assemblage, a heterogeneous multiplicity united by co-functioning, by sympathy.

Having made such a move, our cases suggest that we need to find an alternative role to represent the basis for participation in the public arena as a creator of sociality. Neither the consumer role of the market, nor the already too over-coded 'social entrepreneur' of the 'enterprising society' allows us the kind of openness in which the process of 'becoming-public-entrepreneur' can be conceptualised and practiced. From the case stories we conclude that the

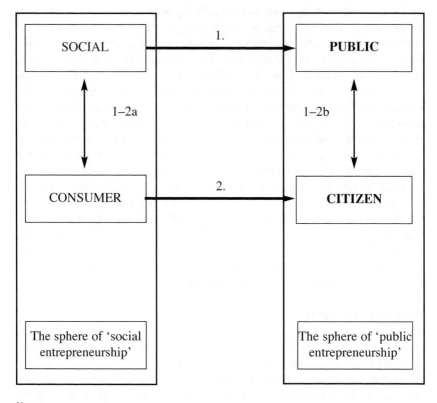

Notes:
1. Through an analysis of the social and the government of the social, we argue for a need to move to the public as the site for what is usually called 'social entrepreneurship'. 1-2a The analysis of the social reveals an increased tendency to populate the social with consumers, corresponding to a re-description of the social as a form of the economic.
2. Having argued for the need to move from social to public leaves us with the need to move from consumer to a more generative role populating the public. We opt for the role of citizen. 1–2b We see a point in relating the citizen to entrepreneurship. From our cases we find support for suggesting that 'public entrepreneurship' emerges out of citizenship rather than from a role as consumer.

Figure 5.1   From social/consumer to public/citizen

role of *citizen* (which has a complex and 'problematic' history, see discussion in 2.1 and 2.3) describes well the way people participate in the public arena when creating sociality.

This chapter proceeds according to the following structure. In the first two sections of part *two* we position our framework against what we have described as the 'ruling social entrepreneurship discourse' so as to build a conceptual framework for which our moves from social to public and from consumer to citizen are central in the third section. We are then ready to turn to the stories of public entrepreneurship (part *three*). These stories emerge from a study in Malmö (the very southern part of Sweden) conducted over sixteen months, from August 2003 to November 2004. We analyse these cases (in part *four*) so as to launch into a discussion that attempts to affirm how our moves can make a difference (part *five*), that is, how 'public entrepreneurship' is a concept allowing us to tell stories of a people presently missing in discussion of entrepreneurship in society. In part *five* we also conclude this study with formulations of new problems, and draw implications from it.

THE PROBLEMS OF UNDERSTANDING PUBLIC ENTREPRENEURSHIP

'Social Entrepreneurship'

There are many names for entrepreneurship performed vis-à-vis society and 'societal needs' rather than as traditionally on a market and for profit only. 'Social entrepreneurship' seems to be the most common one. Other names being suggested are 'civic entrepreneurs' (Henton et al., 1997), 'community entrepreneurs' (De Leeuw, 1999), 'idealistic entrepreneurs' (Piore and Sabel, 1984) or 'mundane entrepreneurs' (Rehn and Taalas, 2004). Typical for the approaches associated with these names is that questions of '*what is* social entrepreneurship' (or civic entrepreneurship, and so on) are almost always answered with discussions on '*who is* the social entrepreneur'. That is, the old convention of limiting entrepreneurship to the individual entrepreneur (criticised already by Gartner, 1988) is reproduced in a new context. This tendency is clearly related to an American culture where individualism is much more central than in European cultures in general and Scandinavian culture in particular.

The model that is ruling the discussions, the US one, is structured by certain lines of reasoning: 'Increasingly, entrepreneurially minded nonprofit leaders are bringing the tactics of the private sector to the task of solving social problems. And with good cause: they need the cash' (McLeod, 1997). This approach operates with a conception of entrepreneurship that makes legitimate a representation of social problems as economic problems with business solutions, something that makes normal the abovementioned tendency to apply business management when solving social problems, for economic reasons. The entrepreneur is reduced to an economic agent with an expertise in business-problem-solving; and the social is without further notice re-described as a form of the economic: 'Social entrepreneurs have the same core temperament as their industry-creating, business entrepreneur peers but instead use their talents to solve social problems on a society-wide scale . . .' (William Drayton, Founder of Ashoka, 2002, pp. 3–5).[14] Like any change-oriented activity in a society, social entrepreneurship has not evolved in a vacuum. It has progressed in a rather complex framework of forces at all levels of our societies: a shift away from a social welfare approach towards a neoliberal, more market-based, approach for the distribution of resources (Johnson, 2000), and the emergence of an increasingly global economic system, where a growing gap between rich and poor has led to many social change initiatives (Reis, 1999). At the national level, traditional government approaches to meet social needs are in question (Dees et al., 2001), and such questioning is used to establish boundaries separating normalities and anomalies. In the example below the traditional welfare-state approach is constructed as a discouraging change not realizing the potential of individuals/communities:

> Traditional welfare-state approaches are in decline globally, and in response new ways of creating healthy and sustainable communities are required. This challenges our social, economic and political systems to respond with new, creative and effective environments that support and reward change. From the evidence available, current examples of social entrepreneurship offer exciting new ways of realizing the potential of individuals and communities . . . into the 21st century (Catford, 1998, p. 97).

The number of non-profit organisations has increased exponentially (Bornstein, 1998; Cannon, 2000). The trend is in effect also in a country like Sweden (Westlund, 2001). By this trend, the boundaries between the tax-based, market-based and voluntary sectors of society have been both highlighted and erased (Johnson, 2003): the sectors have been individualised so as to allow their normalisation according to the norm of 'social entrepreneurship'. The concept of the commercial entrepreneur has been broadened to encompass those who work for social innovation through entrepreneurial solutions – the term 'social entrepreneur' was coined by Drayton, founder of Ashoka (Catford, 1998). The hopes for these entrepreneurs are high:

> There are three different types of benefits which social entrepreneurs can bring to communities. In the short term they can help create new buildings, services and jobs which would not otherwise exist, but they can also improve accessibility, effectiveness and efficiency of existing services. In the medium term they can act as powerful models for reform of the welfare state, and in the longer term can create and invest social capital (Catford, 1998, p. 96).

Descriptions of social entrepreneurs, apart from being individualistic, are most often based on a contrasting effect with business entrepreneurs. Differences between social entrepreneurs and business entrepreneurs are centred on long-term versus short-term focus; profit as means versus profit as end; using profit to serve people versus using profit to gain further profit (Thalbuder, 1998; Westlund, 2001). In summary, social enterprises have a social objective while blending social and commercial methods (Dees et al., 2001): '[Social entrepreneurs] share many characteristics with commercial entrepreneurs. They have the same focus on vision and opportunity, and the same ability to convince and empower others to help them turn their ideas into reality – but this is coupled with a desire for social justice' (Catford, 1998, p. 96).

'Social entrepreneurship' is both complex enough and the literature new enough to prevent consensus (Johnson, 2003). Social entrepreneurship is seen as businesses with a social ethos (Thompson, 2002), as performed by social entrepreneurs that (according to Peter Drucker) '. . . change the performance capacity of society' (Gendron, 1996, p. 37). Most authors, however, follow an old pattern in entrepreneurship research and focus on individual characteristics:

- Bornstein (1998, p. 36) characterises social entrepreneurs as 'path-breakers with a powerful new idea, who combine visionary and real-world problem-solving capacity, who have a strong ethical fiber, and who are 'totally possessed' by their vision for change'.
- Schulyer (1998, p. 1) argues that social entrepreneurs are '. . . individuals who have a vision for social change and who have the financial resources to support their ideas . . . who exhibit all the skills of successful business people as well as a powerful desire for social change'.
- Boschee (1998, p. 1) presents social entrepreneurs as '. . . non-profit executives who pay increased attention to market forces without losing sight of their underlying mission'.
- Thompson et al. (2000, p. 238) describe social entrepreneurs as '. . . people who realise where there is an opportunity to satisfy some unmet need that the welfare system will not or cannot meet, and who gather together the necessary resources (generally people, often volunteers, money and premises) and use these to "make a difference" '.

According to Johnson (2003) one commonality is the social entrepreneur's problem-solving nature, producing 'measurable results in the form of changed social outcomes' (p. 2; see also Boschee, 1998; Dees et al., 2002). 'Social entrepreneurs' are often distinguished by bringing together – often in one person – the creation of 'social value' and a heightened sense of accountability to the constituencies served and for the outcomes created (Dees et al., 2001; Thompson, 2002). These lines of thinking are central to representations of the governable subject. Through individualisation and totalisation, that is, through identifying according to traits and making accountable according to a language of management, control is made possible.

Apart from these management-oriented approaches there are discussions of social entrepreneurship also in the more macro-oriented regional development literature where clusters, rural economies and communities are the central concepts. In this literature, however, the dominance of capital as metaphor effectuates a similar redescription of the social as a form of the economic. Financial capital is accompanied by physical, human, cultural and social (as in Johnson, 2003). Whether this metaphor of capital can do anything for the human, cultural, or social is seldom discussed. One assumes, in accordance with an economised language/society that the use of capital as metaphor brings precision to the discussion and adds weight and importance to these otherwise easy-to-brush-off aspects of human life (those traditionally located as outside the grasp of capital). What we find problematic here is a silent move from citizen to consumer when discussing the social in the context of entre-preneurship. This, in our view, would be to start too much with the *results* of complex historical processes, and we would suggest moving upstream (genealogically) to find a more 'raw' view. Allow us, therefore, a short discus-sion of our two suggested moves: from social to public and (the subsequent) from consumer to citizen.

The First Move: From Social to Public

The present re-description of the social as a form of the economic (Gordon, 1991) rests upon the genealogy of the *social* informed primarily by the post-French-revolutionary (1789) concern with making certain problems of the unequal distribution of power and poverty in the state visible. The invention of the social as a reality, as a level of intervention, accomplished this. Liberal and neoliberal governmentality is a response to this visibility of the social, an attempt to govern the social. Durkheim (and Léon Bourgeois) developed soli-darisme as a doctrine of state targeting the social bond rather than structures of society. Solidarity, understood (by Durkheim) as a general social law of development, and the socialisation of risk resulting in social security systems as central in the welfare state, together provided disciplines as sociology with a new image of society (Dean, 1999). This reshaped the social into a sphere of enterprise on the basis of society as the risk taker *par excellence*.

To the genealogy of the social belongs also the kind of positivity that it acquired through the role played by statistics in the service of the state. Furthermore, the establishment of the private–public dichotomy by the liberal economy delineated a sphere of private authority and autonomy belonging to the private factory owner/entrepreneur and the father as head of household.

'The social' designates a field of governmental action operating always within and upon the discrepancies between economy and society, the princi-ples each of which come to be envisaged in terms of their incipient prejudice to the other's, so that the politics of prosperity (Keynes, Beveridge) centres on the effort to establish positive feedbacks for their reciprocal correction' (Gordon, 1991, p. 34). Keynesian politics – dominant during the decades after the Second World War (a Western-centric term) and up to the early 1980s – made the welfare-state dependent upon a harmonic balance between the economic and the social, but suggesting heavy state intervention along accommodationist lines.

The progress in legislating protective rights for workers during the twentieth century has made us move from a situation in which we define ourselves as employees vis-à-vis capital to a situation where we have become employees of society (in work or not, see Donzelot, 1979). Enterprise discourse (neoliberalism) is also a reaction against this, pushing towards an individualisation of responsibility. Society is then regarded '. . . less as a source of needs that are individually distributed and collectively borne and more as a source of energies contained within individual's exercise of freedom and self-responsibility' (Dean, 1999, p. 152). 'Community', which has become a key term in political discourses, seems attractive for both proponents of Thatcher's 'there is no such thing as society' as well as theorists of social capital (emphasising trust and civic participation) as well as for communitarians promoting reaffirmed shared values (ibid.).

In the welfarist version of the social, the state sought to operate through the economy and upon the 'social' to secure society. In today's society, after the work of neoliberalism, we have the establishment of several markets and quasi-markets which try to make us active as 'players'. There are technologies of agency that try to enhance our capacity for participation, and there are technologies of performance through which the efficiency of our agency can be evaluated and calculated. 'The 'social' is no longer the diverse sector that is subject to the ineluctable logic of bureaucratic rationalisation under the aegis of the welfare state. Rather, the social is reconfigured as a series of 'quasi-markets' in the provision of services and expertise by a range of publicly funded, non-profit and private for-profit, organisations and bodies' (Dean, 1999, p. 173).

In order to make space for entrepreneurship as a societal force, creating sociality, it is not enough to step back from the social and move towards the public, as suggested above. We need also to locate the citizen in the public space rather than in the social, the latter which is becoming an economic place for consumers.

The Second Move: From Consumer to Citizen

At present there is an attempt (by civic republicanism) to reinvigorate a romantic idea of citizenship as a set of practices in the face-to-face relationships of local communities. We do not want to contribute to such a view. Instead we want to contest the neoliberal attempt to limit citizenship to the role of consumer-choices in a market by developing a view of citizenship that high-lights its agonistic history, a creative 'making use' of the public space between state institutions and civic society.

Economic perspectives often provide a limited focus: either on consumers' shift from private consumption to public action (due to frustration), or on their frustration with participation in the public arena (leading to a shift into private concerns). One influential theorist, Hirschman (1977, 1982, pp. 93–96), discusses the differences in these moves (noting that they are not symmetri-cal).[15] However, he focuses on how public action, say political action/activism, is available to the disappointed *consumer*. And he regards this as a 'straightforward deduction from conventional theory', but notably adds the condition: '. . . *provided* we deal with consumers who are also conscious of being citizens and who live in a culture where the private and the public are important dichotomous categories permanently vying for the attention and time of the "consumer-citizen" ' (ibid., p. 63, original emphasis). He also brings in his 'Exit, Voice, Loyalty' theory to suggest that '. . . disappointed consumers have a very different option [from exit] that has been neglected by economic analysis: they can raise their *voice*, and thus engage in various actions that range from strictly private complaining (asking for a refund) to public action in the general interest' (ibid., p. 64, original emphasis). What characterises Hirschman's analysis then?

1. It still is focused on *consumers'* shifts in involvement. In the case of public entrepreneurship we rather witness the process of moving from citizen to *producer* of public services, i.e., we rarely deal simply with consumers making economic choices.
2. He downplays the citizenship side of the issue and thus actually repro-duces the assumed primacy of an economic language when discussing public action. There is a complex history of citizenship that is left out.
3. Hirschman agrees with Weber that capitalism was diffused and embraced due to the desperate search for social order and predictability. Capitalism is assumed to control the passions, create a more one-dimensional human and provide control and predictability while keeping people out of mischief.
4. Hirschman uses economic theory to dissolve the dichotomy of liberal citi-zens as passive[16] and private versus communitarian citizenship as active and public. But he does so by re-describing the issue as one of consumers opting for public action as well as for private silence for economic reasons.

The complexity of citizenship is well described by Michael Harris (1997) who after briefly going through ten different uses of citizenship centres on the need to reformulate citizenship around the tension of 'individual autonomy' and 'universal membership'. White and Hunt (2000), instead focus on a central shift between the nineteenth and twentieth centuries '. . . from a subjectivity rooted in "character" to one based on "personality" that corresponded to changes is the prevailing form of citizenship and the practices of the self' (p. 93). They provide an important historical lesson, pointing out that when character and corresponding public virtues no longer dominated the shaping of a self, a new form of care of the self, organised around 'the quest for a unique self', instead took centre stage. With the help of Burchell (1995), they warn against a 'current nostalgia over citizenship' (2000, p. 94) that we believe is boosted in the discourse on 'social entrepreneurship' where the 'public citizen' is valorised as an enterprising self. Our attempt to make social theory, through a historical perspective, influence the way we discuss the creation of sociality in forms of public entrepreneurship is offered as an example of a more socially grounded discussion. Citizenship is a composite concept that includes individual and group identities, and our study also taught us that discussions of citizenship always have to deal both with rights and values and local practices in which forms of citizenship are practiced (Petersen et al., 1999). In this way you can discover multiplying forms of citizenship, sidestepping traditional political structures in order to create 'effective events' that intervenes with forces shaping societies.

Citizen, it is important to emphasise, is a social concept: it centres on the ethics of social practices. The self as citizen links ethics and public politics and shows how they are always connected. The social (space) between state and citizen was, as we have noted above, invented to make visible a certain level of intervention, a certain reality which is always political in that it accomplishes a certain distribution of wealth and power among citizens. The *public sphere* would then be that arena for intervention with the social that connects the institutionally structured sociality of the state with the mundane and everyday-practices-maintained sociality of civil society. This is where the public entrepreneurs operate to create new forms of sociality in the face of withering state-institutions.

In summary, then, the relational self-forming processes involved in performing citizenship are guided by an ethics of *abundantia* and *aequitas*, central for keeping the public space open, free from forces operating to include it either in civic places or in state-institutional places. Public entrepreneurship, again, operates as a sociality-creating force in the public space, a *space* in-between the civic and the state-institutional.

CASES OF PUBLIC ENTREPRENEURSHIP

With financial support from regional government funds, a series of workshops, lasting between one to two days, have been held (about ten of them altogether over a period of eighteen months in 2003–2005) with about one dozen participants in most projects, where they created sociality in a public space. These workshops have been led by two academics from local universities (of which one is a co-author of this chapter).

Context of Workshops

Some visions guiding these workshops have been:

1. The workshops were to move stepwise and progressively so that experiences from one workshop could provide the inputs to the next one. A lot of searching and trial-and-error have taken place – a true learning process.
2. As all participants in the workshops (except for the two workshop organisers) are practising entrepreneurs (according to how we describe public entrepreneurs in this chapter); the purpose was to bring experience and skills in to and out from the workshops to better promote their own ventures. Learning was indeed generated from the practices of public entrepreneurship. The 'classroom' was a reflective dialogue with peers and ourselves as organisers.
3. The organisers (on the other hand) were mainly interested in finding out how knowledge of 'traditional' entrepreneurship could be improved by learning from the practice and thinking of the participants and, also, to come up with good characterisations of these kinds of entrepreneurs.
4. To give perspective to everything, every workshop was visited by a specially invited speaker who gave a lecture around a favourite topic of his or hers, selected to improve participants' knowledge of common problems in the workshops. These lectures turned out to be real triggers and catalysts for developing a vocabulary and deep sense of understanding of what was going on among the entrepreneurial participants.
5. To give a focus to the discussions, six such cases, all represented among the participants, were selected to be studied in more detail between the workshops. All participants, even if they were not directly involved in a case, participated in studying them. All participants studied around two to three cases each, in a kind of a matrix arrangement. These cases are presented later.

One important activity of the workshops was to develop a specific vocabulary that, according to the participants, would characterise what they were doing in practice. The idea of developing such a vocabulary is based on what we think is important for entrepreneurship today, namely *languaging* (Normann, 2001, p. 253) and even the possibility of seeing *entrepreneurship as a language-making* practice (Bjerke, 2005). The exercise of developing a vocabulary peaked about halfway through the workshops and was genuinely appreciated for providing a terminology to the participants, enabling them to talk about what they were doing and to imagine how it could be moved beyond the limits of the present.

Short Description of Cases and Workshop Outcomes

Aluma
This is a monthly journal in the city of Malmö and its surroundings. This journal is sold only by homeless people in public places (apart from being subscribed to by some regulars and official institutions). The object of the project is, apart from providing some finances and a bit of pride to the sellers, to be a strong instrument in creating opinion in the issue of being without a home. The journal consists mainly of articles on public issues, but it also contains discussions about culture and leisure-time activities in the area. Aluma is not associated with any political party or any religion. The journal sells about 20,000 copies per month in an area of Sweden where a bit more than a quarter of a million people live.

The person who founded Aluma, Elisabeth, had been out travelling and became inspired by and curious of similar types of journals in other parts of the world. As there is a journal of the same type in Stockholm, the capital of Sweden, she went there to study the process. By coincidence she came in contact with a homeless drug addict in Malmö, who became one of her friends. Through him she gained entrance to the world of homeless people.

The old shipyard park
A vision to develop a whole youth park in a former premises of a major Swedish shipyard, now being closed, has grown in Malmö. The main provider of fuel for this process is John. His ambitions include building Europe's largest outdoor skateboard arena in the park. He has gained support for his idea that the city of Malmö can, through such a construction, provide a raw model for co-operation between the city and its young people. The purpose also includes involving these people in creating new public space and to do this in a democratic fashion. John is working hard to get assistance from various sponsors for his project and he is well on his way to realise his dream.

The Brewery
The Brewery (the name comes from the fact that the premises were previously

occupied by a brewery) is an unusually successful example of people getting together to create things of a physical nature (such as an indoor skating arena and space for different educational activities) as well as of a more abstract nature (building networks in the city).

The Brewery was inaugurated in 1998 by the tax minister of Sweden at that time. The main part of its physical space consists of an indoor skating arena – 1,800 square metres large – filled with ramps constructed by the skaters themselves. The arena is seen as one of the best in Europe. There is also a café, an engineering shop, a media shop and 500 square metres of educational facilities.

Home Service
Long term social welfare is a central problem in large-scale big city areas. Home service is a cooperative project where a number of local actors in Malmö are involved in an experimental group aiming at bringing some people out of long term dependence on welfare. The ideal is to assist fifteen long term unemployed immigrants for 22 months in their attempt to be able to start functioning as self-employed entrepreneurs in the home-service sector. The main organisation behind this project is the local community real estate owner and administrator. The main leader of this project in practice is called Stig. The project has suggested that social security money be re-coded as start-up services providing people with support for starting their own home service companies. It is described as a model for 'growth, employment, and integration'. The pilot study comprises four persons being supported in their start-up process (within the home-service sector). The results include being better at speaking Swedish, higher self-esteem, personal networks including people outside their own immigrant group, and higher income. Now fifteen more persons are brought into the same process (and hundreds are standing in line).

The Green Room
The project aims at cooperation between researchers, society, artists and entrepreneurs to establish Österlen (the eastern part of Scania, to a large extent devoted to horticulture) as a centre for knowledge, recreation and therapy nestled among all the fruit trees in the area. This process is driven by Monika, who lives in the area and loves the place.

The tourist industry in the area is based to a large extent on horticulture, among other things through what are called 'Open Gardens', where the public gets access to private gardens in season. A pilot study is underway to find out about similar experiences in other parts of Sweden and abroad, employment numbers in various parts of horticulture in the country, and to find out about ongoing research in the field. The project aims to systematically seek out and exploit knowledge of gardening already developed in the area and create networks and arenas where this knowledge can be diffused in order to boost the development of this horticultural sector and, in effect, create more jobs.

Fair Play

This projects aims at running a program in order to foster an interest in sports in the broad sense (not to screen for the elite) among members in a junior soccer club in Lund. The project started in 2004. There was much turbulence in the club at that time. An ex-juvenile was recruited to lead the program. This was a lucky draw.

The initiator of the program, Gunilla, is proud to say that 'her' team today plays in the first soccer division in Sweden for boys at that age, a level that any soccer team of any kind in that particular city never have reached.

Apart from moving these projects ahead through sharing their stories in the workshops, a *second result* of the workshops is that the participants found it important to elaborate on a vocabulary that they thought could be used to characterise what they were doing – public entrepreneurship is one result of this discussion.

A *third* set of activities of interest to this chapter took place in a two-day workshop in May. After having been part of the process since August 2003, the participants were given the opportunity to tell us what they thought they had learnt about what we refer to as 'public entrepreneurship'. The task was to, in teams of two, work on specific questions like what, in their opinion, characterised 'their version of' entrepreneurship, how they differed from business entrepreneurs, what the obstacles to their kind of entrepreneurship in Sweden today were and what could be done to improve on the situation. Some statements from the presentation of the results were:

- 'Obstacles to public entrepreneurship include nostalgic people, who have a cemented opinion of a "good" society, a society which in their opinion once existed'.
- 'The fact that every expense belongs to an account somewhere complicates a holistic view'.
- 'Differences between public entrepreneurs and business entrepreneurs are part of a moving target for discussion'.

Some opinions among the organisers of the workshops as to what characterises the public entrepreneurs in those workshops are:

- They have no overall plan for what they are doing. Having had one, they would not have succeeded.
- They look at what they are involved in as the most natural thing to do in societies of today and they are very surprised that not more people are doing it.

- They have a humble approach to what they do and look upon their associates and partners as the major contributors to their success.

Interpreting and analysing these results seems to require a more thorough understanding of citizenship, its recent history and present complexity. Our results also suggest that normal–abnormal is a distinction of importance for practicing public entrepreneurship. The results also imply that understanding public entrepreneurship demands from us a sensitivity before the political and ethical sides of citizens-becoming-public-entrepreneurs. The political effort to create space in the public for actualising ideas is intimately related to the ethics of sociality as a life-enhancing collective investment, a heterogeneous multiplicity united by co-functioning, by sympathy.

ANALYSIS: OPENINGS FOR AN OTHER DISCOURSE

Citizenship and Public Entrepreneurship – Understanding a Common Theme

During the nineteenth and twentieth centuries, citizenship became an institution. Citizenship was related to not as something that we needed to achieve but something that was already in place. Citizenship in today's society, as is illustrated by the projects we have reported in our case stories, is less of an institution and more of an achievement. People are constantly asked to position themselves as citizen vis-à-vis specific issues breaching the old left–right dichotomy in politics and instead targeting specific interest groups. Citizenship, as we have concluded above, is therefore a question of identity (Haste, 2004) through which one is relationally defined as 'ingroup' or 'outgroup' in contexts of specific issues: for example, in both Aluma and The Old Shipyard Park, this is central as the former seeks to redefine the identity of the homeless to one belonging to society, and the latter pushes the 'rights' of the skateboarders into the sphere of concerns 'naturally' considered as one of many by the local politicians. Public space – correspondingly – is both inclusive and exclusive. Thus we move from citizenship as a formal status to citizenship as a practice or activity. Our case stories bear witness to this – that public space is inclusive and exclusive. The homeless people selling Aluma on the street create a sociality where the exchange of money and magazine, and exchange of looks during the brief moment, makes the homeless *part of* society – their situation is no longer 'their own', private, but brought into the public sphere.

The genesis of the concept of citizen is characterised by a gradual disciplining – taming of passion (Hirschman, 1977) or eliminating 'harmful belief' through schooling (Burchell, 1999). From Aristotelian and Roman conceptions based on the presence of virtues guiding 'man's building of character', we have moved – with the help of Machiavelli and Hobbes – towards a disciplinary society of citizen-subjects (Foucault, 1979, 1988, 1991a). The neo-liberal redescription of citizenship along lines of individuals' rights to practice their participation in society according to the role of consumer is represented as a move towards freedom and as characteristic of an enterprising society. But the 'enterprising subject' is still a governable subject, the *object* of management knowledge. Our case stories exemplify entrepreneurship changing the ordering forces of public space with its ambition to reorganise and transform what the public is taken to be: Home Service is possible only because 'so-called' public institutions (municipal real estate owner; social security office; job-office) break a number of rules of conduct and re-compose the status of money from simply social security support to funds helping people to start their companies. This exemplifies the citizen-becoming-entrepreneur process that led to us characterises the case stories.

Spinosa et al. (1997) is an example of an attempt to discuss the entrepreneurial aspect of citizenship. In their discussion – *Disclosing New Worlds* – both 'virtuous citizens' and entrepreneurs create social change. Our case stories exemplify what we call 'public entrepreneurs' driven by a desire to arouse a sense of responsibility in their fellow citizens for creating sociality in public space characterised by *abundantia* and *aequitas*. That is, they become public entrepreneurs in the process of uniting the two roles discussed by Spinosa et al. Becoming a public entrepreneur starts with what they name the 'virtuous citizen'. The point is not a universal virtuousness but a locally based practice. A practice of 'virtuosity' is only meaningful when it is based upon the work of translating universals into the local-historical-cultural context. It seems that the universal side, that it is translatable into most contexts, of *abundantia* and *aequitas* is important for *political* reasons of creating space for creation, whereas the local-historical-cultural translation is *ethically* important as sociality anchored in public space.

Public entrepreneurs do not change reality primarily through products/services but by creating the organisational possibilities for people to take up new practices. It is for this reason – that they need new practices to be taken up – that an ethical side of public entrepreneurship is important. The normal has to be relativised in order for public entrepreneurs to change/create sociality. But sociality is where the normal is effective, which makes 'public entrepreneurship' into a creative resistance against forces of normalisation.

As Dreyfus and Rabinow (1982, p. 195) point out, normalisation works through being part of the system of classification and control of anomalies in society. 'Social entrepreneurship' is today used successfully in an increasingly influential discourse on how to 'fix' the problems of the withering 'welfare state'. Accordingly, control and efficiency are now being pursued in 'social sectors' where things and people are normalised according to the knowledge-power of the enterprising citizen's discourse. This 'social entrepreneurship' discourse will therefore, to an increasing extent, determine whether people are to be considered competent members of a political community, that is, whether they are citizens proper. This is characteristic for normalising technologies that '. . . operate by establishing a common definition of goals and procedures, which take the form of manifestos and, even more forceful, agreed-upon examples of how a well-ordered domain of human activity should be organized' (Dreyfus and Rabinow, 1982, p. 198). In contrast to this normality of 'social entrepreneurship', establishing the good examples of practicing management knowledge to solve 'social' or 'public domain' problems, our cases exemplify a much more citizen-driven process. The 'social' is never represented as a form of the economic that lacks a few 'clicking' mechanisms, but instead operates as part of the targeted result.

It is against this background that our cases of public entrepreneurship can further be understood as examples of transforming anomalies into actualities. The normal, according to the 'social entrepreneurship' discourse, would be to respond as a consumer – as Hirschman (1982) has discussed – to 'malfunctions' in society. The organisers of the Home Service project would 'normally' have sought 'external' funds to set up financial means for start-ups. Instead, they chose to suggest an anomaly – to redefine social security money into (part of) a start-up fund. With the help of White and Hunt (2000) and Burchell (1999) we have been able to contextualise such 'normalisation' as part of a certain form of citizenship, practiced as a form of liberal government. However, with Spinosa et al. (1997), we have also seen the creative and productive sides of citizenship, operating between the social – as traditionally maintained and structured by state-institutions – and the civil society of everyday practices. There, in the public, entrepreneurship operates as the creation of sociality through which people can enhance their lives.

Creating Sociality as a Public Entrepreneurship Achievement

Our initial difficulties with reading our cases in conversation with the literature on social entrepreneurship drove us into the project of contextualising two moves (see above): from social to public and from consumer to citizen. This allowed us to problematise 'the social' as a historically situated construct of political potential, used to make visible problems of unequal distribution of power and poverty.

We could then ask how the social is created today in everyday processes. A partial conclusion tells us that the social is predominantly produced as a form of the economic, with the effect that existing political tension is transformed into a discussion of active citizens as responsible consumers. However, this study has told about public entrepreneurs that don't opt for public action for economic reasons as do Hirschman's consumers, but for the kind of opportunities that are created in participating in the public space guided by *abundantia* and *aequitas*. Whereas 'social entrepreneurship' produces the 'social' as something needing to be fixed (re-described as forms of the economic and subject to management knowledge), 'public entrepreneurship' creates sociality as something missing and socialises risk in local communities as part of public space.

The public entrepreneurs studied people as citizens of Southern Sweden and ask them to co-create a sociality that extends the possibilities for people to practice creative citizenship. The driving individuals often seemed moved by frustration over the lack of sociality in public space and lack of collective investments in desired functions.

1. *Aluma*: Why do homeless people not meet people who have homes in ways that help the former to a better life? Aluma creates such a space for interaction in the everyday life of Malmö through the practices of selling the journal;

2. *The Old Shipyard/The Brewery*: Why can't the city of Malmö and its youth interact in creative ways so as to engage young people in democratic processes of co-creating public space? The Skateboard Shipyard Park and The Brewery are both public entrepreneurship stories driven by this desire;

3. *Home Service*: Why must we accept the hopelessness of long-term unemployed and their gradual dependence upon social welfare programs; how can we create a sociality in which these people can find a bridge back to 'society', where they participate in other forms than as passive recipients of money? The Home Service project organises resources in new ways in order to actualise new possibilities for unemployed 'new-Swedes' in this sense;

4. *The Green Room*: How can stressed-out and burnt-out people of big city life get access to space for contemplation and spaces of nature, of gardens where care-taking of life includes ones own? The Green Room project works towards actualising this idea, summoning investments in this common image of nature as recreational;

5. *Fair Play*: How can the joy of doing sports be recreated anew? The Fair Play project has done so, throwing off the shadow of elitism and creating a sociality in which the sport = fun idea rules, and where sports again become part of a useful learning experience – participating and relating are more important than doing your own thing.

The Aluma project illustrates the formation of a necessary community without which the problems of homeless people in Malmö never would have been possible to deal with in a way that provides social, and not simply economic, support. The social opportunity, rather than some market opportunities, drives the project. Aluma creates a public space in between the state-institutionally structured society and civic practices. In this space the possibilities for practising citizenship are extended.

The Old Shipyard Park is more directly targeting the relationships between youth and public space. Also here we find it to be of central importance that the project seeks to provide young people with possibilities to practice citizenship in ways that they can participate in and relate to.

In the case of the Brewery it is the social opportunity of providing a public space that has driven the project. The Brewery does not approach consumers and provide a different choice. They approach people searching for ways to practice their citizenship together with people of their generation and via practices they feel are central to life. Freedom is exercised as social rather than private. This is also, like Aluma, a necessary community in the sense that without it, young people without any prospects for educating themselves or meeting others with similar passions, would most likely have felt excluded from public space.

The Home Service project is stepping in where society traditionally has positioned itself as the risk taker par excellence. Home Service creates opportunities for people to move *from* long-term dependence upon welfare and *to* become self-employed. This is done as a social process, though, and not as a traditional start-up program. There is a whole network of organisations participating in redistributing the social risk, from the wider society to a local sociality constructed by participants in the project and supporting agencies in a network.

In the Fair Play example, *abundantia* and *aequitas* are related to ideas of non-elitism in sport. The common – and often considered quite legitimate – isolation of sport from societal values, making possible the structuring of sport-exercise and training into elitism and pure result-orientation, is here resisted. The Fair Play project seeks to shift focus from results towards the joy of sharing responsibility.

We do not read our cases as exemplifying a Tönnies-inspired claim that we need to move from *Gesellschaft*/society to *Gemeinschaft*/community. The concept of community (see Wenger, 1998) has indeed been revitalised during the last decade, but is well described by White and Hunt as a romantic impulse used by neoliberal concerns for citizenship as a technology of government. If, however, we understand communities as a 'presupposition' as to what being with others means (as in Goodchild, 1996), it instead exemplifies what Deleuze calls 'socius'. As such – as a socius – it represents a virtuality, the fullness of the becomings of new formations of sociality.

PUBLIC ENTREPRENEURSHIP: IN CONCLUSION

Our stories have emphasised that entrepreneurship belongs to society and not primarily to business. We have to understand how everyday living is made possible through entrepreneurship as forms of social creativity, as the creation of sociality in local settings. Local history and culture is far too important to allow for a generalised template as the one circulated in the 'social entrepreneurship' discourse. This template, apart from being insensitive to local historical-cultural specificities, is also overly economic and individualistic in orientation. We need to include social, cultural and historical perspectives in our attempts to understand and participate in developing what we call 'public entrepreneurship' (see Steyaert and Katz, 2004). We believe creativity is a genuinely social force. Our focus should be on the in-betweens, the relationships, and not on individuals. Entrepreneurship is about the everyday, daily life, the civic practices of living, rather than an extraordinary accomplishment.

We agree with critics who might point out that 'public entrepreneurship' is something different from 'social entrepreneurship' and that we therefore have studied something else. This would also imply that our critique of the discourse on 'social entrepreneurship' is unfair, for 'they have never wanted to say anything on public entrepreneurship' in the first place. Let us note, though, firstly that we are anti-essentialists and cannot but operate with an active language, a language that produces when it represents, a discourse that creates the objects of its concern. We do not believe in a 'real' and neutral phenomenon 'out there' which is something like 'social entrepreneurship'. Secondly, we do believe that we have intervened in the discourse on social entrepreneurship and pointed out its centripetal quality. That is, it normalises and harmonises the discussion on 'social problems', representing them as economic problems in need of 'better management'. All these various forms of social creativity today run the risk of becoming targets of this kind of 'social entrepreneurship' discourse.

With our cases we have wanted to point out the need for greater sensitivity before those forms of creating sociality that are based in public space and made possible through practicing citizenship guided by *abundantia* and *aequitas*. To create sociality is to intensify what it is to be human; to socialise risk in processes of creating space for entrepreneurship in public space.

We have tried to exemplify how a hesitation before natural and normal concepts – social, consumer – opens a space for reflection and discussion. This chapter sought to connect citizens (not consumers) desiring socialities. Such connections are not free from problems, and desires easily become interests as they become collective and organised forms. Local desires easily become general interests, which is where a language coding this in economic terms always lies in wait. In an attempt to keep entrepreneurship in life rather than in the economy we have inquired into local desire for a different sociality, one that depends for its becoming on the connection of desiring citizens.

Implications for public entrepreneurship, for policy-makers, and for society, then? Some readers, although we have criticised only a neoliberalist economic politics, have surely located us in an anti-liberalist camp. Our turn now to Rorty (a liberalist philosopher) therefore provides a much needed contribution to forestall such a reading. Rorty (1989, p. 20) believes that '[a] sense of human history as the history of successive metaphors would let us see the poet, in the generic sense of the maker of new words, the shaper of new languages, as the vanguard of the species'. This is because 'to change how we talk is to change what, for our purposes, we are' (Butler, 2004, p. 72). We believe that our suggested move from social to public, and from consumer to citizen is an attempt to change how we talk about entrepreneurship as a *societal* force. Echoing Rorty we would stress that society hasn't got invention on its agenda, but should see as central the task of making it as easy as possible for citizens to achieve their creative goals without hurting each other (Rorty, 1991, p. 196). This, for sure, requires that we/policy-makers believe in people rather than calculate on consumer behaviour. From the perspective of this study, this necessitates a move away from purchaser–provider models as regulating the thinking of policy-makers' view on how society–citizen relations should be conceptualised. We need to respect citizenship as practised in a multiplicity of ways and in local contexts and place '. . . limits on any totalising "common good" ' (Barns, 1999, p. 195) that will always squeeze out minorities and kill heterogeneity. Making space for 'public entrepreneurship', we have created an opening towards a novel discourse on entrepreneurship as a society-creating force. In this way, we have identified the missing people on policy makers agenda – the public entrepreneurs.

6. The rhetoric of social entrepreneurship: paralogy and new language games in academic discourse

Pascal Dey

INTRODUCTION

The proliferation of social entrepreneurship narratives being broadcast on television and published in newspapers, practitioner books and scientific journals represents one of the very latest fashion trends that has penetrated researchers', politicians', and journalists' discourse in equal measure. It is thus noticeable from a cursory glance at the available academic literature that social entrepreneurship gets grounded in such diverse realms as developmental aid work (Fowler, 2000), the voluntary and community sector in the United Kingdom (Pharoah and Scott, 2002), the development of economic communities within the United States (Wallace, 1999), the enrichment of women's work in Sweden (Pestoff, 2000), the promotion of health services in Europe (Catford, 1998; de Leeuw, 1999), non-profit organizations (Mort et al., 2003) and the welfare system more generally (Thompson, 2002). Of utmost importance to me was the recognition that the corpus of texts produced a unanimously positive image of the subject matter.[17] Given, for instance, that many texts stress the univocally positive effects of social enterprises, while providing selective and/or anectotal illustrations of their 'heroic deeds' – such as empowerment (Pestoff, 2000), social transformation (Alvord et al., 2002), regeneration (Thompson, 2002), creation of social benefits (Fowler, 2000), increase of social capital (Leadbeater, 1997), or community economic development (Wallace, 1999) – I was charmed into believing that there was no other option than holding the matter in awe.

Hereon I started to deliberate why and how social entrepreneurship was granted such a self-evidently good image? Doggedly refusing to join the approving choir of academics who endlessly rehearsed their hymn of praise, I opted for what I here call an 'abnormal path of science';[18] I followed a stream of reasoning that puts centre stage the question how texts 'seduce' the reader into one possible interpretation of a situation over a (theoretically) infinite set of alternative possibilities (Westwood and Clegg, 2003). Given the paramount plausibility, trustworthiness and assumed objectivity ascribed to academic statements (Alvesson and Willmot, 1996), I deemed essential a study that puts prime emphasis upon the ways in which the scholarly community has appropriated the term 'social entrepreneurship', and how those constructions serve particular stakes and interests while eliding others. In the adept's mind this might have a familiar ring. The position that I am aspiring to here is that academic discourse[19] rests on skilfully crafted rhetoric, nothing more, nothing less. So, whether you (not WE, because I truly enjoy this vista) 'like it or not, we live in a rhetorical world' (van Maanen, 1995, p. 687).

Discourse and Rhetoric

Admittedly, pinpointing academics' utterances as rhetoric might appear as a denouncement. However, such an impression is comprehensible and tenable only if we take rhetoric to represent that which is not true, as something which stands in opposition to reality, and which aims at seducing compliance and consent (Carter and Jackson, 2004).[20] In contrast to this latter view, my own interest in rhetoric is grounded on the assumption that language is genuinely constitutive and performative. Language in that sense is not something which simply reflects or communicates a particular realm of reality which objectively exists beyond the sign. Rather, while we can dismiss the idea that words might demonstrably mean what they say, that they are 'literally literal' (Eagleton, 1983), using language irrevocably means engaging in rhetoric as the immanent process through which we produce the very realities of which we speak. As we get reminded by van Maanen, '(t)heory is a matter of words, not worlds; of maps, not territories; of representations, not realities' (van Maanen, 1995, p. 134). By implication, all discourse – irrespective of being deemed scientific or not – contains rhetoric as that aspect of language which serves the purpose of convincing the audience of its truthfulness.[21]

Objective

Concurring with Barthes (1967) that no language can ever be 'non-rhetorical', I spotted an opportunity to illuminate the current enunciation of social entrepreneurship in academic texts, and to delineate how science gets to persuade the audience of the sincerity of its utterances (Watson, 2000).[22] As Michel Foucault felicitously pinpointed, interpretations represent a 'violent or surreptitious appropriation of a system of rules, which in itself has no essential meaning', but which tries to 'impose a direction, to bend it to a new will, to force its participation in a different game, and to subject it to secondary rules' (Rabinow, 1984, p. 86). By extension thereof, the ensuing investigation (see below for the list of texts being selected for analysis) will pay prime attention to how texts being deemed 'academic' are organized so as to rhetorically ward off potential counter-arguments (Billig, 1987, 1989). For the present purpose, I strongly identify rhetoric with Derrida's (1976) deconstructive endeavour in that rhetorical analysis irrevocably entails a sensitivity for the indeterminacy of the sign 'social entrepreneurship'. In other words, by virtue of highlighting the rhetorical dynamic of the respective texts, I will try to invoke a space for the tactical other of social entrepreneurship, 'the residue of indeterminacy which escapes the system' (Sipiora and Atwill, 1990, p. 3).

Obviously, instead of grounding social entrepreneurship within a specific theoretical or methodological space, my analysis seeks to evoke a productive crisis, or a 'rupture' to use Derrida's (1966) wording, in which novel cultural interpretations may become possible. To lay bare social entrepreneurship texts' rhetorical dynamic, that is, to expose the binary systems which warrant stability, and to problematize the field's consensus will thus (hopefully) become a transparent strategy for making language the object of its own scrutiny. By implication, after Derrida (1992), it is important to notice that this deconstructive reading is not necessarily an exclusively negative act (Critchley, 1999), but rather a response to, and affirmation of, political struggles against systems pledged to presence. As such, the process of dismantling and constructively deconstructing the rhetoric of scholarly texts on social entrepreneurship serves the aim of laying bare the instability of these texts, and to set in motion some creative playfulness. The last part of this chapter is therefore devoted to making suggestions for the prospective research agenda of social entrepreneurship. Regarding the enrichment of the prevailing truisms, I will argue for a proliferation of deconstructive analysis as well as for the endorsement of new representational practices. New groundings of social entrepreneurship will further be advocated with regress to Lyotard's (1984) concept of paralogy (movements which go beyond or against common reason), aporia (such as paradoxes) and undecideability (Derrida, 1995, 1997, 1999).

RE-READING SOCIAL ENTREPRENEURSHIP TEXTS

Let me begin the present reading with a representative extract from Wallace (1999), in which we are provided with a narrative of social enterprises and the population they are presumed to help.

> These businesses [social purpose enterprises] serve as a necessary bridge into the mainstream business community for their target populations. Educationally and economically disadvantaged populations with sporadic employment histories do not benefit automatically from opened doors to the job market. What non-profit organizations have discovered over time is that many of them lack the very basic skills of how to act and/or contribute to a work environment (Wallace, 1999, p. 164).

On the face of it, we get to hear that social entrepreneurs have spotted that an underprivileged population lacks the necessary skills for traditional employment opportunities, and that social entrepreneurs exhibit the very resources needed to align this population with the mainstream business community. On closer inspection, it is revealed that the excerpt from Wallace's text operates upon the construction of two subjects: social purpose entrepreneurs envisioned through a particular affiliation with mainstream business, and an inchoate population of educationally and economically disadvantaged people. The latter subject is denoted as 'underprivileged' on the ground of its lack of the 'very basic skills' which are necessary to contribute to the workplace (as determined by mainstream business). The relationship between the two subjects is specified through the notion of 'target', which implies uni-directional influence; that is, social entrepreneurs define the target at which they finally 'shoot' their actions and initiatives. Obviously, while the underprivileged group is marked by a lack of specific, and thereby highly relevant (in that it hands those populations to the mainstream business community) resources, it is implied that social purpose entrepreneurs possess those valuable characteristics by virtue of which they are able to 'bridge' the specified populations from an inferior (i.e. underprivileged) state to a superior state (being defined alongside the characteristics of mainstream business).

The Metaphor of Medical Treatment

So far so good. But how then does Wallace's statement appear so agreeable? Peculiarly enough, iteration by iteration I got to recognize that the text was allegorically related respectively to the discourse of (western) medical treatment (Parker, 1992) and development (Frank, 1997). Summoning the former metaphor, we get to see a physician, (social purpose enterprise) representing an all-knowing, incontestable authority, who is infallible in diagnosing (discovering) his (yes, the doctor is male, but more of that later) patient's (underprivileged populations) pathologies (lack of the very basic skills requested for the work environment). Further implied through the medical metaphor is the notion that the physician is able to mitigate the identified problems while the patient gets envisioned as passively entrapped within his/her pathological state. Hence, while the doctor is assumed to have the requisite medical skills to cure (bridge into the mainstream business community) his/her patient, this discourse of medical treatment equally prescribes that those same patients blindly give themselves into the healing hands of their 'redeemer'.

One-sidedness and Dependence

As western medical treatment, specifically its notion of aid, is quasi-naturalized through the image of a needy patient vis-à-vis a skilful help profes-sional, it comes as no surprise that reading the respective social entrepreneur-ship texts (for the first time) did not arouse much suspicion. After all, what would one consider a solid basis for challenging that health is a good thing worth striving for, or that providing help to subjects facing severe problems conforms to higher human standards? However, by applying the analogy of medical treatment, it becomes utterly apparent that social entrepreneurship is premised on an unequal distribution of knowledge. In specific, through the creation of an expert subject (read the social enterprise), and an uninformed and thus helpless subject (read the underprivileged people), the text works to construct a power-knowledge nexus which produces a strategic relationship of dependence between the two subjects.[23] By stressing the dependence and inertness of patients and by means of depicting their pathology as an incon-testable matter of fact, the implicit medical discourse, by association, renders underprivileged populations passive and thus malleable.

Accountability and Blame

While constructing patients as dependent subjects, medical discourse simulta-neously works through a disciplinary stance: 'The need is to innovatively develop new forms of social capital which, in turn, will help empower disad-vantaged people and encourage them to take greater responsibility for, and control over, their lives' (Thompson, 2002, p. 329). Following Thompson et al.'s prospect, it gets delineated that social entrepreneurs provide the medical help needed to leverage (empower) the inferior state of patients, up to the point that patients are finally made accountable to maintain (take greater responsi-bility for, and control over) their own health. By the same token, help profes-sionals are envisioned as restoring the health of their patients while the sustenance of patients' health lies within their own responsibility. On the flip-side of this image, people who do not take care of their health are contestable for acting irresponsible. To be clear on that, wouldn't it therefore appear some-how heterodox to elide the doctor's advice of minding one's health by leading a restful life? Yet, taking into consideration that patients, read social enter-prises, within certain texts (which will be elaborated more thoroughly further down) are held accountable for deviating from the prevailing market ideology, things might start to change their shading.

Entitlement

In academic writings on social entrepreneurship it has become somewhat canonical that business practices (must) serve as criteria for devising social enterprises' governance and for assessing their very performance. However, what is conspicuous, at least for me, is that those texts radiate decisive univocality. The setting beyond dispute of the idea that social enterprises should adhere to the market's logic is achieved within those texts through a particular process of entitlement. As pointed out by Potter (1996), knowledge is culturally and historically linked to categories of actors in a variety of different ways. Certain categories of actors are thereby entitled to know certain things which, in effect, gives their statements particular credence and pertinence. In other words, given that actors are entitled to possess a specific kind of knowledge or skill, it follows that their narratives are warranted pervasiveness and rhetorical intelligibility.

Invoking the metaphor of medical treatment, we thus get to see that the help professional is assumed to perform his cure without hindrance as he knows what health is and how health is to be restored and sustained. Hence, by virtue of envisioning an all-knowing curer who is entitled to heal (in that he has the apposite knowledge) and by conceding to him good health (because he is presumed to govern his own health accordingly), it gets increasingly difficult to envision that the prescription of these practices actually marks a reduction of available treatment opportunities and thus a distinct form of governmentality (Foucault, 1979). However, wise to our text on social entrepreneurship, we get to see that the ascription of expertise is worked up through the dichotomy of knowing–not-knowing. Whereas social enterprises get depicted as possessing indispensable knowledge, namely knowledge which warrants their successful conduct along the lines of mainstream business, those organizations are unquestionably deemed appropriate for their respective positions and tasks.

Progressive Development

A pervasive observation within many articles on social entrepreneurship relates to the strong focus those texts lay on anticipated endpoints. To underscore the important posture of social enterprises and to provide their textual structures a stable centre (Derrida, 1966), such texts operate through the establishment of valued standards towards which social enterprises direct their respective underprivileged populations and help beneficiaries. Conveying the spell of teleological development, it is implied that patients – once they receive appropriate treatment – will evolve in a regular, that is, progressively improving manner. By such accounts, the reader is taught that to achieve a progressive (read healthier), state it suffices to expose the patient to the meticulous interventions of help professionals. Healing, namely the process of development, requires no effort on the part of the patient, which implies that teleology is contained in the action of the help professional!

Importantly, the ideological consequences of this imagery derive from the conflation of social entrepreneurship and mainstream economy. Whereas I have no principle reservation against this respective interconnection, it is the exclusiveness of this truth regime which requires critical heeding. Hence, invoking the image according to which everything gets better once exposed to social enterprises, and taking into account that this dynamic gets sustained by virtue of sweeping eulogies, that is, stories filled with praise and commendation, it is equally important to envision that we have 'sacrificed' a more variegated picture at the cost of stories which univocally provide confidence and hope. However, wouldn't it be all too subversive to call into question an image which warrants such a bright future?

The Demise of our Present

Besides legitimising social enterprises through the celebration of their (to conjure up a forceful metaphor) God-like acts of redemption, other texts foster an exigency for social enterprises by virtue of constantly reiterating the putative demise of our current (welfare) system (e.g. Wallace, 1999). In other words, by perpetually emphasizing that the status quo, in its infernal guise, is no option, those texts achieve to foster a conviction that things have to change immediately. In heralding that the status quo is no longer tenable, this view works pervasively to call into question practices of, for instance, non-profit, voluntary, bureaucratic and governmental, and similar organizations, in that those organizations are made responsible for our crumbling present. In other words, the univocal appeal for increased efficiency, effectiveness and amplified professionalism in the public and non-profit realms are made easily acceptable while being interwoven into a narrative that features these latter organizations as the very reason for our contemporary miseries.

External Pressures

While what du Gay has termed 'modernization hyperbole' (du Gay, 2004) makes us believe that everything in place has to change; this belief is buttressed with respect to social entrepreneurship in the ubiquitously perpetuated story that the environment is turbulent and volatile and shaped by a virtual explosion of complexity: 'The pace of change continues to accelerate globally and traditional attempts to extrapolate from the past are no longer valid' (Catford, 1998, p. 95). This pervasive 'futurology' (Cheney et al., 2004) being revealed in Catford's story predicates that only those will survive (and possibly prosper) who exhibit the aptitude of constant adaptation. Let me illustrate these claims through Mort et al.:

> Within the increasingly competitive market social enterprises are viewed as entities competing with their commercial counterparts and other social enterprises for

survival and growth. Similar to commercial enterprises, NFPs [annotation: non-for profits] are compelled to adopt innovative ways of perceiving and delivering superior value to their clients (Mort et al., 2003, p. 85).

What follows from Mort et al.'s extract is an image that displays a seemingly unchallengeable outside pressure that stems from increased commercial competition. By extension, the image spurs a need to adopt practices traditionally carried out by commercial enterprises. The discourse of economic competition thus gets to justify increased efficiency, customer orientation, corporate accountability, and so on, which seem attainable only through a sound business focus. For instance, 'deinstitutionalization' is depicted in certain texts (e.g. Wallace, 1999) as a reified (a material and therefore not manmade phenomenon) and irrevocable (obscuring the alterability of the phenomenon) force that presupposes economically orientated practices. Remarkably, the belief in the irredeemability of outside pressures is sustained in apprehending them as results of cosmic laws. In other words, being envisioned as a material reality, we get to believe that those pressures are beyond human terms and therefore unchangeable.

Globalisation as the Prescription of Economic Activity

As business-related terms such as re-engineering, financial accountability, cost-cutting, new public management, and so forth constitute an incremental part of our everyday vocabulary, their use (even in relation to issues that formerly operated devoid of such premises) does not make us flinch. On the contrary, while such claims have become part and parcel of lived ideology (Billig et al., 1988), it is somehow commonsense to prescribe, for instance, economic efficiency, smooth management and organizational effectiveness. As suggested in conjunction with the futurology of social entrepreneurship, a Darwinian notion of the environment is being used to support a business mode of conduct in an evolutionary process of natural selection. Envisioning globalisation as a ubiquitous process that presupposes constant competition evokes a threat that can only be counteracted by means of sound business practices. Hence, in many social entrepreneurship texts 'globalization' gets coined as a 'god-term' (Cheney et al., 2004) that is primarily related to (and thereby prescribes) economic activity (Parker, 2004). Consequently, once we get to comprehend social entrepreneurship as an inseparable aspect of the globalized world, the respective globalization-economy nexus works arouse an urge to comply to an economic mode of conduct.

Business–Non-business Binary

While the conflation of globalization and economic activity is unquestionably pivotal for encouraging social entrepreneurship, other texts emphasize the relevance of profit-related practices in social enterprises through a critique of traditional public or third sector organizations. Through the installation of a bureaucracy–social enterprise binary, these texts rhetorically achieve the overthrow of the belief in practices genuinely applied in public, non-profit or nongovernmental organizations as in this typical example:

> Because a bureaucracy practices a high degree of specialization in its tasks (on the assumption that specialization results in efficiency), it can only respond to problems, procedures, and solutions in piecemeal and/or uncoordinated fashion (Wallace, 1999, p. 158).

As follows from Wallace, bureaucracies are not pertinent for meeting public expectations, which implies that these organizations need to be premised on contemporary liberal norms of market-driven responsibilities. While the installation of a Darwinian image of the environment works to condition a belief that social enterprises strive above all to survive, it is implied that those organizations must overcome the natural inclination of the uninspired and lethargic bureaucrat.

Hence, ascribing to (social) entrepreneurial organizations the potential to overcome prevailing calamities (by means of, for instance, their flexibility and innovativeness) works to outdate Wallace's 'bureaucratic organizations'. In this 'epochal schema' (du Gay, 2004) 'bureaucracy' or 'administration' is reduced to a simple and abstract set of negativities contrasted with an equally simple and abstracted, but positively coded, set of 'entrepreneurial' principles. Accordingly, the image of non-entrepreneurial organizations appears univocally disadvantageous whereupon there is virtually no alternative to 'enterprising' unless institutions and persons aim to seal their own fates. Ultimately, how could anyone be for bureaucracy or otherwise non-entrepreneurial forms of organizing if they simply get to represent dysfunctional, outdated and inefficient leftovers?

Universal Claim for Economic Activity

As elaborated above, the discourse of (social) enterprise is normative as it enjoins the conduct of organizations previously seen as non-commercial, including the conduct of government agencies, voluntary organizations, social-purpose enterprises and individuals. A notable number of texts thereby rely upon the proposition that bureaucracies must be aligned to meet the demands of the market, to empower consumers and to create vitalized leaders at the helm of new agencies. While such claims might appear far-fetched, it is revealed on the background of the metaphor of medical treatment that these statements are nonetheless pervasive. As the metaphor of medical treatment

highlights *the* universal way of healing, it follows that this treatment is apposite for all living beings. Taking for granted that all people equally strive for a
healthy life, prescriptions being staged under the spell of 'health' appear
benign and beyond question. However, let us be reminded that health within
social entrepreneurship texts gets to represent the ability to pursue a job and
make money:

> [. . .] working and earning are not merely yardsticks by which to measure 'improve-
> ments' [. . .] rather they are a precondition for these improvements [. . .] an under-
> lying principle is that bearing part of the enterprise's risk produces therapeutic
> effects because it is therapeutic to be able to make mistakes, to learn by trial and
> error, to run the risk of change (De Leonardis and Mauri, 1992, p. 53).

As revealed in De Leonardis and Mauri's utterance, working and earning are
literally circumscribed as therapeutic, meaning that those activities are at the
service of patients' health. Blatantly obvious, working and earning therefore
become quintessential activities in that they teach underprivileged people a
vital lesson for successful living.

Measurability and Technical Rationality

While the penetration of social entrepreneurship texts through business
discourse becomes easily acceptable, we have to bear in mind that our agreement, witting or unwitting, requires strong persuasive buttresses. What finally
gets to appear as natural and inevitable thus relies on constant reiteration.
Additionally, to bolster the respective claims against potential critique one
needs to enrich one's argumentation with easily retrievable commonsense, that
is, lived ideology (Billig et al., 1988). A common rhetorical strategy for immu-
nizing one's accounts thus materializes in allusion to instrumental rationality.
For instance, within its appropriation by Thompson et al. (2000), social entrepreneurship is portrayed as a foremost rational and technical activity which
can be measured and therefore predicted. The notion of 'operationalise', for
instance, represents social entrepreneurship as a calculable undertaking. What
is revealed in such accounts is a kind of 'hyper-realization' (Casey, 2004),
which works to emphasize the merits of technical rationality in the realm of
the third or non-profit sector. The persuasiveness of this particular view is
granted by delineating social entrepreneurship as a programmable and therefore rather easy undertaking (at least as long as sound business practices are
employed), while simultaneously creating the impression that social entrepreneurship operates smoothly, completely devoid of political struggles.

Science

While the invocation of technical rationality as such is already sweeping, some texts on social entrepreneurship additionally strengthen their rhetorical power through recourse to science.

> Although ideas are powerful, people often place too much emphasis on the initial flash of brilliance. [. . .] the bigger challenge is converting an initially appealing idea into a worthwhile opportunity. This step combines rigorous analysis with creative adjustment as social entrepreneurs test and refine ideas through a mixture of action and research (Guclu et al., 2002, p. 6).

Research, within the extract by Guclu and colleagues, gets depicted as a crucial aspect of the social entrepreneurial endeavour. In deeming technological knowledge scientific, and relying on the assumption that science unanimously is (and does) good, there are no sound reasons presented why people working in the third or non-profit sector should reject such a code. Due to the paramount credibility of science (in the western mindset), such texts seek to legitimise the rational calculus of business while simultaneously sidestepping potential criticism of that respective image. Consequently, once social entrepreneurs are delineated as possessing the relevant 'scientific' body of knowledge, these texts are bestowed with a certain cachet of incontestability. And, by implication, any form of knowledge that fails to exhibit the relevant scientific credentials gets judged as worthless. While operating upon the assumption that sound scientific practices lend themselves to evaluation (which stipulates quantitative rather than qualitative parameters), such texts create an urge to provide objectively measurable results in the form of, for example, changed social impacts and outcomes (Johnson, 2000). In effect, such rigorous endeavours of measurement and categorization, as has been shown by Foucault (1988), equally get to represent a process through which objects are rendered amenable to regulation.

Normalization of Business Practices

What follows from equating social entrepreneurship with quantitatively measurable activities (such as number of beneficiaries provided with a job) is that practices and effects of social enterprises which do not materialize in desired numbers are either rendered invisible or are treated as deviant, and thus inferior. This process of normalization–abnormalization is thereby installed through working up a contrast structure which deems particular activities respectively appropriate or inappropriate. Applied to our subject matter, this gets to mean that charging social entrepreneurship of not using quantitative evaluation and scientifically validated practices, business discourse operates to depict traditional voluntary, non-profit and social sector practices as 'flabby' and 'amateurish' (Grenier, 2002). Taking, for example, the statement by Thompson et al.: '[. . .] many typical volunteers will need training in up-to-date information technology skills for some of the needs and tasks involved' (Thompson et al., 2000, p. 336).

As we get to see through the extract of Thompson et al., knowledge of IT is a specific skill which can be acquired through education. The attribute of 'typical' thus points out that subjects working in the social realm normally do not have the requested knowledge (or at least do not exhibit state-of-the-art knowledge). In Thompson et al.'s universe, successful work without the requisite knowledge is bound to fail. To demonstrate the necessity of business modes of conduct, the text has to render those other, read abnormal, practices problematic. The randomness and uncontrollability of such non-business practices has no place in a Tayloristic vision (Morgan, 1997) of social entrepreneurship. As they seem to threaten the survival of those organizations, they get to represent hostile elements that must be destroyed: business practices are privileged, the other practices are denigrated; business is what counts, non-business is the unimportant other, that which needs compulsive appropriation to management. Hence, the normal–abnormal binary calls upon an all-or-nothing logic where you are either for or against business practices. However, it might be unwise to proceed aloof of sound measurement as one would undoubtedly fall prey to the disarrangement of unfunded speculation!

Beyond Profit

As elaborated above, a normal–abnormal division is interwoven into business discourse so as to undermine the appropriateness of social enterprises being premised on non-business practices. There are other texts, though, that install a premium position of social enterprises through notions of 'good intention', 'moral need', 'contributing to society', 'social purpose', 'common good', or even 'passion', 'love', 'honesty', 'empathy'. Following Pearce we get to hear that

> their [social enterprises] common characteristics involve activities centered around a 'social purpose', the regeneration or expansion of local economic activity, collective advancement of the common good rather than solely commercial or private profit (Pearce, 1994).

Texts such as the one by Pearce are rhetorically premised upon a social–non-social divide. While the non-social prospect gets envisioned through monetary issues most frequently exemplified through business entrepreneurs, social enterprises are assumed to account for *both* social and non-social activities and duties. To understand how this seemingly paradoxical combination of features can work without appearing self-contradictory or paradoxical, it is worth looking at Catford (1998) who points out that social and economic entrepreneurs share the same focus on vision and opportunity and the same ability to convince and empower others to help them turn these visions into a reality. In social entrepreneurs, however, these characteristics are coupled with a strong desire for social justice (Catford, 1998, p. 96).

As becomes comprehensible through the extract by Catford, the business-related aspects of social entrepreneurship get depicted in the sense of an add-on criterion. While social entrepreneurs are portrayed as not only exhibiting sound business skills but as additionally embracing social aims, the pursuit of what I here call 'non-social activities' does not seem to collide with their adherence to moral convictions. Remarkably, this particular rhetorical twist seems to reconcile our basic either–or contradiction by means of exchanging it with an inclusionary as-well-as logic. Whereas social enterprises simultaneously are envisioned to carry out profit seeking activities and to retain their social mission (e.g. Pomerantz, 2003), those texts seek to set such organizations aside from those that are characterized by an exclusive, and thereby morally flawed, aim of making money. Hence, as we get to see in the extract below from Dees' (1998) text, it is not monetary activity per se which gets devalued but rather the respective purpose (money, profit, etc.) conveyed in those accounts: 'social entrepreneurs involved in for-profit activities see profit as a means to an end, while economic entrepreneurs see profit as an end in itself' (Dees, 1998).

Through the distinction between means and ends Dees's text aims to bypass inscribing monetary activities an inferior ethical value. Within the above utterance, profit is presented as containing no inherent and pre-existing value. Instead, profit derives its value in conjunction with social entrepreneurship by getting envisioned as a device for achieving particular moral ends. Profit-seeking, according to the text, can be social as long as social entrepreneurs resist the temptation of using it for selfish ends (Guclu et al., 2002). What gets revealed herein is a utilitarian principle, which works to distinguish social entrepreneurs from ordinary entrepreneurs, business people, and the like, despite the fact that all are doing the same thing: earning money. However, by means of its utilitarian 'superstructure', such texts suggest a superiority of social entrepreneurs that makes us so effectively believe that their work, regardless of potentially negative ramifications, gets to serve higher purposes. Overtly criticising such images would thus not only call into question the appropriateness of social enterprises' moral standards but would equally scrutinize their ideal of our common good.

Supernatural Individual

Working up the impression of exclusiveness through an argument of superior morality is one rhetorical strategy. Another strategy creates a similar effect by drawing out a picture of social entrepreneurship on the basis of a singular individual characterized by supernatural talents. For example, as elaborated by De Leeuw, social entrepreneurs comprise multiple talents, including the ability 'to analyse, to envision, to communicate, to empathize, to enthuse, to advocate, to mediate, to enable and to empower a wide range of disparate individuals and organizations' (De Leeuw, 1999, p. 261). Taking into consideration the commonalities this extract shares with other texts, it concludes, to put it bluntly, that social entrepreneurship is largely envisioned through a single person, respectively his/her particularities. By virtue of the accumulated depiction of such traits and aptitudes, an image of social entrepreneurs is created that at one and the same time highlights their power of foresight, their facility for organization and administration, their unusual energy, as well as their more general (but nonetheless valuable) leadership properties. Hence, to gain an understanding of how this effect is achieved through the use of language, let us take a look at the statement following by Thompson et al.: 'In and amongst [social entrepreneurs] will be some non-enterprising people simply committed to doing good' (Thompson et al., 2000, p. 336).

Following this, it is not suffice for successful social entrepreneurs to possess good intentions (as entailed in the morally inclined discourse discussed above). In particular, the addition of 'simply' fosters the impression that the intention of doing good is not only insufficient, but that the intention to do good may even be the most facile part of the whole endeavour. The motive of doing good seems so self-evident and pre-ordained that it does not request any further consideration:

> Others may be sound leaders of some particular venture or organisation, but, lacking vision and charisma, they will never behave in a truly entrepreneurial manner. Such leaders may, for example, lack the courage to take the risks (an issue of temperament) to create growth (Thompson et al., 2000, p. 332).

Within this extract it becomes even more evident how the individualistic enunciation of social entrepreneurs delimits the subject matter from 'sound leaders'. By invoking 'temperament' it is implied that social entrepreneurship is deemed possible only through the possession of certain innate capabilities. Contained therein is the idea that the success of social entrepreneurs is bound to pre-determined (such as genetically defined) capacities. Hence, ascribing to social entrepreneurs prestigious attributes such as 'charisma' or 'the courage to take risks' (both qualities which are conceived as being in short supply) makes it a matter of rare individuals, of 'champions', who sustain their social mission despite upcoming obstacles. In effect, the image of the heroic individual makes us believe that social entrepreneurs are 'sovereign and self-determining beings' (Alveson and Willmott, 1996), and, owing to their grandiose successes, we get to see that social entrepreneurs are in fact indispensable for rebalancing the maladjustment of current societies.

Maleness

Having pointed out that the individualist discourse works by endowing social entrepreneurs with extraordinary personality traits, it will be shown in the ensuing paragraph that certain texts operate upon a gender bias that favours a male perception: '[Social] entrepreneurs display innovativeness, proactiveness and risk-taking propensity in their key decision making' (Mort et al., 2003, p. 82). Examining this statement by Mort et al., we first find a seemingly uncontentious notion of 'risk taking' and 'proactiveness'. While taking into consideration characteristics being employed in other texts such as 'tolerance for insecurity', 'independence, 'determination', 'self-confidence', 'logic', and so on, it becomes increasingly evident that we are entrenched in a stereotypically male narrative. Despite the fact that the gender of social entrepreneurs is mostly not made explicit, such texts, through the employment of male-associated personality traits, nevertheless succeed in erecting an impression of maleness.

The male identity script thereby achieves, seemingly unproblematically, the accentuation of male characteristics as a prerequisite for successful social entrepreneurship. Examined from an ideological vantage point, individualist discourse leads to a gendered division of social entrepreneurs, whereby discourse works to naturalise male qualities and to advocate a demand for free spirit, detachment and rationality. Evidently, the hierarchy works at the expense of those practices and values traditionally attributed to the female domain such as housework, childbirth, child-care, and the like. Such texts, by implication, operate to convince us that these latter qualities obviously do not generate any entrepreneurial spark.

Following from these observations, it seems pertinent to claim that models of social entrepreneurship that are based on an individualist discourse are normative and exclusive in that they marginalize individuals, such as women or ordinary people, who do not comply with the default standards. Accordingly, these particular images contribute to and reinforce the conviction that the sidelined subjects, that is the anonymous others, have psychological and gender characteristics which inhibit social entrepreneurial development.

LOOMING STALEMATE?

We live in this 'reality' and this 'reality' lives with/in us; but so 'obvious' is this reality that it does not arouse much curiosity and/or debate (Prasad, 1997, p. 91).

On the face of it, the discourses examined in the previous deconstructive reading mimic research that has been conducted in the realm of management, marketing, entrepreneurship, and organization science more generally.[24] Contrary to my rhetorical allegation that what I said is important and worth heeding, I thus anticipate being accused of having served old wine in new bottles. However, it is important to recognize that this sense of déjà vu – including its (potentially) associated boredom – is equally to be taken as a revealing reflection of the status quo of social entrepreneurship research. In fact, the prevailing 'objectification of discourse' (Daston, 1992), in my opinion, provides no reason for staging a party. Giving the nascent state of social entrepreneurship research, I feel even more compelled to pose a question regarding the ceaseless perpetuation of management and economic discourses and to instigate new representations, language games and criteria for our future research.

However, there can be no question here of offering exhaustive and definitive suggestions for advancing the field of social entrepreneurship. What I would like to propose, however fragmentary and allusive, as a 'way out' in the ensuing paragraphs follows four distinct, though closely related lines of arguing: first, I will stake out a space for additional reflective, and more specifically deconstructive, studies. Second, some recent developments in entrepreneurship research will be highlighted as potential sources for social entrepreneurship's semantic multiplication. Third, I will hail a paralogical grounding of social entrepreneurship through the employment of styles of writing so far unfamiliar to scholarly representation. And fourth, as a result of scrutinizing the performative grounding of social entrepreneurship writing, I will reclaim a space for ethics and justice through Derrida's work on aporia and undecideability.

Infinite Deconstructive Practice

Departing from the assumption that the 'invisibility' of our common sense rhetorically endows our mindscape with truth-value, my investigation was set up to illustrate how and in what ways social entrepreneurship becomes 'black boxed' (Law, 1994), or disguised in its undecideable complexity. My deconstructive reading was therefore put forward to dismantle the black boxes that render social entrepreneurship incontestable, and, therefore, to disrupt some of its discourse's shiny surface aesthetics. In other words, to see the ordinary with a fresh vision, we first have to make it 'extraordinary' and 'free ourselves of normalized ways of thinking that blind us to the strangeness of the familiar.' (Cooper and Morgan, 1988, p. 101). In line with Derrida (2001) who claims for deconstruction a central position in the 'university of tomorrow', I would like to spur us to see deconstructive and/or rhetorical readings[25] not as something to be avoided or eliminated, but as tactical devices which bear the potential to bring forward a vision of social entrepreneurship that no longer dispenses unclouded optimism but equally radiates ironic antagonism. As critical readings overturn texts' meanings and thereby initiate a de-objectification of social entrepreneurship, we get to create an empty space (Steyaert, 2002) or discursive springboard, on the basis of which we get to see the 'human possibilities' of social entrepreneurship instead of its 'settled certainties' (Bruner, 1986, p. 26).[26]

As deconstruction can never be achieved in any definitive sense, it would be a fallacy to believe that prevailing social entrepreneurship texts and their underlying premises have been dismantled and overcome. Instead, I concede that we are far from beyond the present ideologies, which we probably never will be, and that what is needed is a 'practical politics of the open end' (Spivak, 1990, p. 105), that is the relentless and persistent undoing of the taken for granted and the oblivious supplement upon which they are based. Following Derrida, 'we must join forces to exert pressure and organize ripostes, and we must do so on an international scale and according to new modalities, though always while analyzing and discussing the very foundations of our responsibility, its discourses, its heritage, and its axioms' (Derrida, 2003, p. 126). Deconstructive practice can, against all denunciation, do justice[27] since it effectuates a decoupling from our scholarly heritage and especially its concealed political consequences[28] (Derrida, 1966). Such analysis, I contend, cannot be postponed with regard to social entrepreneurship as it enables an irrevocable concern for indeterminacy, and, by implication, for resistance to what Derrida termed 'exhaustive accounts'. Yet, only if we take upon us this painstaking, and infinite, task might there emerge a chance to change the rules of prevailing language games and thus to reformulate a new grounding for social entrepreneurship.

Inheriting the Other Entrepreneurship

Having mentioned the impression of déjà vu being elicited through the above deconstructive reading, we are foremost reminded of our legacy in respect to entrepreneurship research. Despite having become somewhat disenchanted by the observation that the sign 'social entrepreneurship' equally features strong inscriptions of business and economic discourse, of discourses relating to progressive development and technical rationality, of expert knowledge and individualism, I would nevertheless like to conjure up some anachronistic movements in entrepreneurship research. To this end, I would like to confront the current impasse of social entrepreneurship writing by recommending especially, but not exclusively, a careful reading of the texts by Steyaert and Katz (2004) as well as Hjorth and Steyaert (2003) who have formulated both cogent treatises of the field's foreclosure as well as lines of flight for subverting the prevailing discourse.

Concerning the issue of foreclosure, Hjorth (2005), Hjorth and Steyaert (2003), Steyaert (2000), Steyaert and Katz (2004) thoroughly pinpoint that academic texts reveal a clear bias towards construing entrepreneurship on the background of management theory and business administration. In that respect, I feel much sympathy with Hjorth's (2003) estimate that the dominant representations of entrepreneurship mark a clear limit to our understanding of entrepreneurship as social creativity. Through Hjorth (2005) we further get reminded that by envisioning entrepreneurship as well as the entrepreneur as events of 'controlled creativity' and 'economic managerialism', metaphors of *ludens* (playing), *narrans* (storytelling) and *traditionalis* (tradition) are crudely put aside. Regarding this kind of thematic enrichment, the two texts by Steyaert and Katz (2004) and Hjorth and Steyaert (2003) provide us with additional inspirations concerning how, in other words through what perspectives and in what dimensions, the matter of social entrepreneurship prospectively could, or better should, be conceptualized.

However, as with deconstruction, the task of semantic opening and multiplication (which all of the above articles instigate) is never completed but needs untiring repetition, not only in relation to entrepreneurship (where it only has started) but equally well regarding the matter of social entrepreneurship. It is thus imperative to remind ourselves that we have to insert a question regarding what social entrepreneurship, and especially the epithet 'social', is, and what it ought to be. While this latter issue will be treated further down, I deem it important to emphasize that Steyaert, Hjorth and Katz all contribute to unhitching entrepreneurship from its performative enunciation. In particular, by prescribing multidisciplinary and multiparadigmatic experimentation, and in calling for comprehending entrepreneurship in its everydayness, playfulness, as well as political, cultural, ecological and societal accentuation, the authors make a pivotal plea for paralogical groundings, that is opportunities for innovative enunciations (Brugger, 2001), where interpretations beyond *homo oeconomicus* and technical rationality become possible. To claim new groundings of social entrepreneurship, it is thus not only necessary to instil new contents and theoretical trajectories[29] but also to reflect upon new forms of expressions and representation. Instead of legitimizing knowledge of social entrepreneurship according to whether it can be commoditized and thus made saleable,[30] we must seek criteria that intensify our relationship to the difference that is distinctive about social entrepreneurship. These possibilities shall be elaborated in the following sections.

Paralogy and Style

Derrida (1976) has coined the term 'logocentrism' to depict philosophy's insolence in explaining what words and concepts *really* mean. The assumption that meaning can be grasped by philosophical discourse, unsullied by the imprecision of metaphors is, following Derrida, naive, as the signifiers of language systems cannot refer to any transcendental signified. In line with Derrida's elaboration of the state of philosophy, Czarniawska (2004) has equally made clear that our heritage as organization scholars not only hinders us from seeing fiction, narratives of the self, performance science, polyvocal texts, responsive readings, aphorisms, comedy and satire, visual presentations, and mixed genres (Hardy and Clegg, 1997) as legitimate forms of knowledge, but above all demands that the questions of knowledge status and legitimisation remain unexamined. Hence, the selective admission of scientific discourse and the invocation of absolute conditions of discourse deny difference and multiplicity in respect to academic enunciation. Such a delimitation of ways of thinking and talking is, according to Lyotard (1984), fascist[31] as it forcibly exempts alternative narratives.[32]

Given the totalizing inclination of prevailing metanarratives, what seems to be needed are new criteria for judging knowledge. Regarding the appraisal of the status quo of social entrepreneurship, it is again Lyotard who makes us aware that a large degree of scientific knowledge is legitimated either by invoking truth (in the form of metanarratives) or performativity.

In contrast to those hegemonic codes, Lyotard puts forward an ontological position which stresses that the world is composed of events which give rise to multiple interpretations (or small narratives).[33] In his attempt to formulate an alternative legitimizing principle, Lyotard puts forward 'paralogy'[34] as the kind of movement which seeks new meaning in excluded language games. Lyotard's paralogy thus undermines the determinism aspired to by the two former principles and instead incites a search for instabilities and anomalies yet recognized.[35] Heeding paralogy's concern for pluralism and diversity, it is of central importance (and utterly timely) to consider the issue of its style and its interrelation with knowledge of social entrepreneurship. In other words, to advocate the polysemousness of the signifier social entrepreneurship and to detain its performative legitimization, I would like to search for paralogical groundings through writing styles that feature a sensitivity towards the uniqueness of social entrepreneurial endeavours and thereby sidestep the exclusionary 'terror' of univocal readings.

As outlined by Game and Metcalfe (1996), the practice of writing is actively involved in the production (and not only with mimicking the representation) of knowledge as a result of which (academic) writing becomes an act of cultural production. It follows from Game and Metcalfe's observation that how we are expected to write irrevocably affects what we can write about. Consequently, it might be helpful to temporarily sidestep the distinction between science and non-science and instead instigate a discussion of style and representational practice. Hence, while the kinds of language or discourse we employ in making sense of social entrepreneurship are not reducible to one another (Lyotard, 1988) we get to see that by writing in different ways, each style can bring to the fore a fresh perspective on the phenomenon being studied. While I have tried to liberate us from the myth that there exists such a thing as 'getting it right' (Barthes, 1986), I would like to advocate the introduction of 'breaching' (van Maanen, 1995), or experimentation with styles in order to learn about social entrepreneurship what is unknowable, unimaginable, using prescribed writing formats. In accordance therewith, we are called upon to transcend existing boundaries between disciplinary fortresses and to invent new connections for the sake of understanding social entrepreneurship differently. Grounding the prospective writing of social entrepreneurship in such a 'third place' (Huyghe, 1993) will inspire 'experimenting' with varieties of writing which employ language not only to inform but equally to surprise and to evoke (Lacan, 1977); a language which, by virtue of its tropes, arouses 'imaginative play' (Bruner, 1986, p. 4). In the sense of a rhetorical refolding, the function of new styles and rhetorical tropes is to open the field of social entrepreneurship towards the range of possibilities that a text can refer to. Having located in the field of social entrepreneurship an exigency for 'cool'[36] texts (Linstead, 2003), i.e. texts that 'recruit the reader's imagination – that enlist him in the performance of meaning under the guidance of the texts' (Bruner, 1986, p. 25), I hope for stories of social entrepreneurship which appeal to thinking outside of rational order and prescriptive rhetoric, and which make us hear the 'noise'[37] that might generate novel understandings.

Aporia, Undecidability and Ethics

As the previous deconstructive reading has revealed, staging the neologism 'social entrepreneurship' does not necessarily mean that one has bypassed economic discourse. On the contrary, the ostensible shift towards the social dimension of entrepreneurship might arguably conceal how deeply inscribed exchange relations still are. Quite ironically, while social entrepreneurship is heralded as a moral actor and social benefactor, I have pinpointed that its economic calculus nevertheless reverberates, in fact quite fiercely. In keen contrast to this, paralogy signifies not only a break with established theories and modes of representation but simultaneously incepts a political move by enabling difference in the face of the discourse's 'economic energy' (Steyaert and Katz, 2004, p. 188). Parology's avowed focus on instabilities and the unknown thus directs Lyotards's endeavour away from prescriptive, calculative, or consensual knowledge to the point of immanent instabilities. If we take seriously Lyotard's call to investigate incommensurabilities, undecidables, conditions of incomplete information, and paradoxes, I irrevocably sense revealing associations with Jacques Derrida. In reverting to Derrida, it is therefore of particular importance to see that Derrida, within his latter work, has shifted ground into the terrain of ethics. In what has been hailed as a turn towards ethics (see Dews, 1995),[38] Derrida interrogated the aporiatic, i.e. paradoxical nature of issues such as democracy, law, friendship, hospitality, the gift, and so on. Derrida has thereby conjured up a sensitivity towards the undecidable nature of particular situations, to their 'experience of the impossible' (Jones, 2003b, p. 229).[39]

In conjunction with social entrepreneurship, the previous deconstructive reading has revealed that a fair number of texts operate with an economic logic. Furthermore, epitomized through the quest for technical knowledge and best business practices, those texts prescribe the conduct of social entrepreneurship in a programmable and predictable manner. By implication, social entrepreneurship becomes an endeavour which relies on the application of pre-ordained rules. Yet, as Derrida contends, such programmable applications of rules do not require a decision and thus do not represent an act of responsibility. Derrida made clear that 'there would be no decision, in the strong sense of the word, in ethics, in politics, no decision, and thus no responsibility, without the experience of some undecidability' (Derrida, 1999, p. 66). It is thus through Derrida that we get to see that *the notion of undecidability accentuates the infinite task of responsibility* and, by implication thereof, that prevailing images of social entrepreneurship ignore the point that *a decision which didn't go through the ordeal of the undecidable would not be a free decision.*

Obviously, the notion of undecidability is diametrically opposed to the idea of performativity and pre-ordained rules, in that it indicates that a decision is a 'moment of madness' that must move beyond rationality and calculative reasoning.[40] By extension to social entrepreneurship, we are thus reminded that a decision, to be a decision, must transgress the economic or otherwise calculative rationale, and thereby stretch out to that which is outside of the subject's control. Arguably, a conceptualization which takes seriously the aporiatic feature of responsibility, namely that '*ethics and politics* [. . .] *start with an undecidability*' (Derrida, 1999, p. 66), does not lend itself to the formulation of ready-made rules. In somewhat stark opposition to the mainstream writing on social entrepreneurship and taking recourse to Derrida's ingenious 'Politics of Friendship' (1997), we are thus impelled to concede that *to be(come) social, social entrepreneurship must be able to exceed the economic and performative circles of input–output relations.*

If we are willing to envision social entrepreneurship in relation to societal and cultural creation, the question is what we conceive of as moral or ethical and what kind of relations we thereby endorse, for instance, between social entrepreneurs and its other (i.e. the silent majority of help recipients, jobless, handicapped, underpriviledged, or beneficiaries more generally). While ethics, responsibility and justice have largely escaped the attention of organization studies (Jones, 2003a, 2003b), I would like to conjure up these perspectives for our prospective writing on the matter of social entrepreneurship. Derrida's deliberations thereby seem apposite in respect to social entrepreneurship as the matter has been envisioned by a sizeable number of scholars as a moral or social deed (e.g. Catford, 1998; Dees, 1998; Guclu et al., 2002; Pearce, 1994; Thompson et al., 2000). Derrida, I believe, is indispensable when it comes to deliberating about justice and ethics beyond the boundaries of (performative) prescriptions. First of all, it is implied through Derrida that the moment social entrepreneurship becomes performative about ethics, that is, a matter of strategic rules, the focus shifts from respecting the other to caring about oneself. It follows therefore that ethics cannot be commanded a priori (in the sense of 'before the act') and once and for all. Instead, justice and ethics need to be judged in the moments of their inception, that is against the background of specific events (read small narratives). The ethics of social entrepreneurship thus always has to be created anew, becoming social. Hence, in order to decouple social entrepreneurship from its conditional, performative exegesis, it appears vital to imagine social entrepreneurship as an act that is addressed to the other, devoid of any conditional reciprocity looming in the background. Whereas the clutches of economic calculation undoubtedly still exert a strong hold on academics' perceptions of social entrepreneurship, I nevertheless hope that Derrida's cogent deliberations can lead us to envision the 'social' not as an instrumental, that is calculable, epithet of entrepreneurship, but as the expression of genuine openness towards otherness. On account of this, the 'social' of social entrepreneurship shall be elevated above the level of a 'supplement' (Derrida, 1976) or nice little 'extra' of entrepreneurship through which entrepreneurs (retroactively) legitimize their practices, to become an unconditional hailing of difference, regardless of potentially negative consequences that might derive therefrom.

PART TWO

Contexts of social change

7. Entrepreneurship, shifting life orientations and social change in the countryside

Denise Fletcher and Tony Watson

INTRODUCTION

For much of the history of the social sciences, the most frequently discussed process of social change was that of industrialisation. Closely associated with this was the process of urbanisation and the growth of 'urbanism as a way of life' (Kumar, 1978). As industrialising societies made the transition from *gemeinschaft* to *gesellschaft* (Tönnies, 1963), so people in large numbers moved away from the countryside into the towns. The industrialisation of agriculture played as much a part in this as the growing manufacturing industries around which the modern urban conglomerations grew. However, in recent times in the UK we see the converse of this process with people, and especially middle class people, turning against the old trend of a rural–urban shift and moving from town to country. For a variety of reasons, they leave their urban homes and settle into a different way of life in rural areas. And, in these areas, the industrialisation of agriculture is often continuing in such a way that buildings which previously housed agricultural processes are now coming to house people – especially, middle class people who want and can afford to live in converted agricultural properties. In this chapter we want to complement the range of larger scale studies of these trends with some fine grained analysis of the role which can be played in these processes by the entrepreneurial activities and life orientations of property-developers and the associated orientations of the property-developer's clients.

The research material we are using comes from an ethnographic study of a fairly concentrated area of the English East Midlands, where we are looking at entrepreneurial activities and the role they play in that community. From this broader study we are taking the case of an entrepreneur-developer who is involved in the conversion of former agricultural buildings into high-value rural residential properties. We relate his and his family's experience to that of a family who were his clients. The entrepreneurial family itself made the urban–rural shift, as did the more recent in-migrants who have bought proper-ties in that community. What we are interested in doing is focusing on the *meanings* that these various people attach to their lives and to the moves they have made within those lives. We are thus adopting an interpretive sociologi-cal stance in which we emphasise the *relationality* that plays its part in the *emergent* entrepreneurial and life-shifting processes with which we are concerned (Fletcher and Watson, 2006).

In this chapter we are concerned with the entrepreneurial processes and shifting life orientations occurring as part of the social changes that happened in English rural communities between 1984 and 2004. We focus on the rural community of Kerston. This is a community located between two old coalmin-ing towns in the North Nottinghamshire area of the English East Midlands. We highlight the process by which urban–rural migration trends/patterns facilitate a range of market possibilities in rural communities – possibilities which, when enacted, contribute further to social change in these communities.

COUNTERURBANISATION AND THE TRANSFER OF AGRICULTURAL PROPERTIES TO URBAN–RURAL SHIFTERS IN KERSTON

It was thought for some time that the trend in England after the Second World War whereby significant numbers of people migrated from towns into the countryside was a temporary phenomenon relating to urban business cycles (Champion, 1989). Consequently, it was assumed that the resurgence of the urban economy in the 1980s and 1990s would coincide with a decline in urban–rural migration (Champion et al., 1998; Champion and Atkins, 2000). In fact, demographic statistics indicate a sustained flow of urban migrants to rural areas during this period. According to census figures, between 1991 and 2001, the population of rural England grew at a rate almost eight times faster than that of urban areas (DEFRA, 2002, quoted by Buller, Morris and Wright, 2003). And, interestingly for the present research, the highest percentage growth in rural districts between the 1991 and 2001 censuses was recorded in the East Midlands (ibid.).

The dominant explanatory concept for this demographic trend is 'coun-terurbanisation' (Champion 1989, 1992; Fielding, 1982) – a process of popu-lation 'deconcentration' and 'decentralisation' (Champion, 1989) regulated by planning policy and 'fuelled' by middle class lifestyle choices (Champion and Fielding, 1992). Although it is difficult to unravel social class patterns within this trend, with in-migration and out-migration happening at the same time within the overall population growth, Buller, Morris and Wright (2003) conclude that a socio-economic recomposition has come about – one that can be characterised in terms of *embourgeoisement*. Increasingly, over the recent period, as Champion and Fielding (1992, p. 2) put it, 'it has been those in secure "middle class" professional and managerial jobs, together with those who have a strong expectation of entering such jobs . . . who have come to represent typical inter-regional migrants'. There has been, they continue, 'a sudden up-grading of rural property as villages have been "invaded" by middle-class gentrifiers'.

This interest in 'upgrading' rural properties clearly presents an economic opportunity [for parties who might want to exploit its economic potential]. Moore (2004) describes the conversion of redundant agricultural buildings into residential property as being the 'bread and butter' diversification opportunity for the UK farming community as the agricultural economy has faltered. Such diversification of the farm sector whereby farmers have moved from being 'monoactive' to 'multiple' business owners has been well reported in the small business literature (Carter, 1998, 1999, 2001). But we might also expect such opportunities to be taken up by non-agricultural entrepreneurs, especially in the light of the fact that rural areas have been noted as having higher than average levels of self-employment than urban areas, with urban–rural migrants playing a key role in this area (Keeble and Gould, 1985; Keeble et al., 1992; Keeble, 1993, 1996; Green, 1999; Findlay, Short and Stockdale, 1999; Westhead and Wright, 1999).

As reported in other studies of rural change in the UK (Fuller, 1990; Evans and Ilbery, 1992), in the Kerston district these processes of social change occurred in three stages.

Stage 1

This started in the 1970s, during which time the large land owning estates moved to consolidate the small farming units into larger agricultural enterprises. The smaller farms run by tenant farmers were proving to be no longer economically viable. Most of the tenant farmers were given the opportunity to buy their houses and some land.

Stage 2

The second stage, in the 1980s, saw most of these tenant farmers selling off their properties, typically after only a short period of owning them. Nevertheless some tenant farmers continued to farm the land, coping with economic difficulties by diversifying into other activities. Many of these rural properties – mainly farmhouses – were bought by urban–rural shifters directly from the tenant farmers who had previously lived in them.

An illustration of what occurred at the second stage of social change in the Kerston rural community was given by Maria and Dennis Young who moved to Kerston after living all their previous lives in cities. They moved in 1989 from a semi-detached house in a town on the edge of Nottingham. At that time, Maria wasn't involved in the professional work in which she is now engaged. But as her income began to improve, with promotions at work, she and Dennis decided to move to the country. In moving 20 miles out of the city, they found that they could afford to buy a much larger property. House prices within closer commuting distance were very high as a result of people who had been ahead of them in the urban–rural shift. Maria and Dennis bought a very run-down farmhouse from a couple who had bought it, not long before, from the original tenant farmers. The tenant farmers from whom they had bought the place had put it on the market soon after having bought it themselves from the big estate at a 'knock-down' price. They farmed it for a while but could not really make it pay and so decided to 'cash in' and sell the property on. Maria and Dennis told the researchers that they believed that they had moved 'just at the right time', before developers like Eddie Newhall moved in. They could not have afforded the move to the country with the prices that these houses were to later command.

Stage 3

The third stage, in the late 1980s and into the 1990s, sees the appearance of the entrepreneur-developer. This new figure on the rural scene recognised the market potential for renovating and converting barns into domestic dwellings which had been left to decay through this process.

Eddie Newhall, an entrepreneurial property developer, is part of the third stage of the social change process we are looking at. As we shall see later, he confirms that he was a new type of actor on the Kerston property scene. And, as we shall further see, Eddie and his wife were also in-migrants to Kerston from the city. However, before we look closely at his account of his urban–rural shift and his entrepreneurial activities, we need to establish the style of conceptual analysis that we intend to bring to bear on Eddie, the entre-preneur, and some of his clients – in order to bring out the intertwining ways in which both parties in this entrepreneurial process have 'become other' as part of their involvement in social change processes in the Kerston district. We do this in two stages: first, setting out an 'orientations and meanings' perspec-tive for looking at social change processes and, second, applying this perspec-tive more specifically to entrepreneur–client relationality within the social change processes.

FROM 'MOTIVES AND DRIVERS' TO 'EMERGENT LIFE ORIENTATIONS AND MEANINGS' IN SOCIAL CHANGE PROCESSES

In the above account of how Maria Young and her husband Dennis came to move into the former farmhouse building, we are being told something of the separate and the joint life stories of two people who are part of the 'counterurbanisation' trend. Their move was part of the way they were shaping their individual lives and their relationship – how they were *orienting their lives.* And in shifting attention to this much more fine-grained and complex element of the processes of social change we are filling out a picture that is left incomplete by the more typical literature on urban–rural migratory patterns which concentrates on 'motives', 'drivers' and on 'push' and 'pull' factors which are said to be behind the urban–rural shift process and the *embourgeoisement* trend.

Typical of the kind of analysis in the current literature is the way Fielding (1982) writes of four 'main drivers' of urban–rural migration ('life style preferences, job opportunities, production-led decentralisation and state policy') and that in which Buller, Morris and Wright (2003) discuss a range of structural factors which they see as operating across the various 'drivers and motivations' that have been identified by researchers (p. 23). Buller, Morris and Wright also note how a number of commentators tend to break down the 'range of motives and drivers' into just two 'key explanations' of 'residential preference' and 'employment' (2003, p. 25). Halliday and Coombes (1995) use a less mechanistic type of language when they identify three 'overarching rationales' (the antimetropolitan, the anti-urban and the pro-rural). But, as with the 'motives and drivers' analyses, we get little insight into how these rationales operate at the level of the individuals, couples and families who make these moves. We learn little of the relational contexts in which 'rationales' link to broader life orientations of rural in-migrants. We also learn little about the role that entrepreneurial activities play in enabling peoples' life orientations.

This need to go beyond the concepts and language of 'motives' and 'drivers' in understanding social changes like those of counterurbanisation to look more closely at the social actors' meanings and orientations is very similar to that recognised in the classic sociological study of social change processes carried out in the 1960s by David Lockwood and John Goldthorpe (Goldthorpe et al., 1968; Goldthorpe et al., 1969). An important by-product of this study of changing class patterns in the UK was the development of the concept of 'orientation to work'. Goldthorpe and Lockwood showed it to be necessary to move away from an emphasis on worker 'motives' as 'psychological constants' to a recognition that 'wants and expectations are culturally determined variables' (1968, p. 178). In this, they were relating to the Weberian tradition in sociology, or rather, to the version of that tradition identified by Parsons and Shils (1951) as an 'action frame of reference'.

In the action frame of reference, 'actors' own definitions of the situations in which they are engaged are taken as an initial basis for the explanation of their social behaviour and relationships' (Goldthorpe et al., 1968, p. 184). Later work which utilised the work orientations approach refined it significantly, especially by departing from the Goldthorpe and Lockwood (1968) emphasis on 'prior orientations' and taking full account of the way in which people's orientations change as their circumstances change (Beynon and Blackburn, 1972; Watson, 1977; Watson, 2003). And especially significant here in this shift of emphasis was the seminal organisation theory contribution (Hassard and Parker, 1994) of Silverman (1970) and his refining of the orientation notion by connecting it more closely to the symbolic interactionist tradition in which one is 'encouraged to view subjective experience in process' (1970, p. 185). Thus, in looking at people's orientations one must not 'miss the way in which people's view of themselves and of their situation is one of an ongoing process, never fully determined by one or another set of structural constraints but always in the act of "becoming" as successive experiences shape and re-shape a subjective definition of self and society' (1970, pp. 184–185). And this emphasis is one reinforced more recently in organisation theory, especially by Chia and his call for replacing an ontological posture of 'being realism' which 'asserts that reality pre-exists independently of observation and as discrete, permanent and identifiable "things", "entities", "events", "generative mechanisms", etc.' (Chia, 1996, p. 26) with a 'becoming ontology' as a 'basis for reconceptualising organisation as an emergent process rather than as a stable phenomenon' (Chia, 2003, p. 100). Instead, Chia proposes that we focus on 'organising relationships': 'the dynamic network of implicit assumptions, expectations, social obligations, rules [and] conventions' that 'shape how our individual identities are constructed . . .' (2003, p. 100).

The emphasis on dynamic or emergent 'orientations' has been developed within industrial sociology and organisational theory where, in spite of the concern to link people's work activities to their broader lives, it has restricted its attention to workplace issues. The link between people's work activities and their broader lives needs to be more closely examined (Watson, 2003). For the present study, therefore, we expand the notion of 'work orientation' to give us a concept of 'life orientation': *the continuously emergent meanings attached by people to their life situation and identities which predispose them to think and act in particular ways with regard to their biographies.*

ENTREPRENEURSHIP, LIFE ORIENTATIONS AND 'BECOMING OTHERWISE'

What is also distinctive in our approach is the concern to link this emergent view of life orientations to entrepreneurial activities. In this chapter we highlight the process by which urban–rural migration trends/patterns facilitate a range of market possibilities in rural communities – possibilities which, when enacted, contribute further to social change in these communities.

In particular, we are concerned with how market possibilities are interpreted by knowing actors as 'opportunities' which not only facilitate the emergence of their life and family orientations but which also have effects by enabling the life orientations of their clients. Some of these 'knowing actors' are the tenant farmers themselves, who see the opportunity to make a quick cash sale on the farm buildings they now own. Others are those property seekers who are looking to make new lives for themselves influenced by the 'rural idyll'. But at the centre of our analysis here are the new property entrepreneurs that 'saw' the possibilities in the rural property market and positioned themselves to realise some of these opportunities in the late 1980s.

In our analysis we are concerned to emphasise the relational dimension of entrepreneurial processes. Relational thinking gives primary emphasis to the joint co-ordinations through (and by) which entrepreneurial opportunities are brought into being and realised (Fletcher and Watson, 2005). It challenges the notion that opportunity discovery is the product of cognitive processes (Shane and Venkataraman, 2000) occurring as 'light bulb' moments in individual minds. Instead, opportunity recognition and enactment are the result of interaction processes that develop in a highly relational (and social) context (Bouwen, 2001; Steyaert and Katz, 2004). The relational context incorporates the personal and family identities or life orientations of people as well as the cultural, social and economic context in which they are located. Thus, entrepreneurs, the business ideas they enact and the business enterprises that they establish are not seen as having a fixed being. They are always emergent, in a process of becoming – 'coming ever afresh into existence out of an alternation of events that have gone before and will "become" again' (Steyaert, 1998). The conceptualisation with which we are thus working is one in which we bring the concept of life orientation to entrepreneurship. We approach entrepreneurship as:

> a way of making a living in which people with novel ideas for a product or a service create, develop and realise those ideas as part of their social becoming – something they do through envisaging how those ideas might in some way 'make a difference' and shape or influence the social becoming of their potential customers or clients (Fletcher and Watson, 2005).

This conceptualisation means that we are concerned with the dialogic, interpretive and interactive processes through which market possibilities are
formed into opportunities that enable personal, family and community change.
We shall see the importance of this shortly when Eddie Newhall speaks about
how he enacted an opportunity for property development in the rural location.
Also, by utilising relational thinking this enables us to consider how opportunity enactment is both shaped by and contributes to the social change or
embourgeoisement of rural communities. The two-way nature of this process,
whereby entrepreneurial activity contributes to and is an effect of social
change (at a personal, family and community level), is rarely made explicit in
studies of entrepreneurship. Figure 7.1 represents this process, and the part
played by both entrepreneurs and clients 'becoming other' or 'shifting' their
life orientations. It is upon this that our study focuses.

We now turn to the 'social becoming' of the key property-developing entrepreneur in the Kerston district: looking at how his own shifting life orientation
or 'becoming other' brought him both into the rural location and into entrepreneurial property developing. As we shall see, these two processes are not
only closely interrelated, they are indeed part of a social or relational 'becoming' in that they can only be understood in the light of his relationship with
others in his life, and especially his relationship with his wife, Sylvie. This is
something we are focusing upon to help us answer our key research question:
in what ways, at the level of 'actual' real-life and detailed processes, can entre-

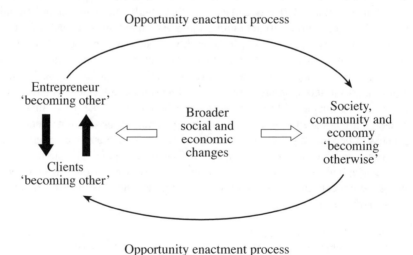

*Figure 7.1   The relationship between social change and entrepreneurs and
their clients 'becoming other'*

preneurial practices facilitate social change at the same time as social change facilitates entrepreneurial practices? The key concepts we are using to address this question are those of life orientations and entrepreneurship as a process involving the interlinked 'becoming otherwise' of the entrepreneur and the 'becoming otherwise' of the entrepreneurial client within the respective life orientations of the two parties. These concepts are applied to what has become a considerable databank of ethnographically-generated materials. Information has been gathered two ways. First, it was gathered by formal field work methods including both targeted and semi-structured interviews. Second, it came from all the informal conversations, participant observations and direct experiences of the researchers, one of whom is a resident of Kerston. This field work material is not only processed by the application to it of social science concepts, it is also inevitably 'moulded' within the writing process as the writers craft their account to give it a narrative shape which makes the account meaningful and manageable for the reader.

EDDIE NEWHALL: RURAL SHIFTER AND PROPERTY ENTREPRENEUR

The involvement of the entrepreneur-developer in that part of rural social change whereby former agricultural properties become residences for middle-class urban–rural in-migrants was shown earlier to be part of a third stage in the change process. At the suggestion of Maria Young, who was a 'second stage' in-migrant, we followed up the various conversations we had had with Eddie Newhall with a specific discussion about the changing pattern of property reallocation in the region.

Within the period that we have characterised as a second stage, Eddie said that the tenant farmers, on taking ownership of their dwellings, made only minor improvements to their properties. This fits with the observation of Maria Young that 'nothing had been done' to the property she and her husband bought. Where changes had been made to the properties, these, Eddie suggested, 'were frequently bodged – they spent very little money on the properties'. And, he adds, the barns and outbuildings on their land, or remaining on the estate lands, were not invested in (newer and more useful barns could readily and cheaply be put up where these were needed).

This still surprises Eddie. 'I can't really understand why tenants didn't do up the properties themselves. Not one tenant took up the development potential of their property.'

He is also surprised that these rural inhabitants 'let people like me in'.

'What do you mean, "people like you"?'

'Well, people like me, I am a scavenger really – a scavenger picking up the bits and pieces. The developer phenomenon was definitely a new element in all of this.'

So, if Eddie Newhall, the entrepreneur-developer, was 'a new element' in the processes of social change in Kerston, how did he come to be there and come to be operating as a property developer in the area? When we asked him to explain this, he chose to go back to his early life, and it is here that we first see him talking in terms which we would conceptualise in terms of 'becoming other'. He initially started work as an apprentice joiner yet, by mentioning that he always liked the idea of having his own business, he implies that the idea of his being an employee of somebody else's company did not fit fully with his broader life orientation.

'Whilst I was still at school, I was interested in building things in woodwork. But I was also very interested in horses.'

'Where did the interest in horses come from?'

'I'm not sure but I reckon it had something to do with my father having been a riding instructor in the army.'

'Anyway', he went on, 'I had two options before me: the building business or the horse business. But I reckoned that the horse business would be a lot of hard work, would have more likelihood of failure and, erm, the chance of it really coming good was very slim.'

In the large construction company where he trained, Eddie became a junior site manager and, whilst still in this, he started to get involved in what he called 'the earliest things that I did that were, I suppose, entrepreneurial'. In the classic sense, opportunities became available to him as a would-be entrepreneur.

'At the time I was managing a small building site of thirty-five or so houses. Then I would hear that "Mrs So-and-So wants a garage adding on to her house" or "Mrs So-and-So wants her drive doing".'

In our terms, here is Eddie 'becoming otherwise' as he now takes on building work 'on my own account, as you might say – doing the jobs at weekends with some of the blokes I brought into it'. But this chance to 'become otherwise' is only there because the residents are themselves 'becoming otherwise' as they improve their properties. The opportunity that is being enacted is an opportunity related to the life orientations of both the entrepreneur and the client. Eddie says he was generally 'bettering himself' in doing this work and that the clients were 'enhancing their lifestyle'.

Eddie is improving his economic position and that of his family. But whereas those workers were surrendering autonomy in the workplace in order to improve the lives of their families, Eddie's orientation was one in which enormous value seems to have been placed on 'running his own show'.

'When I was at school I was already attracted to the idea of running my own company. And now there I was, working for myself at weekends. This made me ask whether I wanted to be a manager in somebody else's company at all – you know, with all that "Yes sir, no sir, three bags full, sir!" thing. And I have to say that I actually enjoyed the whole process, including all the aggravation and the risks involved.'

In our conversations with him, Eddie repeatedly presents himself as someone who thrives on risks and 'beating the challenge of the dangers and all the things that go wrong'. Not surprisingly, in light of this, Eddie soon moved to running his own business full-time. But running a construction business still did not fit with what we would conceptualise as the self-identity element of his life orientation: his idea of himself as someone wanting to be in charge of his own destiny, enjoying the thrills of risk-taking and making a higher level of return.

'I thought, well, why do I build that house for x, y and z and then see them sell it for a lot more money – when it was us who did all the work. I decided I did not want to do what a lot of other builders were doing: working for the developers when you could do the developing for yourself. And what actually enabled me to move in this direction was when I saw the opportunities created by the tremendous amount of government grants that were around that I could take up.'

The early development opportunities supported by these government grants arose in the inner city but, soon, Eddie was looking outside the city for development opportunities. However, the areas in relatively close range to his working and living base in the city were becoming, as he puts it, 'saturated'.

'So I decided that North Nottingham has got to be where it is. Where you could get a cottage for sixty grand south of Nottingham, you could near enough buy a farm up here for that.'

And indeed, with hard-fought-for bank loans, Eddie started to buy properties including the farm in which he stills lives in Kerston. This was 'a dream place for me and Sylvie'.

So why did Eddie and Sylvie move twenty-five mile out to Kerston? Whilst it was a matter of what we would call 'becoming otherwise' in a domestic and non-work identity sense (having a 'dream house' for the family and the space to keep and train horses) this was by no means the whole story: 'It wasn't just a move to live. It was also a move to develop'. And Eddie goes on to make this kind of close link between the 'home and work' aspects of his life orientation. He explained that, at that time, whenever he bought a property he asked himself, 'Could I live in it?' And, at the same time, when he looked at the 'dream house' that he wanted to live in, he also looked at it as an investment – as something that he could sell for a good return. He characterises what he is doing here in terms of 'putting yourself in everybody else's shoes'. This, we would suggest, can be understood as another aspect of the entrepreneur orienting his or her own 'becoming otherwise' by contemplating the 'becoming otherwise' of people who might want to buy the property – even his own dream home – from him at some time.

The element of Eddie's life orientation which so tightly combines the 'personal' and the 'career' aspects of his existence is further illustrated by the way he talks about his 'hobby' of 'having the horses'. Although he recognises that this goes back to some aspect of his childhood identity, he is anxious to stress that he is 'fully focused with it' in a business sense.

'I've focused the horse thing to the market – in the way I've set out the buildings and the paddocks and so on – so that I could eventually sell it to people wanting it for a stud hall. That's where the money is. I'd get a lot more money for it that way than if it was only suitable to go to somebody who just wanted to run a riding school, or something like that.'

Home is work and work is home, it would seem. And the farm also houses the business that Eddie's wife, Sylvie, runs.

SYLVIE NEWHALL: URBAN–RURAL SHIFTER AND PR-ENTREPRENEUR

Although Sylvie's business is primarily a marketing one, it is closely connected to the construction industry. Even Sylvie's original business idea came from Eddie. As she told us:

'When we first moved to this area I was a teacher. But I was feeling increasingly unsatisfied in this role so I was thinking about starting up on my own.

First there was the seed of an idea. This came to me at a dinner party with friends who had their own business. At that point I decided I wanted my own business. [Laughing] I want to become a millionaire. But it was Eddie who really got me going with it. I learned a lot about running a business from him. And, of course, he set up his first wife in a catering business when they split up.

'So, it was my idea to start a PR/marketing consultancy business. But it was Eddie who came up with the idea of specialised consultancy for the construction industry. But don't tell him I told you that. Eddie is good like that. He has lots of ideas and knows what will work. He knows a lot of people and is good at getting new business. He built the office for me here on our farm so that I could have a professional environment to work in – it's all very well working from your living room in the beginning but when you are trying to grow a business, especially a PR one, you need a good image and environment. So Eddie built me an office on our land. This took a bit of doing with the district planning regulations, especially when you live in a conservation area as we do – but the town planning people are keen to encourage rural business development particularly if it has the effect of creating more jobs. So they are reasonably receptive to the building of offices on one's land. And that is where Eddie's skills are exceptional – negotiating with planners is his thing and he always plays to win.'

Sylvie begins her account by informing us that she was previously a teacher and that she was feeling frustrated in this occupation. Shortly after moving to the Kerston district with Eddie, she comments that she started to think about 'starting up on her own'. Interestingly, she does not refer to Eddie as the source of inspiration for this desire to shift occupations. She relates, instead, to another couple who lived in the village at the time who had a successful advertising business. She comments that it was during a dinner party with them that the seed of the idea emerged. However, in the shaping of the business idea, she then relates to Eddie who suggested the niche of 'specialised PR for the construction industry' where there was something of an unfulfilled need. Thus, on moving to Kerston, Sylvie took the opportunity to reassess her identity and life orientation and made a choice about 'becoming other' as a small business owner. But this choice was a relational one brought about through conversations and dialogue with other significant people in her life – including Eddie, although at times Sylvie prefers to play down the relational effect that her husband Eddie has on her life orientation and business emergence. She comments on her 'exasperation' about the way he runs his business, which in her view is 'not systematic' and has 'no procedures in place'. But at other times, as we see in the above account but only when Eddie is not within hearing, Sylvie praises him for his market knowledge, 'gut feel' for the right property purchases and negotiation skills with the town planners, estate agents and other parties. This implies that there is tension in their relationship – a tension which relates to issues of identity, independence and which is heightened by the co-interdependence of their personal and business lives (each has ownership in the other's business).

On the one hand, Sylvie is keen to relate to Eddie for ideas, inspiration and information about her business. On the other, she claims that decisions are 'hers' not influenced by Eddie. He is helping her find the 'right sort of place' to move to in the town location, but she frequently says things like 'don't tell him I said that' and 'I wouldn't want him to know that'. As such there is relational dynamic between the two domestic and business partners which is shaped as much by friction, tension and irritation as it is by mutual respect and cooperation. And it is this energy (that is relationally produced) that sparks their business activities.

In addition, both Sylvie and Eddie have utilised local resources (such as land, building regulations, labour, personal networks) in order to realise their business ideas into action. This interaction and embeddedness in the 'local environment' has been frequently commented on in entrepreneurship and regional studies (Scott and Anderson, 1993; Carter, 1996; Anderson, 2000; Jack and Anderson, 2002). Although, Sylvie began her business from the 'living room', she soon expanded into the office which Eddie built for her on their land. This was constructed at cost and her business paid much less than the market rate for the construction of office facilities that accommodated six members of staff. Likewise, Eddie's construction business benefits from free public relations and general business development consultancy advice. The two businesses are also co-interdependent in terms of the use of secretarial support and professional labour, such as tax and accountancy expertise. Furthermore, Sylvie is now speaking about moving her business to the town as her business 'enters the next phase of growth'. She speculates that growing businesses don't tend to 'stay in the country' because of infrastructure problems. From her point of view, and possibly given the nature of her business, a rural location and the environment it creates, is beneficial for emergent rather than seriously growing business.

In this account we see the importance of the dynamics of the relationship between two people and two businesses in a rural location. We have attended so far to Eddie and Sylvie's shifting life orientation as an entrepreneurial couple. Central to our main conceptual framework, however, is the relationality between, on the one hand, Eddie and Sylvie as an entrepreneurial pair and, on the other hand, Jane and Tom Ford as a client couple. There is relationality at the level of the individuals and couples but this is more than a matter of 'interpersonal' relating. Relationality, here, is a matter of linkages between people in discursively framed social and economic 'roles' – in this case buyers and sellers. Eddie lays great stress on the importance of 'researching' just who his buyers are and where they come from. Two thirds of them, he confirms, are from urban settings. The minority are people, he says, who, 'are from the same rural locality and are upgrading from one house to another invariably on inherited money'.

'But the majority are people who lived in urban housing estates in a Barratt type of house [a relatively modest type of private house] who dream of moving into country. They have either got to the point where their joint salaries are sufficient to move up in the housing market or they are people moving into their first managerial job.'

What this implies is that social mobility as well as geographical mobility is an important factor in the 'becoming otherwise' of Eddie's clients. And a key aspiration of many of them is to provide a better education for their children than they might otherwise have been able to afford. The implication of what he is saying is that many of Eddie's clients have life orientations which involve a rejection of the 'rat race' of big city life, whilst nevertheless wanting to be, as he puts it, 'reasonably prosperous'. His own life orientation, he implies, involves much more ambition than theirs. His clients, he feels, are not 'proper entrepreneurs' like himself and he speaks in a mildly disapproving tone of people being happy in what he calls 'their comfort zones'. He speaks disparagingly of them as people who comfortably settle on a size of business that can be run from a dining room or from 'a bit built on the side of the house'. However, the irony is that Eddie benefits appreciably in business terms from there being people who seek such a 'comfort zone' in the country. An example of this would be Jane and Tom Ford.

JANE AND TOM FORD: RURAL–URBAN SHIFTERS AND ENTREPRENEUR-DEVELOPER CLIENTS

Jane and Tom spoke to us as a couple about their move to Kerston. Jane began.

'We moved up to here from London. It's about two years ago now, isn't it Tom?'

'Oh, it's easily that Jane. Perhaps we should explain, though, that although my family are country people, both Jane and I have lived in the big city since we were teenagers. I was earning good money as an accountant and Jane's money as a part-time teacher was helpful. But this still didn't allow us to have the sort of property we wanted, and especially, the size of garden that we wanted for our three children. Up here not only do we have a big garden but we have a paddock and an orchard. This gives the kids a life much more like the one I had and I want them to be able . . .'

'Just a minute, Tom, you haven't explained how we came to move up here in the first place. Speaking for myself, the crucial thing, I think, was the increasing crime levels in what, otherwise, was a very nice district to live in.'

'All that's true, Jane, but there were much more positive factors weren't there?'

'Yes of course, and the children's education was important here. To be honest, we weren't at first too sure what the implications would be of moving up to North Notts for the kid's schooling. But Eddie Newhall was very helpful on this. As he pointed out, this barn conversion that we have now got is very close to a couple of very good schools. And I've been lucky to get some work in one of those schools . . .'

'Yeah, but we wouldn't be up here in the first place if it wasn't for my job. Let me try to explain this to you. This is very important, I think, for your research. If I remember rightly, it started with a conversation – at a party I think it was – with my cousin. He had this accounting firm in Newark. It was growing and he was keen to interest me in becoming a partner with him. My first thought was "Oh no, down-shifting is not my style". But over time the idea grew on me.'

'Yes, in one sense it is down-shifting. We were losing the big bonuses Tom got in the city firm. In another way, though, it is quite the opposite. We've got a bigger house than we could have afforded in London. We've got all this land. And, above all, we have got a lot more time as a family. Life all round is richer.'

'I think Jane's used a good word there. We are certainly well off here even if the income is lower than before. In some ways this area offers us something – how can I put it? – more socially upmarket.'

'That's right. The riding lessons for the kids are a good example of this. Having a pony is one of those almost cliché middle class things, isn't it. But we could not have dreamed of that in London. And rubbing shoulders with some of the big estate owners at the tennis club gives you more the feeling of . . .'

'I don't agree with Jane about that sort of thing – the social mixing I mean. But, yes, the riding for the kids is something quite different for us. In fact, it was Eddie Newhall who pointed out the opportunities that our kids would have for this kind of thing.'

'And Tom, it was Eddie who told us who to contact about joining the tennis club. And didn't he put us in touch with those people in the church who helped us with the . . . .'

'OK, OK. We got help linking into the local networks. But now we are well able to look after ourselves.'

These closing words of Tom Ford imply a certain edginess towards Eddie Newhall, the entrepreneur-developer from whom they bought their rural property. He is anxious to counter his wife's emphasis on the extent to which Eddie did more than simply sell them a property. She tells of three ways in which he contributed to their 'becoming otherwise' as they moved into Kerston: getting them involved with ponies and riding lessons ('one of those almost cliché middle class things'); introducing them to the tennis club and putting them in touch with 'people in the church'. And Tom is also troubled by Jane's implied pleasure at being part of the rural *embourgeoisement* or 'gentrification' process. Tom is embarrassed by her mention of 'rubbing shoulders' with estate owners, for example. Yet he himself talks of how the area offers them something 'more socially upmarket'. And, note, this cultural upward social mobility has occurred in spite of the fact that Tom and Jane are now living on a lower monetary income. This fits with a pattern observed in research that shows that concerns with quality of life are more significant to urban–rural shifters than employment considerations (Williams and Jobes, 1995). Tom rejects the notion of 'down shifting' suggesting that everything in the life orientations of his family is, in one way or another, 'upwards'.

The relationship between Eddie Newhall, the entrepreneur-developer, and the Ford family of urban–rural shifters and entrepreneur-clients is one from which both parties clearly have benefited. Their mutual 'becoming other' has its roots in both the Newhall and the Ford families changing their life orientations by, at different stages, moving from the city into the country. Each family is in some sense moving 'upwards' as part of their having moved 'outwards'. And, correspondingly, the Sylvie part of the Newhall businesses is moving upwards and outwards. This is apparent in her account of her ambitions for the business:

'I am not sure that businesses stay in the rural outback once the business has taken off. I don't know for sure but I imagine that businesses that are really growing would stay in the countryside whilst the business is emerging, but once you get to 10, 12, 15 employees you start to build an organisational infrastructure, you need bigger premises, broadband technology, and the right image.'

'Are you saying then that you are thinking you might transfer your business soon to a town location like Newark?'

'Well, I am thinking about it. Eddie thinks he gave me the idea for this but I had always planned to start up the business here at home and if things took off, which I am pleased to say they have, I would move to Nottingham or Newark. Newark makes sense for my business because it is only 1 hour and 30 minutes on the train to London. It is really an up and coming town, quite cosmopolitan with lots of bistros and leisure activities. Property prices have really gone up and it has really cultivated its image as interesting historical country/market town – where part of the English civil war was fought. It has waterside properties, warehouse apartments and many large retail outlets are setting up there. So I am looking at re-locating there for the next phase of growth for my business.'

'And what about Eddie's construction business – do you see that moving out of the Kerston district also?'

'Well, I can't see that happening. Eddie is too attached to his farm and horses. And anyway I love living in Kerston. It is just that for my business to really take off I need to be in a town location now. His business is not really going to grow any further. He employs about 4 people full time and has a workforce of 10 sub-contractors. He has plenty of new projects underway. But there is just not the scope within the construction industry to make a lot of money. And that whole building sector is just so chaotic – no systems in place – everything working on an informal basis – no organisation, strategy or vision for the future. But then I shouldn't really complain because he is helping me find the right sort of place to move to in Newark.'

CONCLUSIONS: THE ENTREPRENEURIAL FACILITATION OF RURAL SOCIAL CHANGE AND THE RURAL SOCIAL CHANGE FACILITATION OF ENTREPRENEURSHIP

In this chapter we have examined aspects of urban–rural migration patterns in a small rural area in the East Midlands area of the UK. It is not our intention to generalise empirically from these case studies, suggesting for example that all rural property developers are like Eddie Newhall and that every urban–rural shifting family is like the Fords. However, as pointed our earlier, many villages in the UK are experiencing an influx of urban–rural shifters and our ethnographic study illustrates some of the processes facilitating such migration patterns and their effects when entrepreneurial opportunities are then enacted by people with their changing life orientations as a result of the interaction with the local environment/resources.

In particular, we are keen to generalise theoretically about the types of process (Yin, 1994; Watson, 2001) that occur at the level of the fine grained detail of social change. By using an ethnographic style of analysis, whereby our conversations and interviews are embedded in a close and intimate appreciation of the social context in which accounts are given to us as researchers, we are able to link the changes in life orientations of particular people to broader social and structural changes in rural communities. The basic shape of those changes was established early in the chapter by our use of broader survey-based evidence presented by researchers operating in a more conventional social science research mode. We have shown how, at the level of the meaning-making and life-shaping of individuals and families, these social changes are both brought into being by the actions of members of society – in our case, entrepreneurs and their clients – and how, at the same time, the actions of those social actors are influenced by those social changes.

The lives of the small number of people we have focused upon illustrate this broad theoretical insight. And, within this, we utilise two novel conceptual devices. First, we develop the notion of life orientation – with its emphasis on the ways in which human actions occur in the context of how people's 'whole lives' are shaped through meaning-making processes. And, second, we make use of a concept of entrepreneurship which relates entrepreneurial actions to the life orientation of both the entrepreneur and the clients. We show the interlinked ways in which the entrepreneurial couple, on the one had, and the client couple on the other, 'become other' in the course of transacting with each other. This relationality is represented on the left hand side of figure 7.1. This relationality, however, has to be understood within the broader processes of social change.

In this chapter we have shown social change occurring, in part, through opportunity enactment processes which are an important dynamic component of the figure 7.1 scheme. In particular, we drew attention to opportunity enactment processes in Eddie's migration to a rural location and his realisation of property development potential. We have also considered how opportunity enactment is both shaped by and contributes to the social change or *embourgeoisement* of rural communities. In focusing our analysis on the Kerston district of the East Midlands, we have given an account of three families that have moved into this location from urban situations. At the centre of these families is entrepreneur-developer, Eddie Newhall, who in his life orientation to 'become other' has created and grown a construction business out of property development and conversion of old agricultural buildings. This business, and his role in it, has had a relational effect on the community in which it is located in that these properties have created opportunities for other families (such as Jane and Tom) to make the urban–rural shift themselves. Central to his life and business is Sylvie, who has also started a new business on the farm in relation to her husband's business. Both businesses have had a relational effect on the locality by creating wealth and jobs for the local community (office work, cleaning, gardening as well as professional jobs such as journalism and accountancy). They have also had an effect on the development of the physical infrastructure of the rural village (new tarmac roads and the introduction of broadband technology). And, as Sylvie's business grows further, this will have a 'spillover' effect onto the nearest town.

Our emphasis, throughout, has been on processes and on social, personal and family emergence. In utilising an ethnographic style of research we have highlighted the 'actual' real-life and detailed processes through which entrepreneurial practices facilitate social change at the same time as social change also facilitates entrepreneurial practices. The stories reported here show how the entrepreneur and the client simultaneously shape the process of counterurbanisation and are shaped by them. We hope that we have made a contribution to the understanding of the particular aspect of modern social life in rural locations with which we have been concerned. And, at the same time, we hope to inspire and encourage others to apply this style of analysis to other aspects of the ways in which processes of entrepreneurship and social change interact and influence each other.

8. Women, Mother Earth and the business of living

Kathryn Campbell

REGAINING AN ENTREPRENEURIAL RELATIONSHIP WITH MOTHER EARTH

When we are productively engaged with the land we have the opportunity to fulfil our pre-eminent entrepreneurial responsibility to nurture our bodies, our minds and our relationships with all living creatures. But we do not give sufficient respect or attention to this crucial task. Growing ourselves and our communities in harmony with the land is seldom recognized as an entrepreneurial activity, a conception shaped perhaps by ideological influences but most certainly by practical realities. Although a majority of the world's population lives on the land, only a tiny fraction of the people in industrialized countries maintains an active, economic relationship with the land[41] and it is from these countries that most entrepreneurial theories emanate. Physically distanced from the land, many of us have forfeited the knowledge of how to construct and maintain a creative, life-affirming relationship with Mother Earth. We have discredited our enterprising physical selves and commoditized the business of living. Recreational gardening plots serve as ghostly memorials, marking and mourning our loss of space and place.

To help us regain an entrepreneurial relationship with Mother Earth, the experiences of three strong and remarkably different women – Thuli, Catharine and Anne – are offered to help us remember some of the values, beliefs and behaviours that can be learned through life on the land. These women lead by example, telling how they found sustenance and hope. Each life is idiosyncratic but all three stories are about the opportunities created when Mother Earth becomes a partner in the business of living. The overarching goal is the expansion of the entrepreneurial debate to contemplate the merits of localized, small-scale, non-heroic enterprise that recognizes the necessary interdependence of human development, economic activity and our place on Mother Earth.

To stimulate the relearning process, I first look to our history and factor in women's unrecognized entrepreneurial contributions. Then research methodologies sensitive to the tenets of standpoint feminism (Smith, 1979) are used to quilt together (Campbell, 2004) an unconventional sampling of women drawing upon concepts that were identified in exploratory, sensing interviews with recreational women gardeners who have maintained an emotive and ceremonial relationship with Mother Earth. From the three stories, common threads are discussed as tentative precursors to future theorizing. To push/pull the field of entrepreneurship research, references have been drawn from rather eclectic sources and the chapter concludes with brief commentaries about three theoretical frames – ecofeminism, bioregionalism and survival subsistence – which challenge entrepreneurship researchers to build relationships with other fields of inquiry and thereby strengthen our understanding of that most enigmatic subject – human enterprise.

ARCHETYPAL ENTREPRENEURIAL ACTIVITIES FOR SPECIES SURVIVAL

We exist today because our foremothers foraged and gathered and, later, accomplished the transition to gardening and agriculture (Martin and Voorhies, 1975). Yet that is not how we talk about our entrepreneurial past. 'The general myth is that the male provides most of the food in gatherer-hunter societies, but the truth is that some 80 per cent or more is provided in most societies by the female' (Montagu, [1953] 1999, p. 69). Hunting generated limited human sustenance but it attained cultural and economic significance as its aggressively gendered behaviours were elevated through ceremony and fortified by 'patriarchal myths' (Daly, 1978, p. 47), myths that continue to bolster the 'hunting hypothesis' (Gailey, 1987, p. 39). Modern notions about preferred entrepreneurial behaviours are, in many ways, idealizations of the mythical hunter of old. But our species did not survive by hunting. '[H]umans for most of their history, have actually been omnivores, who ate mostly the leaves, roots, and fruits of plants, as well as insects. The flesh of small or large animals has been the occasional food of festivals, not the staple diet' (Ruether, 1994, p. 52). To this day, subsistence gardening is an essential entrepreneurial activity that sustains a significant proportion of the world's population.[42]

Close study of a subsistence relationship with Mother Earth reveals the quintessential entrepreneurial responsibility, the individual and collective process of self-creation and self-nurturing. We grow ourselves in a life-long endeavour that is strenuous, reflexive, universal and uniquely personal and this business of living is more urgent, more innovative and more rewarding than any business venture. Defaulting on this responsibility is the ultimate loss of opportunity. In the business of living, we literally grow ourselves through the nurturing of our bodies; as well, we grow ourselves through psychological/spiritual identity work and; we grow ourselves through our personal and work relations. Our life's work entails a complex web of relationships 'in which everything is connected with everything, not only across space, but across time as well' (Ruether, 1994, p. 38). Business venturing therefore cannot be a simple or self-contained act of value exchange but is one of many processes by which we intimately build ourselves. Bengt Johannisson describes entrepreneurial practice as 'existential projecting' in which the making of one's identity occurs simultaneously and contiguously with venture development (Johannisson, 2004, p. 3). Work is for life. When we fully comprehend our interdependence with Mother Earth and with all other life forms, our entrepreneurial energies are drawn towards non-hierarchical socioeconomic behaviours that value all resources in a long-term, ecologically sustainable timeframe. Our ancient foremothers lived in this manner.[43]

The woman/earth/life trinity has an honoured history in the religious customs of our ancestors. 'Long before the birth of the modern religions . . . goddess worship . . . the veneration of a Tellus Mater – a great Earth Mother, controller of fertility, and birth, and by extension, of infertility and death' (Bennett, 1991, p. 16) was practiced throughout the ancient world, as evidenced by bone, stone and ivory goddess statues found at innumerable archaeological sites (Bennett, 1991; Stone, 1976). Although archaeological findings are never infallible, there is substantive evidence of matrilineal kinship systems for thousands of years before the arrival of Christianity (Stone, 1976). Over time, these goddess-worshipping societies were overrun by male-dominated religions. Officially, those sustained and bloody campaigns were rationalized in the name of religious conviction – driving out the infidel/witch/heathen – but it now appears that economic dominance was a powerful underlying motive. Drawing together an immense historical and archaeological record, Merlin Stone concludes that 'the suppression of women's rites has actually been the suppression of women's rights' (Stone, 1976, p. 228), the appropriation of women's property through the imposition of a patrilineal system legitimated by the invaders' patriarchal religions. Dispossessed by religious, political and military forces, women today hold/own a disproportionately small fraction[44] of the space on Mother Earth. With increasingly restricted access to food-producing capacity (Boserup, [1960] 1989; Shiva, 1990) and the consequent loss of opportunity to engage in the business of living, women suffer a double jeopardy: loss of space and loss of place.

In everyday usage, space and place are commonly treated as synonymous terms but there is merit in thinking through their distinctive meanings in order to fully delineate the plight of entrepreneurial/self-creating women. Space is typically conceptualized in relation to instrumental attributes; it is inscribed with functionality, physicality and legitimacy; space has stability and usability

(Strid, 2004, pp. 5–6). The plot of ground on which a woman gardens is, in the first instance, a space. However, when that space is imbued with meaning it becomes a place and processes of individual and community identity formation begin to emerge. 'Hudson (2001) contrasts *space*, which is an economic (capitalistic) evaluation of location based on its capacity for profit, with *place*, which is a social evaluation of location based on meaning . . . Places are not simply sites of production and consumption, but areas of meaningful social life where people live and learn; they are locations of socialization and cultural acquisition' (Johnstone and Lionais, 2004, pp. 218–219, emphasis in original). The opportunity to transform space into place is crucial to individual health and to the health and development of a community.

However, land is also power and, while millions of women around the world toil to feed themselves and their children, they are prevented from owning the means of production. And in that power structure three longstanding and tightly interlocking mythological constructs – 'man the hunter-provider-entrepreneur'; 'man the warrior-protector-owner' and; 'man the rational thinker-innovator'[45] – have contributed to the formulation of androcentric economic theory. When combined with an uncritical valorization of technology, these mythologies rationalize the subordination of women (Gailey, 1987) and the domination of nature (Leiss, [1972] 1994; Ortner, 1974) for the purposes of privatized economic gain, thereby effectively alienating women from our past and our space/place on the planet. Consequently, women are 'disproportionately likely to suffer from ecological illness' (Nelson, 1990, p. 177; Philipose, 1989; Hamilton, 1990; Mies, 1993b). Space and place are matters of critical concern to women around the world.

It is therefore both logical and imperative that women assume a leadership role in the practice and promotion of grounded entrepreneurship. If our species is to survive, we must moderate our 'possessive individualism' (D'Souza, 1989, p. 29)[46] and re-craft our entrepreneurial belief system to regain our life-sustaining dependence on Mother Earth. Ecofeminist theologian Rosemary Ruether phrases this transformation as 'an overcoming of the culture of competitive alienation and domination with compassionate solidarity . . . and biophilic mutuality' (Ruether, 1994, pp. 201, 258). Other women have written about 'an ethic of care' (Gilligan, 1982) and 'ecological humility' (Primavesi, 1994, p. 190) and the entrepreneurial experiences of women who live in harmony with the land have much to teach us about who we can become.

ABOUT TELLING A DIFFERENT ENTREPRENEURIAL STORY DIFFERENTLY

Post postmodern narrative and critical realist perspectives, Dian-Marie

Hosking tempts the researcher with her visioning of 'relational construction-ism . . . as a thought style . . . [through which] . . . "research" now has a changed meaning – not to "tell it how it is" – but, for example, to "tell how it might become" ' (Hosking and Hjorth, 2004, pp. 258–259). And joyfully, she proposes that a relationship, or 'inter-action', is not limited to human inter-course. 'Inter-actions involve texts, actions, objects, and artifacts available to be made part of some ongoing process, to be re-constructed, made relevant or irrelevant, meaningful or meaningless, good or bad, *by being put in relation*' (Hosking and Hjorth, 2004, p. 260, emphasis in original). In a sympathetic vein, planetary biologists James Lovelock and Lynn Margulis propound the thesis that Mother Earth, called Gaia after the Greek Earth Goddess, is not simply a sphere of matter but is 'a living system, behaving as a unified organ-ism' (Ruether, 1994, p. 4), an entity with whom it is possible to have an 'inter-action'. In either cosmology, we garden with Mother Earth in a revitalized social relationship that is fraught with physical, intellectual and social signifi-cance, an 'inter-action' that might indeed guide us in becoming, but an 'inter-action' very much in need of voice.

And how might we characterize our 'inter-action' with Mother Earth? To begin to put words to that relationship I decided to survey the recreational gardener, a site of 'inter-action' seemingly irrelevant to the study of entrepre-neurial activity but, in fact, an untapped source of important extant knowledge. In brief, I canvassed a dozen women about what gardening means to them. Two respondents succinctly encapsulated many of the group's sentiments. Sheilagh, a retired banker, said:

> *I read somewhere that 'with a garden there is always hope' and I think that says it all for me. Serenity, creativity, nurturing and a closeness to a higher power are not the reasons I began to garden but they are the reasons I continue* (Fertile, 2004).

Wendy, a lawyer, said:

> *It's a good excuse to spend hours outside, listening to the birds, squirrels, bees . . . Gardening forces me to be patient. I like the fact that the outcome of my efforts is partially dependent on forces outside my control (I hate this in any other aspect of my life). I like best the surprises. It's the process not the results that I most enjoy* (Bird, 2004).

The relationship between the gardener and her garden is not one of ownership and control but of sound and silence, respect and reciprocity,[47] hard work and spiritual healing. This ancient and paradoxical behaviour has no voice in mainstream economic or entrepreneurial research but these insights are urgently needed as we seek new ways to look at the problems of our world.

Faced with an 'ingenuity gap . . . between our ever more difficult problems and our lagging ability to solve them' we need to look at our situation '. . . in a multitude of ways – analytically, empirically, emotionally, and spiritually' (Homer-Dixon, 2001, p. 2), seeking out all possible sources of innovation as well as respecting 'ideas that though not fundamentally novel are nonetheless useful' (Homer-Dixon, 2001, p. 21). Finding our way will be made easier if we could temper societal adulation of the heroic and adopt a more egalitarian view of entrepreneurial potentiality, an approach Chris Steyaert (2004) calls 'the prosaics of entrepreneurship'. 'A prosaics acknowledges the importance of the everyday and the ordinary, the familiar and the frequent, the customary and the accustomed, the mediocre and the inferior, in short, the prosaic' (Steyaert, 2004, p. 9). Combining a 'prosaics of entrepreneurship' with a belief that 'creativity is . . . not an exceptional condition but an everyday occurrence' (Steyaert, 2004, p. 13) will help us to re-member the entrepreneurial community to embrace all possible sources and types of creativity. The stories of Thuli, Catharine and Anne are indeed prosaic but nonetheless illuminating. And, remarkably, their experiences share many commonalities despite the differences in their backgrounds.

Using research methodologies sympathetic to emerging research topics (Hjorth, 2004), this chapter looks at three women who come from different cultures, different eras and different economic systems. Rejecting the strictures of objectivity and random sampling (Vickers, 1989) and adopting a stance of 'conscious partiality . . . partial identification with the research objects' (Mies, 1993a, p. 38), I have chosen women whose stories, in turn, draw attention to the physical/survival (Thuli), mental/spiritual (Catharine), and communal/relational (Anne) elements of entrepreneurial self-creation. Ecofeminist Judith Plant would call these 'stories of place', 'stories of women who have made contributions to social change movements . . . [and] progress towards truly sustainable human community' (Plant, 1997, p. 134). These 'stories of place' are unique in their particulars but each of the women profiled shares a common bond with the land. Thuli tells us how she gardens to feed herself, her children and her grandchildren. We learn how Catharine nurtured her mind and spirit by writing about the plants she found in an often hostile new country. And finally, we meet Anne, a modern eco-businesswoman. She runs a successful gardening business but she does so with considered attention for the land and for the well-being of her family, her employees and her customers, thereby nurturing a complex web of relationships necessary for a healthy community.

I admire these women and am in awe of what they have accomplished, but telling their stories is not easy. Denied the authority and opportunity to craft publicly legitimated inspirational female heroines, women writers have struggled with the art of representation, resulting in unusual and oblique forms in many genres (Lerner, 1986, 1993; Heilbrun, 1988). Women's story-telling is

often situated in daily, lived experience, with limited attention to the articulation of grand, hegemonic ideas and theories, paralleling attributes found in
'genealogic storytelling' (Hjorth, 2004).[48] To honour the tenets of standpoint
feminism (Smith, 1979) these stories begin with biographical details to
provide some context for each woman's respective experiences; then,
extended verbatim reporting is used to try to capture each distinctive voice.
The data for Thuli and Anne have been abstracted from transcripts of lengthy,
open-ended interviews while Catharine's story fragments were chosen from a
volume of her personal correspondence.

In all cases, the women speak in their own words. Narrative synopses
attempt to fill the gaps but, inevitably, the stories will still be incomplete. As
well, by selecting them and 'inter-acting' with them, I become 'part of the
story' (Hosking and Hjorth, 2004, p. 265) evoking possible concerns about the
impartiality and trustworthiness of the data. This weakness inherent to qualitative research is not easily overcome, particularly as this study focuses on the
positive/commendable aspects of each respective life for the purpose of drawing out that which is possible/desirable and does not attempt to be a complete
and objective record. The justification is pedagogic. These are medicine
stories with lessons about healing (Orenstein, 1990, p. 286) – healing the self,
healing others and healing the community. These are stories about the work we
all need to be doing in order to heal the world. Living at the margins of their
economic and intellectual systems, these women offer perspectives which
could add richness and diversity to entrepreneurship theory (Campbell, 2004).

To bring together stories that span the Atlantic Ocean and over two hundred
years of human history, I propose a quilting analogy (Campbell, 2004), the
sewing together of distinctive pieces/stories into a creative whole. The quilting analogy invites the reader to experience these lives through sight and
touch, to see and feel their vibrant/colourful textures, to feel their warmth, to
value their individuality and, at the same time, to appreciate the common
threads of their juxtaposed lives. To stimulate the auditory senses, I propose an
additional analogy – jazz improvisation. Jennifer Coates, feminist ethnogra-
pher and socio-linguist, describes the construction of talk among women
friends as 'a kind of jam session . . . [where] all participants share in the
construction of talk in the strong sense that *they don't function as individual
speakers* . . . the group takes priority over the individual and the women's
voices combine (or meld) to construct a shared text' (Coates, 1996, p. 117,
emphasis in original). The attributes of such talk include collaboration, turn-
taking, minimal responses, partial utterances, non-competitive overlapping
comments, and lots of laughter (Coates, 1996, pp. 117–151). Obviously, the
women in this study did not talk to each other but I believe that they each
speak as if they were part of a 'jam session' and that their words are best
understood as part of a 'shared text'. The contributions of every speaker are

uniquely valued and their collective endeavour 'permits a more multilayered development of topics . . . [referred to in classical music as] polyphony . . . where two or more different but mutually reinforcing things are said at the same time' (Coates, 1996, p. 133).

Thuli is the first voice in this polyphonic, 'shared text'.[49] Research for this story was conducted when Botswana was still seen as an exemplar of entre-preneurial possibility in sub-Saharan Africa. Additionally, the !Kung-San of the Kalahari desert had attracted considerable research attention as a 'matrifo-cal hunting gathering society that has lasted into the twentieth century' (Ruether, 1994, p. 159). It seemed an ideal site to study women entrepreneurs. I went to Botswana ostensibly to review field notes with my research assistant Antoinette Ratang Dijeng but, thanks to Thuli and the other women we inter-viewed, I learned to view my own farming ancestors with respect as entrepre-neurial, pioneering settlers in rural Ontario. Up until that time, I had self-reported my heritage as farming rather than entrepreneurial. I also had to confront my limited Western notions of progress in the presence of a viable subsistence life.

NURTURING THE BODY THROUGH 'PRUDENT SUBSISTENCE' IN THE INFORMAL ECONOMY OF BOTSWANA

Thuli lives in Serowe, Botswana. She is fifty-four years old, a mother of three girls, a step-mother to three sons and a grandmother of four. She cares for two of her grandchildren because their mother lives and works in the capital city of Gaborone. Her husband died in 1974. Her home is a mud and cow-manure rondavel. She has three years of education and expresses deep disappointment that she was prevented from obtaining further schooling: '*I was ill but later on when I wanted to proceed they refused to accept me. I loved school and it always bothered me that I did not continue.*' For the past eight years, Thuli has had a garden in her yard, growing and selling fruits and vegetables. '*Most of my customers are women*' and they compliment her gardening skills: '*They always remark that trees grow better in my yard.*' Botswana has near-desert conditions and, at the time of the interview, the country was just beginning to recover from the effects of a seven-year drought. Thuli investigated the requirements for obtaining her own water tap and had accumulated the neces-sary 250 pulas (one pula being worth about 50 Canadian cents) but, when there were delays, she was unable to hold the money in reserve. Three years ago she opened a *semausu* (a convenience store) in an adjacent hut; there are no local competitors. Thuli paid one pula for a business license to operate the *semausu* and she is eligible for that license because she '*did not have a formal job*'.[50]

Thuli routinely manages her finances through barter. Local school children carry water for her garden from a communal borehole and she pays them with produce. She 'purchases' manure deliveries with fruit trees as payment. Thuli is frustrated that the lack of money is inhibiting her business and that her usual resourcefulness is no longer sufficient. '*I do not know what my limitations are – maybe money. If it was something I could fetch and find then I could look for it. I wanted to fix my hedge. I cannot do it because I do not have the money.*' Thuli's garden is a source of business revenue but, more importantly, it provides food for personal consumption. '*Last year I did not have to buy anything. I just ate from the garden.*'[51]

As head of her household[52] Thuli is aware of disadvantages faced by Botswana women farmers: '*You know men plant in larger areas but we do it at home*'. As well, draught animals are crucial to farming the larger plots of land but 'women from female-headed households [are] less likely to have timely access to draught power obtained through the traditional systems of loaning cattle (*mafisa*)' (Cownie, 1991, p. 12). No access to transportation further limits her business; '*If I had a vehicle I would use it to get some good soil for my fruit trees*'.

Thuli is optimistic about the future – '*I am improving and I have some money these days*' – but she frames her future plans in the long-term context of her death. '*It is my interest, that, before I die, things will get better.*' She is cautious. '*I have no time limit. It is better to be patient and slowly achieve your goals.*' She strategizes about improvements to her garden – '*I want my business to be bigger and also offer more products*' – and her *semausu* – '*I would like to make homemade jams out of those fruits. I mean marmalade jams. I am going to talk to this other lady to show me how I can make that jam.*'

She takes pride in her independence. '*I plan my days and do exactly what I have planned . . . I never worked. I work for myself. I choose to do something and I do that for the whole day . . . I like doing things for myself. I am strong.*' She scoffs at the notion that the Headman might be helpful. '*The chief has no interest in what we are doing.*' She also prides herself in being a hard worker. When asked about how much time she spends in relaxation, she declares, '*I do not relax even if there is no gardening. I would rather renovate my hut.*' She continues in the traditional migratory lifestyle, travelling from her garden to the lands to plough in January and February and back again in June for harvesting. '*At the lands, I knit a little, not too much. It is difficult to do that because life is hard there.*'

There is no direct Setswana word for success. When asked about her business goals, she says, '*I would like to improve my living standard by selling and eating well. My business provides me with good food. I get dignity from my good health and my children included. When my children eat well and people see us healthy that is very pleasing indeed.*' When asked about her personal goals she gives essentially the same answer. '*I would like my life to be better, to eat well together with my family.*'

The second story is about Catharine Parr Traill, who, many years ago, immigrated to Canada in search of a more secure life for herself and her family. Consistently cheerful in the face of severe hardship, she seemed to draw strength and an indefatigable *joie de vivre* from the land. Today Catharine is regarded as a national literary icon, proof that European settlers could not only survive in the harsh Canadian climate but could also lead productive intellectual lives.

NURTURING AN ECOLOGICAL MIND IN THE BACKWOODS OF ONTARIO – THE STORY OF CATHARINE PARR TRAILL

Catharine Parr Traill was born in London, England in 1802 into an erudite but impoverished family of six girls and two boys. Writing was one of the few occupations approved for women of her class and, by 1825, Catharine had published numerous children's books. At the advanced age of 30 years, she married widower Thomas Traill, a retired and half-pay officer of the Royal Scottish Fusiliers, who was 'encumbered with debts, teenage children and a morose temperament' (Gray, 1999, p. 46). Pressed by their limited prospects in England, Thomas and Catharine immediately set sail for Canada to claim Lieutenant Traill's free grant of land. In regular missives to family and friends,[53] Catharine glossed over the difficulties they encountered and even before their first log cabin was built, she had begun to collect plant specimens: '*I am never weary with strolling about, climbing the hills in every direction, to catch some new prospect or gather some new flowers, which, though getting late in the summer, are still abundant*' [Peterborough, September 11, 1832] (Traill, [1836] 1966, p. 41). This was no idle dalliance with pretty things; Catharine was an avid naturalist and scrupulously collected, documented and published details of Canadian plants and trees. During her lifetime, Catharine's considerable knowledge was not recognized by the scientific community and she, therefore, took special delight in the power to name new plant discoveries: '*I am glad to discover the Canadian or even the Indian names if I can, and when they fail I consider myself free to become their floral godmother, and give them names of my own choosing*' [April 18, 1833] (Traill, [1836] 1966, pp. 53, 61).

By 1839, with their financial affairs steadily worsening, the Traills gave up their first farm and moved to the town of Peterborough, where Catharine turned her hand to a number of business ventures. The economy of the region was neither well established nor fully monetized, forcing its citizens to depend on barter and self-provisioning. Catharine struggled to acquire the things her family needed and she was never appropriately compensated for her work, but each small sum helped her beleaguered family. 'She started a small school, and she also began to act as the local nurse and midwife, relying heavily on the herbal remedies on which she was already an expert' (Gray, 1999, p. 175). But Nature study remained her passion. In 1857, when their log house caught fire and burned to the ground, Catharine saved nothing but 'a half-finished manuscript on plants' (Gray, 1999, p. 288). Over the years, she used her considerable literary and scientific skills to write extensively about her newfound Canadian landscape, always with the general reader in mind. She was determined to offer useful information, particularly for women who might, like her, emigrate to this strange new land.

Catharine sensed that men set themselves against nature. On November 1833, she commented on '*the total absence of trees about the dwelling-houses and cleared lands* . . . [and opined that] *Man appears to contend with the trees of the forest as though they were his most obnoxious enemies; for he spares neither the young saplings in its greenness nor the ancient trunk in its lofty pride; he wages war against the forest with fire and steel*' (Traill, [1836] 1966, p. 71). She, on the other hand, aligned herself with her natural environment. Although surrounded by seemingly endless forest, she tried to limit the damage caused by the '*choppers*' and worried that, '[s]*ome years hence the timbers that are now burned will be regretted*' (Traill, [1836] 1966, p. 106]. 'In 1852, she protested to the editor of the *Genesee Farmer* that in the rush to clear land, stock greenhouses and cultivate annuals for gardens, indigenous forest plants were disappearing' (Gray, 1999, p. 290) thereby qualifying her as Canada's premiere ecofeminist.

Catharine's correspondence contained prim religious sentiments typical of the era: '*It is a study that tends to refine and purify the mind, and can be made, by simple steps, a ladder to heaven* . . . *to look with love and admiration to that bountiful God who created and made flowers so fair to adorn and fructify this earth*' (Traill, [1836] 1966, p. 92). However, when alone in the bush, she lived by a code of stalwart self-reliance and hard work. Determined to be brave for the sake of her nine children and her emotionally fragile husband, she never admitted defeat to her family back home. '*I must say, for all its roughness, I love Canada, and am as happy in my humble log-house as if it were courtly hall or bower*' (Traill, [1836] 1966, p. 114). Beneath this saccharine cheerfulness lay an unshakeable practicality that bolstered the family's circumstances through innumerable misfortunes.

Catharine invoked the power of the garden to draw women together to share whatever bounty they had; '*If you have more than a sufficiency for yourself, do not begrudge a friend a share of your superfluous garden seeds*' (Traill 1855, quoted in Bennett 1991, p. 86). Her herbal expertise was gleaned from the local Aboriginal women with whom she had a respectful relationship (Cole, 1975, p. 75). Widowed in 1859, Catharine maintained a close association with her sister Susanna and a large circle of female friends and relatives. Assisted by her oldest daughter Kate, she continued her writing and gardening until her death in 1899. It was during this latter period of comparative security that Catharine completed her most important botanical writing, works that she thought of as a legacy for her grandchildren. '*I wished to leave something myself for my grandchildren as I have neither gold nor silver nor any personal property to leave*' (Traill, quoted in Gray 1999, p. 339). The legacy she left all Canadians is remembered annually during a literary festival hosted by her home town of Lakefield.

In diverse but significant ways, Thuli and Catharine were both alienated from the capitalist system of ownership (Cohen, 1988), a common plight for women around the world even today. It was well into the twentieth century before Canadian women could legally own land and conduct business in their own name and Anne, who owns and operates Anne's Perennials a thriving garden center, is the beneficiary of that emancipatory legislation. I have known Anne for four years. Her business start-up is a classic blend of necessity and opportunity entrepreneurship. She is full of delightful contradictions. She has a grade-ten education and, for eight years, has run a successful business in a high-risk and increasingly competitive industry. She is boisterous and shy, irreverent and caring. She describes herself as 'laid-back' but works herself to the point of exhaustion. She has a wonderful, infectious laugh. Interviewing her was an adventure.[54]

WOMEN GARDENERS AND BUSINESS OF BUILDING COMMUNITY – 'ANNE'S PERENNIALS'

'Anne's Perennials' opened in 1996. Anne had been '*out of work for quite some time and . . . was trying to figure out what to do*'. She was pessimistic about her employment prospects, '*I am over forty and really nobody wanted me*', she said with a boisterous laugh. She '*wanted to do something that* [she] *really enjoyed*'. '*My husband [Jim] and I were always bigtime into gardening*' and, one evening, their favourite business show on television ran a feature on business opportunities in the gardening industry. Interest, need and opportunity coalesced into an idea '*to grow flowers from seed and sell them at the side of the driveshed* [barn]'. They started out with '*three rows of pallets . . . a little wooden sign on the road out there and people just started coming . . . It went from a hobby into a little business and it just kept growing and growing.*'

Anne's business/life philosophy is pragmatic: '*I just believe that the world is not a perfect place'*; yet she remains joyful about her work: *'I really enjoy it, I enjoy the people and I enjoy being outside . . . you're surrounded by beautiful things, so if that doesn't make you feel good then what does?'* She has a very tolerant, non-competitive life-view. With obvious distress, she talked about the impact 'Anne's' had on another woman's garden business, *'when I started this up I didn't even know she was over there . . . I put a dint in* [her] *business . . . but I never intentionally set out to'*. Anne is pleased that the woman is now doing *'freelance gardening'* and regularly purchases gardening materials from her *'and gets them on a real deal'*.

Anne eloquently defines success. *'Success in business means different things to different people . . . yes, if you're making a profit at the end of the year, you're successful . . . but I also think that if people enjoy coming to your place of business, if they really enjoy being there, doing business with you . . . I think that's being successful . . . you know when people say good things about you that's being successful.'* Her business is more than a business; it is a destination, a place. *'People that come here to look at the plants, it's like a totally different world, a different atmosphere . . . when we put up the lathe house . . . people would stay longer . . . just wandering like they don't even want to leave.'* Customers are even welcome to walk through her personal garden. Her rural location is a particular advantage, *'you couldn't have this in the city . . . this sort of space . . . when people come out here they are looking to get away from the hustle and bustle'*. Success is also linked to the fostering of long-term personal relationships: *'I like to see the people come in year after year, you know, the familiar faces, talking and laughing'*.

Laughter is a significant ingredient in Anne's personality. She has a wonderful laugh and I was not surprised to hear her say that *'all we do here is laugh'*. The identification of a strong female work-culture was a further, complementary insight.[55] *'*[T]*here is a lot of camaraderie going on around here when it comes to the women . . . I really look forward to when we start transplanting . . . when we are in the greenhouse and there are no customers around that's when we have our most fun . . . with the girls it's just a laugh a minute.'*

Anne does not express any overtly feminist views. In fact, she is uncomfortable when she acknowledged that most of her employees are women, *'this sounds terrible but . . . men do the grunt work* [because] *women are more well versed in the fine art of gardening . . . the women are more meticulous . . . they will do a much better job than the guys'*.

She relates to her business in a physical and sensual manner, valuing its seasonality – *'the adventure every spring . . . waiting for* [the perennials] *to come up through the soil'* and the *'peace and quiet'* of fall and winter. She revels in the physical labour, *'it's not like sitting in an office . . . you're out there in the mud . . . a lot of digging in the dirt . . . and the black flies!*

[laughs]'. For her, even weeding is relaxing; '*It would be raining but it would be on a warm day and I'd be out in the rain pulling weeds and the girls would be looking at me like I was nuts . . . and I was enjoying it so much* [thoughtful tone]'.

When asked about her future plans, Anne first gives a textbook strategic analysis: '*I've only got about five acres . . . we can't do much more expanding . . . we were thinking about putting a gift shop into the upstairs of the barn*'. Then her focus shifts to a practical assessment of their physical stamina; '*I don't know . . . because I'm 54 now and Jim's 58 . . . so you have to think about how long can you keep this pace up [sigh]*'. Later, in a moment reflective of her Scottish ancestry, she talks about dying '*in the gloaming*'. '*One day I was sitting out here in a lawn chair and the sun was going down and it was such a warm day and I said, "this is where I would like to die, sitting with the sun going down, in a chair in the garden"*.' Perhaps you need to be both Scottish and a gardener to fully appreciate that wish. Never one to be gloomy, she quickly jokes that, instead of her ideal death, she would '*probably drop dead out there in the lathe house and one of my customers will come in and find me and come* [screaming] *up to the house, "Anne's dead out there"*.' She then laughed as only Anne can.

The garden is a special place for her. She talks about it as '*a sanctuary . . . a get-away . . . an escape . . . an open space* [of] *peace and quiet . . . a form of relaxation*'. Her daughter worries that the business keeps Anne too much at home and is too '*confining*' but Anne thinks that '*it's just a little bit of heaven*'. Although not given to philosophical reflection, she thoughtfully inverted the causality of my question, 'are people who garden happy people?' She looked at me rather warily and, after a long pause said, '*that's really a loaded question because I think you're happy when you're in the garden, I think a garden is like a place where you can get away from it all*'. With simple words, she instinctively valorizes the healing power of the garden.

READING THESE STORIES AS 'SHARED TEXT'

Feminist story-telling radically challenges the conventional researcher-subject-reader relationship. The 'subject' is recognized as the expert who shares her knowledge with the researcher; the concepts and the words belong to the 'subject' and are not appropriated or altered unilaterally by the researcher. And the reader is not viewed as a passive recipient of expert knowledge. 'If one person's theorizing is sound and correct enough to be useful to another, the other still has to make use of her own knowledge to transpose and interpret it, to adapt it to the details of her own life and circumstances, to make it her own' (Frye, 1983, p. xiv). Lengthy verbatim extracts encourage the reader to respond to the data at a personal level, both intellectually and emotionally. Thus, feminists encourage the writing of research outcomes in a manner that is accessible to the lay reader. The roles and responsibilities of researcher, 'subject' and reader are thereby reconceptualized as a nuanced, non-hierarchical alliance. There is, however, a difference of opinion among feminist scholars as to the desired/target audience for feminist research. For example, liberal feminists are keen to educate men into an appreciation of gender equity and tend to write for a male audience. Radical and social feminists believe that women's first priority is to 'speak profoundly to one another' (Heilbrun, 1988, p. 43). Ecofeminists, the group with whom I affiliate my thinking, are the most ecumenical, arguing that women and men alike need to be more respectful of Mother Earth.

Mindful of the intent of feminist research, I will nonetheless point out some of the common threads emerging from this 'shared text', as the reader is disadvantaged by having access to only a selected number of interview/correspondence fragments. In such a circumstance, the researcher must assume a more proactive interpretive role. In keeping with the jazz improvisation analogy, the individual threads, while often not identical, reflect and modify each other. The values, attributes and attendant behaviours are not necessarily unique to grounded entrepreneurial work but they are central to the life experiences reported here. Further data collection or the critical reassessment of already collected data may confirm or refute the definitive validity of these threads.

Multifaceted, Meaningful Work

For all three women, their work is, simultaneously, a means to honour Mother Earth and an opportunity to provide for the present and future needs of their families. More than simply capitalist asset acquisition and revenue generation, 'gardening' with Mother Earth is conducted within an ethical/religious/values-based context. A grounded enterprise is both a space and a place where these women become, accessing an opportunity that has been lost for many workers in industrial societies. Localization and re-ruralization initiatives could, according to their proponents, 'strengthen and diversify economies at both the community and national levels' (Norberg-Hodge, 1996, p. 394; Mies and Shiva, 1993). More urgently, reuniting with the land could bring spiritual/ psychological relief to alienated workers.

The Healing Power of Physical Work

Working on the land fosters the holistic interdependence of body, mind and spirit such that hierarchical distinctions between body work and mind work are muted. Through strenuous physical labour Thuli, Catharine and Anne all experienced the healing power of Mother Earth and were justifiably proud of their accomplishments; yet those accomplishments would typically be deemed life-style businesses and not worthy of an entrepreneurial designation. As entrepreneurship theory shifts towards valorization of mind work, our theoretical frameworks are weakened and we lose sight of essential, meaningful enterprise. These stories are cautionary tales, reminding us of important human experiences.

Reconceptualized Time

Earth time has a rhythm that supersedes the unnatural constraints of quarterly/annual business cycles. On the land, seasons/years are recognized as benchmarks, marking patterns, but working the land is a continuously regenerative process. Death is not an ending but a transition point. While the agendas of the Enlightenment, modernism and postmodernism embrace a naive desire to decouple life and death, Mother Earth teaches that life and death are one and inseparable, an insight that Hjorth and Steyaert astutely observe to be endemic to the entrepreneurial process in which 'creativity and pathology are inevitably interwoven' (Hjorth and Steyaert, 2003, p. 300). In the garden, death is not a taboo subject. Reflecting upon their life's work, Thuli and Catharine envisaged a multigenerational timeline in which their children and grandchildren would benefit from their hard work. For Anne, her garden is an ideal place to die; she knows that new life will appear with the changing of the seasons.

Non-monetary Success

In subsistence and imperfectly monetized economies, success equals the physical survival of oneself and one's family. For Thuli and Catharine, hard work and pride in a job well done are proxy phrases for success. In a harsh environment, measurement against effort expended, rather than outcomes achieved, establishes pragmatic goals within the individual's control. These goals align with what organizational behaviourists call intrinsic rewards. Reciprocity and altruism replace individualistic consumption, not as an assertion of moral superiority, but as consistent with the realities of the work situation. Working in a monetized economy Anne must meet necessary financial standards in order to stay in business; however, she does not set profit as her personal measure of success. Instead, she defines success as the creation of a peaceful destination and the building of long-term relationships with her customers.

Power Through Female Support Systems

Denied public influence by androcentric systems of ownership and economic control, Thuli and Catharine cultivated supportive relationships with women in their respective communities. As they engaged in cooperative endeavours they enacted power as a shared, collective resource, which enhanced prospects for group survival. With comparatively better legal rights and greater economic security, Anne was still uncomfortable with the notion of power over others. She talked about a relaxed work environment with her female employees; for her cooperation, even with a competitor, was a preferred strategy. When power is shared it empowers everyone and it can transform a community.

Building Relationships and Community

Unlike industrial production or knowledge work, grounded work – work that occurs with and for the land – is axiomatically concerned with space and place. Grounded entrepreneurial activity becomes a mutually beneficial inter-action between and among individuals as they collectively create meaning for themselves and for their community. In Thuli's village, these transactions were non-monetary; she needed the help of young neighbourhood children to manage her garden; in turn, the children earned food, a win–win exchange. Superficially, Anne's relationship with her customers is a profit-creating economic value exchange and, as her business prospers, she contributes to a stronger local economy. However, she works hard to transform her space into place. She offers her customers a destination, a place of quiet and beauty and reflection; she encourages them to linger and is rewarded by the camaraderie and affection offered in return. As most of her customers are women, Anne is informally nurturing a vibrant, although transient, female community. Spoken of with affection within the gardening community, Anne does not have a pres-ence in the local business community.

About Strong Women

With limited public support, Thuli and Catharine and Anne succeeded in their chosen endeavors, exhibiting along the way strength and courage and patience and insight. But, because historians have not attended to our entrepreneurial foremothers (Bird, 1968; Lerner, 1986) and because entrepreneurship theories focus very narrowly on selected forms of enterprise, we are unaccustomed to reading about strong women[56] who engage in the essential, everyday business of living. Our collective entrepreneurial record needs reconstruction.

WE NEED MORE STORIES ABOUT ENTREPRENEURIAL, SELF-CREATING WOMEN

The merits of narrative and discourse analysis in organization and entrepreneurship studies have garnered extended consideration but it is worth noting that stories are particularly helpful in thinking about women's entrepreneurial activities. Stories are a vital, first-round strategy to recover women into economic history and render our accomplishments formally visible to ourselves and to the world. Stories are, by definition, idiosyncratic; they insist on the value of the particular, the individual woman; good stories do indeed have some universal applicability but they cannot easily be appropriated/distorted into hegemonic theory. Stories can be trusted for exactly what they are, partial representations of something and/or someone that feels familiar. And like a memory fragment or a familiar tune they evoke an emotional response that heightens our sense of connection and communion with others. Stories do not tell us how to live but they can tell us how others, like ourselves, have dealt with the important business of living. Stories offer comfort. They reposition our own experiences within a wider context. They render the impossible possible. They exhort. They caution. They entertain. They inspire.

Thuli tells us about surviving under difficult circumstances and about being driven to make a better life for her children and grandchildren. She comes from a long, unbroken line of subsistence farmers and, as did her ancestors, Thuli lives *from the land*. Through her, we are reminded of our own roots in the land. We are the sum of our collective human experience and we forget that at our peril. Catharine began with a very gentrified view of nature and, when faced with physical and financial privation, she and her husband were unable to support themselves by farming. However, Catharine was continuously engaged *with the land* through her botanical studies; she fully accepted that Mother Earth was neither benign nor blindly vengeful. She saw her surroundings as an unbounded classroom offering a lifetime of learning and delight. Anne's story is not so readily parsed/dissected. Like the other women, she lives *from the land* and is continuously involved *with the land* but it is much too easy to see only her successful business enterprise. Anne's gift to us is the reminder to look beyond the obvious, to seek out the complex, multifaceted dynamics of entrepreneurial self-creation and not just the superficial, instrumental business activities, the subject of most current economic and entrepreneurship research. Body, mind and community – each woman, in turn, illuminates a possible self-creating, entrepreneurial relationship/'inter-action' which we can have with Mother Earth. Theorizing that more complex entrepreneurial activity is ongoing, with a number of promising initiatives; and three theoretical frames – ecofeminism, bioregionalism, and a survival subsistence perspective – are each briefly discussed.

Thoughts on the Ecofeminist Movement

Many business and economic theories applaud the entrepreneur who is driven to consume any and all available resources in the pursuit of immediate, personal monetary gain and who, therefore, shows limited regard for long-term collective well-being. Women and nature have been indiscriminately exploited in this system of domination (Ortner, 1974). To overcome this misogynist and narrowly materialistic ideology, the scholarly/activist movement known as ecofeminism invites a radical reconstruction of entrepreneurship through a multi-disciplinary investigation of the context, motives, processes, agents, beneficiaries and victims of present and future economic activity. 'An ecofeminist perspective propounds the need for a new cosmology and a new anthropology which recognizes that life in nature (which includes human beings) is maintained by means of co-operation, and mutual care and love' (Mies and Shiva, 1993, p. 6). With an 'emphasis on spirituality . . . [and] the rediscovery of the sacredness of life (Mies and Shiva, 1993, p. 17), ecofeminism 'locates production and consumption within the context of regeneration' (Shiva, 1993, p. 33).

Ynestra King has characterized ecofeminism as 'the third wave of the women's movement . . . [following on] the first-wave nineteenth-century women's movement and the second-wave women's liberation movement of the 1960s and 1970s' (quoted in Sturgeon, 1997, p. 260). That genealogy affirms women's extended commitment to social change, with ecofeminism our most revolutionary initiative to date. 'The term *ecofeminisme* was coined by the French writer Francoise d'Eaubonne in 1974 to represent women's potential for bringing about an ecological revolution to ensure human survival on the planet. Such an ecological revolution would entail new gender relations between women and men and between humans and nature' (Merchant, 1990, p. 100). Initially, the ecofeminist alliance brought together 'feminism, indigenous knowledge and appropriate science, development and technology' (Wells and Wirth, 1997, p. 304) in a direct challenge to the tenets of neoclassical economics, a discipline that has persistently ignored the economic contributions of women (Boserup, [1960] 1989; Waring, 1990; Nelson, 1996) and has insisted on the legitimacy of economic models devoid of values, emotions and spirituality. As work in the field has progressed the women and men who identify with ecofeminism have embraced an ever-larger roster of issues, including 'feminism, environmentalism, antiracism, animal rights, anti-imperialism, antimilitarism, and non-traditional spiritualities' (Sturgeon, 1997, p. 263). The enlarged mandate recognizes that all forms of oppression are inextricably intertwined and, therefore, seeks inclusivity and redress for all oppressed groups.

With a multi-disciplinary perspective and an inclusive spectrum of participants, ecofeminism promotes respect and harmony amongst peoples and with

Mother Earth. 'If we look upon ecofeminist literature as medicine stories, we can understand that its function is to teach us lessons about healing. These stories illustrate ways in which we can reconnect with the sources of our powers of transformation' (Orenstein, 1990, p. 286). For example, Catharine's story illustrates how women can achieve power in unexpected and positive ways, in a manner consonant with the feminist ideal of '*transforming* power . . . [as] the truly significant and essential power . . . not *power over others*' (Rich, 1986, p. 99). She did not consciously chose a life of social activism yet has exerted significant influence. Through her love for the land, Catharine was able to keep her family together and eventually to achieve a measure of personal acclaim. Her work was powerful enough to compel respect from the literary and publishing communities in Canada and Britain. By teaching the poor and inexperienced working class immigrants how to survive in the bush, she inadvertently helped to undermine the class system in which she had been raised. Ecofeminists strive 'not just to change who wields power, but to transform the structure of power itself' (Starhawk, 1990, p. 76) in order to affect a 'social reordering' (Ruether, 1994, p. 2). Born before the label was invented, Catharine was nonetheless an ecofeminist.

Bioregionalism

Bioregionalism dramatically reframes the entrepreneurial process, shifting the perspective away from humans as the pivotal agents of change towards Mother Earth, the non-human partner/agent, and towards an ecosystems[57] orientation. 'Bioregionalism calls for human society to be more closely related to nature (hence 'bio') and to be more conscious of its locale, or regions, or life-places (thus 'bioregion') . . . It is a proposal to ground human cultures within natural systems, to get to know one's place intimately in order to fit human communities to the earth, not distort the earth to our demands' (Plant, 1997, p. 132). Bioregionalism thus encourages a micro, embedded, local perspective.

Key to the success of a bioregional initiative is a change in attitude. 'Becoming native to a place – learning to live in it on a sustainable basis over time – is not just a matter of appropriate technology, home-grown food, or even "reinhabiting" the city. It has very much to do with a shift in morality, in the attitudes and behaviors of human beings' (Plant, 1990, pp. 158–159). To the new mind-set of bioregional development women bring proven expert knowledge that is 'relational', 'inherently collaborative', 'transparently situated', and 'temporal' (Curtin, 1997, p. 90). With its goal of healthy communities, bioregionalism is a powerful tool to turn space into place and to direct entrepreneurial energies in a life-affirming manner. Blissfully unaware of these concepts, Anne's approach to her business, her employees and her community of customers and neighbours is helping to build a number of healthy communities. As mentioned above, community building is occurring at the economic level and also among female gardeners. The bioregional construct brings into focus a third community which is benefiting from her business – the rural economy, which is being regenerated through the employment of local workers and the inflow of revenues from city customers. Anne believes that her rural location gives her business a competitive advantage and, in return, her business is helping to strengthen the rural community. Bioregionalism is successful when relationships create reciprocal benefits.

A Survival Subsistence Perspective

Ecofeminism and bioregionalism are initiatives that are principally drawn from and designed for Western societies. Building upon and radically adapting these philosophies, Maria Mies and Vandana Shiva (1993) look around the world and address the concerns of billions of people living in survival subsistence circumstances. Deeply critical of the capitalist commodity market, they work to help people 'regain self-reliance and subsistence security, that is, to become ecologically, socially, and economically more independent from external market forces' (Mies, 1993b, p. 312). They propose a people-oriented development that obliges entrepreneurial activity to focus on the 'creation and re-creation of *life*' (Mies, 1993b, p. 319, emphasis in original). They document projects from around the world and compile a dossier of principles to guide a subsistence economy that respects and sustains the individual and sets the health of the human community ahead of profit. Maria Mies (1993b) delineates the following key principles of the survival subsistence perspective:

- 'self-reliance, self-provisioning, food self-sufficiency, regionality, the need for re-ruralization, participatory democracy, inter-regional co-operation' (p. 302)
- 'autonomous [community] control of the subsistence base . . . the land, water, forests, hills . . .' (p. 303)
- 'a paradigm of science, technology and knowledge that uses grass-roots, women and people-based knowledge to achieve greater social justice . . . using locally based ecologically sustainable alternatives' (p. 320)
- 'the reintegration of culture and work as both burden and pleasure, along with a reintegration of spirit and matter' (p. 320)

Maria Mies and Vandana Shiva are advocating on behalf of Thuli, who is not a quaint anachronism but is a standard-bearer for billions. With a substantive proportion of the world's population immersed in subsistence work, researchers have a responsibility to craft entrepreneurship theory and practice to reflect/respect their needs and their many contributions to society. Enacted, the principles of 'subsistence work as life-producing and life-preserving work' (Mies, 1993b, p. 297) promise a radically new economic order. These are not new ideas. As Mies points out, the development community has been promoting these principles for a long time; entrepreneurship researchers (Schumacher, 1973; Peterson, 1977; Hawken, 1987) have proposed complementary ideas but also to no avail. Why should we contemplate such radical change?

GROUNDED ENTREPRENEURSHIP – TOWARDS A SUSTAINABLE ENTREPRENEURIAL ETHIC

The 'blue planet' is in crisis. If our species is to survive, we must craft a new entrepreneurial belief system that has as its core principle the recognition of our life-sustaining dependence on Mother Earth. Egalitarianism, communalism, cooperation, patience and humility will be some of the supporting operational beliefs. Aboriginal peoples talk about 'living in a good way' by which they mean living in harmony with each other and with the land, a lifeview worth emulating. The economy is not driven by any natural/immutable laws; it is a 'man-made' belief system, carefully bolstered by legal, political, social and religious ideologies; and it can, therefore, be altered to reflect preferred values.

The current resurgence of the 1970s concept of Corporate Social Responsibility seems to suggest a renewed commitment to responsible entrepreneurship. Unfortunately, the sustainable development/ 'green' capitalism/ 'natural capitalism' (Lovins et al., 1999) movement has done little more than replace the old notion of *working against nature* with a slightly improved mantra of *working with nature* but always with the intent of protecting profits (Mies, 1993b). Only when we are *working for nature* will we have reset our priorities so that we are protecting and promoting all life as our first and most urgent entrepreneurial responsibility. If we are to survive and prosper as a species we must set the 'business of living' ahead of business for profit. And for that Journey, women gardeners can serve as expert guides. Thuli, Catharine, and Anne, individually and idiosyncratically, encourage us to think about what each of us might do and what each of us might become.

Change can, and must, begin at the micro level, at the level where we 'can understand and take responsibility for the ecosystem of which [we] are a part' (Ruether, 1994, p. 201). By encouraging praxis at the micro level, we resist the dogma of totalizing theory (Quinby, 1990) while simultaneously recognizing the potential impact of local action. And always, we need to aspire to grounded entrepreneurship, that is, enterprise that is working for the self, for the community and for Mother Earth. In a classic tale of aspiration, we are told that Icarus wanted to fly but failed when he flew too close to the sun. An ecofeminist re-interpretation of that tale suggests rather that he flew too far away from Mother Earth and lost connection with his human community. Really important changes can happen at home. In a matter-of-fact, nonpolemical style, my local newspaper recently reported that Abby, an eighteen-year old high-school student, had coordinated the donation of materials and the volunteer labour of 900 cadets over six weekends to build a butterfly garden, an edible plants garden and a memorial garden on the site of a long-term care facility for senior citizens. She saw a way to make a better future and she acted on those beliefs. What have you done for Mother Earth today?

9. The dynamics of community identity making in an industrial district: the spirit of Gnosjö revisited

Bengt Johannisson and Caroline Wigren

ROCKING A LOCAL WORLD

Entrepreneurship as economic and social value creation, through imaginative organising, is usually associated with renewal processes that are enacted by interacting individuals or corporate structures. However, local communities may accommodate entrepreneurial processes as well (Johannisson and Nilsson, 1989; Steyaert and Katz, 2004). Relating entrepreneurship to self-actualisation (Kostera, 2005) as an existential quest reveals its connections to identify formation. The launching and the absorption of challenging initiatives are not only constitutive for individual identity construction (Giddens, 1991a; Jenkins 1996), but for organisational (Eccles and Nohria, 1992) and community (Hjorth and Johannisson, 2003) identity formation as well. In spatial contexts where economic activity is deeply embedded historically and culturally and carried out by (small) family businesses, everyday social practices make individual and collective identity construction intertwine closely.

Our concern here is the need for the (re)making of a strong community identity due to a changed commercial and social context. Our focus is an 'industrial district', a concept that was coined by Marshall (1890/1922) and revived by Piore and Sabel in their seminal work *The Second Industrial Divide*, published in 1984. It has been especially elaborated on in the Italian empirical context (for example Goodman and Bamford, 1989; Pyke et al., 1990). Here we will report from the Gnosjö region, the only fully-fledged industrial district in Sweden. It is located in southern Sweden and consists of four municipalities (in addition to Gnosjö also Gislaved, Vaggeryd, and Värnamo) with 80,000 inhabitants and about 1,500 manufacturing firms altogether at the turn of the millennium. As late as the 1990s a number of conventional 'objective' criteria confirmed that the region thrived on substantial growth, whether in terms of economic wealth, high start-up frequencies in the dominant manufacturing industries (light engineering and plastics) or low unemployment. In addition, the region accommodates a high portion of immigrants, who are/have become well integrated in the labour force. At the turn of the millennium about 26 per cent of the people living in the municipality of Gnosjö were immigrants (Wigren, 2003, p. 108).

Elsewhere we have argued that Gnosjö as an entrepreneurial setting relates to the region as an organic whole, its business community amalgamating with other 'worlds' that social, cultural, and institutional textures nurture (Johannisson, 2000; Wigren, 2003). In Gnosjö entrepreneurship appears as a genuinely 'collective' phenomenon, i.e. it is associated with the very interactions between individual firms and their embedding in the socio-cultural context, as a historical construct. Accordingly, the great majority of the firms are multi-generation family businesses with modest growth ambitions. Few firms have their own strong brand creating a potential for growth (the great majority of them operate as subcontractors to larger (multi)national companies). Nevertheless, the socially embedded small-business fabric and its 'spirit' has for centuries brought prosperity and visibility to the region.

Until recently the public discourse, produced by the mass media institutions as much as by researchers, enforced and legitimated the image of the Gnosjö region as unique and successful. It was the emblem of a place where neither high-tech firms and financial capital nor highly educated managers and employees were needed to create (economic) wealth. It has also been used as a prototype for the enactment of sustainable small-family-business communities (Johannisson and Nilsson, 1989). A collective identity has thus been enacted (Hjorth and Johannisson, 1997), which has enhanced local self-confidence as well as enforced and legitimised existing practices. Accordingly, people in the Gnosjö region became more concerned with celebrating and thus reproducing historical times than with developing the self-reflexivity needed to envisage alternative futures (Spinosa et al., 1997).

Now, only half a decade after the turn of the millennium, norms and values that once guided work-related practices in the Gnosjö region have radically changed. The entry of China as a key player on the global market has amplified the already fierce competition from (East) European low-cost countries. In recent years, the start-up frequency has decreased (though turning up again in 2005), and unemployment has increased to the average Swedish level. The dominant manufacturing industry, forced to invest in more efficient production equipment, offers fewer jobs than before. Gnosjö thus seems to have lost its lead in economic achievement. Furthermore, the public discourse on growth and economic progress, as driven by formal knowledge, venture capital, and high-technology, penetrates society more pervasively than ever before. The media have quickly acknowledged and amplified the setbacks of the region into a rival image. Today they present the region as lagging because of the low level of education, a gathering need for succession in the many family businesses, and increasing external ownership. Intended successors in the local firms are neither committed to a career in the family business, nor to the local way of life (Davidsson, 1995). Academia has made its contribution to the deconstruction of Gnosjö as an ideal setting for entrepreneurial processes. Two recent doctoral theses on Gnosjö have given devastating reports on the silencing of women entrepreneurs (Pettersson, 2002, 2004) and on the region as a segregated community (Wigren, 2003).

While the public discourse has quickly furnished the Gnosjö region with an emerging new image, the local self-image and (business) practices building the strong collective identity have become an imprisoning curse. In a global world that is furnished with a knowledge economy, the logic of the industrial era still dominates the Gnosjö region. As much as corporations may become ossified by their own success (Miller, 1990), attempts to break out of this mental lock-in seems to be hindered by Gnosjö's own success story, until recently reproduced in the public discourse. The new order on the global market has created a totally different game, where the Gnosjö firms do not seem to qualify as players.

Local voices proposing an alternative future are not being listened to and radical events are not recognised as a seedbed for new initiatives, for new openings (Spinosa et al., 1997; Hjorth and Johannisson, 2003). For example, the fact that all unemployment caused by the close-down of the largest plant was absorbed by the collective local industry is not used to enhance self-confidence. There are a few who see the potential for new business, such as those local firms that deal successfully with the Chinese invasion on the world market by cooperating with Chinese firms. On one hand, these firms are not recognised as prototypes for business-owner managers in the Gnosjö region, presumably because they do not create local jobs, on the other, the contributions of externally owned firms in terms of new products, markets, and local employment are overlooked. Thus, a vicious circle is triggered, which strikes the business community with collective exhaustion and helplessness.

So, is it time to give up the supposedly invincible Spirit of Gnosjö and proclaim the community and its logic as nothing else but an anachronism, a relic from great historical times, or can its once vibrant self-organising processes be resurrected? Here we will propose an answer to this key question by 're-visiting' Gnosjö literally as well as by excursions into the different images of the region that various existing (own) texts on Gnosjö provide. Our aim is to identify countervailing forces that may reconstruct entrepreneurship and seed as well as feed social change in an industrial district under siege from both its own history and external forces. The forces that create inertia are disentangled by way of Unruh's (1979) model of 'social worlds', but we also expand his cast of 'participants' as we try to identify forces that may guide the region when trying to break out of its social and mental prison.

We will first introduce the reader to the 'Spirit of Gnosjö', which we address first as a 'master narrative' that has colonised the collective identity making process in the region. Unruh's (1979) notion of 'social worlds' – communities with shared values and norms – is introduced next as a vocabulary able to demonstrate (re)making of the Spirit of Gnosjö. Searching for more basic influences on individual and collective identity construction we then reflect upon the family as a generic value source in a community where owner-managed firms dominate. Following this, contradictions in the everyday lives of the natives as well as tensions between them and strangers as triggers for change are identified. After that, Unruh's (1979) cast of participants who inhabit social worlds is broadened by introducing the 'outsider' on the stage. The latter character acknowledges community-wide generic values and practices on the one hand, but on the other practices a divergent style. The final section provides concluding comments concerning how the Gnosjö region may regain self-organising by recasting the participation in an ongoing dialogue, within and across its spatial boundaries.

A few words have to be said about how our (re-)visit to the research field was enacted. We will first provide comments on our re-appearance in the field before and during the preparation of this chapter, and then reflect upon our re-visits in a transferred sense.[58] In a figurative sense, our re-visits can be arranged and reflected upon in different ways. These include, first, a systematic review of interactions with/in the field. Alvesson and Sköldberg (2000, p. 255) suggest four levels of interpretations in their agenda as a guide for reflexive qualitative research: empirical accounts/construction of data; interpretation; critical interpretation; and self-critical and linguistic reflection. They encourage multiplicity in interpretations and a critical view of dominating interpretations.

We argue that the composition of the research duet, the very dialogue between the two authors, provides a potent base for reflexive interpretation. For both researchers, conversations with people in the field have been close and prolonged indeed, inviting alternative interpretations of field experiences. The two authors relate in contrasting ways to the 'Spirit of Gnosjö' and its enactment, the senior one by contributing to its enactment and the junior one by explicitly challenging it. Obviously, critical interpretations have invited themselves to the authors' dialogue. Close readings of each others' research texts are supplemented with joint conversations with local subjects in order to temporally recontextualise and complete our original accounts from the field. Since as researchers we are recognised as being familiar with and committed to the region, these supplementary talks, staged in informal settings and using an everyday vocabulary, took place in, as we see it, a close and confident atmosphere.

THE MAKING OF A MASTER NARRATIVE

Organising the roles of narratives in social science research, Czarniawska (2004, pp. 3–12) proposes three perspectives as she distinguishes, in addition to narratives as directing the enactment of social life also narratives as modes of knowing and communication. As much as life stories guide personal quests (McAdams, 1993), locally shared norms make people take everyday social life for granted. 'The Spirit of Gnosjö' as imagining the region as an ideal setting not only organises people locally but has, as part of the public discourse, made sense to most grown up Swedes. Trading on the concept of 'master idea' as dealt with by Czarniawska and Joerges (1996), we address the Spirit of Gnosjö as a 'master narrative'. 'The power of master ideas resides in the fact that they are taken for granted, are unproblematic and used for all possible purposes' (1996, p. 36).

We propose the following criteria when applying the notion of a 'master narrative' to a (physical) place. *First*, a master narrative not only constitutes a local self-identity but produces a 'global' image as well. The story the master narrative tells about Gnosjö is how industriousness, close family ties and strong religious beliefs make local businesses successful. Since the imprint of the narrative is even stronger outside than inside the region (Johannisson, 1978), it (also) becomes externally controlled. This means that local identity reconstruction has to fight not only local prejudice and practices but global mental lock-ins as well. The existence of a penetrating master narrative means that the collective identity that it envelops is not enacted by but also imputed on the local people. Obviously this hampers the re-construction of a collective identity and 'block sensitivity to what is happening in local situations' (Spinosa et al., 1997, p. 33).

Second, in the public discourse a master narrative is codified as an entry in encyclopedias and reference books. In the early 1990s, the proposed life-bringing features of the Gnosjö region were stated in the *Swedish National Encyclopaedia* as follows (our translation):[59]

> The Spirit of Gnosjö is the name for the atmosphere of enterprising that prevails in the Gnosjö municipality and its neighbouring municipalities in Småland. Self-employment as a way of life dominates the region. This implies that the local authorities, banks, and trade unions adjust their behaviour to the way the businesses are operated. The region has a unique manufacturing industry and a very low level of unemployment.

At the same time the Spirit of Gnosjö was also presented in the reference book *What Every Swede Needs to Know*:[60]

> The Spirit of Gnosjö is the spirit of enterprising that has developed in the western part of Småland [including the municipalities of Gnosjö, Gislaved, Värnamo, and

Vaggeryd], the centre of one of the country's leading areas for small-scale industries. The Gnosjö owner-managers are known for their reliability and for their unconventional methods.

Third, locally as well as globally, the master narrative embraces diverse communities of practice – globally, for instance, in the business world, the political system and academia. Politicians as well as researchers are intrigued by the mode of doing business that contrasts against conventional economic thinking. The inclusion of the Spirit of Gnosjö as a special entry in the *Swedish National Encyclopaedia* itself reflects that it was proposed as an ideal to guide local and regional development. It so happens that this interpretation of the Spirit of Gnosjö is constructed out of a (face-to-face) dialogue between an insider (a local autodidact historian) and the senior author of this text (Johannisson), an (academic) visitor to the setting. Words such as helpfulness, cooperation, solidarity, personal networking, and positive rivalry and envy – reflected in the local saying 'if he (yes, he, not she) can, I can' – were then used to furnish the Spirit of Gnosjö. This labelling is apposite considering that the region is part of the Swedish 'Bible Belt', that is a larger area inhabited by many free churches.

A *fourth* feature of the master narrative, as the concept literally indicates, is that it reflects power structures. Researchers and media have primarily listened to and reproduced the voices of male family business managers, taking for granted that everyday life in the region is dominated by the practices of the male business world. Both codified entries of the Gnosjö Spirit presented above also focus on the conduct of family business owner–managers. The stories collected and interpreted by Wendeberg (1982) are mainly told by (male) business persons as well. When women are heard it is usually as wives to owner–managers. Other voices that are silenced belong to immigrants, international as well as domestic.

If this is how a master narrative is constructed, what message about the unique Gnosjö region as an industrial district does it communicate? It tells us that renewal emerges spontaneously in the business community, marking an evolutionary path rather than a revolutionary trajectory. Change is associated with interactive learning and spin-offs, collaborative as well as competitive, jointly constructing a game of *co-opetition*. Bianchi (1998) sees the industrial district as constituted by a production system, a social system, and a spatial system. The very point, though, is that they are jointly constructed and define each other, as an owner–manager reveals (Wigren, 2003, p. 92):

When I go to the kiosk to buy a newspaper, I pass by the office. Private lives and business lives are interwoven. Those managers who do not live in the community have another perspective on their private life; when they leave the community they are free. We who live here are never free. But, it is not altogether either a good or a bad thing.

The industrial district as a general phenomenon also invites academics to story-telling, using colourful language. Metaphors that are used include putting the local norms for exchange 'in the air' (Marshall, 1890/1922), turning relations into 'untraded interdependencies' (Storper, 1995) and making regions into contexts for 'learning' (Maskell and Malmberg, 1999; Gustafsson, 2004). These tropes may still tell a superficial, if not idealised, story, that in a functionalist tradition calls for substantiation (Johannisson et al., 1994). Relational accounts reporting on interconnected dyadic relationships can, as we se it, be both used for analytical comparisons between communities and as an interpretative bridge between representational data and the self-organising metaphor, as used for example by Morgan (1993) and Hjorth and Johannisson (2003). Recent research on industrial districts, however, mainly concerns the impact of the increasing dominance of major, 'well-managed', global companies that threaten the established production logic of the district and welcome the formalisation of what used to be mutual-aid services (Carbonara, 2002). The need for these changes is often 'seen' as acknowledged by researchers using a functionalistic mind-map that hides managerial ideals and a technological turn.

CASTING THE LOCAL WORLD OF BUSINESS

Business obviously has a strong impact on everyday life in the Gnosjö region. In order to come to grips with what may trigger a local review of the master narrative, we will therefore inquire into the business community as a 'social world'. According to Unruh's work, social worlds are constructed on shared norms and values, creating trust and providing guidelines for behaving and acting, thus constituting communities of practice. In order to unpack the image of Gnosjö as hosting a homogeneous business community we will, as indicated, with the help of Unruh (1979) introduce four types of participants in the regional business world: insiders, regulars, tourists, and strangers. We want to inquire into whether the different participants, and how they are constructed and how in turn they construct, nurture stability or instigate general social change in the business community.

According to Unruh (1979), an *insider* is a person who fully identifies her- or himself with the social world to which s/he belongs. If the social world dissolves, the insider will lose her/his identity. *A regular* is a person who produces and reproduces everyday life. The social world appears as a home to regulars who nurture relationships that are 'characterized by a high degree of familiarity' (1979, p. 120). *Tourists*, following Unruh, are those people who approach existing social worlds to have exotic experiences which often concern finding the 'essence' of a destination. Tourists do not stay, they move

Table 9.1 Participants in social worlds – a typology

Types of participants	Orientation	Experiences	Relationships	Commitments
Insiders	Identification with the social world	Creation of the world for others	Intimate	Recruitment of others
Regulars	Habituation	Integration into the local world	Personal	On-going practices
Tourists	Curiosity	Searching for authenticity	Transient	Entertaining encounters
Strangers	Naivety	Disorientation in the social world	Superficial and ephemeral	Detachment

Source: Unruh (1979, p. 122), Figure 1, *Characteristics and Types of Participation in Social Worlds* (modified by the authors).

on to new social worlds. *Strangers* are people who approach 'an already-established social world with an attitude of objectivity and detached indifference' (1979, p. 116). While some strangers would prefer to be included and to participate in their new social setting, that is to become a regular, others prefer to stay detached. In Table 9.1 the significant features of Unruh's (1979) different types of participants in social worlds are summarised.

Some business-owner managers are publicly recognised as *insiders* in the local business world. As indicated, they play an important role in the construction of the master narrative of Gnosjö. Some insiders are significant enough to be given the honourable title 'Mr. Gnosjö'. For reasons elaborated by Pettersson (2002, 2004) the master narrative (or 'discourse' in her terminology) allows no women to appear as 'Mrs. Gnosjö'. The 'Mr. Gnosjö' epithet came out in the 1999 local theatre play, where it was ascribed to the main character, Johan-August, who thus embodies the Spirit of Gnosjö itself. The play was written and directed by locals in cooperation with the County Theatre in Jönköping and the scriptwriter and actor Carl-Johan Seth. In the play the grandson of Johan-August reveals his character (Wigren, 2003, pp. 189–190):

> [he] knows everything and everybody. Everybody trusts him. He has all the credits one aspires to in Gnosjö. He gets the expert advice he needs within a radius of five hundred meters and whenever he wants to. He knows almost about every machine in the community since, in one way or another, he contributed to their construction. He has given many people advice and he has lent out money. Everybody listens to grandpa and he listens to everyone. He almost knows everything. It is there in his blood. He **is** the Spirit of Gnosjö.

This story tells us of an insider who has access to information; he furthermore has technical skills, which are highly respected in the community, for example inventiveness. Most of the few people who have earned the Mr. Gnosjö nickname have founded or taken over and vitalised a family business, nurturing paternalistic, even Schumpeterian (1911/1934, p. 93), ideals of creating a dynasty. An entrepreneur who (jointly with his brother) turned their father's small firm into one of the leading businesses in the region is one of the more prominent members of the virtual 'Mr. Gnosjö Club'. When an external investment company acquired the firm in 1979, he stayed for seven more years as the CEO. Then he set up a local investment company jointly with other owner managers, and he has also personally acquired two local companies, later handed over to his sons. He has served on several regional and national boards of companies and organisations supporting small and medium-sized companies. For two decades an active Pentecostalist, Mr. Gnosjö was for more than three decades also active in local political life. Epitomising the master narrative he tells us how work and life are inseparable in Gnosjö:

I am allowed to work as many hours as I can manage – nobody tells me to go home. A lot of work is not a problem as long as it makes fun. Any job that does not make fun means overtaxing, independent of hours spent.

Regulars share the same history and form the core of the local culture by internalising and reproducing jointly defined norms and values. Since Gnosjö is quite a remote place, strong informal ties have developed between the inhabitants in general and those in the business world in particular. Many people have local roots that go several generations back and by tradition they have become absorbed by the intense personal networking that has evolved over the years both inside and outside the family. A local owner–manager states succinctly (Wigren, 2003, p. 86): '*You know who knows when you need to know.*'

The regular participants in the social business world take the master narrative for granted. People who have lived their entire lives in Gnosjö, are members of free churches, or have married into a local family are anchored in the well-established local networks and they see themselves as regulars (Wigren, 2003, p. 314). When asked about the Spirit of Gnosjö and what it means to them, they spontaneously turn into spokesmen of the master narrative, reproducing the stories they have been told by colleagues as well as by visitors to the region. As regulars businesspeople nurture their trade by visiting different types of local arenas, for example the Rotary lunches, meetings organised by the local trade association and, if members, a church. Neither access to, nor participation on, an arena, however, means that trustworthiness is gained. It is rather rooted in the concrete actions taken by the person and the ability to add value, economic or, for example, political, to the region.

Tourists in the business social world obviously include researchers who visit the Gnosjö region with the intention of experiencing its culture in general and its business community in particular. Business consultants are constructed as tourists and therefore they have difficulties in approaching potential customers in the community. Successful interventions, though, are quickly spread by word-of-mouth, which means that once a consultant has become accepted by one firm, doors to the others are open.

The professional managers at externally owned companies who usually only stay for shorter periods of time in the community (Wigren, 2003, p. 98) are constructed as *strangers* in the Gnosjö business world. In order to gain legitimacy and fully benefit from the local milieu it is thus necessary for immigrant business leaders to spend time in gatherings such as breakfast meetings set up by the local trade association or events organised by the local sport associations. A former CEO of a large externally controlled firm was so anxious to attend the monthly breakfast meetings that he stayed overnight at the local inn only for that reason (Wigren, 2003, p. 127).

As indicated, strong indigenous values jointly with different immigrant groups craft a multiethnic community – of strangers. There is even a small Chinatown in Gnosjö, where apartments are mainly occupied by Chinese immigrants who also have their own shops in the centre of the town. Those immigrants who become members of a church or marry into a family may travel socially and become accepted as regulars, thus becoming genuinely integrated. However, people who move to Gnsojö mainly socialise with other immigrants, and this goes for old as well as new Swedes. Strong local institutions, such as the family, uphold a divide between community members and those not belonging – between on the one hand insiders and regulars, on the other tourists and strangers.

Our experiences suggest the delicate social tissue that the different types of interacting participants create within and across social worlds, feeding the ongoing collective-identity construction processes. Strangers look for recognition, tourists for the spectacular experiences, regulars for arguments for reproducing history, while enlightened insiders by way of personal networking 'on the spot' connect the local and the global, the past and the future. A positive reading of this experience might be that lock-ins due to strong local ties (alone) are avoided and instead a collective absorptive capacity is created that can be used for challenging the world of business in such a way that diversity emerges and change forces are released (Grabher, 1993). However, as indicated, insiders appear as caretakers of the past and the present, not as creators of the future.

However dominant the social world of business is in the Gnosjö region, local norms and values are also influenced by other social worlds. In order to come to grips with the local forces that maintain the Gnosjö collective identity as an invincible machine for dedicated and effective manufacturing production and determine its (lacking) ability to disclose an alternative future, we have to inquire further into the family as a paramount social institution in the Gnosjö region.

THE FAMILY AS A BASIC VALUE SOURCE

A value source, according to Wigren (2003, p. 206), has 'an institutionalised power, i.e. it has played a prominent role in the community for decades and it is well-known to the community members'. Among many optional value sources, we focus on the family, that is a group of people that are welded together by marriage (or any other kind of partnership) and kinship. Kinship includes all the individuals who belong to the family, including both generations gone and generations to come (Trost, 1993). The family is a generic institution in most cultures but it is paramount in the Gnosjö region as well as

being an important discursive resource when researching small firms
(Fletcher, 2002, p. 5). The nuclear family is the core social unit, but the
extended family also organises local social life. People know each other by
way of kinship ties and are trusted by virtue of their family bonds.

In Gnosjö the families thus organise both the private sphere and business
life. A great majority of the firms are privately owned by different constellations of family members. Many people are proud of their family links, especially if they belong to established families that have participated in the
founding of prominent firms in the region. It is important not to drag the
family name into the dirt. Traditions have resulted in many companies being
run by the second or third generation of owners and this often means compli-
cated ownership structures and in-breeding. Where the retired family members
have kept their stocks, passive ownership emerges, which occasionally
becomes a stumbling-block in the development of the firm. Whatever problems have been around, the priority seems to have been given to kinship.

The family as an institution represents a definitive social order, revealing in
the Gnosjö region a patriarchal society. Thus, while the men dominate the
business world in Gnosjö, the women carry family life. In line with our findings Pettersson (2002, 2004) argues that, according to what she addresses as
the local discourse, family life has to submit to business life and women to
men. Even if one third of the firms in Gnosjö are family businesses with
women as formal leaders, men represent them in public life. The father is head
of both the family and the firm and this makes the family business a convenient construct. The struggle for the survival of the firm then seems to be more
important to the women than breaking out of their own social prison does.
Conversing with Wendeberg (1982, pp. 127–128), a woman in a family business describes what made her and her husband keep on working hard:

> What it is? Primarily it is nice to find out if you will succeed. This is very exciting.
> Also, there is a pressure to carry on, you cannot imagine anything else. Dear me,
> how many around here fight side by side against an adverse wind – and it works.
> With joy, funnily enough.

Young women in the Gnosjö region either adapt to prevailing values and
norms or leave the community (Wigren, 2003, p. 211). Returning exiles challenge what is taken for granted, making the Gnosjö community members
aware of their sociocultural embedding. Even if Pettersson's (2002, 2004)
disclosure of the patriarchal Gnosjö community initiated an intense local
debate, the women of Gnosjö do not seem to have taken the opportunity to tell
a different story and stand up for alternative futures.

The paternalistic ideology reinforcing the image of the entrepreneur as a
builder of a dynasty and not as a hands-on caretaker of children becomes

apparent in the rumour about a man who decided to take paternity leave. According to hearsay, he was one of the first men in Gnosjö who enrolled for this experience. On his return to the company, he was told that in the meantime he had been given notice. When he came to the unemployment office he was informed that it probably would be best for him if he looked for a job outside the region. Even today, it is not taken for granted that a father should stay at home with his children. Most inhabitants feel that this is a task for the mother. The wife of a business owner–manager with young children provides a different perspective (Wigren, 2003, p. 142) :

> I have seen the other side of the picture and all work that it [running a firm] implies. My husband was only at home during Sundays, when the children were young. He started working at six o'clock in the mornings and finished at eleven in the evenings. He spent Friday evenings at home; otherwise he worked all day. It is a characteristic of the region, people work too much.

Voices like this one reveal how the family institution, as much as it has brought order and stability to the social world of business, may become a stumbling block when the Gnosjö region tries to bring about social change. Only if the heart of the local culture – the interrelationship between the business and the family – is challenged will the need for change be seen and acted upon accordingly. By talking about their wives being responsible for the household and for the children, male owner–managers separate their businesses from their private lives in line with traditional norms for business ownership (Ahl, 2002).

WEATHERING THE TAKEN-FOR-GRANTED STORY

However locked the Gnosjö region seems to be into the norms and values of (family) business it currently contains many conflicts and tensions – between locally and externally owned companies, between natives and newcomers, between the educated and non-educated. So far, though, the master narrative dressed as the Spirit of Gnosjö seems to have silenced voices with alternative messages and keeps seducing regulars as well as insiders to reproduce traditional values and behavioural norms. In spite of continued progress, but facing external threats due to technological changes in the global environment, the business community in the 1990s was placed under a guardian. Formally this was done voluntarily, but in practice under the pressure of national institutions, the business community joined with the trade unions and the local municipality to establish a support structure, a regional industrial development centre in the Gnosjö region. Its aim is to enforce technological change and (formal) training. Energetically 'educating' the region by way of a managerial rationale and vocabulary, the centre, however, appears to be a Trojan horse that has brought in an ideology that threatens to undermine the subtle everyday negotiations that constitute the local order (Johannisson, 2000). Although many native owner–managers still are sceptical of the centre, considering its staff as strangers, it presages a promise of an alternative future, that of a 'knowledge district' (Hjorth and Johannisson, 2003).

As much as any change towards the making of a sustainable community must be triggered from inside/below (Hjorth and Johannisson, 2003), the Gnosjö region thus has to find ways to reconstruct its collective identity by creating visible norms and values that are hidden by the master narrative. One intrinsic source of social change is that local people, however parochial, have a global outlook. Local commitment to place does not exclude wide networking and broadmindedness – physical, social and mental spaces do not have to coincide (Hernes, 2003). People in Gnosjö see themselves in relation to countries such as Japan and the United States. Japan as a manufacturing and commercial system has served as a role model for Gnosjö. The US influence is present in everyday local life. A miniature copy of the Statue of Liberty has been erected in the main street of Anderstorp, a small town in the Gnosjö industrial district. Some fly the American flag. In the United States as well as in Gnosjö, cars play an important role in society and so do free churches (Wigren, 2003, p. 83). People use their cars on a daily basis, even if the distance to cover is less than a few hundred meters. In both the USA and the Gnosjö region, free churches organise a considerable part of the population. Early on Wendeberg (1982, p. 24) pointed out that in Gnosjö, as well as in the United States, it is acceapble to show a healthy self-esteem. However, it is not permitted for one to become ostentatious or arrogant – the Jante Law, whose first paragraph says that you should not believe that you make a difference, rules here as well as in any other small (Scandinavian) town.[61]

The public discourse also feeds challenges to the basic values and norms in the Gnosjö community as a social space. When a Swedish tabloid some years ago published an article about the Swedish jetset in Båstad, a small town located on the Swedish coast west of Gnosjö, it included a report of a group of young people from Gnosjö. Huge restaurant and bar bills accompanied their stay. When confronted with this news, people in Gnosjö reacted very differently. Some said that the reported excesses did not matter, since those concerned were still young. What counts is what the young people do at home and what they achieve at work. But in other people's eyes this behaviour was shameless and not forgivable at all. This story communicates how people in Gnosjö cope with contradicting values and norms. The Swedish West Coast is not just a playground for young people but also a refuge for many Gnosjö adults. Going west, people leave the Gnosjö area and its prohibiting social and mental spaces behind (Wigren, 2003, p. 188). The outdoor local theatre play that was launched in 1999 ridiculed the Gnosjö people who were staying on the West Coast. This refuge was billed as Heaven, where all the millionaires could really enjoy life in their weekend houses, not necessarily entailing a richer social life. The many Gnosjö cottages on the West Coast, though, are distributed among different places depending on what social group you belong to in Gnosjö (Wigren, 2003, p. 115). In any case, different rules apply outside the community, on the West Coast for example, and back home.

In the social/mental space back home, religion infuses the local community with distinct norms and values. There are also stories about people who act and talk differently in Gnosjö on weekdays and on church days. An active Pentecostalist argues (Wigren, 2003, p. 160):

> There are those who are known to say one thing in church and then behave differently outside the church. I do not think they know how wrongly they act. They act in one way, they misbehave, and then they go to church and ask for forgiveness. Other people question how they can behave like that, mainly those who are not church-goers themselves.

Beyond the harmonious façade that the Spirit of Gnosjö builds according to the master narrative there are obviously many contradicting social processes going on, whether we consider that certain groups, such as immigrants (managers) who are constructed as strangers or natives going (ab)normal when on the West Coast. On the one hand, this means that basic values and norms, as well as the associated mutual trust, are eroding, on the other, that contrasting practices emerge and produce variety. Where individuals, due to multiple memberships on social arenas, interrelate and practices intertwine, new images of reality emerge. Internal and external pressures jointly determine whether conformity then (again) arises or multiple voices are kept alive, creating a new collective identity based on diversity. Today foreign newcomers are not perceived as aliens, which suggests that regulars and strangers acknowledge each other.

Hannerz (1987) elaborates on the metaphor of 'creolization' and considers it useful for capturing how meanings are constructed through the interplay between those actors close to the centre and those who are more peripheral, insiders and strangers in the language we have borrowed from Unruh. Creolization is a creative interplay and not a one-way influence from the centre to the periphery as the local attitude towards university studies suggests. Earlier, people in the region did not consider higher education to be important, while today they do. Structural changes in society and on the market, such as the increasing demand for technical development and knowledge-intensive products have influenced how and what people in the region think about university studies. If local people do not see academic logico-scientific knowledge as a threat to their narrative, tacit knowing (Czarniawska, 2004; Johannisson, 2000), the very interface between the contrasting modes of understanding will enrich local insight.

THE OUTSIDER/INSIDER RELATIONSHIP AS BROKERAGE

In social worlds, like in the business community's social world in Gnosjö, there may be participants who work against what insiders promote and regulars take for granted and tourists/strangers try to grasp. The Unruh vocabulary obviously restricts the search for local dynamics to areas that submit to the rules of the game, that is to already dominant values and norms. In order to break free from them and construct a different collective identity, participants are needed, who on the one hand question the very culture that has fed them, and on the other are marginalised by the community members. We thus expand the original cast in Unruh's model by introducing the 'outsider'. An *outsider*, as defined by us, is a participant who takes the role of challenging the established social world as experienced by insiders and regulars and reflected in their norms and practices.

The outsider thrives on ambiguity, and by protesting against what is taken for granted she/he constructs a territory of her/his own, founded on a balanced use and abuse of the values of other participants in the social world concerned. People are constructed as different, as outsiders, by those who consider themselves to be 'normal', here insiders/regulars (Becker, 1963). The outsider, though, may use this marginalisation and associated discretion to articulate ongoing change (Spinosa et al., 1997, p. 25). To the extent that the latter is referred to as an example, the outsider defines what is not considered as (not yet) proper social conduct. This means that the outsider is important when the boundaries of the community as a social and a mental space are defined (Hernes, 2003). In Table 9.2 the outsider is characterised as an insurgent, a rebel who takes his own initiatives that often challenge what is taken for granted. Nevertheless the outsider is recognised as a (permanent) community member and allowed to, even expected to, ridicule the values and norms of the community, that is, to enact the role of a jester.

Gnosjö accommodates an outsider who is extremely visible in Sweden: 'Big' Bengt Erlandsson. Born on a farm in the early 1920s, and a habitual entrepreneur ever since his teens, he has been a very active and visible contributor to the post-World War II economic expansion in the region. Himself a

Table 9.2   The outsider as an insurgent

Type of participant	Orientation	Experiences	Relationships	Commitment
Outsider	Identification/ denouncement	Challenging the TFG world	Glocal	Attraction of tourists

habitual entrepreneur, 'Big Bengt' has helped many others to get started. His visibility in public life can be ascribed both to his commercial activities (production and trade) and to his constant heckling of the Swedish authorities. Big Bengt has also created one of the original attractors in the Swedish experience economy: the Wild West town of High Chaparral. Constantly and carefully nurturing his identity as 'somebody', he walks streets far beyond his amusement park dressed in his white cowboy hat and matching boots. It goes without saying that the Wild West of North America has inspired Big Bengt in building both High Chaparral and his own image.

Big Bengt is as talkative as he is industrious, telling as many stories – also about himself! – as stories are told about him. Walking his Wild West town of High Chaparral with us on a sunny summer day he reveals both his belonging to and detachment from basic values and norms in Gnosjö. 'The Bible is my guideline', he tells us from the pulpit in his own town church, further stating that '[a] believer, a person who believes in God and has faith, reveals through his deed if he is religious or not'. Big Bengt obviously embodies the Protestant ethic that rules in the Gnosjö region. When asked about what really makes him happy he quickly responds: 'It is making a person fully committed to starting a manufacturing company of his own and raising a family as well.' Not surprisingly, he reinforces/the paternalistic family model: 'A really wise woman does not interfere with her husband and his business as long as he manages to run it.' Already at the welcoming coffee table, with his wife standing behind him, he had stated: 'Thank God for giving me two boys. If I got a girl too it would all go wrong.'

As indicated, Big Bengt has for decades fought the national Swedish legal system as well as the (local) authorities (Johannisson and Wigren, 2006). He spent some years in jail for alleged fraud, but he certainly has won some battles as well. One disagreement was settled when, after having repeatedly ignored the local building regulations, he was authorised to organise his own construction activities within the territory of High Chaparral, his sanctuary (Sköldberg, 2005, p. 141). The resistance he originally met he seems to appreciate as it encourages sparring in his venturing career:

> Thank God that the local authorities opposed me, because that gave me inspiration to do what I have done. If the local authorities had not done what they did this [High Chaparral] would not have existed. If you think that what is here is good, then you should thank the local authorities.

When one asks Big Bengt about Gnosjö and its spirit, he argues that it has changed and that it is not what it historically was. Like a jester, he frankly states that Gnosjö and its well-known spirit is about hypocrisy, about envy, about imitation. But he realises that it is difficult to write and talk in public about those things; it is easier to keep to the myth, stick to the master narrative. Now it seems to be time to re-construct his outsidership and find ways of making its boldness and folly an opening in the creation of space for a changed collective identity.

Although the extrovert outsider, like Big Bengt, is constantly exciting the (business) community and its context, the wild forces that thereby are created need to be acted upon. Otherwise the outsider and her/his passion will remain marginal, ridiculed or silenced. We argue that, due a partially shared world-view and practices, insiders have the capability to make intelligible the words and deeds of the outsider. We will therefore return to the insider introduced as Mr. Gnosjö above and draw a parallel between his and Big Bengt's approach to local (business) life. Considering that the two have been directly related, our constructed 'dialogue' seems to qualify. Epitomising the power of initiative, the rebel Big Bengt also needs to relate to the local organising context: 'Stifle initiative in an organization, and you get a petrified colossus; stifle dialogue and you get a moving zombie' (Sköldberg, 2005, p. 135). Big Bengt and Mr. Gnosjö once jointly bought a company and ran it for a couple of years. The latter even gives Big Bengt, 20 years his senior, credit for facilitating his own entrepreneurial career:

> He certainly is a very special person. He has had the courage to acknowledge himself. He is a man of action. He has meant a lot to the community and its small firms. I remember being 16 or 17 years old going to Big Bengt to buy some machinery. He told me to pay as much I then could afford and the rest later. His High Chaparral has literally put this region on the map.

Mr. Gnosjö in his turn is seen as a mentor by a number of younger local business owner–managers (here presented as regulars). However, while Big Bengt challenges norms and values, Mr. Gnosjö negotiates between different groups of participants in the business community. One example is his conversation with us as visiting researchers. Another example of his mission as a 'translator' is his socialising with CEOs of externally owned firms (by him obviously constructed as strangers). Thanks to his background as the CEO of an externally owned firm he can 'educate' the employed managers about the local rules of the game. Thereby he reinforces established norms and values in Gnosjö. One of the local projects initiated by Mr. Gnosjö and his colleagues is the establishment of a local hotel and restaurant. Only the broad commitment of the local firms made this orchestrated community effort possible. Initially, the non-local managers are indifferent to such initiatives but Mr. Gnosjö asserts (with a laugh):

> Well, if I get an hour or so on my own with them, telling them who I am and what I have accomplished, it is very difficult for them not to contribute. Sometimes the laying on of hands is needed.

Big Bengt, the outsider, and Mr. Gnosjö, the insider, share a number of further norms and practices. They are both strong believers and esteem hard work. Both are successful habitual entrepreneurs who have handed over their businesses operations to their sons. Contrasting with the local norms, they keep their public and private lives apart, which means that that in public they never talk about their wives. Officially Big Bengt and Mr. Gnosjö have both retired but they both consider what were once their firms as personal social arenas. Both appreciate experiential and social learning, Big Bengt, by stressing that High Chaparral, has been a springboard for hundreds of new ventures, Mr. Gnsojö, by giving prominence to the company he once was part of building up and then selling off, acknowledges how much he and his sons learned from working there. Both have been involved in ventures without any equity interest, Mr. Gnosjö as board member and Big Bengt by selling second-hand machines to nascent entrepreneurs on easy terms. Both are true salesmen and think highly of others who are.

Also, both Big Bengt and Mr. Gnosjö, caring for those who are marginalised by society, extend their creative organising into the social sphere. High Chaparral has always been a place where people perceived as odd have been welcomed. Mr. Gnosjö's concern for the unfortunate comes through in the story he tells about caring for the physically, mentally, or socially disabled in the community:

> My religious belief and membership in an independent church reinforce a special view of humanity. I voted against and managed to make the majority of the local council join me every time it was proposed that an independent sheltered workshop should be established in Gnosjö. I argued that if there is some place in Sweden where these people can be really cared for then it is here in our small manufacturing firms. I managed to establish a sheltered workshop accommodating eight people at my former company. I was very pleased, because not all people are given the same chances in life. (. . .) This concern [for the disadvantaged] obviously evolves most easily where you live. You get closer to these people.

During his spare time Mr. Gnsojö is engaged in an organization that aims at supporting and helping addicted people. Big Bengt does the same but in a different way, he says:

> I take care about a lot of people who have problems with alcohol and similar things that make them crash and go bankrupt. Here I have the saloon, where they may drink as much as they want for free, then they are in heaven. That is the reason why I have the Gate of Heaven (Pärleporten) here, they come here, they pass by the gate and they are in heaven, here is everything, for free, they do not have to pay, it is included in their salary . . . but they do not drink anything!

Albeit using different tactics, both the outsider and the insider are completely dedicated to their social worlds in words as well as in deeds. As the business community is integrated with the other social worlds in the industrial district, insiders typically cross boundaries between the different local social worlds as well as the boundary between the community and the global context. Carrying the role of a reformer, the insider contrasts with the outsider, who appears as an expressive revolutionary. We propose that their coexistence, their very mutual relation, combine into a brokerage between not only the local and global worlds, indeed an entrepreneurial mission (Barth, 1963, p. 16), but between the ruling master narrative and those silenced voices that carry the seeds of an alternative collective identity.

ACKNOWLEDGING DIFFERENT STORIES

We have indicated that the Spirit of Gnosjö can be seen as a conspiracy set up by a brotherhood of male owner–managers, well supported by outside conspirators including the mass media and researchers. This master narrative has hindered local people in Gnosjö from becoming disclosers of new worlds (Spinosa et al., 1997). Obviously there are, however, other stories to be told, for example by silenced women and immigrants and a very garrulous Big Bengt. What has been said about the double life of Gnosjö natives on the Swedish West Coast suggests that instead of confronting different value systems and associated practices in order to gain momentum from the tensions created, the two worlds are kept apart. Considering that the two generic spaces in everyday life – the workplace and the private sphere – coincide in the Gnosjö region, arenas that can provide a 'third space' where creativity thrives seem to be much needed.

The cage that keeps the Gnosjö region trapped by the master narrative is strong. Parents expect their children to work at the family business during weekends and vacations, and upon finishing school to take on a position in the firm. The local theatre plays and industrial museums make people attend to those days when male inventiveness and ingenuity alone built economic wealth. The question is whether the next generation will stay loyal to the historical heritage, leave or reflect, and give voice and commit themselves to a different future. As Davidsson (1995) states, the answer cannot be taken for granted. There is a great risk that the young generation will leave the Gnosjö region behind, both literally and in a transferred sense.

When trying to break out of the Spirit of Gnosjö both discursive and concrete measures are needed on the part of researchers also. In 2003, the authors of this chapter tried to arrange a seminar on women entrepreneurship in the Gnosjö context. When told that Katarina Pettersson, the recent critic of paternalistic Gnosjö (Pettersson, 2002, 2004), was going to attend, none of the about ten Gnosjö female owner–managers who were asked to join a panel could spare the time (although the meeting was staged in a neutral arena outside the region).

The very idea that local norms and practices can remain as a basis for sustainable entrepreneurship in a changing world is unrealistic, if not genuinely naive. Diversity and movement, rather than the homogeneity and stability that are associated with any master narrative, must rule. If the very fact that immigrants and professional managers are constructed as strangers is made part of an ongoing local multilogue about the future, a new collective identity may emerge and by enacted by way of changed practices. Different stories appropriated from elsewhere should be told, beginning with the locals themselves as narrators (Hjorth and Johannisson, 2003). New local vocabularies are needed to accomplish this changed worldview. For example, locally Big Bengt is presented as a dealer in second-hand machinery and crazy organiser of an amusement park. A different language would present him as a venture capitalist, promoting the concept of lean production, and as a pioneer in the experience economy. In partnership with Mr. Gnosjö, Big Bengt conveys the message that the creation of an identity that 'makes sense' and constructs collective entrepreneurship calls for both reinforcement and denial of the rules of the game, both the construction and destruction of master narratives.

The strong sociocultural legacy of the Gnosjö region suggests that rationalisation of ways of identifying the local change potential is not sufficient. Following Czarniawska (2004), another way to gain insight is to reflect on the way local people dramatise their own history. In the theatre play written and performed by the local theatre association in 1999, one of the characters, Catrine, enacted what it is like to be different in Gnosjö. Her role was mainly modelled after Caroline, whose father was the managing director and proprietor of the local bobbin industry. Staying unmarried, Caroline spent her life in the house where she was born. She did not have a traditional job but gave piano lessons, wrote novels and painted.

For people in the community Caroline was surrounded by mystery. It is said that Caroline once left for America, only to return a few years later. She was reported to enjoy swimming naked in the small pond close to the 'Love Path' in Gnosjö. This was considered to be a strange and unusual act in a community where, for quite some time, the church has had a dominant position. Caroline was narrated as being too sophisticated for the community and she never became part of it. Caroline/Catrine seems to manifest the fear of the unknown, which fetters the Gnosjö region. Even though inhabitants probably do not really think about what that means for the community, it tells a visitor that Gnosjö is still a community tied to its past. On the other hand, the very fact that Caroline reappears on the (theatre) stage foster increasing local awareness and, to supplement Big Bengt's carnivalesque words and deeds, possibly announces a revised collective identity produced by narratives that deliver and liberate the region from its past and instigate social change.

10. Entrepreneurship as boundary work: deviating from and belonging to community

Monica Lindgren and Johann Packendorff

ENTREPRENEURSHIP AS BOUNDARY WORK: A SOCIAL CONSTRUCTIONIST PERSPECTIVE

Entrepreneurship is usually seen as a solution to problems in community development – through new firms, new industries and community mobilization, stagnating regions and cities are expected to return to growth and prosperity (Cornwall, 1998). While this solution is almost undisputed, the question of what entrepreneurship is and how it emerges often remains unanswered or neglected (Spinosa et al., 1997). There is also an underpinning positive assumption that all new firms or entrepreneurial acts are good for any local community and that they are well received by the locals (Welsch and Kuhns, 2002). Moreover, it is said that industries should be built on local resources, competencies and culture – the question is how we can develop our town and local area out of our existing traditions, culture and habits? We can find this ideal of the embedded industrial cluster throughout the world.

In France there are different wine and food districts, there are US cities where all activities are built around car manufacturing (e.g. Detroit), there are regions inhabited by numerous glass and crystal manufacturers (Småland in Sweden, Bohemia in the Czech Republic). There are the famous local specializations of northern Italy with their emphasis on civil society, not to mention the notorious US case of Silicon Valley (Saxenian, 2000). We have thus many examples of clusters where traditions and cultures are part of how to and what to produce, and where people have been able to construct affluent communities out from their local culture. Behind the visible products and local specialities, the inhabitants of these areas have together created strong regional cultures that support and maintain certain behaviours, identities and social relationships – enabling but also limiting individuals in relation to tradition. In less fortunate areas, economic activities are likely to be more diverse (Welsch and Kuhns, 2002), but still performed in a close and harmonical relation to the local community (Mort et al., 2003). Not surprisingly, many regions have been convinced about this harmonic cluster strategy and actively try to reinvent them at home.

Entrepreneurial action that means deviations from culture and traditions or bringing new ideas in from the outside are rarely considered in these analyses (Hjorth and Johannisson, 2003), despite the fact that entrepreneurship is often described in terms of change, newness and deviation. Not least in the sub-genre of entrepreneurship literature that deals with the fates and fortunes of successful individual entrepreneurs, it often stands clear that being an entre-preneur is about deviating from norms that others follow and in the creation of new norms. Still, this is a masculine image characterized by conflict and conquest that is unusual to find in the social entrepreneurship and/or commu-nity entrepreneurship literature. What should be of interest to entrepreneurship research is thus a discussion about how entrepreneurial action can be embed-ded in local history and tradition at the same time as it challenges and stretches these taken-for-granted boundaries of how and what to think, and how and what to act. The aim of this chapter is thus to contribute to a developing under-standing of the phenomenon of entrepreneurship as boundary work in relation to local cultural context.

Taking a social constructionist view, we argue that entrepreneurship, both as concept and practice, emerges dynamically in social interaction between people. People always interact in different forms with each other through meetings, through reading what others have written, through the Internet and so on. Even in those cases when one entrepreneur has indeed 'singlehandedly' performed the entrepreneurial act, interaction with a social context has still taken place (through upbringing, local culture, inspiration, idea generation, support, resistance and so forth). Although different persons have different impact, and differ in their importance to the process, we could recognize the entrepreneurial process as a complex web of reciprocal interactions between culturally embedded actors closely connected to each other (Jack and Anderson, 2002; Lindgren and Packendorff, 2003; Hosking and Hjorth, 2004). With a social constructionist view entrepreneurship is something 'in becom-ing', a movement, in which pluralism and emancipation from structures are consequences (Spinosa et al., 1997; Steyaert, 1997; Chia and King, 1998; Janssens and Steyaert, 2002).

The notion of entrepreneurial action as a process of constructing and recon-structing the cultural boundaries of everyday life is extensively discussed by Spinosa et al. (1997). They maintain that entrepreneurship is a way of making history (that is, changing the way in which we understand and deal with ourselves and with things), and that it rests upon certain entrepreneurial abili-ties. These can be found in almost any human being, and are based in the sense of an anomaly or disharmony in any of the worlds in which life is lived. They adopt a Heideggerian view of worlds – that a world is a self-contained set of interrelated socially constructed meanings that link things, purpose and identity to each other – and find such disclosive worlds in tribes, professions, subcultures, academic fields and so on. While the usual human behaviour may be to live on with such an anomaly or disharmony, getting used to it and even making it a part of one's identity, entrepreneurial action would imply hanging on to it in order to change the way in which the world is perceived.

This is done, Spinosa et al. claim, through handling the anomaly/disharmony by innovation and social interaction with others in the same world, socially constructing the innovation as both sensible and strange. Sensibleness is about constructing belongings to the world, about changing practices, and strangeness is about constructing deviations from that world, about making history. Entrepreneurship as boundary work is thus a process of socially constructing deviations and belongings in a certain world and maintaining these tensions long enough for historical changes to materialize – establishing a new way to see the world rather than constructing a brief diversion that in the end reinforces tradition.

Entrepreneurship is thus about changing the way we see the world, that is, that our style of relating to people and things are changed. While most new products and services and the subsequent changes in daily practices do not imply a change in style, entrepreneurial acts do. Spinosa et al. discuss three different ways in which styles in our way of viewing our world are changed. Entrepreneurial change – a change in style and not merely a change in practices – in/of these worlds happen through articulation, reconfiguration and cross-appropriation. Articulation means that a style is changed as its practices become explicit, which in the case of social/community entrepreneurship would imply, for example creating awareness about some aspect of local culture and its importance to future development. Reconfiguration means that a style is changed as a marginal part of established practices gradually becomes dominant following some sort of practical transition, for example local patriotism is redefined from being old-fashioned small-mindedness into becoming a common force in mobilizing and uniting people. In the discussion about entrepreneurship as boundary work, the notion of cross-appropriation is perhaps most important in the sense that practices are brought in from other worlds (that is, from outside the boundaries) and made useful, thereby stretching and redefining boundaries.

THE STUDY OF ENTREPRENEURIAL PROCESSES

In this chapter, entrepreneurial processes are studied through narratives – in order to get an understanding of individual participants' interpretations of them. These data are then subjected to an analysis where the story – the narratives of the participants – are re-written by the researcher in order to cover the events, conflicts and such that convey an understanding of the entrepreneurial processes (see also Steyaert and Bouwen, 2000; O'Connor, 2002; Fletcher, 2003). We can understand how/why problems arise, how/why people can perceive obstacles, how/why new ideas emerge, how identities are constructed, co-constructed and re-constructed and so on (Johansson, 2004). Since we view entrepreneurial acts as collective experiences, the empirical basis concerning an entrepreneurial act cannot be the 'visible' entrepreneur's narrative only. If different narratives from different actors involved are brought together in the analysis, understanding of events could be much broader (Lindgren and Packendorff, 2003). However, it is also very important to carefully handle interrelated questions such as how language is viewed and used, the notion of discourses, and the importance of reflexivity throughout the research process (Potter and Wetherell, 1987; Alvesson and Sköldberg, 2000; Lindgren and Wåhlin, 2001; Fletcher, 2003).

In the following, we present an in-depth study of the Hultsfred rock festival in Sweden and how the actors behind the festival – organized through the voluntary non-profit association RockParty – have initiated a number of entrepreneurial processes over the years. The study is based on recurrent interviews, participant observation and documentation from the actors themselves. From the narratives we understand where problems appear, where obstacles have emerged, why some ideas are realised and others not (Kupferberg, 1998). Since we view entrepreneurial processes as collective interaction, it is also important to speak to several of the inter-actors (Lindgren and Packendorff, 2003). The interviewees were asked to speak openly about the development of their operations, how they had worked together, what problems they had experienced, how they constructed and re-constructed the boundaries of their local context themselves, including their interpretation of the external reactions and attitudes towards them. In total, ten of the central actors in Hultsfred have been interviewed in-depth on at least one occasion. They have also read and commented upon the material, which is ethically important in this kind of approach.

The boundary work studied here is thus the ongoing interactions between a number of people that together construct boundaries for the sake of testing and stretching them. Their narratives are a part of their construction and co-construction of the content and context of their daily work, and give us as researchers a chance to understand how and why their common interaction unfold as it does. They convey to us their relational realities: the realities that they are creating together, the realities that are 'in becoming' – which is something different from factual correspondence between what is and what is said (Hosking and Hjorth, 2004).

THE HULTSFRED CASE: FROM PUNK REBELS TO MUSIC INDUSTRY DEVELOPMENT

Hultsfred is a small industrial town in the Småland region of Southeast Sweden, characterized by forests, lakes, farms and pittoresque villages. The municipality counts about 15,000 inhabitants, half of them living outside the town. The social life of the town had not much to offer the young men growing up as punk rebels during the 1970s, and in 1981 some of them formed their own music club, RockParty, in order to arrange concerts and other happenings. Rock music, a reliance on voluntary work, and a determination that nothing was impossible were – and still are – mentioned by all interviewees as the foundation of RockParty.

Today, RockParty is the arranger of the Hultsfred Festival that has been held annually since 1986. The festival has steadily developed into one of the major summer rock festivals in Europe, and set a new record in 2005 with 31,000 visitors. RockParty also arranges several other recurring festivals with separate themes. The club has its own concert hall, which they had to build by themselves when the municipality ended their lease of the sports hall in 1990. It is situated at the edge of the town, in a small industrial block between the deep forest and the regional highway.

In the middle of the 1990s, the group realized that the success of the festival could be used for the good of the whole town. At the same time, the club was constantly close to bankruptcy and some of the employees were forced to form companies out of their specialities in the festival organization (catering, advertising, booking, call centres and the like) and sell their services to external customers too. With some exceptions this worked out fairly well, and it spurred RockParty to invest some small amounts in other business ideas related to the music industry, and they managed to attract public funding to establish an industrial development centre for the music industry. Today, the concert hall has been expanded with the addition of a large office building called RockCity, housing a number of small entrepreneurial companies, a national music industry centre, a business incubator, a university education programme in music management and a high school with a music profile. RockCity has also become the common brand name for the whole group that is owned by RockParty. As of 2004, the group had 44 employees and total revenues of 72 million SEK.[62] In 2003, RockCity CEO Putte Svensson was elected Creative Entrepreneur of the Year in Sweden, but he immediately noted that he was just the front member of a group of people that had worked together for decades: RockParty was started by Håkan Waxegård and Per Alexandersson, the former being the 'front face' and the latter the organizer. As the festivals grew in scope, more people joined the inner circle. Gunnar Lagerman became responsible for signing up artists,

Putte Svensson organized the voluntary work needed to build the festival area, and Per Alexandersson specialized in marketing.

In the beginning of the 1990s, Per Alexandersson left Hultsfred for a career in Malmö, and Håkan Waxegård was ousted from the board and replaced by Patrik Axelsson. Waxegård left both RockParty and Hultsfred, and it was then decided that Putte Svensson was to become the charismatic 'front face', and Patrik Axelsson the thoughtful administrator. RockParty still owns the festival and all the companies of the group, and Putte, Patrik and the others are regular employees with ordinary salaries. Since the club was created out of voluntary work, no one will ever be allowed to use RockParty to amass personal wealth.

After Putte becoming the driving force in the creation of new firms related to the festival – a strategic direction that is still a major source of conflict and discussion within RockParty – he gathered a new network around him to pursue the ideas on business development, educations and music industry research. The effort was called Project Puzzle, and they rapidly developed a set of complementary identities. In this network, Erkki Lahti was the opportunity searcher and idea generator, Putte the charismatic motivator, and Lasse Rönnlund the action-oriented 'doer'. They also placed their old friend Per Kågefors as business developer in the regional authorities, which meant access to all sorts of financing and funding.

In order to maintain the dynamics in the RockCity building, they try to question their roles and what they do, and they actively seek to involve new persons both as employees and as network contacts. Being a group consisting of men only, they made efforts to recruit women (Putte was replaced by Frederika Svensson as CEO of the largest company, Metropol), which has also generated projects aimed at improving the possibilities for young female rock musicians, led by Hanna Rotelius.

Since the members of the original team have now become fathers with families, they have had to redefine their way of working. They are not available around the clock anymore, and they need to plan for their interaction. Still, a lot of ideas and decisions happen informally around coffee tables, but they have also begun to see the drawbacks of too much informal networking in an organization with 44 employees. Hence, they are forming a professional board for the whole group and establishing a development company to handle all new ideas. Many employees outside the inner circle find RockCity to be the most creative and inspiring place they have ever worked at, but they also say that informal power, traditions and history are important – you need access to certain key actors if you really want your ideas to come true.

NARRATIVES ON DEVIATING AND BELONGING

In the interviews with the (inter)actors in the Hultsfred organization, a number of narrative themes on the relation between the entrepreneurial processes and context emerged. One such theme was the image of rock music and rock culture as rebellious and different as compared to the local culture of sports. Another theme was the perceived massive lack of local understanding for the special characteristics of the music industry, which was explained with reference to the traditional industrial structure of the region. The relation between the RockCity people and their context has also been characterized by an ongoing debate on the relation between culture and commercial business (see also Mort et al., 2003), which has also led to severe internal conflicts. It appeared that having been met with scepticism in the local arena, RockCity has instead focused on networking and collaboration in other arenas; regionally, nationally and internationally. Still, they all share a basic desire to make Hultsfred a better and more prosperous place to live, which represents an aim to contribute and be respected, to be seen as an important and relevant part of community development. These themes are described below through the voices of the (inter)actors in the RockCity organization.

Rock Music Culture as Deviation

The leading actors behind the club RockParty were all born in the end of the 1950s or in the first half of the 1960s. Those who grew up in Hultsfred tell the story of a quite traditional and stagnating industrial town, where almost every family was dependent upon a few large factories. All the factories had benefited from the Swedish postwar boom, and the local youth knew that they would get jobs right after school and be able to buy their own house before the age of 30. In that sense, life was easy and predictable, despite the economic stagnation during the 1970s.

When not working, the Hultsfred people got together in sports clubs and numerous other voluntary associations, but the teenagers not interested in sports had not much to do. During the punk wave at the end of the 1970s, Putte and others arranged concerts in their school and noticed that the interest in music was growing:

> Most of us played in bands and we brought together the bands to concert evenings. The dean had a big meeting with us on how to stop violence and drinking among the pupils, and we started to arrange a new form of parties where the music was in focus. And then we graduated, and had no reason to continue to arrange school concerts. We then formed the club RockParty. December 16th, 1981. (Putte S)[63]

From the beginning they were seen as outsiders, but they also think that that has helped them in their ambitions:

> Sometimes I think that it was good for us that everybody worked against us; crazy young rebels were not really popular in the beginning of the 80s. Well, perhaps they didn't work against us, but nobody ever listened to us. The local politicians lived in the old days; they were not bad people, but they did not understand that the local youth wanted concerts and festivals. Today, the official policy is that the festival is good for Hultsfred, but we have never seen any decisions to support the festival. I have been to some awkward meetings with the municipality board ... It has become our strength that we have had to fix everything by ourselves. (Patrik A)

The RockParty board was a group of friends, which has meant a strong sense of collectivity but also difficulties in handling conflicts:

> I think it was an initial strength that we were a bunch of old friends that were behind a lot of things. But it has meant difficulties in handling budget overruns or layoffs; we have not been professional in such occasions since we are all old friends. This is a sensitive thing, we must be professional but it shall also be fun to work here. (Patrik A)

The board of RockParty was relatively small, and the way to make big things happen was to use voluntary forces when needed. Voluntary work for RockParty became the opposite thing to spending time in school:

> Our friends became the tools. At high school I was not popular among the teachers, because when we had concerts in the sports arena a lot of people were away from school helping us out. I've been at the dean's office several times and promised to stop doing this [laugh]. But today, many of our old teachers come up to us in the street and congratulate us to the successes. It was not that school was boring; we just did not see the practical use for all the theory. It was a relief to be able to slip off and do something practical. (Patrik A)

The club and the festival grew fast, and since nobody had any knowledge of accounting or business matters, they used a very simple business model:

> We had indoor concerts every week around the year and outdoor concerts every second week during summer season. The tactic was to make a profit out of the outdoor concerts and to spend the money on our favourite bands at the club. Some sort of anarcho-capitalism, as I used to say. (Gunnar L)

Rock music and rock culture is not that deviant anymore, and the actors seem to think more carefully about when and in terms of what they want to challenge their context:

> We are not that rebellious anymore, we are more of an institution now. We are forty instead of twenty years old, and we have assumed a more politically correct view

on things like teenagers getting drunk during the festival. We often did not listen to criticism before, today we do understand it in another way. (Nisse J)

The festival is still an independent thing, so in that sense we are still rebels. A feminist rock association is now being started up, and they have had a rookie-camp with Marit Bergman.[64] We will work more with things like that. (Putte S)

Music Industry as Deviation

In Hultsfred, the RockCity building represents a deviance from the traditional way of working and living. When the members of the original RockParty board grew up, they felt predestined to lives as factory workers. The years they spent building up the club and the festival was something they did as a part of their youth rather than as a part of their working lives. Hence, even after more than a decade of festival organizing, they saw themselves as just a bunch of rockers unable to do real business. The festival was not growing so much anymore, and they had constant problems in matching revenues and costs. However, they got indications that their experiences could be useful for other sorts of operations as well:

> One day when I came down to the Unemployment Agency, there was a new adviser there that just had come to town, and she said that the battery factory needed a new CEO. 'I can't apply for CEO at the battery factory', I said, my high school grades didn't really match that job. And then she said that I had led festival projects with thousands of people involved, and at the factory there were only 400 employees. Then, we realised that we could start other business operations besides just arranging concerts. (Putte S)

The festival was also met by scepticism by banks and other institutions. When they built their first concert hall, they were forced by the bank to fully own the building themselves, since the bank did not trust the RockParty club to be a responsible debtor. The music industry represented a different economic logic from traditional industrial manufacturing, a logic that did not suit established models for credit evaluations:

> We have had festivals where we lost big money, and we have tried to solve it by selling inventory and taking personal loans. The festival business is risky, you know. And the bank has not been keen to help, not even with temporary credit for costs that will be re-paid when the festival entrance fees flow in. The characteristics of traditional manufacturing are built into the bank world; it has shaped their view on judging business risks. We are different, which means that they must have trust in us instead. Which they don't. (Patrik A)

In some instances, there were also serious mistakes made, often due to over-optimistic assumptions on future revenues:

> I was among those who were sceptical about this building, I thought it to be too large for Hultsfred. You don't really want to come down on the enthusiasts, but it appeared that our indoor concerts resulted in a loss of about one million the first year. The indoor concerts we have today are not at all of the same scope as intended from the beginning. We had a loss of about 40 or 50 thousand every weekend. (Gunnar L)

Music industry is still not fully understood, the actors claim. The only support and competence available is to be found in Stockholm, which is where the major companies in the industry are located. When they started IUC (the national music industry centre), the money came directly from the government, not from venture capitalists and banks, and the RockCity spin-offs also deviate in the sense that they aim for survival rather than fast growth:

> Say that we have 60 per cent of our venture capital left in three or four years, then we will be really satisfied. But everybody around saw us as idiots; banks, venture capitalists, authorities. We had to break all these prejudice saying that you cannot do anything with music outside Stockholm. Our companies are not that profitable, they live on a level suited for self-employment which means careful spending habits and survival despite recession. These people are here because they want to be here. The business development manager at the municipality is not really happy about this; he now has dozens of small companies to take care of instead of a single big one as it was before. (Lasse R)

The actors themselves do not, however, think that their industry is that different. Instead, they want to be seen as a complement to other industries in the area, and they also want to learn from them:

> We travel around a lot, everywhere in fact. We have stolen a lot from the manufacturing industry, they are 100 years ahead of us. They have been working with strategic development since the beginning of twentieth century, and the music business started to make money in the 1950s. We are lagging 50 years behind. So we look at what they do, what they are good at, and then we try to steal it. (Putte S)

Maintaining the Balance: Culture vs Business

The decision in the middle of the 1990s to create spin-off operations from the festival reawakened an old ideological dilemma in the actor network. RockParty had always been different both in terms of lifestyle and music and as a form for economic value creation, and the general opinion was that they were a cultural association where money was a secondary thing. When it was suggested that some of the existing operations within the festival (such as catering) were to be transformed into companies aiming for profit, many feared that traditional economic thinking would become the norm for the whole festival:

There is a history here governing what you can do and not, a conflict between cultural and commercial values. The festival culture is still around, and some people have had rough times when trying to deviate from that. I think that it is important to stick to the original foundations for what we do. RockParty is the cultural part and the Metropol companies are the commercial part. (Frederika S)

Even though the festival has remained a non-profit activity, economic thinking has indeed influenced and changed their way of doing things:

Before, when you wanted a certain band, you just went for it. If someone younger wants to bring in an unknown band to the festival today, it might not be that easy. Today, everybody has a more developed sense of economic responsibility. Before, we brought in two famous artists and used the profits to pay for a bunch of unknown bands. We don't do that to the same extent anymore. (Nisse J)

Patrik Axelsson, longtime chairman of RockParty, has a dual role in both preserving the original ideology built on voluntary work and maintaining financial stability:

We earn decent salaries, but nobody has become rich. Some people in Hultsfred has earned a lot of money, like those owning the festival grounds, coffee shops, restaurants and so forth, but we are not among them. If we had owned this some difficult decisions could have been easier to implement, but the spirit in this building might not have been the same. In the end, it is about daring to test ideas. (Patrik A)

I'm a big critic and always ask who is going to pay for all this and who is going to make it happen. It's a pity that I always assume that role. But I can live with that, in the end it's always better not to let the visionaries run ahead all the time. I also have visions myself, but mostly I keep things together. (Patrik A)

The conflict became even more serious when Putte brought in Lasse Rönnlund to support a number of small independent ventures in the house:

Putte had decided to create spin-offs from the festival. The person that decides to do such a thing must be able to handle the reactions from the rest of the organisation. When he declared that we were going to do other things using the festival brand, a gigantic conflict broke out. If it had not been Putte, he had been thrown out at once. They wrote angry letters to each other and called me to meetings where they told me that I destroyed the festival brand and so on. My first year here mostly meant working internally to get permission to do new things, and I use to remind people about that now. It was just to take it cool, explain and deliver. (Lasse R)

No one at RockCity does, however, claim that they are mainly interested in money and business. Putte's view of this seems to be quite common among most of the actors:

Like everybody, I have had to work elsewhere and I've also been registered as unemployed. I worked at the paper mill, for example. I don't own anything of this, and that is a good thing. I was part-owner for a time, and that was not good; people started to think that we were earning money for ourselves. The envy that we have seen is rather a part of the mentality of an old industrial town, where no one was allowed to rise above others. I like doing a nice deal, but a nice deal is primarily an acknowledgement that I have done a good job that someone appreciates and put a high value on. Money is not interesting unless it can be used for something funny. (Putte S)

Still, Putte is most aware of the tensions, and knows that there will be future conflicts on the subject:

What happens if the commercial parts of RockCity become bigger than the festival? A lot of people work with the festival and are proud of that, and what happens if something else appears that is bigger and consumes more resources? If it is put that way, there will definitely be a hot debate. (Putte S)

Belonging to What? Local, Regional, National and International Arenas

Relations with the local context have been problematic since the beginning. Rock music and rock culture was strange in itself (as compared to the traditional local focus on sports and dance), and they interpreted the municipality as reluctant to support what was happening:

Then [1990] we had a debate with the municipality about us having destroyed the floor in the sports hall. It later appeared that it depended on a construction mistake, and that it had been actually destroyed by the athletes. But it was really not about who was to blame, they just didn't want us on the premises. (Putte S)

The perceived lack of understanding has – among other things – implied that they feel that the festival is accepted, but never embraced:

The relations with the town are really bad; the expression that you never become a prophet in your hometown is an accurate image of what we have experienced. Look here, here's a new brochure from the municipality intended to promote Hultsfred. Look at the pictures. Forests, forests, an airplane, a lake. And on the back side, a small picture from the festival. The Jante law[65] still applies, and some people don't like that we have received public funding. Even though all the money has been well invested. (Hanna R)

Most of the blame for RockCity not having become an established part of the local business life is put on the local politicians, who do not understand that the rest of Sweden have forgotten about the traditional industries and equates Hultsfred with the festival:

In five years, there will be twice as many students, I think. And the festival, of course. 95 per cent of the Swedish population think of the festival when they hear 'Hultsfred', they don't think of any manufacturing industry. We have had a better relation with the inhabitants of the town than with the politicians; the politicians have not been seen as representative in this matter. They are very positive when media direct their attention to the festival, but when you scratch the surface you sees otherwise. (Gunnar L)

The leading actors also think that their ambitions have taken them to another level, where the natural collaborators are to be found elsewhere. Two members of the actor network, Erkki Lahti and Per Kågefors, work with projects that include RockCity in developing the entire region, and through the music industry centre they seek to play a central role on the national arena:

The bigger we get, the more distance we get to the start of all this. It is not the same local connection as it used to be, and we are looking elsewhere for contacts and ideas. We don't pile up money in bank accounts, it is re-invested in new projects. There are other values to care for here. (Frederika S)

We have discussed a pure development company in which to gather all new projects, and we have also discussed to form our own venture capital firm here in Hultsfred for music industry ventures. There are no venture capitalists here, they are in Stockholm. But in Stockholm they know too little about the music industry and too little about working outside Stockholm, so that makes it even harder. (Putte S)

They also try to use different 'front persons' depending on what context they operate in. Some people are the faces of RockCity locally, Gunnar Lagerman symbolises the festival internationally, and Putte operates on the national level:

My strategy is not to be seen locally. I might be on the cover page of *Entreprenör*[66] and looked upon as the great businessman and all that, but at home I'm not seen at all. Instead, it is always the one that has been responsible or actually did the job that is to be seen. It's important that you always try to put the others in the light, and I've tried to do that for five or six years now. (Putte S)

Even though they are critical of the local connections, they are convinced that RockCity will nevertheless have a major impact on the town. In a way, this is already happening through the subsidiary RockCity AB, which is a joint venture between RockParty and the municipality. This conviction that their boundary work will one day be of central importance is even formulated in geographical terms:

In a long-term perspective, our relation to the town will change through the students. I'm not even sure that the traditional city centre will be the centre in the future, but that is an unimaginable thought for the locals who built the big centre blocks in the 1970s. To us, the city centre is the road out here, and it might be more blocks of flats and businesses along that road than in the traditional city centre. (Putte S)

The long-term vision is far beyond Hultsfred, at the same time as it means expansion in Hultsfred. If Hultsfred does not go to Europe, Europe will have to come to Hultsfred:

The national music industry centre here has formulated a development programme for the Swedish music industry that we are now presenting to the government. It is a plan on how to develop the whole Swedish music industry, and in due time we will establish a European music development centre here in Hultsfred. That is the long-term target. (Putte S)

In Search of Relevance: Contributing to Society

Already from the outset, the RockParty gang both loved and hated their home town:

The idea was that you should stay here in Hultsfred; you should be able to live here and still go to concerts with your favourite bands. That became even more important when the local factories here started to downsize. After high school, people moved to Stockholm, especially the women. The guys stayed here to a greater extent. We somehow felt that we should work against that trend. And our way of doing it, it was through music. (Putte S)

The problem with Hultsfred was – and is – economic stagnation and a lack of visions:

To many, this house might be a way to stay here in town. As compared to the days when I ran the record store, the town has stagnated. There are no commitment and enthusiasm there. This house is growing and there is rapid development here, but the city centre lags behind. The only thing you notice is that all houses are inhabited nowadays. Hultsfred has no business tradition, Vimmerby is the town of the merchants in this region. (Nisse J)

What they like about Hultsfred is knowing everybody, feeling that they are part of a community:

I have become a real Hultsfredian; you can actually find most things here. I'm not a big city guy, I don't like anonymity. I really enjoy staying and speaking to people I meet in the supermarket. In Hultsfred, everybody always say hallo to each other in the street, which astonishes my friends from other towns. I have travelled a lot in the world and have friends at many places, but it is nice to come home and know everybody you meet. I like life in the small town. (Patrik A)

Using RockCity as a tool for local development was not a natural thing, but it came to be through both emotional and business-related arguments:

> It was not a natural thing to expand during the 1990s, but we saw that we have had many people working for us during the festival that then ended up in Stockholm. We wanted to give them possibilities to live and work here in Hultsfred. It was both about keeping competence and friends here; it is not so fun to see the removal vans driving away. We do have a responsibility to society; it is about keeping up shops, schools, childcare and so on. (Patrik A)

In this sense, business and culture unites in the struggle for their hometown:

> Good business means you can invest in new projects, make your dreams come true, bring in more entrepreneurial people. We are trying to change our whole life here through establishing new businesses. I know several people who have said to me that they have stayed in town because of what we do here in RockCity. This house is for Hultsfred, anyone can borrow a key and go here! (Putte S)

BOUNDARY WORK AND IDENTITY CONSTRUCTION IN ROCKCITY

In the Hultsfred case, the question of deviating is central to the actors' conceptions of themselves in relation to society. They cherish their own self-image as deviators as a kind of prerequisite for their success, that is, their entrepreneurial processes imply co-construction of both the content of the process and its relation to the context. The relation to the context is mostly twofold, though, in the sense that it is usually constructed both in terms of deviating and belonging. In the early years, deviating implied rebellion, and rebellion implied that belonging was something sought for internally in the actor network and in the rock music culture. Today, deviating is to them the same thing as moving ahead of the rest of community, and belonging to society is taking responsibility for its future development rather than being conformist. In order to summarize this development and contribute to the ongoing discussion about how boundary work is socially constructed in entrepreneurial actor networks, we have identified three forms of boundary work that also imply re-creation and change of the world(s) they inhabit – including how they see themselves.

Re-constructing the Traditions of Local Community – Hultsfred

The leading actors at RockCity constantly complain about the local community not using the Hultsfred festival as a marketing tool and not focusing any school education on music. The image of Hultsfred is rather constructed as not being the RockCity and festival. Another problem with this relation between the local community and RockCity is that young people growing up in Hultsfred do not involve themselves locally to any significant extent. Instead people come from outside the town, for example the coast, and work or study for a while in RockCity. They then leave after some years for careers elsewhere and remain valuable network contacts to RockCity, but they do not improve the local community of Hultsfred.

If we only focus on the relation between RockCity and its local environment, the Hultsfred case could be seen as a case of 'liability of newness' (Stinchcombe, 1965, Aldrich and Fiol, 1994), where deviance from institutionalised norms implies problems for the entrepreneurial process. It is still not easy to convince the community of the benefits of what they are doing; compared to all the steady jobs at the local factories, rock festivals and music management is not really expected by the average citizen to imply any significant advantage for the town. In this case, however, newness has also been an asset for everybody involved – so much an asset that the RockCity gang has tried to preserve parts of it. Instead of conforming to norms, they build networks with those that share their view of reality – and their 'degree of deviance' also fluctuates over time. Their legitimacy and sense of belonging seem to rest not in the different entrepreneurial processes that they initiate – those are usually met with scepticism – but in the long-term ambitions and ideals that they try to maintain.

The local community of Hultsfred has been a threatened and stagnating environment throughout their lives, but it is also an environment that they cherish and want to protect. Through their interest in rock music they deviate from traditions about how and what should be done in this community; they create something new and unexpected in this peaceful little town. At the same time, you cannot live in a small community just as a deviant, and the members of RockParty soon realized that they also had an important mission where they lived. Still deviating at the same time as they are constantly networking to find allies and supporters, they actively work to make Hultsfred a part of the emerging TIME[67] sector in Sweden. In this work, the images of the local community as still focused on traditional forest industry and the town centre as a stagnating housing area are maintained as 'the other' to which they want to contribute.

Our interpretation of this boundary work is thus that the actors at RockCity are persistently working with changing the way people in Hultsfred view themselves and their community. From the very beginning, they have strived to make rock music a part of the local culture, initially through estranging rock culture from local traditions, later also through sensible and responsible interaction with the rest of the population in terms of business development, university educations and so on. Still, after almost a quarter of a century, there is much more to do, not least because most Hultsfredians do not see the same anomalies and disharmonies in their society as do the RockCity actors. Disclosing the new world of the youthful, entrepreneurial TIME sector Hultsfred community seems a long process.

Re-constructing the Boundaries of Actor Networks – RockParty and RockCity

The core of the entrepreneurship definition – to be outsiders at the same time as they remain connected to and involved in the community – can be interpreted as central for the RockCity actors' identity construction. They have always had problems with legitimizing their industry in the eyes of the common Hultsfredian; people cannot identify with rock music because they cannot link their own lives to that lifestyle. In the words of Spinosa et al. (1997), they succeed estranging themselves but fail to connect in a sensible way to actors outside their network. As an instance of entrepreneurship it is also outside traditional local identities, since it deviates from local traditions in terms of industry and through its emphasis on equality. From the beginning, the actors have also deviated as persons since they were punks, which meant that they looked different, acted different and thus created a distance between themselves and 'ordinary people'. Over time, they have become 'ordinary people' in the sense that they have bought houses, formed families and normalised their dress-code. It has meant that they are more likely to be accepted for who they are, even though their business deviates. Deviation is thus now an eternal process of trying to challenge boundaries, not least the ones that they themselves erect.

The actors at RockCity also see their organization as a haven for continuous entrepreneurship; they never want to become just an ordinary firm. The founders still want their organization to take risks, to challenge, and to contribute to the Hultsfred community. Newness is a part of the internal culture of the organization, and a lack of external legitimacy is to a large extent something that strengthens their internal view of what is legitimate. They organize their new project ideas in a special department and they also have individual 'idea banks' for potential ventures that can be picked up later on. Often ideas rest for a while and are used when the timing is right (Cohen et al., 1972).

The notion of entrepreneurship as fun, creative – but responsible – deviations is also central to the culture within the RockCity organization. They constantly strive to bring in young, enthusiastic people that will challenge and change taken-for-granted perspectives, but the long successful past is not always supporting this. A major internal conflict emerged when some of the members wanted to create a group of profit-seeking companies out of the festival brand; it was seen as too much of a deviation from the RockParty ideals.

And there are also examples of individuals that have left the organization because they were too individualistic and that way of being is not accepted in the organization. There are also examples of people that left because of the lack of structure and rules; there is an internal story about a man who continuously asked for a work description, and resigned when someone handed over a blank sheet of paper and a pen to him.

For a small group of deviant people whose ambitions are met by scepticism from others in the local context, it is definitely a challenge not to become victims of groupthink (Janis, 1972), and the focus on basic values (such as entrepreneurialism) rather than consensus on single projects seems to make this work. Externally, RockCity embraces all kinds of network contacts wherever possible. This kind of boundary work – constructing and re-constructing the limits of the actor network – implies the disclosure of new worlds of identities. Since the beginning of the 1980s, they have relied much on each other, and as deviators the construction of limits between themselves and 'ordinary people' has been central to their collective identity construction. In this process, they have sought external strangeness and internal sensibility. On the other hand, many of the problems that they experience (such as the debate on commercialism vs culture or the lack of women in leading positions) seem to be rooted in some of them being more strange to others in the actor network than they are to some 'outsiders'. Identities are thus always in the making, constantly becoming rather than being ready, which means that the basic anomalies and disharmonies always appear anew in other terms.

Re-constructing the Boundaries of the World to be Changed – from Local to International

Deviating in terms of international networks and building trust and belonging outside the local community is also something new in the local business life of Hultsfred. They work together with other towns in the region and with the regional authorities. They have established the national music industry centre IUC, which is based in Stockholm and Hultsfred. The market for the festival and RockCity is not limited to southeast Sweden; people come to it from all over Europe. In that sense the RockCity group deviates from local industries, which produce local services and compare themselves with other companies in Sweden. RockCity orient themselves towards big festivals in Europe and the international music industry, and in that sense they deviate from how a typical Hultsfred industry would act in relation to local society. To protect and build industries upon local culture resources are important for many provinces in Sweden and other countries. RockCity use the name Hultsfred as a brand for the festival, but the resources they use are not traditional resources from that area in Sweden.

Ever since the start of RockParty, the central actors have identified themselves as part of something bigger or other than the local community. In
several of their fields of operation, their natural collaborators are to be found
elsewhere. At the same time, they do not see this as either surprising or
discomfiting; it is rather that they want to widen the conceptions of what kind
of world Hultsfred is, and is part of. From the sensed disharmony between
what Hultsfred is and the positive consequences of making it become a part of
something bigger, the RockCity actors have tried to re-construct the notion of
locality. While that has been successful internally (that is, it is perceived as
sensible), it has so far seemed strange to others in the town.

ROCKCITY VS THE HULTSFRED COMMUNITY –
PROMISES AND PROBLEMS IN COMMUNITY
ENTREPRENEURSHIP

In the words of Spinosa et al. (1997), entrepreneurial action and identity
construction in RockCity in relation to the Hultsfred community involves
articulation, reconfiguration and cross-appropriation. To a quite large extent,
their boundary work and self-image as deviants seem to consist in articulating
and making use of basic values that have been a part of local community for
decades. They describe Hultsfred as a place where people are loyal to the
town, where it is not acceptable to rise above others in terms of status and
wealth, where people come together in clubs and associations and create
things on a voluntary basis, where music and parties have always coincided.
When constructing the RockParty/RockCity spirit as something different and
radically new, they make use of many of the same values and practices that
have always defined the Hultsfred community (cf. also Hjorth and
Johannisson, 2003).

The entrepreneurial actions in the RockCity network have also involved
reconfiguration – i.e. that hitherto marginal aspects of a style become central.
As a small industrial town, Hultsfred has always been dependent upon national
and international demand for wood houses, batteries and pulp, and the region
is still the home of wood house manufacturing in Sweden. Still, the people at
RockCity maintain that Hultsfred has been far too locally and regionally
focused, and no one had any idea on how to keep the local youth from moving
away to Stockholm. From the RockCity perspective, Hultsfred needed to
embrace and make use of the national and international orientations that had
always potentially been there, making the world coming to Hultsfred rather
than the other way around. By explicitly defining their own operations as
directed towards national and international markets, they wanted to show the
rest of the community how such a re-configuration could happen.

In the relation between RockCity and the Hultsfred community – as it is perceived by the people at RockCity – there are thus several instances of more or less 'successful' cross-appropriation of values and practices (that is, the taking over from another world a practice that could not be generated in the present one, but that is still found useful). Within itself, the RockCity organization has been moderately successful in combining an idealist, rebellious, left-oriented notion of rock music culture with the harsh, ultra-commercial realities of the modern music industry through articulating and appropriating practices and values from local community. Even though this has involved serious conflicts in the organization – and even the threat of splitting it up into parts – it has still been a source of what is seen throughout Sweden as something new, exciting and challenging.

In relation to local community, cross-appropriation of what has been learned in the world of RockCity for the development of Hultsfred has not been that straightforward, though. In RockCity they think that their way of organizing both voluntary work and business operations are things that other industries and the local society should try, and they also think that they provide access to the TIME sector and other knowledge-intensive, fast-growing segments of the economy – things that should be essential and most useful to a small, stagnating industrial town far away from bustling 'regions of excellence'. This has not been easy; they have worked with their own role as an anomaly in local community for years without finding a way to 'get through'. Instead of their practices and values becoming new normalities after a temporary deviance, they are still stuck in a situation of seemingly eternal cross-appropriation without the construction of any other normalities apart from the traditional ones. This is visible not least in their maintenance of a self-identity as deviant rebels and their perceptions of the 'local people' as 'others' – a kind of dichotomization useful in many business-related situations but less so in processes of community development and change. On the other hand, Hultsfred has never experienced any major economic crisis like a sudden closedown of a major factory – which might otherwise have created an arena where the deviant voices of the RockCity people could have attracted a wider local audience (Hjorth and Johannisson, 2003).

From the example of Hultsfred and RockCity, it might be concluded that community entrepreneurship in the form of establishing new organizations intended to move ahead of the community is not that easy. New organizations may help communities to articulate and re-configure practices and values, thereby changing the style with which inhabitants look upon themselves and their common concerns. As sources of new practices and values to be cross-appropriated into communities, new organizations like RockCity might be too homogenous, simple and un-bounded by history to be able to make substantial contributions to something as heterogeneous, complex and history-dependent as a whole local society. Unlike the common business entrepreneur, community entrepreneurs must perhaps get used to the idea that work is done in an eternal process of constructing deviations and belongings, rather than expecting that their communities will, in a not-too-distant future, assume new values and practices and change the style by which they perceive people and things.

To conclude, entrepreneurship means doing boundary work in several ways, and boundary work means balancing sensibility and belonging for the sake of changed practices, rather than strangeness and deviation for the sake of re-defining how we see the world and handle it. This also means that entrepreneurial processes in communities may take much longer than processes of bringing new innovations to the market – if they finish at all. What keeps the community a community are the shared traditions and values with which its members identify, and the disharmonies that may appear are usually not more serious than ones that most people can live with throughout their lives. Community entrepreneurs must always assume the values and practices of their communities in order to belong, and they can never count on their fellow citizens to become part of deviating actions – other than during brief periods of crisis and confusion. Community entrepreneurship can, in the long run, be described as an eternal balancing act between deviation and belonging – constantly striving to make history without being able to leave anyone or anything behind.

11. Discursive diversity in fashioning entrepreneurial identity

Karin Berglund

INTRODUCTION

It is late summer 2001 and we find ourselves in Katrineholm, a small town which, with two other municipalities, make up a region[68] in central Sweden. The freshness in the air this morning encourages the drawing of deep breaths, which the managing director of the local trade and industry office does on his way to work. The summer flowers and foliage are pleasing and on the point of changing into the display of colours that the autumn offers. This is exactly what they emphasized in the promotion of the borough's vision of 2010 he thinks, with the beautiful countryside and many lakes hereabout.

His good mood at the start of the day changes considerably later on when he is informed that two of the largest companies in the community are planning to close down. When it is time for the press conference, about a week later, another large company – perhaps also historically the most influential – announces its intention to transfer the major part of its business to another town. Torchlight processions, banner headlines and television broadcasts characterize these chaotic days, a turbulent period that inhabitants describe as 'the great catastrophe', which results in 1,500 people being made redundant. At the same time, an EU project application awaits approval at the European Social Foundation (ESF) Council; the ESF in Sweden is responsible for programs aimed at strengthening the individual's position in working life in a way which contributes to growth and increased employment. Some weeks later the application is granted and the project, Diversity in Entrepreneurship (DiE), becomes a reality.

DiE is a project which aims to create and promote entrepreneurial activity by means of group processes and, as it is an Equal initiative (one part of the European Union's strategy to combat inequality and discrimination with regard to the labour market), its overall purpose is to combat all kinds of inequality and discrimination in the labour market. For DiE this involves the promotion of entrepreneurial activity among women from ethnic minorities, school-leavers, disabled people, and cultural workers who are underrepresented in business in the region. In the regional debate about entrepreneurship a new voice is heard. An equality discourse enters the debate in which all inhabitants are seen as potential entrepreneurs, and where entrepreneurship becomes the 'things' that are created in relations between people.

The equality discourse challenges prevailing conceptions of entrepreneurship in the region – the enterprise discourse – rooted in historical, social and political processes, where economic rationality is both a means and a goal, managed by the men who (to a certain degree have) run the large manufacturing companies in the region in which the inhabitants have participated as industrial workers. A mostly implicit conversation begins of what entrepreneurship could – and should – mean, which touches on what is to be included and excluded. A crucial debate, it seems, for inhabitants who are all affected – directly or indirectly – by the changes occurring within their region. In both discourses there seems to be an agreement about the need for people who can somehow replace the loss of the companies. However, different, and perhaps also conflicting, goals and means are emphasized in the two discourses. Nevertheless, the hunt for entrepreneurs has begun.

During this period Lena and Sara are both about to start their companies. In this chapter, their entrepreneurial endeavours are described via their own accounts and those of others, which have been gathered during a two-year long ethnographic study in the region. Both Sara and Lena tell of their new situations, and how their ideas have brought them into a new way of life. For Sara, who was previously an entrepreneur in Denmark, it is the context which is new, whereas Lena is involved in business for the first time in her life. The transition from one stage to another, for instance from employee to entrepreneur, from unemployed to employed or from student to entrepreneur, could be regarded as a journey where increased self-reflection occurs, raising such questions as 'who am I?' and 'where am I going?' (Wåhlin, 1999, p. 126). To realize a business idea is certainly not an act performed in a vacuum; to a great extent it involves interacting with the world, as discussed by among others Hjorth and Johannisson (2000).

During this interaction one is suddenly positioned as an entrepreneur; if not in one's own eyes then in those of many others (Lindgren and Packendorff, 2003; Warren, 2004). Starting a company is thus a process which – among other things – also involves becoming surrounded by discourses of entrepreneurship which offer certain identity positions. As in all life-changing situations, this entails identity implications. Johansson (2004) and Lindgren (2000) hold that the study of identity construction could bring new insights to entrepreneurship research. What we learn from Lena and Sara is that although they have different business ideas, visions and expectations they also have some things in common: both live in the community depicted above, both describe their companies as a venture which changes their lives, and both face the enterprise and the equality discourse prevalent in the region. However, it is the case that they seem to relate to the discourses quite differently which is of interest in this chapter.

The fashioning of a new identity is understood as involving two sides of a coin. On the one hand it is a process in which individuals interact, communicate and draw upon discourses in the reality construction of a self (Lindgren and Wåhlin, 2001). On the other hand it is a process in which we, in order to become subjects, must relate to certain given versions of the world – discourses – that put us in certain positions. One can thus compare discourse to a linguistic inter-play where 'people use language – and sometimes – where language uses people' (Alvesson and Kärreman, 2000, p. 1126). And as Gergen (1991) concludes, it is the language of the self which constitutes the self, and not the other way round. This reasoning departs from a linguistic approach where conversation is seen as the principal vehicle of reality-maintenance, as people construct their reality thereby (Berger and Luckmann, 1966).

Conversation, language and text are not neutral, transparent media but exert effects, since they both set up boundaries and constitute resources for what is possible – not solely to speak – but also to do. Starting a company is, hence, an act which, inter alia, means to become an entrepreneur and this identity raises some expectations of Sara and Lena, which emphasize the co-constructed nature of identity. It is thus of interest to study how Sara and Lena relate to the enterprise and equality discourse when they describe themselves and their relations to their entrepreneurial endeavours. We must also pay atten-tion to the positions in which they are put during their interactions with people in the region. The purpose here is to elaborate on the relation and potential displacement between the enterprise and the equality discourse by focusing on the identity construction process by asking: *how is the enterprise and equality discourse present in Lena and Sara's stories as entrepreneurs?*

To this end, the regional context and field work will first be introduced. Secondly, the relation between discourse and identity will be elucidated. Thirdly, the enterprise and equality discourses are sketched in more detail. Fourthly, I will come back to Sara and Lena by interpreting their stories as those of entrepreneurs. This should, hopefully, give us something to reflect upon in considering what it might mean to become an entrepreneur. This chap-ter is thus not about telling 'how it is' but rather 'how it might become', and thereby encouraging us all to consider our involvement in (re)producing certain stories about entrepreneurship.

THE FIELD OF TEXTS

The region KFV constitutes the context here, which should remind us about the many *con/texts*[69] that relate to the catastrophe, entrepreneurship, and Sara and Lena's endeavours in the region. I intend here to give a first overview of some of the texts of importance, which are gathered in a two-year long ethnographic study following the project Diversity in Entrepreneurship. DiE is a regional attempt to increase the entrepreneurial spirit where about thirty different organizations have joined forces to 'develop strategies, methods and practices to create an organizational infrastructure that promotes entrepreneurship characterized by diversity' (Application, 2002, p. 1). The ethnographic study is one part of the DiE project, which has provided access to formal and informal meetings, seminars, conferences and activities, all connected to entrepreneurship in the region (see Berglund and Johansson, 2003; Berglund, 2003). Consequently, contacts with actors from the organizations as well as participants from the target groups were straightforward. By this I do not mean that the empirical material was easily accessible but that the research project was never questioned, which made it easier to establish contacts with the general public.

The field work involved personal participation, and on these occasions I observed and took field notes. I paid special attention to interactions among the people involved, to differences of viewpoints, to which voices are heard and which are ignored, and to the topics discussed. Since I do not live in the region, which is one hour distant, I have had plenty of time to read through the field notes and reflect upon the happenings of the day on my way home. Alvesson and Deetz (2000, p. 187) discuss the relation between proximity and distance as an important part of illuminating empirical phenomena, and thereby putting them in a state of tension between the established order and borders that could be crossed in order to problematize what is taken for granted. Geographical distance has enhanced such tensions, not to mention moving from one context to another; for instance, I have travelled from meetings at the national agency that handles issues concerning industrial policies to meetings with the mobilization group consisting of women from ethnic minorities and disabled people. This interplay between contexts, and the proximity and distance to the field, have not only enhanced reflection but has also made it easier to avoid involvement in everyday work, and to keep uppermost in my mind the question: what do the natives do when they carry out – or support – entrepreneurship?

The loss of companies in the region and the structural changes this has entailed has lead to a situation where inhabitants are leaving and where an increasing number of inhabitants have become unemployed. This topic – or text – has been a recurring theme during the field work, which has also been disseminated to other arenas. In a publication by NUTEK[70] (2002) and in the Regional Growth Program (2003), the region is pointed out as one of the most vulnerable areas in Sweden with regards to the labour-market. In the environmental reports complied at the instigation of the Swedish government the region is characterized in the same way (Engström, Larsson and Wigren, 2002a; Engström, Larsson and Wigren, 2002b; Engström, Stenberg and Wigren, 2002). There is certainly a need for those who are left behind to start to do something, and one inhabitant expresses the following view of what is needed in the region:

> So we have to work so as not to become a dormitory suburb . . . but we want, of course, entrepreneurs to move here and bring their companies, so that the region can grow and so that we will get many more small companies than the large ones we had before (Comment from a focus group interview).

The hunt is on for entrepreneurs that could 'save' the region from its troubled situation. The desire for new companies and people who could start and run them was frequently voiced during the field work. These people – the entrepreneurs – are, however, not expected to be found locally:

> You know, we have never been entrepreneurs here . . . (Comment from a focus group interview).

> This is a place where ordinary people don't do anything; instead they are all waiting for a new industry to show up (Comment from a focus group interview).

After all, large companies dominate ideas of enterprise and their patriarchal culture is said to have deeply wounded the self-esteem of the inhabitants. It is not difficult to understand why inhabitants look elsewhere for entrepreneurs when the latter are perceived as risk-taking, independent, imaginative and creative individuals, as this picture stands in sharp contrast to the characteristics of an industrial worker.

Early in the project I felt that many questions were raised, and the more I participated the more unanswered they seemed to become; I was studying a scene, but I could not make sense of the drama I was following. For instance the local authorities were not interested in participating, although the project description emphasised that its main goal was to change the structures in the community and thereby promote entrepreneurial activity among its inhabitants. Presumably they neither regarded themselves as part of the project nor of the structures (see also Stridh, 2002). Moreover, the project team were constantly troubled trying to anchor the project among the organisations in the development partnership, which are the organizations that have joined forces to develop a more entrepreneurial region. Furthermore, the inhabitants expressed that they were not comfortable with the discussions on entrepreneurship, and as research shows many people do not like the epithet 'entrepreneur' (e.g. Warren, 2004).

At that time all this was a major obstacle to different processes in the project, so I wanted the inhabitants to talk about their region and its potential, as well as incidents, issues and questions which had emerged during the field work in order to capture what was taken for granted with regards to entrepreneurship. For that reason, eight focus group interviews[71] were staged, where twenty-four actors from the organizations in the partnership were offered an arena for discussion. On these occasions the interviewees were asked to reflect on the future prospects for their region. All focus group interviews were transcribed and, together with DiE project documents, newspaper articles, public documents and the Regional Growth Program[72] in the county, they make up the corpus of text which has been analysed. The texts that make sense of the equality and enterprise discourse were thus gathered from many sources in order to include the different voices of entrepreneurship in the region.

THE INTERPLAY BETWEEN IDENTITY AND DISCOURSE

Departing from a social constructionist understanding, the epithet 'entrepreneur' is an identity created at each and every turn of life: 'it is from the myriad forms of language exchange between people that the person emerges', writes Burr (1995, p. 53). Self-identity is continuity, across time and space, as interpreted reflectively by the agent (Giddens, 1991b). Identities are thus not 'fixed' entities but are always in process, and discourses constitute our common linguistic resources from which we draw in order to represent our selves in a certain way; or to resist such representations, and which simultaneously put us in certain positions (Wetherell and Potter, 1992). Remember here that we both make up our selves by discourses – the active part of the subject – and are made up by discourses – the passive part in which we are made subjects. Discourse here refers to a set of meanings, metaphors, representations, images, stories and statements which together produce a particular version of the world (Foucault, 1972; Laclau and Mouffe, 1985).

A frequently referred to definition by Foucault (1972, p. 49) says that 'discourses are practices which form the object of which they speak'. Burr (1995) invites us to consider that this apparently circular statement also sums up the relation between discourses, ourselves, and the world we inhabit. In this vein, a discourse constitutes simultaneously both a resource and a restraint for what we can say and do (see Ainsworth and Hardy, 2004). On the one hand, a discourse driven subject appears, while on the other, agency appears, viewing people not only as products but also as producers of discourse. Following a line of thought of Hosking and Hjorth (2003), there are always multiple texts available to produce a story of our selves but not anything goes, they remind us, as 'there are limits to what will be socially certified' (p. 262). From this standpoint, the fashioning of an entrepreneurial identity depends on what versions of the world we relate to at a certain time in history, in a particular place, and in a particular social situation.

In everyday life we are caught up in a flow of discourses and the identities in which we are positioned are seldom called into question. Since no such thing as one fixed self exists we constantly relate to different identities; sometimes we are men or women, mothers or fathers, and brothers or sisters. But identity construction goes beyond these basic epithets and in our working lives we usually identify with what we do; for instance we are dentists, lawyers, plumbers, researchers and so on, but we also tend to identify with our private interests and tastes. The list of potential 'identities to become' seems endless, something we rarely consider in the daily routine where we perceive the self as a whole and disregard the fact that our identities are constantly shaped and transformed.[73] Consequently, talk of the self reveals how we draw upon available discourses in our reality construction and how we imagine ourselves free to create different identities depending on the discourses at our disposal.

Nevertheless, 'one is not totally free to fashion one's identity since some discourses combine better than others' states Ahl (2002, p. 59), and demonstrates how well the identities 'white', 'man', 'father', 'entrepreneur' and 'industrial leader' are combined. If we are about to become entrepreneurs then this is an identity that must fit our set of existing identities. Moreover, it is not only our own conceptions of entrepreneurship that are of importance, we must also relate to other people's conceptions as well. Identities do not grow within us but *between* us. The creation of a new identity depends, therefore, on socially constituted identities, social relations and social representations of the world (Wetherell and Potter, 1992). The notion of positioning acknowledges the active mode in which people locate themselves within a particular discourse during interaction; 'who one is, that is, what sort of person one is, is always an open question with a shifting answer depending upon the positions made available within one's own and others' discursive practices and within those practices, the stories within which we make sense of our own and others' lives' (Davies and Harré, 1990, p. 35). The concept 'identity work' is used by Svenningsson and Alvesson (2003, p. 1165) in their study of a middle manager's identity work in a knowledge intensive firm which refers to 'being engaged in forming, repairing, maintaining, strengthening or revising' the self. Identity work highlights the *active* positioning in the fashioning of an identity. Hence identities derive from adjustments of the self, from multidimensional work in (re)negotiating the self since we are always subject to other people's expectations and conceptions, which both facilitate and limit the identity construction process.

DISCOURSES OF ENTREPRENEURSHIP

'One does not need an extensive discourse analysis to illustrate that approaches of entrepreneurship and entrepreneurs are affected in a mainly economic discourse', write Steyaert and Katz (2004), who use an example from an OECD report to demonstrate how entrepreneurship is regarded in society: 'Entrepreneurship is central to the functioning of market economies. Entrepreneurs are agents of change and growth in a market economy' (OECD, 1998, p. 11). The European Commission's Green Paper on entrepreneurship in Europe states that 'entrepreneurship is multidimensional and although it can occur in different contexts, economic or other, this Green Paper focuses on entrepreneurship within a business context' (ibid., 2003, p. 5). Entrepreneurship *can* occur in different contexts but these are not relevant. It is the business context which is relevant. Entrepreneurship involves economic consequences as it has the potential to create new jobs and ensure that the Western World does not disappear. There is no denying that a hunt for entrepreneurs is in progress in society, not the least of which can be seen within the European Union, where programs with a focus on innovation and renewal are launched for the purpose of putting Europe on the centre of the global stage. Entrepreneurship is chiefly seen as the panacea for economic dilemmas, and most public efforts to promote it incorporate a general assumption that entrepreneurship means bringing new, or growing, companies into the market. In the same vein, new ventures and business start-ups are ascribed a considerable significance within entrepreneurship research. Accordingly, entrepreneurship is equated with the creation or growth of new companies.

The hunt for entrepreneurship and entrepreneurs is distinguished by a zeal for categorization in order to trace the 'true' individuals, companies, lines of business and so forth. From the Green Paper (2003, pp. 5–6) we learn that there are certain common characteristics of entrepreneurial behaviour, as those pursuing such activities are ready to take risks, have a taste for independence and self-realization, and regard themselves as more imaginative and creative than others. There is an obsession with 'dividing the world into entrepreneurs and non-entrepreneurs', according to Sarasvathy (2004), and this division focuses our attention on the characteristics of the people who fulfil the requirements associated with entrepreneurship. However, to construe the world in terms of those people who are entrepreneurs and those who are not produces one particular type of knowledge, which brings power inequality between different social groups. This notion is significant inasmuch as the separation of entrepreneurs and non-entrepreneurs leads us to think of two different categories of 'people with inborn attributes' (Ogbor, 2000, p. 618).

Categorization, thus, has power implications since we must contend with the conceptions of some groups of claims and ideas, so that power is to be understood as 'power over the thought' (Lukes, 1990), or 'power as productive' (Foucault, 1974), rather than power possessed by a few individuals. We need, therefore, to consider what positions the discourses of entrepreneurship offer, as they serve as a guidance for what one is up against if one is about to act entrepreneurially. The distribution of entrepreneurs among separate social groups suggests a view of these groups and their acts as isolated processes without any point of contact with each other. When, for instance, we speak of entrepreneurs, young entrepreneurs, women entrepreneurs, ethnic entrepreneurs, solo entrepreneurs or high-tech entrepreneurs we also divide these groups into diverse categories and, simultaneously, create different, demarcated, analytical rooms. In these rooms the division of significance for each group and the search for explanations of specific conditions take place. It is, thus, a challenge to see how these rooms are created and changed in relation to each other, since they affect those who are in the process of fashioning themselves in an entrepreneurial identity. Furthermore, if these rooms are neglected – what new insights can we then obtain?

'Entrepreneurship' and 'entrepreneur' are words that have been with us since the sixteenth century (Landström, 2000) and are, thus, concepts shaped by historical, social and political conditions; as a result we perceive them to signify objective features of the world. However, these words are all contingent; that is why there is never a 'true' meaning, only *different* meanings which can be more or less fluid in society's currents (Laclau and Mouffe, 1985); some are more fixed and perhaps taken for granted, while others become stabilised in the context of their construction. There seems, however, to be some consensus with regard to entrepreneurship in society, namely that the entrepreneur is a special breed who is very good and useful to the community, and that this is a creature for which to be on the look out as it enables us to live in a prosperous society; moreover, it is involved in financial pursuit which leads to economic growth and the creation of new jobs. This discourse corresponds well with how entrepreneurship is represented in the scientific community (Ahl, 2002; Ogbor 2000).

Another assumption must also be added here, which is the construct of gender, as the creature to be sought is clearly a man who is strong-willed, determined, persistent, resolute, detached and self-centred (Ahl, 2002). To quote Ogbor (2000): 'Entrepreneurship is conceptualized by this ideological orientation as if it were a concrete means by which the rational European/North American male model exhibits the propensity to take risks, to conquer the environment and to survive in a Darwinian world' (p. 618). The entrepreneurship discourse discussed, contains some of the overall assumptions in society where the economy seems to have become both a means and a goal, and where the man is represented as the superior living being who behaves in a rationally economic manner (du Gay, 1986; Hjorth, Johannisson and Steyaert, 2003; Hjorth, 2003).

This overall description of entrepreneurship represents a mega discourse and can be seen as a standardized way of referring to entrepreneurship in society, which does not capture the newly begun regional conversation of what entrepreneurship could, and should, mean. So in order to understand the regional context I will move from this mega representation of discourse to meso representation, as this is the level of use as a researcher who is interested in broader patterns in similar contexts (Alvesson and Kärreman, 2000). The regional corpus of texts has been of value here as it constitutes the material for contextualizing the entrepreneurship discourse, an analysis which is inspired by Laclau and Mouffe (1985) according whom the starting point in mapping a discursive field is to trace special concepts called *nodes*, which have a privileged status, to see how they are defined in relation to other signifiers. A discourse, or a 'chain of equivalence', is thus established through signifiers that are equivalent to the node, but not the same as the node, and drawn upon in speech of (in this case) entrepreneurship (ibid., p. 112). One of these chains is the *enterprise discourse*, which arguably draws from the mega entrepreneurship discourse in society:

> *Enterprises* – are – *industries* – which – *employ workers* – and – *produce products* – with – *profit* – run by – *business owners* – who are – *men*.

The enterprise discourse incorporates some features of the entrepreneurship discourse, although it derives its distinctive character from the region's historical, political, social and ideological systems and norms. The other approach to entrepreneurship is found in the discussions in DiE where equality is stressed as a main goal that has resulted in an *equality discourse*, which is meshed with the entrepreneurship discourse as follows:

> *Entrepreneurs* – are – *all humans* – that – *use opportunities* – to – *self-fulfilment* – in – *relations* – which bring – *economic value*.

This discourse is most clearly expressed in the DiE documents and is later extended to the regional development program. In the equality discourse, entrepreneurship is emphasized as belonging to *all* humans, though they have some unique qualities as 'renewal expects great things from entrepreneurs who can make *use* of opportunities' (RDP, 2003, p. 19, emphasis added). The use of opportunities is, however, a process also involving other people, institutions etcetera, so that the entrepreneurial act is conceived as an inter-relational phenomenon which includes people. But all people are not included, yet. The RDP (2003, p. 43) says that 'odd businesses, ideas from youth, women and immigrants are met with scepticism despite having great potential', which indicates that these groups hold a separate position in discursive practices fixed by the enterprise discourse. When Atkinson and Davoudi (2000) discuss the concept of social exclusion within the European Union, they conclude that there is a tension between enhancing economic performance and combating social exclusion, and that the former is consistently dominant. The equality discourse thus challenges the enterprise discourse in the regional playground, and in the 'discourse order' (Fairclough, 1992) it is the runner-up as it emphasizes equality and other social values, instead of economic rationality (see also du Gay, 1999).

In the light of the enterprise discourse both Lena and Sara are players who, because of their gender and ethnic background, play in a separate division. The region's scenario for development – socially and economically – is undoubtedly affected, which is an argument used in both the enterprise and the equality discourse to motivate people to act entrepreneurially. In local parlance both discourses are employed, more or less entwined, but the enterprise discourse seems to set the agenda with its rationale of economic growth. On some few occasions, the differences between the discourses have been made visible as they have ended in antagonistic relations when people refer to entrepreneurship in two completely diverse ways, which have brought forward the 'other' rationale calling for an egalitarian society (Berglund and Johansson, 2003). The awareness of the difference between the enterprise and the equality discourses is, though, expressed by a few and as a rule the shifts between them are subtle. However, Sara seems to employ both discourses at their extremes.

A FIRST ENCOUNTER

One of the focus group interviews is coming to an end and the usual follow-up discussion is taking a long time. All three participants are entrepreneurs who, besides running companies of their own, are also involved in different business associations and interested in what could – or should – be done to develop their community. I have an interview appointment with Sara in half an hour which I mention, as time is running out. Suddenly all of them are involved in the following conversation:

> A: Do you mean the innovative mushroom firm?
> B: I helped her to restore her premises . . .
> C: This is exactly the kind of company that this community needs!
> B: Yes, there you have a true entrepreneur. Nothing holds her back . . .
> (Field notes)

This is not the first time during the interviews that I have been informed about

Sara and her new mushroom company in town. On this occasion one of the interviewees had been restoring the old dairy in which Sara's business is situated. On other occasions I have met her bank contact, a local politician who is enthusiastic about the business under construction, a project leader for another EU project in which she participated when she first moved here and a many other people who have told me about 'the crazy business idea'. All seem eager to tell me about this new venture. 'If you can cultivate mushrooms *here* you can do practically anything', I am told. Sara's entrepreneurial endeavours seem to involve a large number of inhabitants who talk about this 'woman who cultivates mushrooms', how 'well she is doing' and how she 'thinks differently'. One could say that the mushroom company has become a regional affair and some people are even involved practically in the attempts to establish her company, for instance the local politician mentioned above who encouraged her to play off the employment office against the social welfare service in order to introduce a course on mushroom cultivation for new employees. So when I was invited to the opening ceremony of her company I was really looking forward to meeting Sara for the first time as I, among others, had become fascinated with the stories told about her and her company; her idea, visions, plans – well, her whole appearance – seemed intriguing.

At Sara's opening ceremony, strangely enough, I also encounter Lena for the first time. At that time both of them are about to start their companies and eagerly describe their business ideas and what they seek to accomplish. But when Lena discusses the different keep-fit treatments and measures she will offer and the benefits they can confer, she becomes more anxious when the conversation touches on her company. Sara, on the other hand, is by no means as vague when she says that her fresh Thai mushrooms will be in every other Swedish supermarket in five years, employing five hundred people and next heading for the European market. In the interview with Sara a few months later, she describes her company and her plans before I have time to ask, and describes herself as follows: 'I'm sort of like the water that flows around the rocks that emerge. If a rock comes in my way I just try to find a way around it . . . How can one otherwise break new ground?'

In contrast, in my interview with Lena I have plenty of time to introduce myself and she does not start to tell her story until I ask her to. Then, the first thing she says is: 'Well, at this time I feel I've spread myself too thinly.' This statement recurs frequently during my conversation with Lena. While Sara refers to herself as 'the water running' Lena speaks of herself in terms of division and fragmentation. Sara seems neither to accept nor to reject her position as an entrepreneur; instead she moves on and assumes different positions during the conversation, while Lena feels split in her position as an entrepreneur.

Remember here that we are never the sole authors of our own narratives as discourse is part of every conversation, constituting our linguistic resources (Czarniawska, 2004). Sara and Lena are about to become the desired entrepreneurs so that there are certain hopes and expectations of their endeavours, which both the enterprise and equality discourse report; without including them in the conversation. This is what power in a Foucaultian view is about, putting people in certain positions, and in the dominant enterprise discourse the 'proper' position is held by the money-making man offering vacant jobs in a large manufacturing company. This should raise a degree of inconvenience for both women; the question is how they try to resolve this position. Following Burr (1995, p. 125), who argues in favour of viewing people *both* as actively producers, manipulators, *and* as products of discourse, makes it possible to understand that we can also resist the discourses of which we are subjected. We should, thus, be open to the capacity to identify, understand and resist the dominant discourses by which we are surrounded; a troublesome question also for the researcher interested in identity work.

STUDYING IDENTITY WORK

During the field work, I not only encountered Sara and Lena but also came across other 'prospective' entrepreneurs in the KFV region. I met them all on one formal interview occasion where I asked them to tell me about themselves, their ideas and companies. These interviews can thus be seen as a complementary identity study to the ethnographic study. According to McAdams (1993) the 'personal myth', which is here designated the self, is a kind of life story that integrates the diversity of role expectations common in modern life. 'We do not discover ourselves in myth, we *make ourselves* through myth', writes McAdams and 'our sources are wildly varied, and our possibilities vast' (p. 13). A self-presentation thus says something about our identities as it reflects how we relate to the world around us. Sveningsson and Alvesson (2003) beautifully illustrate what it takes to study identity: 'In order to understand identity in depth we need to listen carefully to the stories of those we claim to understand and to study their interactions, the discourses and roles they are constituted by or resist – and to do so with sensitivity for context' (p. 1190).

I do not claim to have followed Sara and Lena over a long period as I only met both once where they were asked to give a spontaneous account of their journey through working life, though there have been other occasions during the field work where our paths have crossed. Nevertheless, the contextual understanding is thorough and an intention to *listen* to the stories was definitely my guiding principle. My interest was, thus, to listen to their narratives and hence to trace elements of change, contradiction and fragmentation in their life-stories in order to discern how they tried to fashion themselves in an entrepreneurial identity. They were therefore asked to talk freely about themselves and their business ideas and, as interview situations are often perceived as complex and somewhat artificial, I invariably sought to attain a 'normal' conversational tone to encourage candour.

My experience from all of my conversations with the prospective entrepreneurs is that while some, like Sara, willingly shared their stories – one story merged into another – others, like Lena, found it difficult to talk freely without direction in the form of detailed questions. This notion is important, since the task was to deliver a story about themselves *and* their company. Hence, a 'who-am-I' story with regard to business was requested which raised serious misgivings for some. My first impression from the interviews thus consisted of their differences in producing their stories. At first this was confusing as I tried to make sense of *what* they said and not *how* they said it. So besides listening to what was said, their ease in telling a story relating to themselves and their businesses was observed. Differences in producing stories were also noticed by Johansson (2004) in his study of nine small business owners; he writes: 'some entrepreneurs I have encountered have seemed eager to tell their stories while others have been more reluctant' (p. 286). He mentions several factors that may have disturbed the interview situation in different ways and thereby affected both the narrator and the narrative, such as my presence as a researcher (with certain attributes which have particular meaning for particular people), how the first contact was established and the occurrence of different interview contexts (Johansson, 1997, pp. 184–187). These are naturally acceptable reasons to question certain statements that were made, but a narrative always contains a self-presentation which somehow comprises the narrator's self (Mishler, 1986). The intention here it to interpret how stories were *produced* and how the enterprise and equality discourses were drawn upon and integrated in Sara and Lena's life stories.

THE FASHIONING OF AN ENTREPRENEURIAL IDENTITY

I step out of the car outside the old dairy that has been converted into premises for local companies. Presumably I seem somewhat lost, as a man emerges and calls to me. This turns out to be Lars, Sara's partner in business as well as privately. Both of them take part in the interview eagerly, presenting their intention to grow fresh Thai mushrooms in Sweden, the opportunity to create a new market, the opportunities for this company to expand and how they expect Thai mushrooms to become an everyday commodity throughout Europe. The enterprise discourse is obviously drawn from their discussion of market plans, the number of future employees needed, how to appoint a board of directors and so forth. In the next moment Sara refers to 'the things that matter', and explains that their future staff is of utmost importance as it is hard work to grow mushrooms ecologically:

> You know, this company is going to be an arena for integration. There are so many people in this community who are excluded from the labour market. It's a great shame! In my company there will be a mix of immigrants, Swedes, old workers, school-leavers, different ethnic minorities and so. And here they must all have respect for their co-workers. Otherwise they can look for a job elsewhere . . .

Apparently she uses the equality discourse to describe the purpose and the goal of the company, I muse. In the next sentence she returns to the different expansion strategies, and is then interrupted by her first employee who needs some practical guidance.

Sara leaves the room for a while and I feel confused as I try to grasp the different turns in the conversation. One moment she is talking about how her company will serve as a small society guided by equality, and the next she emphasizes that she will conquer the whole European Thai mushroom market. These goals stand out as being full of contradictions, and Sara ends up the same way. When she returns I give up trying to understand her and instead listen to what she has to say. The way Sara composes her story, by constantly drawing from different discourses, as if arbitrarily, seems to confuse more people than me. She is not only puzzling but a puzzle to solve, and while people try to solve this puzzle she moves on with her efforts to start a company of the size, vision and purpose she has in mind. Sara actively takes a stand as an entrepreneur as she refers to herself as a serious businesswoman, while the next moment she rejects what she perceives to be dominant conceptions of entrepreneurship. For instance she asserts what she *is not* or does *not do*: 'You know, I'm not a man. I don't run one of those large manufacturing companies and I'm definitely not in this only for the money [laughing].' These are all topics pertinent to the enterprise discourse, which is drawn upon but simultaneously rejected on the grounds of 'otherness'. However, she never turns into 'the other' but seems to use the two discourses to escape dominant conceptions and move on with what matters to her: to build an organization which is based on heterogeneity, trust and respect, and to create a successful company which can expand to produce mushrooms all over Europe.

These are ideas and goals that people around her regard as ambiguous, in the same way that they perceive her. The portrayal of the self as an entrepreneur is in Sara's case obvious, though she does not entirely 'buy' the conceptions brought by the enterprise discourse. On the contrary, if a conception does not fit her self it is actively rejected, a reaction which closely resembles that of the women farmers in Fournier's (2002) study who use categories at whim, which made every attempt to understand them impossible as they worked actively to disconnect from people's perceptions by continuously moving 'somewhere else'. This strategy to reject dominant conceptions by being on the move is also found in other contextual settings. In their study of identity work in a knowledge-intensive company, Sveningsson and Alvesson (2003) describe how an R&D manager 'actively positions herself apart from what she views as trivial matters' (p. 1180). Sara seems to move unconcerned into and out of different positions by way of active work to both connect and disconnect to the enterprise and the equality discourses.

On my way to the interview with Lena I recall my conversation with her about a year ago at Sara's opening, and her enthusiasm about the different treatments and their effects. She seemed well-informed about her products and services and what good they could do, but was more reticent about her plans to start a company. It will be interesting to hear her story, I think, before I enter her premises, which are centrally located. 'I have recently moved here to be able to have some contact with other entrepreneurs', she tells me. Apparently she shares the premises with two other women who have similar business ideas. 'It's perfect, because then I can learn from them'. Well, that is good I think and am curious about what she can learn, as there must be a fine balance between being a colleague and being a competitor. 'I need to learn to be in business', she continues, 'because I am not that, an entrepreneur, you know'. Lena seems to try to find a text to which she can relate, a text which offers her status in the business community and which also fits her personal preferences. So, I ask her to describe such a person to me: 'That is a strong businesswoman who is self-confident and that picture doesn't fit the rest of me. I sometimes wake up in the morning and wonder if I am still going to run this firm.'

Once the struggle to become this person, whom she describes as risk-taking and brave, who is in business for money, is articulated, she continues for another half an hour and the conversation becomes somewhat introspective. She almost seems to forget that I am in the room and that the interview time has run out. The point here is not that she is doing poorly – she has acquired more and more customers and she seems to have made a living from her idea of running a keep-fit measures company – but her story reveals that she is struggling to relate to herself as an entrepreneur, which is even articulated as follows: 'To set a price is the same as to set a price on oneself. When a customer complains about a service it really hurts me – personally – and I don't want to charge.' One crucial struggle is to set a price for the services she offers as these are closely connected to her identity as an entrepreneur, an identity with which she is not comfortable (see also Ahl and Samuelsson, 1999). She therefore finds it difficult to raise the prices and realizes at the same time that she must do so otherwise the company will collapse.

She only has one body to use, and she already works both evenings and

Saturdays to make ends meet. The level of pricing proves to be a balancing act between opposite claims as she does not perceive herself to be a person who could charge very much for her services. It is striking how Lena falls foul of conflicting goals, which creates an identity dilemma that is difficult to solve. Lena says she likes what she is doing and also seems content with her new colleagues and the new place. Yet she constantly reconsiders her entrepreneurial endeavours as she needs to become the 'tough businesswoman' and charge more for her services, and her colleagues turn into role models and teachers in her struggle to become more entrepreneurial. Obviously Lena is struggling to produce an integrated and meaningful identity connected to entrepreneurship, an identity that is constituted by the enterprise discourse and which – at least partly – is in conflict with her perceptions of herself. In the case of Lena the puzzle of identity is not to be solved by someone else but by herself; while Sara positions herself as an entrepreneur Lena struggles, and while Sara moves on Lena gets caught.

AT THE CROSSROAD OF ENTREPRENEURIAL DISCOURSES

Becoming an entrepreneur should be seen as a complex collection of processes, intertwined and woven together, since they are connected to and interlinked with diverse arenas in life. This process does not imply that there is one single road to follow; though there seems to be two prominent 'walking styles' since discourses are drawn upon in different ways. One could say that both Sara and Lena ask the questions outlined in the effectuation theory: Who am I? What do I know? and Whom do I know? (Sarasvathy, 2001). Except, they do it differently.

In the case of Lena she illustrates her struggles in walking towards the epithet 'entrepreneur' as constituted in the enterprise discourse. Lena is positioned by the enterprise discourse in a way which retains its status in the discourse order and, despite feeling uncomfortable, she nevertheless seems to accept the standard definition of an entrepreneur and struggles to equip herself with a socially constituted identity befitting a person who is determined, rational, and self-confident and so on. The fundamental features of the dominant enterprise discourse are reproduced unintentionally, referring to entrepreneurship as a primarily economic act.

In contrast, Sara walks into and out of the epithet 'entrepreneur', and by using both the enterprise and the equality discourse, she disconnects from dominant conceptions of entrepreneurship using a walking style which is interpreted as an act of disconnection in order to move freely. Sara seems to relate to both the enterprise and the equality discourse to move on with her ideas; moreover, the fact that she is becoming known as 'the mushroom woman' who does something new and that the local newspaper has published several articles about this new, exciting venture, challenge the perceptions of what entrepreneurship could mean as well as of what an entrepreneur can be. Her story has thus, so far, similarities with history-making, which means that entrepreneurs, through their innovations, change the way we see particular things (Spinosa, Flores and Dreyfus, 1997).

Johansson (2004, p. 278) concludes that the entrepreneurs in his study '*not merely* tell stories as an account of their experience. They *also* live out their affairs in storied forms'. But we should also remember that those stories are always negotiated in relation to others, as we are never the sole authors of our life stories. Looking at the manuscript that Sara and Lena have produced so far gives an impression of having found a 'good' and a 'bad' solution, respectively, to how to deal with the enterprise discourse if one does not fit its description. I would, though, argue that this is an illusion where one would easily look for some form of causality regarding how to 'behave', which holds us back from seeing identity work as a relational process.

Following Sara and her endeavours in the region for almost three years has certainly been a roller-coaster experience. One moment, she is expected to produce the new jobs, growth and equality that are sought after in the region. Her organization could very well be described as heterogeneous, employing about twenty-five people of all ages, of both sexes and from different social, ethnic and religious backgrounds. Yet, the next moment she suffers from setbacks, such as a conflict with the landlord, which forces her to move the company to another town, followed by production problems and bankruptcy. Next she is back making new deals as a contractor supplying mushrooms to two of the largest grocery chains in Sweden, and last year she also received the 'Entrepreneur of the Year' award from a national organization that supports entrepreneurship and business start-ups. However, again she has suffered a major setback as she has gone bankrupt a second time, and what she will do in the future is uncertain.

Sara's entrepreneurial endeavours have become highly ambiguous as she draws from both discourses. It is in conversations with inhabitants that the difficulties in moving the enterprise discourse towards the equality discourse become visible. The story of Sara and her company, as told by inhabitants, shifts from a heroic tragedy to comic irony and she is used as an example of both 'what is possible to do' and 'what could happen if you start a company'. In my conversation with two sisters who were advised not to go through with their business idea, they legitimated their actions referring to Sara's bankruptcy, which put them in a favourable light as 'responsible people' acting rationally, and in an economically well thought-out way.

Changes such as those in Sara's process are not part of Lena's entrepreneurial endeavours, which are neither paid such attention to – nor filled with any certain hope – in the region. When I recently met the new managing director for the office of local trade and industry in Katrineholm, she told me about an idea to transform a central building into a 'market place':

> This should be an arena for everyone so that they can try out their ideas collectively with other people who are in the same situation. One will never be alone here [at the 'market place']. There will always be some kind of social support available, such as a day-care centre. The idea is not only to foster new companies. No, it deals with making entrepreneurship available for all the people (Field notes).

The equality discourse seems to gain ground and, unexpectedly, Lena's story becomes rewritten; she can become an entrepreneur on her own terms. Lena has recently served as a model of an entrepreneur in a newly started network which aims to support entrepreneurship among women from ethnic minorities in the region, and she is no longer reconsidering whether she is going to continue her life as a self-employed person; instead she seems to reappraise her new entrepreneurial identity:

> This is more independent work. I can decide myself how I want to work, develop myself and so. There is no longer anyone who says that you cannot be that person, or that one, or that one. No one gives me money at the end of the month saying; here is your salary thank you for working for us and goodbye.

MOVING ENTREPRENEURSHIP

To move entrepreneurship into new realms we need to make the different ways of discussing and conceiving entrepreneurship visible in society, state Steyaert and Katz (2004). By paying attention to identity work among prospective entrepreneurs, this chapter has provided a glimpse into how the enterprise versus the equality discourses work in both changing life in the community as well as the lives of certain people. From the equal discourse we learn that there are alternatives to the overall economic discourse in society, whereby new opportunities involving values other than purely economic ones could be created if people start to perceive entrepreneurship in unconventional ways (see Rehn and Taalas, 2004; Johnstone and Lionais, 2004). In a world in which entrepreneurship seems to have become *the* solution to bringing about growth in order to maintain our system of welfare, with the equality discourse there is a gleam of hope as it addresses equality, interaction and the mundane. In contrast to the enterprise discourse, it includes us all in the world of entrepreneurship. By means of the equality discourse, there is perhaps a small chance to move a step further away from the economic rational human being to a more playful one (Hjorth, 2004), making values other than economic ones an alternative rationale for our decisions, and making us perceive the relational component in the creation of opportunities. This is probably a journey to Utopia; however, what we can do if we want to be part of such a journey is to repeatedly remind ourselves that there are other options regarding how one can perceive entrepreneurship in society. So each and every time we are about to tell a story of entrepreneurship, or when we talk to friends who are considering starting a company, or when we are engaged in staging a new entrepreneurship project, I would suggest that we stop for a moment and reconsider the alternative ways there are of talking about entrepreneurship.

12. City of enterprise, city as prey? On urban entrepreneurial spaces

Timon Beyes

A: I don't have any idea what this is, here, this prey I live in. What sort of PREY is this, I'm LIVING IN! THIS HERE! There is this city and it is prey, and suddenly location marketing is transferred to human organisms.
(. . .)
A: But in this thing here, this . . . city, it wasn't just marketing that was announced all the time, was it? Some time or other something else was sold in this city, wasn't it? It cannot have been selling just itself all the time! This shit! City development policy cannot have been location marketing and the transformation of public spaces into real estate all the time.
(. . .)
P: In face of the reduction of industrial workplaces communities see themselves forced to developing entrepreneurial profiles. (. . .)
A: This SHIT-COMMUNITY HERE IS DEVELOPING AN ENTREPRENEUR-IAL PROFILE! We're lying around in this community hooked on location market-ing or city development policy – I DON'T KNOW FOR SURE ANY MORE! And some entrepreneurially driven gas has taken over from the physical manifestations of factories. And all the demands for self-fulfilment and autonomy have been real-ized by this community out there. (. . .) Suddenly there are all these service firms lying around in this community.
P: SHIT! THIS SHIT-COMMUNITY HERE IS DEVELOPING AN ENTRE-PREURIAL PROFILE! And its management philosophy is transferred to human organisms. THIS HERE! And all you walk through, here, is city management. The city as company. Here you stroll through MANAGEMENT! And anyway you just stroll through management. Your walking is MANAGEMENT! You walk through this town, and your walking is regulated through consumption, milk coffee and architectural design, that you can take a look at or SWALLOW.
F: Shit. And that I'm working within a body-less factory here. In a company fluidizing itself. It's all around me, here, this SHIT! Somebody has called this new, growing form of power, HERE! That you're sprinkled in, that I AM sprinkled in, somebody has called it gas, gas that's taking over from the physical manifestations of factories. WHO WAS THAT AGAIN? SHIT! I don't have a damn life anymore, it must have sold itself when I wasn't watching. (. . .) There used to be something, and sometimes things reminded me of something I had once, but it has somehow vanished into air. And where I used to live once, there's some sort of retail area now
(. . .)
B: All we talk is corporate gas, and that's clouding our social displays. This here.

This PREY! This face, of which I love the fluid technology of power. But I thought this would be yours, this would be your technology of power or self, or mine, but it's just your company's!
(René Pollesch, *Stadt als Beute*, my translation)

DISCOURSE THEATRE

Who was that again? 'Damn Deleuze', an actor shouts laughingly, having lost his line again, unable to keep up with the bewildering cut-ups and samplings of recent social theory and fragments of entrepreneurial 'lingo' that make up the plays of German writer René Pollesch (2002a, 2003). Pollesch, who writes and directs his plays mostly at the *Prater*, side stage of Berlin's *Volksbühne*, has created a theatrical approach some critics have dubbed 'discourse theatre'. In a way, it is a theatre of entrepreneurship. Instead of focusing on individual subjects as entrepreneurs – this being the dominant approach in entrepreneurship research (Holmquist, 2003) – Pollesch's plays dig into the discourse of managerial entrepreneurship that is apparently so hegemonic these days (du Gay, 2004). Borrowing Yeats' famous line – How can we know the dancer from the dance? – it is not the dancers of entrepreneurship that are of interest, it is the dance of entrepreneurship (Gartner, 1988). With Pollesch, dancing is in focus instead of individual subject positions: Regardless of the topic his actors grapple with, they cannot avoid falling into managerial/entrepreneurial semantics, throwing fragments of 'business-speak' at each other, ever so often, as in the examples cited above, questioning their lives through excerpts from recent social theory, but in the end unable to escape the seemingly all-encompassing enterprise discourse. Drawing on poststructuralist theories, Pollesch mostly de-individualizes his texts. There are no 'characters' or 'persons' being developed on stage, it is just texts: assemblies of popular management and entrepreneurship literature and 'postmodern' theory. What seems to be missing is any 'Brechtian' lesson and subsequent code of practice pressed upon the audience. The actors throw themselves against the walls of the discourses constructing them as entrepreneurs of themselves, so to speak, without ever finding a way out.[74]

In *City as Prey* (*Stadt als Beute*), Pollesch turns his attention to urban spaces. Drawing on an article by the afore-mentioned Deleuze (1993) and a reader by critical German urban sociologists and city planners, from whom he borrows the play's title (*Die Stadt als Beute*, Ronneberger, Lanz and Jahn, 1999), the play deals with 'the production of space' (Lefebvre) through the discourse of managerial entrepreneurship and its consequences. It addresses how what used to be perceived as a city has turned into something else, something new (Becker et al., 2002), something the 'discursive apparatuses' on stage desperately circle around – something Edward Soja calls

'Postmetropolis', signalling the transition from what has conventionally been called the modern metropolis to something significantly different (Soja, 2000). Instead of factories and clear hierarchies, manifestations of the Foucauldian disciplinary society, the actors in *City as Prey* find 'announcements inside of themselves' demanding that they always behave entrepreneurially. Although at times desperately yearning and searching for an alternative, they stumble on nothing but entrepreneurial spaces, be it their bodies, their homes – another Pollesch play is called *Insourcing of Home* – or cityspace.

With Pollesch's plays, then, there is a master narrative, a discourse dominating and absorbing other possible discourses, and it is a narrative of entrepreneurship having taken the form of enterprise discourse (Hjorth, 2003). It lays down the rules and regulations for what to say, for what role to enact. It provides us/the actors with 'regular' practices. It produces reality (Hjorth, Johannisson and Steyaert, 2003; for this notion of discourse, see Foucault, 1971; Bublitz, 2003). In *City as Prey*, the topic of urban spaces is sucked into this master narrative, leaving nothing to talk (or scream) about but retail areas, privatization of public spaces, shopping malls, favourable conditions for corporate headquarters and start-ups, deregulated urban labour markets and place marketing.

UNGROUNDING ENTREPRENEURSHIP RESEARCH

At least with regard to his take on entrepreneurship, Pollesch has his point. In reading the historiography of entrepreneurship research, Hjorth and Steyaert (2003) diagnose a central line of thought commanded by economic theories and presently dominated by studies in management theory and business administration. In discussing representations of entrepreneurship within entrepreneurship research, Hjorth (2003) concludes that the dominant enterprise discourse, being composed of managerial notions of what is entrepreneurial, limits our understanding of social creativity to a set of managerial tools. Instead, Hjorth calls for other concepts, other lines of flight, from both students and practitioners. For that, we should look for other sources of knowledge and concepts in order to open entrepreneurship research to different forms of entrepreneurial activity. Moreover, as Hjorth, Johannisson, and Steyaert remark, the arena for entrepreneurship may surpass technology and economy (Hjorth, Johannisson and Steyaert, 2003). It may be treated as a societal rather than an economic phenomenon, thereby steering observations toward manifold forms, practices and concepts of entrepreneurship. It might be seen as 'a model for introducing innovative thinking, reorganizing the established and crafting the new across a broad range of settings and spaces and for a range of goals such as social change and transformation far beyond those of simple commerce and economic drive' (Steyaert and Katz, 2004, p. 182).

The purpose of this chapter is to explore a possible opening in entrepreneurship research through a spatial perspective: by focusing on urban spaces. After all, when it comes to urban entrepreneurialism, the unit of analysis, the city, is wholly different from, say, a start-up company. Also, rather than assessing the entrepreneurial city as a site of economic production or as an object of governance (Liggett, 2003) urban spaces may be regarded as potential 'lived spaces' (Lefebvre) – as potential sites for reorganizing the established and crafting the new. Interwoven with this text, then, is the assumption that it takes sites and spaces for social change and transformation to happen and that sites and spaces may be constituted through entrepreneurial activities. 'What spaces have we privileged in the study of entrepreneurship and what other spaces could we consider?' Steyaert and Katz ask, looking for other places than Silicon Valley to study entrepreneurial activity (Steyaert and Katz, 2004, p. 183). And, it might be reformulated here: what kind of spaces have been observed in the study of entrepreneurial cities, and what *other spaces* could be observed?

Pollesch's staged claim of converging spatial and entrepreneurial discourses, leading to the social production of cityspace through the dominant narrative of enterprise, sets the stage for the search for different entrepreneurial spaces. What do we talk about when we talk about possibly converging discourses of entrepreneurship and urban spatiality? For that, I will look for other traces of convergence, couplings of territorial and entrepreneurial tellings, to undermine or cast doubt upon what the actors in *City as Prey* scream out in disgust or toy with. Also, the two central concepts are in need of closer scrutiny: what is generally being described with the notion of entrepreneurship in urban contexts? And what might be observed with the concept of socially produced spaces?

There are different ways to read Pollesch's plays, of course. In the following, to explore answers to the questions raised, I will attempt two different readings: Firstly, perceived as an *apocalyptic tale*, the writer/director's texts convey a bleak message: there is no escaping the hegemonic reign of enterprise discourse. Cityspace is produced, controlled and commonly interpreted through this master narrative. On the foil of recent developments in spatial theory, however, I will attempt to propose a different story: an *exemplary tale* of Pollesch's theatre as an other entrepreneurial space. For this, I will pick up on the above-mentioned critique of the notion of entrepreneurship as used by scholars and practitioners alike. There may be more to the concept of entrepreneurship and urban entrepreneurialism than the enterprise discourse, indeed. 'Space' may become the site where the (re)production of dominant narratives is interwoven with the inevitable production of alternatives, of 'lived', 'third', 'heterotopic' – and in this sense, entrepreneurial – spaces (Liggett, 2003).

Proceeding along Foucault's notion of heterotopic space (Foucault, 1991b, 2005), the search for other entrepreneurial spaces will be tentatively applied to Pollesch's theatre itself. After all, a 'discourse theatre' makes a difference. It interferes with the world. Hence, this will also be a political story about seeking engagement (Law, 2004), about 'not [to] be blind to what is out there' (Pollesch, in Monroe, 2005, p. 12), about taking issue with the circumstances of everyday life as well as about changing the process of how a theatre play is developed, rehearsed and staged.

Art and literature, like science, are possible fields of second-order observations, hence generating descriptions, producing knowledge (Luhmann, 1999). Science and poetry are knowledge in equal measure, writes Deleuze (1987), and every literary text appears as part of orders of knowledge if it reproduces, confirms, corrects or moves the borders between visible and invisible, sayable and unutterable, as Joseph Vogl (2002) beautifully points out in his 'poetology of knowledge'. Dealing with a variety of sources, exploring possible openings through connections between different forms of knowledge as well as evading a fixed disciplinary vessel calls for an open, essayistic form of writing. Being methodically anti-method and continually discontinuous, as Adorno (1984) puts it, an essay nourishes its anti-systematic impulse and privileges fragments and fractures instead of totalities. For Adorno, writing essayistically means proceeding experimentally, taking detours, questioning, reflecting and examining the topics in question from diverse angles without achieving closure, without proceeding from a fixed starting-point to a predefined ending. Seen this way, crossing research on entrepreneurship and entrepreneurial cities with thoughts on and observations of socially produced spaces suggests a form of writing that echoes the simultaneous presence of difference and its immanent conditions of indeterminacy and possibility (Deleuze and Guattari, 1997). 'This puts research back in the position of search' (Hjorth and Steyaert, 2003, p. 291).

A FIRST, APOCALYPTIC READING: THE DRAMA OF ENTERPRISE DISCOURSE

> Every culture has its characteristic drama. It chooses from the sum total of human possibilities certain acts and interests, certain processes and values, and endows them with special significance . . . The stage on which this drama is enacted, with the most skilled actors and a full supporting company and specially designed scenery, is the city: it is here that it reaches the highest pitch of intensity (Lewis Mumford, *The Culture of Cities*).

The notion that urbanization and urban life are closely interlinked with market mechanisms is far from new. In Max Weber's work on the sociology of urbanity, the existence of commerce and trade, as well as associated activities such as the establishment of markets and exchanges, account for the rise of modern cities. The city basically is a market settlement, complemented with a certain degree of political and administrative autonomy (Weber, 1980). In Georg Simmel's seminal essay 'The Metropolis and Mental Life' the sociologist/philosopher argues that the modern metropolis allows for such a high concentration of capital that the integration of space, time and social actors reaches a hitherto unheard-of complexity and that speed and intensity of social and economic interactions in the city has led to the advent of a new, modern society (Simmel, 2002). The essay, which is widely seen as the empirical essence of Simmel's grand theory of modernity as laid out in his 'Philosophy of Money', presents the metropolis and its inhabitants' behaviour as embodiments of the money economy's procedures and doings (Lindner, 2004) – a century before Pollesch would deny his actors any way out of the enterprise discourse.

For Marxist urbanists, the key to understanding cities is to be found in the dependence of the configuration of space on the domination of capital and hence on the commodification of space into an asset that can be bought and sold. In short, the capitalist production of cityspace determines the urban environment (Parker, 2004; Harvey, 1985). Departing from his earlier, more orthodox Marxism, the sociologist Castells has come up with the *space of flows* as analytical concept to account for contemporary urban processes, exchanging the focus on capital flows for a network perspective. Nevertheless, one of the central layers constituting the space of flows refers to the spatial organization of the dominant, managerial elite exerting the dominant spatial logic (Castells, 2002). Building up on these arguments and studies, contemporary 'postmodern' researchers like Soja diagnose a profound change in what the city represents, a 'simultaneous interplay of deterritorialization and reterritorialization' resulting in a 'hub of fusion and diffusion, implosive and explosive growth, a First-Second-Third World city wrapped into one' (Soja, 2000, p. 153), a postfordist, globalized, fractal postmetropolis.

It is on this foil that Pollesch's texts can be read as resigned, apocalyptic tales paying tribute to the notion that in the realm of capital, every kind of opposition emanates from the very powers it supposedly revolts against (Sloterdijk, 2004), echoing the classic Marxist admiration for capitalism's ingenuity, recently revived through a healthy dose of Foucauldian and Deleuzian theory by Hardt and Negri's bestselling treatise *Empire* (Hardt and Negri, 2001). With Pollesch, though, one will not find much of socialist theory's belief in inevitable change and progress. In the writer Don Dellilo's work *Cosmopolis*, this argument is beautifully captured by the protagonist and entrepreneurial *wunderkind* Eric Packer, who watching an anti-globalization riot, muses:

> Even with the beatings and gassings, the jolt of explosives, even in the assault on the investment bank, he thought there was something theatrical about the protest, ingratiating, even, in the parachutes and skateboards, the styrofoam rat, in the tactical coup of reprogramming the stock ticker with poetry and Karl Marx. He thought Kinski was right when she said this was a market fantasy. There was a shadow of transaction between the demonstrators and the state. The protest was a form of systemic hygiene, purging and lubricating. It attested again, for the ten thousandth time, to the market culture's innovative brilliance, its ability to shape itself to its own flexible ends, absorbing everything around it (Delillo 2003, p. 99).

Coming back to the notion of managerial entrepreneurialism figuring so prominently in Pollesch's plays, the notion of companies taking over artistic and counter-cultural modes of production and work in order to further enhance their productivity is a recurring theme running through the writer/director's texts. In his 'Heidi Hoh' plays, the actresses talk about their 'irregular lives' – once a progressive utopia, now a decreed lifestyle in deregulated markets: the revolution as a company offer. Echoing the romantic artistic notion of art and life falling into one, Heidi Hoh is invited to fully bring in her subjectivity and feelings, to realize herself in her job, exploiting the most private spaces as economic resources (Pollesch, 2003). Do so-called 'counter-cultural' strategies of living or arts really deserve their title when, in the end, they supply the rough, reterritorialized, entrepreneurially promising diamonds of the 'official' urban cultural economy (Diederichsen, 2002)?

Very much a Pollesch question; indeed, a question that on stage would probably be 'resolved' by some screamed obscenities – before going back to the entrepreneurial business. In his *Postscript on Control Societies*, Deleuze (1993) picks up Foucault's writings about disciplinary societies, trying to describe an upcoming form of power and control. Foucault, claims Deleuze, knew about the relatively short span of historical time his concept of the disciplinary society would be an apt description for, culminating at the beginning of the twentieth century in robust milieus of enclosure, like family, school, hospital, prison and factory (Foucault, 1998). After the Second World War, these technologies of discipline started falling into a major crisis. According to Deleuze, as of today – read 1990 – the milieus of enclosure are in permanent crisis, exemplified by the rhetoric of decline and the struggles for reform organizations like prisons and factories have found themselves in. But new powers are at the doors: control societies are taking over from disciplinary societies. Whereas the enclosures work like different stable casting molds that form the individual, the controls resemble modulations, casting molds forming and deforming themselves, changing from one moment to the next.

Whereas the factory assembles individuals to a framed corpus, says Deleuze, in a control society it is replaced by the concept of business or entrepreneurship that works like a soul, a gas that passes through the individuals, splitting them within itself – 'the instrument of social control is now called marketing' (Deleuze, 1993, p. 260, my translation).

One feels tempted to relate this critical notion to the discourse of managerial entrepreneurialism that is targeting the employees' selves. To become successful and make a contribution to the organisation's well-being, according to the presently reigning managerial knowledge, the employee's self-management should be directed towards the ideal of an initiative-taking, opportunity seeking, enterprising – but nevertheless, of course, of a responsible and reliable individual. Entrepreneurship in the form of enterprise has become the dominant force within the technologies of the self, the controlling mode of assembly producing the contemporary subject (Hjorth and Steyaert, 2003; Bröckling, 2004; Bröckling, Krasmann and Lemke, 2004).

While the French philosopher supplies the conceptual framework for *City as Prey*, Ronneberger, Lanz and Jahn come up with empirical descriptions on how conventional politics of urban development have turned to location marketing for the 'entrepreneurial city' and thus to 'new urban politics' (to borrow the title from Hall and Hubbard, 1998) in German agglomerations. Being in constant competition with other cities, city management focuses on becoming an attractive location for corporate headquarters, start-ups and tourists, this way turning inner cities as well as suburbia into landscapes of consumption, malls and theme parks, a corporatization of cityspace which the artist Nils Norman has called 'urbanomics' (Ronneberger, Lanz and Jahn, 1999; Ronneberger, 2001; Norman, 2005). Much in line with Deleuze's suspicions, the German researchers diagnose that in entrepreneurial cities, social space is increasingly observed and discussed on the foil of security and order, thus provoking rhetorics of social warfare about missing safety, urban poverty, inner-city decay, drugs and organized crime, discourses that lead to gentrification, measures of exclusion and the advent of gated communities at the same time.

Observation of social stratification and changes in the urban social order has 'traditionally' been home turf for urban sociology. Hence, one of the major academic discourses around the contemporary western metropolis circles around the notion that newer urbanization processes go hand-in-hand with intensified socio-economic inequalities, taking shape in the immigration of global labour, a postindustrial underclass or the rise of the black economy (Häußermann, Kronauer and Siebel, 2004; for an overview see Eckardt, 2004; Soja, 2000). And on a global level, Lanz and Becker (2003) angrily observe the consequences of entrepreneurial governance by assembling a disturbing array of urban 'orders', or rather, disorderly produced conditions of violence and poverty: descriptions of urban realities that on the foil of so-called Good Governance (Bundesministerium, 2000) would simply, far too simply, be interpreted as results of competitive deficits and bad administration – as in Medellín, Kampala, Lagos, Sarajevo, among others.

CITY OF ENTERPRISE

> The city of enterprise has boomed and busted. Partly in consequence, the fate of the permanent underclass has if anything worsened; but, strange accompanying trend, the city of theory has become even more academically detached from the city of globalized, polarized reality (Peter Hall, *Cities of Tomorrow*).

When it comes to urban discourses, then, the concept of entrepreneurialism has become a veritable movement, albeit a floating one, in itself. As Jessop (1998) remarks, the thematic of the entrepreneurial city is often linked to neo-liberal discourses (as, critically, in *City as Prey*). If one looks through the literature, though, it might also be linked with neo-corporatist, neo-statist, or even community-based modes of governance. To broaden the scope to a possible common denominator, these diverse approaches usually agree in conceding that the success of entrepreneurial city-strategies depends on market forces (Jessop, 1998). According to Hall and Hubbard (1998), producing a legitimate standalone argument to tie up the approaches to urban entrepreneurialism or even coming up with any definition of *the* entrepreneurial city would be difficult, if not impossible. Broadly, two characteristics of urban entrepreneurialism are defined: 'a political prioritization of pro-growth local economic development' and 'an associated organizational and institutional shift from urban government to urban governance' (Hubbard and Hall, 1998, p. 4).

Painter, understanding entrepreneurial urban regimes as reflexively constructed political phenomena, has mixed feelings about the concept of an entrepreneurial city: Who is being entrepreneurial here? The city? Its residents? The politicians? To give an idea what this concept might connote, Painter comes up with a range of meanings (Painter, 1998, pp. 260–261):

- 'The city as a setting for entrepreneurial activity' implies that a city resembles a location for investment and risk-taking by private businesses.
- 'Increased entrepreneurialism among urban residents' would lead to a growing proportion of residents becoming entrepreneurs themselves.
- 'A shift from public sector to private sector activity' would mean that an increasing amount of urban activity is undertaken by the private sector.

- 'A shift in the values and meanings associated with urban living in favour of business' – exemplified by the figure of the 'yuppie' back in the 1980s.
- And Painter's own definition: 'A shift in urban politics and governance away from the management of public services and the provision of local welfare services towards the promotion of economic competitiveness, place marketing to attract inward investment and support for the development of indigenous private sector firms'.

From a discursive point of view, one is tempted to add to Painter's list a narrative perspective, tackling the phenomenon that – whether local economic developments have recently been reoriented or not – entrepreneurial rhetorics have been widely adopted by urban politicians and city planners. Furthermore, as Hall notes, one of the most obvious manifestations of entrepreneurialism among city governments has been the attempt to transform, or at least enhance, their city's image – in other words, to tell stories, to invent or reconstruct an image, a 'carnival mask of late capitalistic urbanism' (Harvey) – a strategy that has been dubbed 'boosterism'. Somewhat attesting to Deleuze's suspicion about marketing having become the contemporary instrument of social control, marketing cities has been identified as 'the principal driving force in urban economic development' (Bailey as quoted in Hall, 1998, p. 29). As Dobers shows by analyzing the narrative of Stockholm as an IT city, creating images of cities has become progressively important in so-called entrepreneurial cities (Dobers, 2003).

Hence, although (or perhaps because) the entrepreneurial city refuses to yield a generally accepted definition, today the notion of cities being run in an entrepreneurial manner is widely subscribed to, serving as a regular part of local politicians' and public administrators' semantics. Similarly, Hall and Hubbard diagnose, the idea of urban entrepreneurialism is currently in fashion among academics, especially in urban geography, but also among planners, sociologists and cultural theorists. In recent years an impressive array of studies has emerged, analyzing the rise of entrepreneurial cities throughout the western world and the growing importance of so-called entrepreneurial policies (Hubbard and Hall, 1998).

TOWARDS SPATIAL OPENINGS

It is at this moment that the mode of production dominates the result of history, takes them over and integrates within itself the 'sub-systems' which had been established before capitalism ... without, however, managing to constitute itself as a coherent system, purged of contradictions. Those who believe in the system are making a mistake, for in fact no complete, achieved totality exists ... (Henri Lefebvre, *The Survival of Capitalism*).

If the dominance of enterprise discourse is this culture's characteristic drama, to borrow Mumford's phrase, then for Pollesch it appears to be a disconsolate drama being enacted in urban realities as well on the *Prater* stage. Having tentatively looked for and mapped connections between a 'discourse play', a poststructuralist theory of power, critical observations by urban sociologists and descriptions of the entrepreneurial city by other urban theorists, one could stop here, content with reading *City as Prey* as an apt apocalyptic tale. After all – and judging from the gathered empirical and conceptual evidence – discourses of urban politics and entrepreneurship seem to have converged and formed a practically powerful and theoretically fascinating, if somewhat broad, notion of urban entrepreneurialism – a strong movement or, as Pollesch would probably register it, a totalizing discourse producing entrepreneurial narratives and great efforts in place promotion as well as turning public spaces into private real estate, shopping malls, landscapes of events, and so forth. Solely under the conditions of entrepreneurial city development, it appears, can progress be made (Becker, 2001).

But there seems to be more in urban theory – and in entrepreneurship research. As to the latter, Hjorth, Johannisson, and Steyaert point towards a dominating enterprise discourse in entrepreneurship texts that comes equipped with a particular vocabulary: a managerial one (Hjorth, Johannisson and Steyaert, 2003). Looking at the writings on entrepreneurial cities, one recognizes that the approaches to urban entrepreneurialism – critical or affirmative – are drenched in business semantics. By leaving his actors trapped within enterprise discourse, Pollesch's texts echo this discourse's rules and regulations. And on the side of critical urban theory as cited above, the enterprise discourse is equally dominating, assigning these texts the role of examining the entrepreneurial cities' underbelly.

Putting aside an apocalyptic reading, its grand theory and close-to-totalising epistemology, one could also (and more carefully) read the writer/director's plays as important pieces of social criticism pointing towards possible social consequences of the perceived rise of entrepreneurial managerialism. More specifically, Pollesch's harsh grasp of entrepreneurialism may direct one's attention to the one-sidedness of the enterprise discourse itself, suggesting the need to think differently about the concept of entrepreneurship, reminding us that there is more to the entrepreneurial city than being a site of economic production or an object of governance (Liggett, 2003), and that there might be more to entrepreneurship research than the enterprise discourse (Hjorth, 2003).

To explore such an opening, I suggest considering approaches dedicated to the social production of space, conceptualizations of space that grapple with 'the play between desire for order and the need to reach what escapes it' (Liggett, 2003, p. 38). For what Foucault calls 'the dangers of discourse' always leave room for other narratives, for innovative thinking, for reorganizing the established and crafting the new – for entrepreneurial activities. And when searching for these phenomena, we usually look to cities as arenas of activity (of multiple contradictions and interlocking spatial practices). The tyranny of conventional representational forms is never complete. Space appears to be a suitable analytical category to deal with questions of social change, for example by observing where and how the (re)production of dominant narratives are interwoven with the inevitable production of alternatives, of 'lived', 'third', 'heterotopic', and in this sense, entrepreneurial, spaces (Liggett, 2003).

At present, the so-called *spatial turn* figures quite prominently in social scientific circles, denoting a renaissance of 'space' as conceptual and analytical category; renewed attention is being paid to the spatial side of the historical world and to the spatiality of human life (Crang and Thrift, 2000; Schlögel, 2003: Maresch and Werber, 2002; Soja, 1996). Through the writings of, among others, Lefebvre (1991, 2003), Castells (1983, 2002), Harvey (1985), Soja (1996, 2000), and, in Germany, the texts of Schlögel (2003) and Löw (2001), spatial analysis is back in the social sciences.

Relating Lefebvre's ideas of the 'production of social space' (Lefebvre, 1991), as well as Soja's Lefebvre-influenced writings on postmodern geographies (Soja, 1996, 2000), to urban entrepreneurialism, adds spatial thinking as an alternative interpretive thread to the existing body of entrepreneurship analysis. Lefebvre perceives space as both physical and social: an area of activity to be analyzed rather than an empty void or a pre-existing area to be fulfilled. In a three-part model of spatial processes, he distinguishes between three kinds of spaces: spatial practice or perceived space; representations of space or conceived space; and representational spaces or lived spaces (Lefebvre, 1991). In trying to relate Lefebvre's 'conceptual triad' to urban entrepreneurialism, I will focus on Soja's 'trialectics of spatiality' that entails – closely related to Lefebvre's triad – firstspace, secondspace and thirdspace epistemologies (Soja, 1996).

Within *firstspace epistemologies*, human spatiality is primarily seen as outcome or product, what Lefebvre calls perceived space,

> a material and materialized 'physical' spatiality that is directly comprehended in empirically measurable *configurations*: in the absolute and relative locations of things and activities, sites and situations; in patterns of distributions, designs, and the differentiation of a multitude of materialized phenomena across spaces and places; in the concrete and mappable geographies of our lifeworlds (. . .) (Soja, 1996, pp. 74–75).

Firstspatial knowledge has the qualities of a text to be read and understood in all its details, with spatial configurations being more or less causal effects of historical and social variables. For example, analysing urban entrepreneurial-ism by observing and describing the perceived 'physical' consequences of urban entrepreneurial governance (privatization of public spaces, amusement parks, shopping malls, gated communities as well as shanty towns or other islands of poverty) – would, in Soja's spatial theory – fall under firstspace epistemologies.

Secondspace epistemologies can be distinguished from their firstspace counterparts by focusing on conceived rather than perceived space, implicitly assuming 'that spatial knowledge is primarily produced through discursively devised representations of space, through spatial workings of the mind' (Soja, 1996). These 'representations of space' (Lefebvre) tend to define and order realities: the imagined geography tends to be perceived as 'real'. Whereas Soja, looking at the history of spatial thinking, assigns secondspace episte-mologies to the subjective imaginaries of the creative artist, the artful archi-tect, the utopian urbanist and the philosophical geographer, among others, when turning to entrepreneurial cities one thinks of the 'urban spin-doctoring' figuring so prominently in the literature on urban entrepreneurialism. To invent stories, to try to construct an alternative, investor-friendly image of one's city is seen as a central component of entrepreneurial governance; hence, according to Hubbard and Hall it might be best to consider the entrepreneur-ial as an imaginary city, constituted through an abundance of images and representations (Hubbard and Hall, 1998) – a secondspace mode of thought.

Using Lefebvre's and Soja's concepts, existing approaches to studying urban entrepreneurialism can be interpreted as applications of firstspace and secondspace thinking, while privileging an enterprise discourse. The point I try to make is that *thirdspace epistemologies*, or representational spaces, open up new possibilities for entrepreneurship studies, both conceptually (by accounting for a widened spatial perspective) as well as in terms of treating entrepreneurship as a societal rather than a purely economic phenomenon (by being able to add observations of different forms and practices of entrepre-neurship to the existing body of research).

Next to perceived and conceived spaces (or firstspace and secondspace, to use Soja's terminology) Lefebvre develops the idea of representational spaces 'embodying complex symbolisms, sometimes coded, sometimes not, linked to the clandestine or underground side of social life, as also to art' (Soja, 1996, p. 67; Lefebvre, 1991). What we have here is space that is *directly lived* – dominated space which the imagination tries to change and appropriate, inter-twining the real and the imagined without preferring the one over the other. In other words, we have marginalized 'counterspaces', resisting dominant (first-space or secondspace) orders – thirdspace, the space of radical openness, of creativity, of activism, of social struggle (Soja, 1996). *Thirdspace epistemolo-gies* resemble what Lefebvre once called the city: a 'possibility machine', a study of a third by looking at tensions between a perceived first(space) and a conceived second(space).

To deepen his understanding of thirdspace, Soja turns to Foucault's concept of heterotopias, 'other spaces' which are something like 'counter-sites' or 'enacted utopias' that simultaneously represent, challenge and invert 'real sites' (Foucault, 1991b). One could also point to Deleuze and Guattari's notions of deterritorializing and reterritorializing, conceiving society less through its antagonisms and contradictions (like the dualism of firstspace and secondspace) than through its 'lines of flight', its movements of deterritorializing producing new, different 'continuums of intensity' (Deleuze and Guattari, 1997).

What these ideas suggest is to study cities as territories where thirdspaces are emerging, connecting real and imagined spaces, contesting dominant discourses, producing subversion, provoking transformation, enabling social change. Coming back to the concept of entrepreneurial cities, what these ideas also imply is that it is in such in-between places where opportunities are sensed and tackled, and where new practices are invented. And if in entrepreneurship studies one stepped back from the enterprise discourse, looking out for lived, paradoxical spaces, for inventions or transformations of practices as examples of everyday or social or artistic entrepreneurship, then alternative forms and concepts of research into urban entrepeneurialism could emerge (Hjorth, Johannisson and Steyaert, 2003). This search should by no means be limited to art or a theatre stage. But it seems promising, for example, to look for 'art firms' that produce their own spaces of experience such as the *Volksbühne*, Pollesch's home-base, which has been beautifully described and analyzed as a special and very entrepreneurial case of how to organize the labour of art by Guillet de Monthoux (2004). Moreover, if social change is about producing other spaces, then Pollesch's theatre itself can be read as an *exemplary tale* of urban entrepreneurialism.

A SECOND, EXEMPLARY TALE: A LIVED SPACE

We just talk about it. We talk about representative theatre, what it means. My favourite example for it is a theatre play by Peter Turrini, called *Ich liebe dieses Land* ('I love this country'). It refers to Germany and its asylum practices. The main role is a black character, a migrant who tries his luck in Germany and ends up getting kicked out. Because they think we should criticize the immigration policy of Germany, the theatre people stage an evening, telling us a story about an immigrant who goes through all the hell of detention centres in Germany. So we see him being hit by white policemen, who take down his trousers, look in his ass to see if there are drugs in there and so on. They want to expose all these practices. They think that's how they can criticize the policies of Germany; they think they are being progressive. What I see in the show is that a white director, a white playwright tells a black actor to take off his clothes. . . .

. . . and show his ass.

Exactly, and that's what people forget, because art is always an excuse for doing again and again what is already out there, and they think they are left-wing progressive people[. . .] They are racist when they do it (René Pollesch, interviewed by Liz Monroe).

Upon hearing that the Berlin stage where his brand of theatre is played would be part of a chapter on urban entrepreneurialism, René Pollesch would treasure the irony, or so I imagine.[75] Nevertheless, and relating to entrepreneurship as the emergence of lived spaces, one is tempted to identify aspects of thirdspace by applying Foucault's principles of heterotopology (1991b, 2005) to Pollesch's *Prater* stage, thus reading his theatre as an exemplary tale – an example for artistic entrepreneurship. For Lefebvre, artistic activities are recurring examples of representational spaces, enabling involvements that generate social and physical possibilities (Lefebvre, 1991). Or, as the sociologist Luhmann once dryly pointed out, art demonstrates that there always is an other way (Luhmann, 1999).

In the by-now famous opening to *The Order of Things*, Foucault (1971) introduces the concept of heterotopic space, provoked to an almost Nietzschean laughter by the deliberate violation of coherence and closure in a passage by Borges quoting a 'certain Chinese encyclopedia' – apparently a comprehensive compilation of knowledge, but one sidestepping the common perception of an encyclopedia by leaving out a table or site or space where the given categories and creatures might be arranged next to one another to make sense. From here, Foucault develops his image of heterotopias as opposed to utopias: whereas the latter are unusual, consoling, coherent spaces that do not exist, the former are real, disquieting spaces that violate coherence. But it is not a violation of simple opposition: 'it is the violation of mixed use that sidesteps the societal common ground while standing in it' (Liggett, 2003, p. 44), a perspective echoing Lefebvre's notion of lived space intertwining the real and the imagined.[76]

In a later speech, Foucault sketches his principles of heterotopology, starting from the assumption that heterotopias are connected to the problematics of the society in question, thus taking different forms in different societies (Foucault, 1991b, 2005). By staging one of this culture's perceived characteristic dramas and depicting the 'actors' as puppets on the strings of (and with their lives produced by) a hegemonic enterprise discourse, unable to find their own language to deal with their situations and surroundings, Pollesch's theatre relates to a common contemporary unease about the power of entrepreneurial/

managerial narratives – maybe even more so in Berlin, a city on the ropes with
debts of about 41 billion Euro, the number of unemployed at 19.3 per cent and
more than 270,000 people on welfare, a metropolis rather desperately struggling to compete on regional and global levels (Eick, 2003). At the same time,
the writer/director's plays violate the commonsense notions of self-handling
and choice through radically reducing the 'characters' on stage to discursive
apparatuses and fragments of business semantics. For Pollesch, however,
theatre is not about conveying messages or teaching content:

> On stage we are interested in reflecting, and we just try to show that, we try to show
> that it's useful, to not be blind to what is out there, and we want to know what it's
> all about. We don't say we know what it's all about and we tell it to our audience.
> We try to find something out, we are curious (Pollesch, in Monroe, 2004, p. 12).

In *City as Prey*, 'what is out there' is the collapsing border between private and
public space and the production of cityspace and subjects through the regime
of enterprise discourse. Hence the rebuke to conventional critical agitprop-
theatre and to a Brechtian notion of *Lehrstück*: there is no flesh-and-blood
political opponent 'out there' to document and confront. Clutching at thin air,
in *City as Prey* despair and anger turn to collective outbursts of 'shit!'
(Lengers, 2004). But then again, as Diederichsen (2002) notes, trying to find
out what is out there with Pollesch results in knowing which life one does *not*
want to live and thus results in an existential I becoming able to name his/her
despair. Seen this way, turning one's despair into a desire for change is only
one step removed; for some, Pollesch accordingly becomes the 'Turbo-Brecht
of the post-economic age' (as quoted by Lengers, 2004). Whether one is
inclined to perceive *City as Prey* as journey of reflection, resigned apocalyptic tale or even call to arms, by forming a language with which to reflect upon
a dominant entrepreneurial (enterprise) discourse and by playing out this
language in a temporarily secluded place, a space of illusion is created. Like a
heterotopia, it comprehensively relates to the space that remains outside,
unmasking all the other managerial-entrepreneurially produced spaces as in
their own way also being illusory.

Although heterotopias do not follow any universal model, 'deviation' is a
characteristic of the more modern ones (Foucault, 1991b). Physically, the
Prater-space itself is not about the classic model of theatre at all. Housed in a
rundown, small hall in the former East Berlin, the audience – in the current
stage setting – is sitting on the floor (on cushions) in the middle of the room
in full light, while the play is decentralizedly going on around them. Moreover,
reflecting upon social change (on the one hand) is linked to inventing a new
form of theatre (on the other). In a way, this is 'theatre without theatre'
(Pollesch), a post-dramatic (Lehmann, 2005) doing-away with the classic

Aristotelian notions of embodied drama personalities whose traits are developed through dialogue, of a linear narrative enacted on stage, of representative theatre (Lengers, 2004). Hence, the plays' texts as well as their stagings withdraw from traditional definitions (Wirth, 2003), inventing a language of their own, one that is developed together with the actors – who are also asked to study the texts the plays are assembled of – in the process of rehearsal (Diederichsen, 2002; Pollesch, 2003). Actors are also encouraged to please not 'play theatre', not to embody the text, but rather to try to find out if and how Pollesch's ideas resonate with their thoughts and experiences – and to show the results, to bring these thoughts and experiences into the play: 'I don't direct, the actors organize their text themselves' (Pollesch as quoted by Lengers, 2004, p. 144). This means changing the very foundations of conventional representative theatre, that ever so often goes hand-in-hand with the image of a towering, authoritarian, god-like director-figure. In other words, this means finding new practices of work:

> *We* decide. I don't say I'm a director. I say I'm a partner in the rehearsal process, who can say a lot about the text he wrote. A man who can tell actors what's in the text. But I'm not a director who tells an actor, 'You go from there to there.' It's totally unimportant whether they sit or lie or stand. Our rehearsal process is that we know what we are discussing, that we are interested in the discussion, that we need it really, and that the actors have the motivation to go on stage and discuss it. [. . .] and the process is political. We try to organize the research process totally differently, we try to do it very democratically. We think everyday life is worth our concern . . . if an actress needs a babysitter and can't get one, there can't be a rehearsal – the rehearsal has to be when the babysitter is there. So we organize people around our everyday lives (Pollesch, in Monroe, 2005, p. 12).

Heterotopias, Foucault writes, are linked to slices of time, for example transitory, fleeting spaces of time. Pollesch's plays are developed through and for a couple of months, with and through a certain stage setting built into the *Prater*, disappearing with a changed stage setting, sometimes to resurface in different spaces/stages entitled 'bootlegs' of themselves, having changed through a new production process with different actors, in a different setting. (This mode of operation has led Pollesch to the curious move of banning other directors from working with his texts.) Also, according to Foucault, a heterotopia is able to blend several different spaces into one, which Pollesch does for example by using video screens showing an interplay of live close-ups and film excerpts, inviting the audience to selectively tracking the play or the screens. Through quoting film, through being inspired by film and through integrating cinematic techniques into the unfolding of the play (Lengers, 2004) a strange, hybrid body emerges that challenges and transforms our notions of a 'nice evening out' in the theatre.

To empirically come closer to the abstract notion of thirdspace, then, one can turn to Foucault's – still quite loosely coupled – principles of heterotopology, looking for heterotopias as other, entrepreneurial spaces not being sucked into a dominant mode of assembly – sites that bring forth new practices and possibilities. This way, Pollesch's 'theatre for metropolitan indians' (Wirth) appears to be an example for an artistic way of urban entrepreneurialism, creating, for a time, a third, 'lived' space.

Reading *City as Prey* solely as an apocalyptic tale, one reflects upon how contemporary cityspace is constructed and maintained through the demands of enterprise discourse dictating – in Lefebvre's words – the rules of assembly, thereby trying to understand relations of dominance in society embodied in concrete spatial processes. However, according to Foucault (1971) every discourse runs the danger of exhausting itself as the context of its production shifts and changes, bringing forth a fresh set of myths on which to build other narratives. Following Liggett (2003), a city can be perceived as a cohabitation of the larger normalizing spatial order and heterotopic space – as a possibility machine. In this vein, one can also use Lefebvre's and Foucault's theories as an invitation to return to urban spaces in order to look for alternative productions of space. From this perspective a second reading emerges, one that perceives Pollesch's theatre as a heterotopia, as an other, entrepreneurial space engendering artistic creativity and innovation, and bringing forth change. Tracing emerging thirdspaces thus opens up a space of possibilities for an entrepreneurship research that is looking for the entrepreneurial in artistic, cultural, social, everyday or political settings: entrepreneurship studies ungrounded in the enterprise discourse.

SPACES FOR OTHER READINGS AND WRITINGS OF ENTREPRENEURSHIP

> Rather than remaining within the field of a discourse that upholds its privilege by inverting its content . . . one can try another path: one can analyse the microbe-like, singular and plural practices which an urbanistic system was supposed to administer or suppress, but which have outlived its decay; one can follow the swarming activity of these procedures that . . . have reinforced themselves in a proliferating illegitimacy, developed and insinuated themselves into the networks of surveillance, and combined in accord with unreadable but stable tactics to the point of constituting everyday regulations and surreptitious creativities that are merely concealed by the frantic mechanisms and discourses of the observational organization (Michel de Certau, *The Practice of Everyday Life*).

Cities are laboratories for the configurations and significations of modernity, brimming with creativity and entrepreneurial behaviour. Nowhere are there so many potential fields of interaction as in the urban habitus – and it follows that any specialist or different vocation, disposition or lifestyle as well as any form of social change will find its articulation somewhere within urban spaces (Parker, 2004). With regard to the notion of urban entrepreneurialism, then, it takes sites and spaces for entrepreneurship to happen, and at the same time sites and spaces are constituted and reorganized through entrepreneurial activities. Applying a spatial perspective therefore offers myriad opportunities for exploring the ways in which manifold forms, practices and concepts of entrepreneurship emerge – be they socially, artistically/culturally, or, indeed, technologically and economically grounded. However, if the reasons for venturing into urban spaces are expanded far beyond the city's familiar functions as suburb's other and as the site of economic aspirations and growth, as Liggett (2003) argues, then different stories of entrepreneurship emerge.

To approach these possible other stories, I have proposed an analytical framework that draws upon the notion of socially produced space. With Lefebvre, space is perceived as both physically and socially produced and hence as an ongoing area of activity rather than an ensemble of mere physical manifestations (Lefebvre, 1991). Lefebvre's crucial question, namely *how* space is produced, becomes the angle from which to analyze the social production of entrepreneurial spaces. In analytically distinguishing between perceived, conceived and representational spaces (or fist-, second- and third-space epistemologies, to use Soja's rewriting of Lefebvre), the first two can be regarded as dominant modes of the writings on entrepreneurial cities: space as conceived, produced and perceived through the enterprise discourse.

Although an impressive array of valuable research has been done and is being done in that vein, one might also sense how, both theoretically and practically, space for life is reduced to a master agenda – and one might feel the urge to look for *other spaces*. To give voice to what is left out in this master narrative (and thus to expand the ways entrepreneurship is reflected upon and written towards questions of social change) I suggest applying the third pillar of Lefebvre's perspective on spatial processes: lived spaces of representation, 'counterspaces', marginalized spaces, sites where the other side of entrepreneurship is created.

Recycling entrepreneurship as a solution to managerial problems creates a silence (Hjorth and Steyaert, 2003). Likewise, reserving the notion of urban entrepreneurialism to neoliberal forms of urban politics, to a general shift from public to private sector and to cityspace as a location for risk-taking by private business (Painter, 1998) silences urban processes of social, cultural, voluntary, political, civic and ecological innovation. Like Calvino's fictive Marco Polo in his beautiful reports on *Invisible Cities* (Calvino, 1997), the urban researcher will always sense that there is more to a city than its physical manifestations, its street maps, its architectural plans, its latest poll statistics, its first- and secondspace epistemologies. When it comes to the entrepreneurial city, there, too, is more beneath the thick coating of signs that read place marketing, events, promotion of economic competitiveness and urban governance. For inquiring into entrepreneurship as social change, then, our task becomes that of writing these invisible cities: looking for sites where thirdspaces are emerging and real and imagined spaces are connected, where dominant discourses are subversively contested – provoking transformation, enabling change.

If we add thirdspace epistemologies to its first- and secondspace counterparts – or to put it more broadly: if we pick up on developments in spatial thinking as important contributions to social theory – we can open up possible lines of research that might contribute to a wider and richer agenda of entrepreneurship studies, denoting a generalized model for introducing innovative thinking, rearranging the established and producing the new across many sites and spaces, and for a range of goals exceeding those of the enterprise discourse. A theatre of entrepreneurship has a lot more to offer than commerce and economic drive.

> A: But in this thing here, this . . . city, it wasn't just marketing that was announced all the time, was it?

Notes

1. The research on which the study is based is financed by *Östersjöstiftelsen*, the Baltic Sea Foundation, and the European research project *PERSE*, financed by the European Union.
2. Portes and Sensenbrenner declare: 'We begin by redefining social capital as those expectations for action within a collectivity that affect the economic goals and goal-seeking of its members, even if these expectations are not oriented towards the economic sphere'. (1993, p. 1323) This definition differs from Coleman's, where the emphasis is on social structures facilitating individual rational pursuits.
3. For a critique of Putnam's approach, see Portes (1998). Portes' criticism is directed to the logical structure of Putnam's analysis. Nonetheless, he concedes (1998, p. 21) that redefining social capital as a property of larger aggregations is thinkable in principle. An important dimension of Putnam's work which is not dealt with here, deals with political participation and political institutions.
4. This attitude towards charitable organizations and donations, is also reflected in the taxation system (Quarsell, 1993; Lundström and Wijkström, 1997).
5. Primarily the *Cooperatives in the Welfare Market* project (1994–1998) and the respective Sweden studies within the European Thematic networks and projects *ESSEN-CGM*, *EMES ELEXIS* and *PERSE* (1994–2004). To minimize tedious self-referencing in this text, other authors than myself that studied the same, or similar organizations were quoted wherever this was possible.
6. At the time, municipal kindergartens operated within a duble system of municipal funding and dedicated state subventions, that were allocated by the municipality. Parent co-operatives consented in many cases to make do with state subventions only.
7. The Stockholm association's formative stages, and the Gothenburg association were documented by Gough (1989, 1994). I was personally involved in a number of seminars with the group in 1984/5 and followed its development throughout the 1980s and early 1990s. Current information on http://www.stil.se, 17 August 2004.
8. This and the following section are based on Stryjan (2002, 2004), and on material collected by the Sweden study of the European project *PERSE*. Interview material, wherever quoted, was collected for the said project by E. Laurelii of *Kooperativ Konsult*, under my supervision.
9. In Swedish labour authorities' parlance, they are not considered as 'standing at the labour market's disposal', and thus are not entitled to apply to the employment agency or for labour-market grants. Taking an occasional job would disqualify them for social assistance of pension, resulting in a serious permanent income shortfall without changing their labour-market classification. Some of the institutional features of this field, and of the organizations themselves, were discussed in Stryjan (2004).
10. According to a comprehensive evaluation (Samverkan inom rehabiliteringsområdet, 2000) that balances the gains and expenditures for individuals, local government and social care organs in 16 labour-market integration projects, (two of which are included in this study) the economic benefits of moving to employment are marginal to negative for most categories of the marginalized. Typically, the ICS's economic controller LH, chose to remain on disability pension throughout the 15 years of his involvement in the cooperative.
11. This is naturally an oversimplification. Tutors voluntary overtime contribution is often crucial, not the least in securing the cooperative's contacts with the community. Nonetheless, seeming anomalies, such as marginalized people working without pay to earn up their tutor's salary can only be grasped from this perspective.
12. *Förankring*, the expression used, literally means 'anchoring', being anchored. From interview transcripts, the *PERSE* project.

13. Both cases of pure economic reproduction and pure social reproduction are intuitively famil-
    iar. The potlatch ceremony is an unsurpassed example of a one-way, one-time reinvestment;
    likewise, confidence tricks are extreme cases of one-way conversion of social capital to
    economic capital. With some reservations, since opportunistic actors may seek a way to reit-
    erate their gains, this may be said about 'opportunistic behaviour' as well.

14. Drayton – who is said to have coined the concept of 'social entrepreneur' – emphasises the
    ethical element and does so with reference to trust. He points out that maximising social
    value is only possible in an atmosphere of trust (Drayton, 2002).

15. Hirschman does relate to the terms used by Aristotle and up to the Renaissance: *vita activa*,
    understood as active involvement in public life; and *vita contemplativa*, understood as with-
    drawal from the public life for purposes of contemplation and philosophical meditation. He
    then notes that his distinction between public action and private interest only partly main-
    tains the old distinction: instead his distinction is a distinction between two varieties of
    active life – the one concerned with public affairs, and the other with the pursuit of a better
    life for oneself and one's family.

16. We should not be quick to limit consumption to passivity. Consumption also has its forms
    of creativity. Everyday practices 'silently' harbour creative tactics of 'making use' of domi-
    nant orders (strategies) and 'consumption as production' is one such tactic (de Certeau,
    1984). Our aim here is not to debate with Hirschman. Rather we would like to balance the
    picture by emphasising the social sides of the problem of citizenship.

17. Notice that Ahl (2002) has discussed similar effects in relation to texts on entrepreneurship.
    See also Jones and Spicer (2005) who provide a readable genealogy of the positive valua-
    tion of the entrepreneur.

18. Taken to represent the opposite of what gets referred to as 'normal science' (e.g. Case, 2003),
    that is, positivist and post-positivist science (Burrell and Morgan, 1979).

19. The term 'discourse' is used here to pinpoint socially organized frameworks of meaning that
    define categories and specify domains of what can be said and done. Consequently,
    discourse delineates the constitutive force of reality as it simultaneously frames how a topic
    can be expressed in acceptable and intelligible ways and, on the flipside, 'rules out', i.e.
    limits and restricts what can be said on a particular issue (Hall, 2001).

20. As pointed out by Symon (2000), a favoured subtitle for academic publications is 'rhetoric
    versus reality', where rhetoric is seen to be inaccurate and even manipulative, i.e. the oppo-
    site of a truthful, honest account.

21. See Callon, Law and Rip (1986) who contend that the publication of scientific text is both a
    goal of scientific activity and a means to build actor-networks for persuading and enrolling
    others.

22. Notice that the conventions which scientific texts follow and the stylistic devices which they
    use make its rhetorical underpinning less than obvious. However, it is exactly that which is
    displayed as a non-rhetorical style, which by itself represents the rhetorical device that
    deflects its own dynamic.

23. Though Foucault (1980) has scrutinized the notion of ideology on the grounds of its presup-
    position of truth, ideology gets employed here to describe a form of relationship that entails
    hierarchical ramifications.

24. For instance, in the realm of critical entrepreneurship research one finds an abundance of
    texts highlighting the 'fact' that the entrepreneur emerges as essentially more masculine than
    feminine (e.g. Holmquist and Sundin, 1988; Mirchandani, 1999).

25. In a readable interview, Gayatri Spivak outlines the interrelatedness of the two analytic
    endeavours (Sipiora and Atwill, 1990).

26. Apparently, critical discursive readings get to fulfil a political and ethical function in social
    entrepreneurship research in that they, by dismantling unexamined assumptions and by
    making accepted concepts strange, enable 'human beings to transcend the conventional and
    create new approaches and policies' (Gusfield, 1976, p. 32).

27. Since Derrida's 'Force of Law' (1992), which Dews (1995) has codified as his 'ethical turn',
    Derrida related his deconstructive strategy to issues of, for instance, justice and law. Through
    a cogent deconstruction of prevailing legal systems, Derrida at the same time decoupled
    justice from law while introducing a undeconstructible ideal of justice which is not founded

on violence. In opposition to existing legal systems, genuine justice, as Derrida pinpoints, is the very movement of deconstruction.

28. By means of deconstructing the binary oppositions which hold together a respective structure one simultaneously destabilizes the entire structure or, following Derrida, puts its elements into play.

29. As this would in itself not warrant the circumvention of performativity.

30. Which is one of the prevailing objectives of contemporary business schools.

31. Michel Serres (1997) is equally dismissive in his appraisal of the state of research, describing current university curricula – and especially their enforcing of conformity, rules and norms – as intellectual terrorism which despise creativity and invention.

32. In 'The Differend' Lyotard (1988) took a forceful stance by illustrating the terror of hegemonic forms of speech on behalf of Auschwitz and the extermination of the Jews.

33. In Lyotard's view the little narratives (must) become the 'quintessential form of imaginative invention, most particularly in science' (1984, p. 60).

34. Which is not to be mistaken as 'false reasoning'.

35. Paralogical groundings, following Lyotard, warrant justice by way of countermanding excluded language games.

36. 'Hot' and 'cool' are taken to refer to the level of definition of a particular media performance. It is thereby the cool performance, i.e. the soft, shadowy, blurred, and interchangeable, which evokes (and requires) more involvement on behalf of the audience.

37. For Serres (1995), noise is the medium for creative ambiguity. Whereas the concept at first glance might appear in the sense of an interruption it can, following Serres, actually lead to a new order.

38. However, as Jones (2003b) warns us, it is not the case that Derrida made deconstruction ethical, but that he (deconstructively) reflected on the meaning of notions as, for instance, 'justice' and 'law'.

39. What I have tried to show with respect to social entrepreneurship is that however 'logocentric' a particular sign might appear, close inspection will irrevocable reveal its paradoxical grounding by virtue of which its solid standing gets undermined.

40. As circumscribed in relation to 'The Gift of Death' (Derrida, 1995a), a decision irrevocably requires a courageous 'leap of faith' beyond the facts at hand.

41. For example, in the United States 'only 2 per cent of the population lives on the land' (Norberg-Hodge, 1996, p. 396).

42. 'About half the people on the planet – some three billion, all told – rely on agriculture for their main income, and . . . perhaps one billion of these agriculturalists are mainly subsistence farmers, which means they survive by eating what they grow.'(Homer-Dixon, 2001, p. 31).

43. Archaeological records of the Sumerian society of 2300 BC document reforms, called *amargi*, endorsing activities which were land-based, matricentric, communally oriented and intended to 'free' the citizenry (Stone, 1976, p. 41). Religious leaders in the prevailing goddess-based theology followed precepts of egalitarianism and the blending of economics with spiritual values.

44. Although the data is difficult to tabulate, the conventional estimate is that women own well less than 10 per cent of the world's land.

45. These are some of the constructs camouflaged within the patriarchal cosmology which feminists call the 'Master Narrative' (Campbell, 2004).

46. 'The political creed and philosophy of European liberal thought . . . emphasized the importance of private endeavor, private interests, private profits: competition and utilitarianism were its cornerstones. A philosophy based on the concept of possessive individualism generated an image of an individual who owed nothing to society' (D'Souza, 1989, p. 29).

47. In *Good Nature: Animal Origins of Human Morality*, Frans deWaal defines reciprocity as the exchange of benefits with short-term costs but long-run gains, behaviour he believes to be essential to morality. Claims for immediate/mass consumption are moderated by commitment to sharing and to intergenerational exchange, namely communal and future gains.

48. Genealogic storytelling 'cultivate[s] a concern for details and accidents that accompany

every beginning . . . [G]enealogists seek discontinuities, play, avoid the search for depth, and do not practise interpretation' (Hjorth, 2004, p. 212) . . . [The goal is to] 'avoid fixation/ossification . . . [so that] the narrative . . . as a form of writing and knowledge . . . is allowed to be carried to the reader/listener with its liveliness, fervour, excess, potentiality, and passion still breathing us' (Hjorth, 2004, p. 221).

49. Verbatim quotes for Thuli are taken from an in-depth interview conducted, in the summer of 1991, in a mixture of Setswana and English, and later translated by Antoinette Ratang Dijeng, a Setwana speaking research assistant who was born and raised in Thuli's village. This interview was part of a larger study on women in the informal economy of Botswana (Campbell, 1992).

50. Thuli works in the informal sector, defined by the Botswana government as 'any enterprises which have no fixed location or operate from owner's home and have less than five persons employed' (Alexander, 1991, p. 45). This sector is a significant source of employment for Botswana women. Of the 1985 female population over 12 years of age 31 per cent were employed in the informal sector, 9 per cent were employed in the formal sector, 18 per cent were unemployed and 42 per cent were not in the labour force (Alexander, 1991, pp. 42, 47, 53). Their system of labour tabulation is more far more comprehensive and inclusive than classical, 'first-world' economic data.

51. The economic value of the informal sector garden is critically underestimated (Cohen, 1988; Nelson, 1996; Ross and Usher, 1986).

52. 48 per cent of rural households and 42 per cent of urban households are headed by women (Cownie, 1991, p. 11).

53. Some 136 of her 500 extant letters have been edited and published. All verbatim quotes attributed to Catharine are taken directly from this extensive personal correspondence (Traill, [1836] 1966).

54. Verbatim quotes for Anne come from the transcript of an open-ended, in-depth interview conducted in May 2004.

55. Elsewhere I have discussed the contagious presence of laughter when women enterprise together (Campbell, 2002).

56. Freudian stereotypes of the neurotic and/or engulfing mother have been major impediments to theorizing about strong women who are worthy of emulation. The Gaia hypothesis portrays Mother Earth as neither malevolent nor benign; she is watchful and caring and resilient, attributes which might form the basis for more enlightened prototypes of strong entrepreneurial women.

57. Social ecologist Murray Bookchin defines an ecosystem as 'a fairly demarcated animal-plant community and the abiotic, or nonliving, factors needed to sustain it. I also use [ecosystem] in social ecology to mean a distinct human and natural community, the social as well as organic factors that interrelate to provide the basis for an ecologically rounded and balanced community' (Bookchin, 1991, p. 23).

58. A few words about our earlier visits. The senior author has over three decades repeatedly travelled to the area, mainly as a researcher (Johannisson, 1978, 1983, 1984, 1988 and 2000 as well as Johannisson et al., 1994), but also as a teacher and debater. In addition to research in the logico-scientific tradition, he has tried out different interactive approaches, including 'transformative insinuations' (Hjorth and Johannisson, 2003) in order to get backstage insight into the world of native owner–managers and to instigate change. The junior author has spent almost a year doing ethnographic field research in the community (Wigren, 2003) and since then paid it several visits as an organiser of different development activities. As a woman, academically trained in the social sciences, and in the patriarchal setting of an industrial district, she certainly was alien (Wigren, 2003, pp. 58–60).

59. All translations from Swedish to English are done by the authors.

60. In Swedish: *Vad Varje Svensk Bör Veta.*

61. The Jante Law was 'enacted' by the Danish-Norwegian author Aksel Sandemose in his 1933 novel *En flyktning krysser sitt spor.*

62. 1 EUR corresponds to about 9 SEK at the time of the study.

63. This and all subsequent quotes in this chapter are taken from interviews with the RockCIty actors.

64. Emergent Swedish rock star that has collaborated with RockParty to find ways to help young women to enter the rock music industry.
65. The Jante Law is a set of aphorisms by the Norwegian author Aksel Sandemose, intended to describe small-mindedness and contempt for those who deviates in society. In Sweden, the Jante Law is a widely known concept for the attitude that nobody should think that they are special and that nobody should be more ambitious and deviant than the rest of us.
66. A leading Swedish business magazine on entrepreneurship and business creation.
67. Telecommunications, Information Technology, Media and Entertainment.
68. The regional concept can be envisaged from three different perspectives; first the region as a geographical concept, second the region as an expression of an administrative unit, i.e. a county, and third the region as a functional unit. Salomonsson (1996) combined all these into a functional region and this is how the KFV region is discussed here; a region in which 58.193 people lived 1st of November 2003, according to SCB.
69. A text is regarded here as 'any printed, visual, oral or auditory production that is available for reading, viewing or hearing (for example, an article, a film, a painting, a song)' (Denzin, 1995, p. 52). Relating to one text will probably involve *multiple con/texts* (Hosking and Hjorth, 2003) which make up a discourse on, as in this case, entrepreneurship. The meaning of a text is always indeterminate, open-ended and interactional as people constantly create, interpret and interact with texts. Hence, it is in everyday life that texts are co-constructed and where realities are (produced) and changed.
70. NUTEK is the Swedish Agency for Economic and Regional Growth whose task is to contribute to the creation of more new enterprises, more growing enterprises and more strong regions.
71. In the focus group interviews, different actors who are directly or indirectly involved in regional development work were provided with an arena for dialogue. Groups of two to five people met on eight occasions in their own organizations. The interviews opened with a presentation of an illustration of two circles tied by an arrow, where the first circle represented the region today and the second the region in three years. This illustration was followed by the question: What do you think about when looking at this illustration? The actors were then allowed some time alone to reflect over the illustration, drawing and/or writing on the papers given to them. After this time of individual reflection the discussion could start, and each of them presented their thoughts. My role during the interview was to act as a moderator, give fuel to the discussion and keep it on track when necessary. In most of the interviews I was silent, but occasionally mentioning concepts such as entrepreneurship, diversity, enterprise and equality proved to be helpful to guide the dialogue. The actors represented the three municipalities (politicians and officials), the employment offices, cultural workers, small companies, industry organizations, banks, a firm of accountants, the county administrative board, an organization that promotes co-operative development.
72. The regional growth program (RGP) is coordinated by the county administrative board. Many hundreds of people from several organizations in the region have participated (p. 2). The purpose of the RGP is to guide the regional development such in a direction that the living standards can be retained, and also improved. The county administrative board in Södermanland is in charge of this work.
73. Identity is not to be confused with the role concept which involves more casual dress and is thus transitory. The number of roles is larger than the number of identities, e.g. customer, patient, client, guest, visitor and so forth (see Kärreman, 2003, p. 129).
74. If this sounds drab, it is not. The plays are short, usually not longer than 70–80 minutes, very energetic and exhausting, and often mordantly funny, e.g. when the actors try to talk about the concept of love: 'Or that I let anybody realize his or her feelings by interacting with me socially, and he experiences something and that counts as NORMAL! I DON'T WANT THAT! I want this to be PAID FOR! . . . I want to BUY experiences. It can't be normal to just HAVE experiences and feelings . . .' (Pollesch, 2002b, p. 47).
75. Pollesch is not only well aware of so-called counter-cultural innovations that are sucked into enterprise discourse but also, specifically, the role of his theatre with regard to the issues discussed in *City as Prey*: '. . . we know that it's a problem to be part of the *Standortfaktor*

thing and we try to reflect on it, but we don't make less interesting theatre in order not to be part of the *Standortfaktor* problem . . .' (Pollesch, in Monroe, 2005, p. 11).

76. It should be noted that Lefebvre was highly critical about Foucault's use of the concept of space (as he was rather unforgiving about existing conceptualizations of space in general). According to Lefebvre, Foucault would never explain what space it was that he was referring to, nor how it would bridge the gap between the theoretical (epistemological) realm and the practical one, between mental and social, between the space of philosophers and the space of people who dealt with material things (Lefebvre, 1991). However, Lefebvre directs his criticism at Foucault's early writings, especially *The Archeology of Knowledge*, thus not being able to take into account Foucault's 1967 lecture that is referred to in this chapter, *Of Other Spaces*, published much later (Foucault, 1991). Departing from this text, the similarities between the ideas of lived spaces and heterotopias seem quite striking.

References

Ackroyd, S. (1992), 'Paradigms lost: Paradise regained?', in M. Reed and M. Hughes (eds), *Rethinking Organization: New Directions in Organization Theory and Analysis*, London: Sage, pp. 102–19.

Acs, Z.J. and D.B. Audretsch, (2003), *Handbook of Entrepreneurship Research*, New York: Springer.

Adams, G. (1966), *The Age of Industrial Violence, 1910–1915*, New York: Columbia University Press.

Addams, J. (1910), *Twenty Years at Hull-House*, New York: Macmillan.

Adorno, T.W. (1984), 'Der Essay als Form', in T.W. Adorno, *Philosophie und Gesellschaft: Fünf Essays*, Stuttgart: Reclam, pp. 5–33.

Ahl, H. (2002), 'The making of female entrepreneur: A discourse analysis of research texts on women's entrepreneurship', Dissertation, Jönköping International Business School.

Ahl, H.J. and E.F. Samuelsson (1999), 'Walking a tightrope: Women entrepreneurs on the pricing decision as a delicate act of balancing inner and outer forces', in S. Kunkel (ed.), *Sailing the Entrepreneurial Wave into the 21st Century*, Proceedings of the USASBE Entrepreneurship Conference, January, San Diego, CA.

Ainsworth, S. and C. Hardy (2004), 'Discourse analysis and the study of identities', in G. Grant, C. Hardy, C. Oswick and L. Putnam (eds), *The Sage Handbook of Organizational Discourse*, London: Sage, pp. 1–36.

Albrecht, J. (2002) , 'Environmental issue entrepreneurship: A Schumpeterian perspective', *Futures*, **34** (7), 649–61.

Aldrich, H. and M. Fiol (1994), 'Fools rush in? The institutional context of industry creation', *Academy of Management Review*, **19** (4), 645–70.

Aldrich, H. and M. Martinez (2001), 'Many are called, but few are chosen: An evolutionary perspective for the study of entrepreneurship', *Enterpreneurship Theory and Practice*, **25** (4), 41–56.

Alexander, E. (1991), *Women & Men in Botswana: Facts and Figures*, Gaborone, Botswana: Central Statistics Office.

Alvesson, M. and H. Willmott (1996), *Making Sense of Management: A Critical Introduction*, Thousand Oaks, CA: Sage.

Alvesson, M. and K. Sköldberg (2000), *Reflexive Methodology: New Vistas for Qualitative Research*, London: Sage.

Alvesson, M. and S. Deetz (2000), *Kritisk samhällsvetenskaplig metod*, Lund: Studentlitteratur.

Alvesson, M. and D. Kärreman (2000), 'Varieties of discourse: On the study of organization through discourse analysis', *Human Relations*, **53** (9), 1125–49.

Alvord, S.H., L.D. Brown and C.W. Letts (2002), *Social Entrepreneurship and Social Transformation: An Exploratory Study*. Working Paper No. 15. The Hauser Center for Nonprofit Organizations and the Kennedy School of Government, Harvard University.

Alvord, S.H., D. Brown and C.W. Letts (2004), 'Social entrepreneurship. Leadership that facilitates societal transformation – an exploratory study', Working Paper, *Center for Public Leadership, Kennedy School of Government*, www.ksg.harvard.edu/leadership/workingpapers.html.

Amin, A. and A. Malmberg (1994), 'Competing structural and institutional influence of the geography of production in Europe', in A. Amin (ed.), *Post-Fordism: A Reader*, Oxford: Blackwell, pp. 227–48.

Anderson, A.R. (2000), 'Paradox in the periphery: An entrepreneurial reconstruction?', *Entrepreneurship and Regional Development*, **12** (2), 91–109.

Anderson, R.B. (1999), *Economic Development Among the Aboriginal Peoples of Canada: Hope for the Future*, Toronto, Canada: Captus University Press.

Anderson, R.B. (2002), 'Entrepreneurship and aboriginal Canadians: A case study in economic development', *Journal of Developmental Entrepreneurship*, **7** (6), 45–65.

Anderson R.B., D.W. Wingham, R.J. Giberson and B. Gibson (2003), 'Indigenous economic development: A tale of two wineries', *Small Enterprise Research: The Journal of SEAANZ*, **11** (2), 49–62.

Anderson, R.B. and R. Giberson (2004), 'Aboriginal entrepreneurship and economic development in Canada: Thoughts on current theory and practice', in C. Stiles and C. Galbraith (eds), *Ethnic Entrepreneurship: Structure and Process*, Amsterdam: Elsevier Science, pp. 141–70.

Anderson, R.B., R. Camp II, J.M. Nkongolo-Bakenda, L.P. Dana, A.M. Peredo and B. Honig (2005), 'Indigenous land rights in Canada: The foundation for development?', *International Journal of Entrepreneurship and Small Business*, **2** (2), 104–33.

Anderson R.B., L.P. Dana and T. Dana (2006), 'Aboriginal land rights, social entrepreneurship & economic development in Canada: "Opting-In" to the global economy', *Journal of World Business*, **41**(1), Forthcoming.

Antonucci, M. (2005), 'In search of heroes: Robert Redford and ex-eBay executive Jeff Skoll team up to nurture documentaries that make a difference', *San Jose Mercury News*, 22 June.

Asian Development Bank (2000), *Policy on Indigenous Peoples*, www.adb.org/Documents/Policies/Indigenous_Peoples/ippp-002.asp?p=policies (viewed 15 June 2004).

Atkinson, R. and S. Davoudi (2000), 'The concept of social exclusion in the European Union: Context, development and possibilities', *Journal of Common Market Studies*, **28** (3), 427–48.

Backhaus, J. (ed.) (2003), *Joseph Alois Schumpeter: Entrepreneurship, Style and Vision*, Boston, MA: Kluwer.

Badelt, C. (2003), 'Entrepreneurship in nonprofit erganizations: Its role in theory and the real world nonprofit sector', in H. Anheier and B.N. Avner (eds), *The Study of the Nonprofit Enterprise. Theories and Approaches*, New York: Dordrecht, pp. 139–60.

Bailey, L. (1966), *Native American Slave Trade in the Southwest*, New York: Tower Publications.

Barber, K. (ed.) (1998), *The Canadian Oxford Dictionary*, Toronto, Canada: Oxford University Press.

Baritz, L. (1965), *The Servants of Power*, New York: Wiley.

Barns, I. (1999), 'Technology and citizenship', in Petersen et al. (eds), *Poststructuralism, Citizenship and Social Policy*, London: Routledge, pp. 154–98.

Barth, F. (1963), 'Introduction', in F. Barth (ed.), *The Role of the Entrepreneur in Social Change in Northern Norway*, Bergen: Norwegian University Press, pp. 5–18.

Barthes, R. (1967), *Writing Degree Zero*, trans. A. Lavers and C. Smith, New York: Hill & Wang.

Barthes, R. (1986), *The Rustle of Language*, trans. R. Howard, Oxford: Blackwell.

Bartilsson, S., G. Gillberg, H.E. Hermansson and P. Olofsson (2000), *Arbete I Egen Regi*, Göteborg: Daidalos.

Bauman, Z. (1993), *Postmodern Ethics*, Oxford: Blackwell.

Baumohl, J. (1996), 'Introduction', in J. Baumohl (ed.), *Homelessness in America*, Phoenix, AZ: Oryx Press, pp. xiii–xxii.

Baumol, W.J. (1990), 'Entrepreneurship: Productive, unproductive and destructive', *The Journal of Political Economy*, **98** (5/1), 893–921.

Becker, H.S. (1963), *Outsiders. Studies in the Sociology of Deviance*, New York: The Free Press.

Becker, J. (2001), 'BIGNES? Kritik der unternehmerischen Stadt', in J. Becker (ed.), *BIGNES? Size does Matter. Image/Politik. Städtisches Handeln. Kritik der unternehmerischen Stadt*, Berlin: b_books, pp. 6–28.

Becker J. et al. (2002), 'Das Material fragt zurück', in B. Masuch (ed.), *WOHNFRONT 2001–2002*, Berlin: Alexander Verlag, pp. 221–37.

Becker, M. and T. Knudsen (2002), 'Schumpeter 1911: Farsighted visions on economic development', *American Journal of Economics and Sociology*, **61** (2), 387–403.

Bennett, J. (1991), *Lilies of the Hearth: The Historical Relationship Between Women and Plants*, Camden East, ON: Camden House Publishing.

Berger, P.L. and T. Luckmann (1966/1991), *The Social Construction of Reality*, London: Anchor Books.

Berglund, K. (2003), 'A public initiative towards an entrepreneurial region – An ethnographic study with a focus on release and evolution of creative processes', paper presented at RENT XVII, Research in Entrepreneurship and Small Business, University of Lodz, Poland.

Berglund, D. and A.W. Johansson (2003), 'Entreprenöriella processer – kan de skapas?', paper presented at HSS conference, Ronneby, Sweden.

Berglund, K. and A.W. Johansson, 'Hegemony and *conscientiazacao* in processes of regional development', Unpublished document.

Bernasek, A. and J.R. Stanfield (1997), 'Grameen bank as progressive institutional adjustment', *Journal of Economic Issues*, **31** (2), 359–66.

Beynon, H. and R.M. Blackburn (1972), *Perceptions of Work*, London: Cambridge University Press.

Bianchi, G. (1998), 'Requiem for the Third Italy? Rise and fall of a too successful concept', *Entrepreneurship & Regional Development*, **10** (2), 93–116.

Billig, M. (1987), *Arguing and Thinking: A Rhetorical Approach to Social Psychology*, Cambridge: Cambridge University Press.

Billig, M. (1989), 'The argumentative nature of holding strong views: A case study', *European Journal of Social Psychology*, **19**, 203–23.

Billig, M., S. Condor, D. Edwards, M. Gane, D.J. Middleton and A.R. Radley (1988), *Ideological Dilemmas. A Social Psychology of Everyday Thinking*, London: Sage.

Bird, C. (1968), *Born Female The High Cost of Keeping Women Down*, Richmond Hill, ON: Simon & Schuster.

Bird, W.J. (2004), Personal correspondence.

Bjerke, B. (2005), *Förklara Eller Förstå Entreprenörskap?* ('Explaining or understanding entrepreneurship?'), Studentlitteraur, Sweden.

Blawatt, K. (1998), *Entrepreneurship: Process and Management*, Scarborough, ON: Prentice Hall.

Blumer, H. (1971), 'Social problems as collective behavior', *Social Problems*, **18** (3), 298–306.

Boli, J. (1991), 'Sweden: Is there a viable third sector?', in R. Wuthnow (ed.), *Between States and Markets The Voluntary Sector in Comparative Perspective*, Princeton, NJ: Princeton University Press.

Bonus, H. and G. Schmidt (1990), 'The cooperative banking group in the Federal Republic of Germany: Aspects of institutional change', *Journal of Institutional and Theoretical Economics*, **146**, 180–207.

Bookchin, M. (1971/1991), *The Ecology of Freedom: The Emergence and Dissolution of Hierarchy*, Montreal, Canada: Black Rose Books.

Bornstein, D. (1998), 'Changing the world on a shoestring', *The Atlantic Monthly*, **281** (1), 34–9.

Bornstein, D. (2004), *How to Change the World: Social Entrepreneurs and the Power of New Ideas*, New York: Oxford University Press.

Borzaga, C. and Defourny, J. (2000), *The Emergence of Social Enterprise*, London: Routledge.

Boschee, J. (1998), 'What does it take to be a social entrepreneur?', www.socialentrepreneurs.org/whatdoes.html.

Boserup, E. (1960/1989), *Women's Role in Economic Development*, London: Allen and Unwin: Earthscan.

Bourdieu, P. and L. Wacquant (1992), *An Invitation to Reflexive Sociology*, Cambridge: Polity Press.

Bouwen, R. (2001), 'Developing relational practices for knowledge intensive organisational contexts', *Career Development International*, **6** (7), 361–9.

Boyer, K. (1999), 'Evolutionary patterns of flexible automation and performance: A longitudinal study', *Management Science*, **45** (6), 824–42.

Brazeal, D.V. and T.T. Herbert (1999), 'The genesis of entrepreneurship', *Entrepreneurship Theory and Practice*, **23** (3), 29–45.

Bröckling, U. (2004), 'Unternehmer', in U. Bröckling, S. Krasmann and T. Lemke (eds), *Glossar der Gegenwart*, Frankfurt am Main: Suhrkamp, 271–7.

Bröckling, U., S. Krasmann and T. Lemke (eds) (2004), *Glossar der Gegenwart*, Frankfurt am Main: Suhrkamp.

Brown, K.M. (2001), 'New voice, same story? Social entrepreneurship and active social capital formation', *Third Sector Review*, **7**, 7–22.

Brugger, N. (2001), 'What about the postmodern? The concept of the postmodern in the work of Lyotard', *Yale French Studies*, **99**, 77–92.

Bruner, J. (1986), *Actual Minds, Possible Worlds*, Cambridge, MA: Harvard University Press.

Bublitz, H. (2003), *Diskurs*, transcript, Bielefeld.

Buckingham, S. and L.P. Dana (2005), 'Focus on regulation theory', *International Journal of Entrepreneurship and Small Business*, **2** (2), 178–87.

Buller, H., C. Morris and E. Wright (2003), 'The demography of rural areas: A literature review', *Research Report to DEFRA*, Countryside and Community Research Unit, University of Gloucestershire.

Bundesministerium für Verkehr, Bau- und Wohnungswesen (2000), *Urban 21 – Weltkonferenz zur Zukunft der Städte: Dokumentation*, Berlin: Bundesministerium für Verkehr, Bau- und Wohnungswesen.

Burchell, D. (1995), 'The attributes of citizens: Virtue, manners and the activity of citizenship', *Economy and Society*, **24**, 540–58.

Burchell, D. (1999), 'The disciplined citizen: Thomas Hobbes, neostoicism and the critique of classical citizenship', *Australian Journal of Politics and History*, **45** (4), 506–24.

Burkey, S. (1993), *People First: A Guide to Self-Reliant Participatory Rural Development*, London: Zed Books.

Burr, V. (1995), *An Introduction to Social Constructionism*, London: Routledge.

Burrell, G. and G. Morgan (1979), *Sociological Paradigms and Organizational Analysis*, London: Gower.

Busenitz, L.W., West, P.G.III, Shepherd, D and T. Nelson (2003), 'Entrepreneurship research: Past trends and future directions', *Journal of Management*, **29** (3), 285–308.

Burt, R. (2001), 'Structural holes versus network closure as a social capital', in L. Nan, K. Cook and R.S. Burt (eds), *Social Capital: Theory and Research*, New York: Aldine de Gruyter, pp. 31–56.

Butler, B.E. (2004), 'Rorty, the first amendment and antirealism: Is reliance upon truth view-point based speech regulation?', *Journal of Moral Philosophy*, **1** (1), 69–88.

Callon, M., J. Law and A. Rip (eds) (1986), *Mapping the Dynamics of Science and Technology*, London: Macmillan.

Calvino, I. (1997), *Invisible Cities*, London: Vintage.

Campbell, K. (1992), 'From Botswana to Canada: Entrepreneurship lessons from a third world country', *Best Paper Proceedings 1992: The International Council For Small Business Canada*, Victoria, BC, pp. 31–42.

Campbell, K. (2002), 'Theorizing matrilineal business enterprises to add mother/daughter businesses to the entrepreneurial mix', paper presented at 2002 *ICSB World Conference*, Puerto Rico, USA, 16–19 June.

Campbell, K. (2004), 'Quilting a feminist map to guide the study of women entrepreneurs', in C. Steyaert and D. Hjorth (eds), *Narrative and Discursive Approaches in Entrepreneurship*, Cheltenham, UK and Northampton, MA, USA: Edward Elgar, pp. 194–209.

Cannon, C. (2000), 'Charity for profit: How the new social entrepreneurs are creating good by sharing wealth', *National Journal*, 16 June 1898–1904.

Carbonara, E. (2002), 'New models of inter-firm networks within industrial districts', *Entrepreneurship and Regional Development*, **14** (3), 229–46.

Cardoso, H. (2001), *Charting a New Course: The Politics of Globalization and Social Transformation*, ed. M.A. Font, Lanham, MD: Rowman & Littlefield.

Carson, M. (1990), *Settlement Folk: Social Thought and the American Settlement Movement, 1885–1930*, Chicago, IL: University of Chicago Press.

Carter, P. and N. Jackson (2004), 'For the sake of the argument: Towards an understanding of rhetoric as process', *Journal of Management Studies*, **41**, 469–91.

Carter, S. (1996), 'The indigenous rural enterprise: Characteristics and change in rural areas?', *Entrepreneurship and Regional Development*, **10** (1), 17–32.

Carter, S. (1998), 'Portfolio entrepreneurship in the farm sector: Indigenous growth in rural areas?', *Entrepreneurship and Regional Development*, **8**, 345–58.

Carter, S. (1999), 'Multiple business ownership in the farm sector: Assessing the enterprise and employment contributions of farmers in Cambridgeshire', *Journal of Rural Studies*, **15** (4), 417–29.

Carter, S. (2001), 'Multiple business ownership in the farm sector – Differentiating monoactive, diversified and portfolio enterprises', *International Journal of Entrepreneurial Behaviour and Research*, **7** (2), 43–59.

Case, P. (2003), 'From objectivity to subjectivity: Pursuing subjective authenticity in organizational research', in R.I. Westwood and C. Stewart (eds), *Debating Organization: Point – Counterpoint in Organization Studies*, Malden, MA: Blackwell, pp. 142–56.

Casey, C. (2004), 'Bureaucracy re-enchanted? Spirit, experts and authority in organizations', *Organization*, **11**, 59–79.

Castells, M. (1983), *The City and the Grassroots: A Cross-cultural Theory of Urban Social Movement*, Berkeley, CA: University of California Press.

Castells, M. (2002), 'The space of flows', in I. Susser (ed.), *The Castells Reader on Cities and Social Theory*, Oxford: Blackwell, pp. 314–67.

Catford, J. (1998), 'Social entrepreneurs are vital for health promotion – but they need supportive environments too', Editorial, *Health Promotion International*, **13**, 95–8.

Champion, A. (ed.) (1989), *Counterurbanisation: The Changing Pace and Nature of Population Deconcentration*, London: E. Arnold.

Champion, A. (1992), *Patterns and Processes of Counterurbanisation: A Study of Population Deconcentration in Advanced Western Societies*, London: Belhaven Press.

Champion, A. et al. (1998), 'The determinants of migration flows in England', *Report to the DETR*, University of Newcastle-upon-Tyne and the University of Leeds.

Champion, T. and T. Fielding (eds) (1992), *Migration Processes and Patterns. Volume 1: Research Progress & Prospects*, London: Belhaven Press.

Champion T. and D. Atkins (2000), 'Migration between metropolitan and non-metropolitan areas in England and Wales', in R. Creeser and S. Gleave (eds), *Migration within England and Wales using the ONS Longitudinal Study*, London: HMSO, pp. 1–15.

Cheney, G., L.T. Christensen, C. Conrad, and D.J. Lair (2004), 'Corporate rhetoric as organizational discourse', in D. Grant, C. Hardy, C. Oswick, N. Phillips and L.L. Putnam (eds), *The Sage Handbook of Organizational Discourse*, Thousand Oaks, CA: Sage, pp. 79–103.

Chernow, R. (1998), *Titan: The Life of John D. Rockefeller*, New York: Random House.

Chia, R. (1996), *Organizational Knowledge as Deconstructive Practice*, Berlin: DeGruyter.

Chia, R. (2003), 'Ontology: Organization as "world-making"', in R. Westwood and S. Clegg (eds), *Debating Organization: Point-Counterpoint in Organization Studies*, Oxford: Blackwell.

Chia, R. and I. King (1998), 'The organizational structuring of novelty', *Organization*, **5**, 461–78.

Christie, M.J. and B. Honig (2006), 'Social entrepreneurship: New research findings', *Journal of World Business*, **41** (1), 1–5.

Coates, J. (1996), *Women Talk: Conversation between Women Friends*, Oxford: Blackwell.

Cohen, M.D., J.G. March and J.P. Olsen (1972), 'A garbage can model of organizational choice', *Administrative Science Quarterly*, **17**, 1–25.

Cohen, M.G. (1988), *Women's Work, Markets, and Economic Development in Nineteenth-Century Ontario*, Toronto, ON: University of Toronto Press.

Cole, J.M. (1975), 'Catharine Parr Traill – Botanist', in G. Corbett (ed.), *Portraits: Peterborough Area Women Past and Present*, Woodview, ON: Portraits' Group, pp. 73–9.

Colebrook, C. (2002), *Gilles Deleuze*, London: Routledge.

Coleman, J.S. (1987), 'Norms as social capital', in G. Radnicky and P. Bernholtz (eds), *Economic Imperialism*, New York: Paragon, pp. 133–55.

Coleman, J.S. (1988), 'Social capital in the creation of human capital', *The American Journal of Sociology*, **94**, Supplement: Organizations and Institutions: Sociological and Economic Approaches to the Analysis of Social Structure, 95–120.

Collins, D. (1998), *Organizational Change: Sociological Perspectives*, London: Routledge.

Commission of the European Communities (2003), *Green Paper Entrepreneurship in Europe*, Brussels: European Commission.

Conference Board (1999), 'The 1990s: Strategic philanthropy and community development', in S.A. Muirhead (ed.), *Corporate Contributions: The View from 50 Years*, New York: The Conference Board, pp. 40–57.

Cooper, R. and G. Morgan (1988), 'Modernism, postmodernism, and organizational analysis: An introduction', *Organizations Studies*, **9**, 91–112.

Corbridge, S. (1989), 'Post-Marxism and development studies: Beyond the impasse', *World Development*, **18** (5), 623–39.

Cornwall, J.R. (1998), 'The entrepreneur as a building block for community', *Journal of Developmental Entrepreneurship*, **3** (2), 141–48.

Cownie, D. (1991), *The Effects of Gender on Access to Credit and Grants in Botswana*, Gaborone, Botswana: Social Impact Assessment and Policy Analysis Corporation.

Crang, M. and N. Thrift (eds) (2000), *Thinking Space*, London: Routledge.

Crewe, E. and E. Harrison (1998), *Whose Development? An Ethnography of Aid*, London: Zed Books.

Critchley, S. (1999), *The Ethics of Deconstruction: Derrida and Levinas*, West Lafayette, IN: Purdue University Press.

Cruikshank, J. (1987), *A Delicate Experiment: The Harvard Business School, 1908–1945*, Boston, MA: Harvard Business School Press.

Curtin, D. (1997), 'Women's knowledge as expert knowledge: Indian women and ecodevelopment', in Karen J. Warren (ed.), *Ecofeminism: Women, Culture, Nature*, Bloomington, ID: Indiana University Press, pp. 82–98.

Czarniawska, B. (2004), *Narratives in Social Science Research*, London: Sage.

Czarniawska, B and B. Joerges (1996), 'Travels of ideas', in B. Czarniawska and G. Sevón (eds), *Translating Organizational Change*, Berlin: de Gruyter, pp. 13–48.

Daly, M. (1978), *Gyn/Ecology: The Metaethics of Radical Feminism*, Boston, MA: Beacon Press.

Daston, L. (1992), 'Objectivity and the escape from perspective', *Social Studies of Science*, **22**, 597–618.

Davidsson, P. (1995), 'Culture, structure and regional levels of entrepreneurship', *Entrepreneurship and Regional Development*, **7** (1), 41–62.

Davidsson, P., M.B. Low and M. Wright (2001), 'Low and MacMillan ten years on: Achievements and future directions for entrepreneurship research', *Entrepreneurship Theory and Practice*, **25** (4), 5–15.

Davies, B. and R. Harré (1990), 'Positioning: The discursive production of selves', *Journal for the Theory of Social Behavioural*, **20** (1), 43–63.

Davis, A. (1967), *Spearheads for Reform: The Social Settlements and the Progressive Movement*, Oxford: Oxford University Press.

Dean, M. (1999), *Governmentality – Power and Rule in Modern Society*, London: Sage.

de Certeau, M. (1984), *The Practice of Everyday Life*, Berkeley, CA: University of California Press.

de Certeau, M. (1997), *Culture in the Plural*, Minneapolis: University of Minnesota Press.

Dees, J.G. (1998), *The Meaning of 'Social Entrepreneurship'*, draft report for the Kauffman Center for Entrepreneurial Leadership, Stanford University.

Dees, J.G., J. Emerson and P. Economy (2001), *Enterprising Nonprofits. A Toolkit for Social Entrepreneurs*, New York: John Wiley & Sons.

Dees, J.G., J. Emerson and P. Economy (2002), *Strategic Tools for Social Entrepreneurs. Enhancing the Performance of Your Enterprising Nonprofit*, New York: John Wiley & Sons.

Defourny, J. (2000), 'From third sector to social enterprise', in C. Borzaga and J. Defourny (eds), *The Emergence of Social Enterprise*, London: Routledge, pp. 1–28.

De Leeuw, E. (1999), 'Healthy cities: Urban social entrepreneurship for health', *Health Promotion International*, **14** (3), pp. 261–9.

De Leonardis, O. and D. Mauri (1992), 'From deinstitutionalizaton to the social enterprise', *Social Policy*, **23**, 50–4.

Deleuze, G. (1987), *Foucault*, Frankfurt am Main: Suhrkamp.

Deleuze, G. (1993), 'Postskriptum über die Kontrollgesellschaften', in G. Deleuze, *Unterhandlungen 1972–1990*, Frankfurt am Main: Suhrkamp, pp. 254–63.

Deleuze, G. and F. Guattari (1997), *Tausend Plateaus: Kapitalismus und Schizophrenie II*, Berlin: Merve.

DeLillo, D. (2003), *Cosmopolis*, London: Picador.

Derrida, J. (1966), 'Structure, sign, and play in the discourse of the human sciences', in *Writing and Difference*, trans. A. Bass, London: Routledge.

Derrida, J. (1976), *Of Grammatology*, trans. G.C. Spivak, Baltimore, MD: Johns Hopkins University Press.

Derrida, J. (1992), 'Force of law: The mystical foundation of authority', in D. Cornell, M. Rosenfeld and D.G. Carlson (eds), *Deconstruction and the Possibility of Justice*, trans. M. Quaintance, New York: Routledge.

Derrida, J. (1995), *The Gift of Death*, trans. D. Wills, Chicago, IL: University of Chicago Press.

Derrida, J. (1997), *Politics of Friendship*, trans. G. Collins, London: Verso.

Derrida, J. (1999), 'Hospitality, justice and responsibility: A dialogue with Jacques Derrida', in R. Kearney and M. Dooley (eds), *Questioning Ethics*, London: Routledge.

Derrida, J. (2001), 'The future of the profession or the unconditional university', trans. P. Kamuf, in L. Simmons and H. Worth (eds), *Derrida Downunder*, Palmerston North, New Zealand: Dunmore Press.

Derrida, J. (2003), 'Autoimmunity: Real and symbolic suicides', in G. Borradori (ed.), *Philosophy in a Time of Terror: Dialogues with Jürgen Habermas and Jacques Derrida*, Chicago, IL: University of Chicago Press.

Dews, P. (1995), *The Limits of Disenchantment: Essays of Contemporary European Philosophy*, London: Verso.

Dey, P. (2006). 'On the name of social entrepreneurship: Business school teaching, research, and development practice', Unpublished Dissertation, Université de Neuchâtel.

Dicken, P. (1992), 'International production in a volatile regulatory environment', *Geoforum*, **23** (3), 303–16.

Diederichsen, D. (2002), 'Denn sie wissen, was sie nicht leben wollen', *Theater heute*, **3**, 56–63.

DiMaggio, P. and W. Powell (1983), 'The iron cage revisited: Institutional isomorphism and collective rationality in organizational fields', *American Sociological Review*, **48**, 147–60.

Dobers, P. (2003), 'Image of Stockholm as an IT city: Emerging urban entrepreneurship', in C. Steyaert and D. Hjorth (eds), *New Movements in Entrepreneurship*, Cheltenham, UK and Northampton, MA, USA: Edward Elgar, pp. 200–221.

Donham, W. (1936), 'Training for leadership in a democracy', *Harvard Business Review*, **14** (3), 261–71.

Donzelot, J. (1979), *The Policing of Families*, New York: Pantheon.

Drayton, W. (2002), 'The citizen sector: Becoming as competitive and entrepreneurial as business', *California Management Journal*, **1** (1), 3–5.

Dreyfus, H.L. and P. Rabinow (eds) (1982), *Michel Foucault – Beyond Structuralism and Hermeneutics*, London: Harvester Wheatsheaf.

Drucker, P.F. (1985), *Innovation and Entrepreneurship*, New York: Harper & Row.

D'Souza, C.M. (1989), 'A new movement, a new hope: East wind, west wind, and the wind from the south', in Judith Plant (ed.), *Healing the Wounds: The Promise of Ecofeminism*, Toronto, ON: Between the Lines, pp. 29–39.

du Gay, P. (1986), 'The conduct of management and the management of conduct: contemporary managerial discourse and the constitution of the "competent" manager', *Journal of Management Studies*, **33** (3), 263–82.

du Gay, P. (1999), 'The tyranny of the epochal: Change, epochalism and organizational reform', *Organization*, **10** (4), 663–84.

du Gay, P. (2004), 'Against "Enterprise" (but not against "enterprise", for that would make no sense)', Organization, **11** (1), 37–57.

Dunning, J.H. (2003), *Making Globalization Good: The Moral Challenges of Global Capitalism*, Oxford: Oxford University Press.

Eagleton, T. (1983), *Literary Theory: An Introduction*, Oxford: Blackwell.

Eccles, R.G. and N. Nohria (1992), *Beyond the Hype. Rediscovering the Essence of Management*, Cambridge, MA: Harvard University.

Eckardt, F. (2004), *Soziologie der Stadt*, transcript, Bielefeld.

Economic and Social Council Commission on Human Rights (1993), *Draft United Nations Declaration on the Rights of Indigenous People*, United Nations, viewed 30 June 2004, www.cwis.org/drft9329.html.

Eggertsson, T. (1991), *Economic Behaviour and Institutions*, Cambridge: Cambridge University Press.

Eick, V. (2003), 'Berlin on the ropes: Nonprofits in transition and under pressure', in V. Eick, M. Mayer and J. Sambale (eds), *From Welfare to Work – Nonprofits and the Workfare State in Berlin and Los Angeles*, Berlin: Department of Politics, Freie Universität Berlin, pp. 51–60.

Eikenberry, A.M. and J.D. Kluver (2004), 'The marketization of the nonprofit sector: Civil society at risk?', *Public Administration Review*, **64** (2), 132–40.

Elam, M. (1994), 'Puzzling out the post-fordist debate', in A. Amin (ed.), *Post-Fordism: A Reader*, Oxford: Blackwell, pp. 43–70.

Engström, L. and C.J. Engström (1982), *Kossan: ett Föräldrakooperativt Daghem*, Stockholm: LiberFörlag.

Engström, A., A. Larsson and A. Wigren (2002a), *Omvärldsanalys för Katrineholms kommun*, Stockolm: Inregia AB.

Engström, A., A. Larsson and A. Wigren (2002b), *Omvärldsanalys för Flens kommun*, Stockolm: Inregia AB.

Engström, A., P. Stenberg and A. Wigren (2002c), *Omvärldsanalys för Vingåkers kommun*, Stockholm: Inregia AB.

Evans, M./CONSCISE project team (2003), *The CONSCISE Project Final Report*, mimeo, Framework V Research Programme contract HPSE-CT-1999-00016.

Evans, N.J. and B.W. Ilbery (1992), 'Farm-based accommodation and the restructuring of agriculture: Evidence from three English counties', *Journal of Regional Studies*, **8**, 85–96.

Evans, N.J. and B.W. Ilbery (1993), 'The pluriactivity, part-time farming and farm diversification debate', *Environment and Planning*, A, **25**, 945–59.

Evers, A. and M. Schultze-Böing (2001), 'Germany. Social enterprises and transitional employment' in C. Borzaga and J. Defourny (eds), *The Emergence of Social Enterprise*, London: Routledge, pp. 121–35.

Fairchild, G. and P.G. Greene (2004), 'Wealth creation in distressed inner cities: What can business schools contribute?', in H.P. Welsch (ed.), *Entrepreneurship: The Way Ahead*, New York: Routledge, pp. 211–24.

Fairclough, N. (1992), *Discourse and Social Change*, Cambridge: Polity Press.

Fertile, S. (2004), Personal correspondence.

Fielding, A. (1982), 'Counterurbanisation in Western Europe', *Progress in Planning*, **17**, 1–52.

Fiet, J.O. (2002), *Systematic Search for Entrepreneurial Discoveries*, Westport, CT: Quorom Books.

Findlay, A., D. Short and A. Stockdale (1999), *Migration Impacts in Rural England*, Report to the Countryside Agency, Cheltenham.

Fleck, L. (1979), *Genesis and Development of a Scientific Fact*, Chicago, IL: University of Chicago Press.

Fletcher, D.E. (2002), 'Introduction', in D. Fletcher (ed.), *Understanding the Small Family Business*, London: Routledge, pp. 1–16.

Fletcher, D.E. (2003), 'Framing organisational emergence: Discourse, identity and relationship', in C. Steyaert and D. Hjorth (eds), *New Movements in Entrepreneurship*, Cheltenham, UK and Northampton, MA, USA: Edward Elgar, pp. 125–42.

Fletcher. D.E. and T.J. Watson (2006), 'Entrepreneurship, management learning and negotiated narratives: 'Making it otherwise for us – otherwise for them', *Management Learning* (in press).

Foreman, G. (1970), *The Five Civilized Tribes*, Norman, OK: University of Oklahoma Press.

Foscarinis, M. (1993), 'Beyond homelessness: Ethics, advocacy and strategy', *Saint Louis University Public Law Review*, **12** (1), 37–67.

Foscarinis, M. (2000), 'Homelessness and human rights: Towards an integrated strategy', *Saint Louis University Public Law Review*, **19** (3), 327–55.

Foucault, M. (1971), *Die Ordnung der Dinge*, Frankfurt am Main: Suhrkamp.

Foucault, M. (1972), *Diskursens Ordning*, trans. M. Rosengren, Stockholm/Stehag: Brutus Östlings Bokförlag.

Foucault, M. (1974), *Discipline and Punishment*, Lund: Arkiv Förlag.

Foucault, M. (1979), 'On governmentality', *Ideology and Consciousness*, **6**, 5–26.

Foucault, M. (1980), *Power/Knowledge: Selected Interviews and Other Writings 1972–1977*, trans. C. Gordon et al., New York: Pantheon.

Foucault, M. (1988), *Madness and Civilization: A History of Insanity in the Age of Reason*, New York: Vintage.

Foucault, M. (1991a), 'Governmentality', in G. Burchell, C. Gordon and P. Miller (eds), *The Foucault Effect: Studies in Governmentality*, Chicago, IL: University of Chicago Press, pp. 87–104.

Foucault, M. (1991b), 'Andere Räume', in K.H. Barck, P. Gente, H. Paris and S. Richter (eds), *Aisthesis: Wahrnehmung heute oder Perspektiven einer anderen Ästhetik*, Leipzig: Reclam, pp. 34–47.

Foucault, M. (1998), *Überwachen und Strafen: die Geburt des Gefängnisses*, Frankfurt am Main: Suhrkamp.

Foucault, M. (2005), *Die Heterotopien. Der utopische Körper. Zwei Radiovorträge*, Frankfurt am Main: Suhrkamp.

Fournier, V. (2002), 'Keeping the veil of otherness: practising disconnection', in B. Czarniawska and H. Höpfl (eds), *Casting the Other: The Production and Maintenance of Inequalities in Work Organizations*, London: Routledge, pp. 68–88.

Fowler, A. (2000), 'NGDOs as a moment in history: Beyond aid to social entrepreneurship or civic innovation?', *Third World Quarterly*, **21** (4), 637–54.

Frank, L. (1997), 'The development game', in M. Rahnema and V. Bawtree (eds), *The Post-Development Reader*, London: Zed Books.

Frederick, H. and E. Henry (2004), 'Innovation and entrepreneurship amongst Pakeha and Maori in New Zealand', in C. Stiles and C. Galbraith (eds), *Ethnic Entrepreneurship: Structure and Process*, Amsterdam: Elsevier Science, pp. 115–40.

Frye, M. (1983), *The Politics of Reality: Essays in Feminist Theory*, Trumansburg, NY: Crossing Press.

Fuller, A. (1990), 'From part-time farming to pluriactivity: A decade of change in rural Europe', *Journal of Rural Studies*, **6**, 361–73.

Gailey, C.W. (1987), 'Evolutionary perspectives on gender hierarchy', in B. Hess and M. Ferree (eds), *Analyzing Gender A Handbook of Social Science Research*, Newbury Park, CA: Sage, pp. 32–67.

Galaskiewicz, J. (1997), 'An urban grants economy revisited: Corporate charitable contributions in the Twin Cities, 1979–81, 1987–89', *Administrative Science Quarterly*, **42**, 445–71.

Galbraith, C. and N. Kay (1986), 'Towards a theory of multinational enterprise', *Journal of Economic Behavior and Organization*, **7**, 3–19.

Galbraith, C. and A. DeNoble (2002), 'Advanced manufacturing technology, flexibility and the strategic scope of high technology firms', in C. Galbraith (ed.), *Strategies and Organizations in Transition*, Amsterdam: JAI Press.

Galbraith, C. and C. Stiles (2003), 'Expectations of Indian reservation gaming: Entrepreneurial activity within a context of traditional land tenure and wealth acquisition', *Journal of Developmental Entrepreneurship*, **8** (2), 93–112.

Game, A. and A. Metcalfe (1996), *Passionate Sociology*, London: Sage.

Gartner, W. (1988), 'Who is an entrepreneur?' is the wrong question', *American Journal of Small Business*, **12** (4), 11–32.

Geertz, C. (1973), *Peddlars and Princes*, Chicago, IL: University of Chicago Press.

Gendron, G. (1996), 'Flashes of genius: interview with Peter Drucker', *Inc.*, **18** (7), 30–37.

General Assembly The United Nations (1995), *The Rights of Indigenous Peoples, Office of the High Commissioner for Human Rights*, Fact Sheet No. 9 (Rev. 1), www.unhchr.ch/html/menu6/2/fs9.htm, viewed June 2004.

Gentile, M. C. (2002), *Social Impact Management and Social Enterprise: Two Sides of the Same Coin or totally Different Currency?*, New York: Aspen Institute for Social Innovation through Business.

George, S. (1988), *A Fate Worse Than Debt*, London: Penguin Books.

Gergen, K.J. (1991), *The Saturated Self*, New York: Basic Books.

Giddens, A. (1991a), *Modernity and Self-Identity. Self and Society in the Late Modern Age*, Cambridge: Polity Press.

Giddens, A. (1991b), *Modernitet och Självidentitet: Självet och Samhället i den Senmoderna Epoken*, Göteborg: Daidalos.

Giddens, A. (2000), *The Third Way and its Critics*, Cambridge: Polity Press.

Gillespie, R. (1991), *Manufacturing Knowledge: A History of the Hawthorne Experiments*, Cambridge: Cambridge University Press.

Gilligan, C. (1982), *In a Different Voice: Psychological Theory and Women's Development*, Cambridge, MA: Harvard University Press.

Goldman, S. (1995), *Agile Competition: The Emergence of a New Industrial Order*, Hamilton, ON: The Society of Management Accountants.

Goldthorpe, J.H., D. Lockwood, F. Bechhofer and J. Platt (1968), *The Affluent Worker: Industrial Attitudes and Behaviour*, Cambridge: Cambridge University Press.

Goldthorpe, J.H., D. Lockwood, F. Bechhofer and J. Platt (1969), *The Affluent Worker in the Class Structure*, Cambridge: Cambridge University Press.

Goodchild, P. (1996), *Deleuze and Guattari – An Introduction to the Politics of Desire*, London: Sage.

Goodman, E. and J. Bamford (eds) (1989), *Small Firms and Industrial Districts in Italy*, London: Routledge.

Gordon, C. (1991), 'Governmental rationality: An introduction', in G. Burchell, C. Gordon and P. Miller (eds), *The Foucault Effect: Studies in Governmentality*, Chicago, IL: The University of Chicago Press, pp. 1–51.

Gough, R. (1989), 'Personlig assistans under eget ansvar', *Stencil*, Stockholm: Arbetslivscentrum.

Gough, R. (1994), 'Fem år med Göteborgsföreningen för självständigt liv och GIL-Projektet', Report, GIL, Gothenburg.

Gourville, J. and V. Rangan (2004), 'Valuing the cause marketing relationship', *California Management Review*, **47** (1), 38–57.

Grabher, G. (1993), 'The weakness of strong ties: The lock-in of regional development in the Ruhr area', in G. Grabher (ed.), *The Embedded Firm: On the Socioeconomics of Industral Networks*, London: Routledge, pp. 255–77.

Granovetter, M. (1992), 'Economic institutions as social constructions. A framework for analysis', *Acta Sociologica*, **33**, 3–11.

Grant, P. and L. Perren, (2002), 'Small business and entrepreneurial research. Meta-theories, paradigms and prejudices', *International Small Business Journal*, **20** (2), 185–211.

Gray, C. (1999), *Sisters in the Wilderness: The Lives of Susanna Moodie and Catharine Parr Traill*, Toronto, ON: Penguin.

Green A. (1999),'Employment opportunities and constraints facing in-migrants to rural areas in England', *Geography*, **84**, 34–44.

Grenier, P. (2002), 'The function of social entrepreneurship in the UK', *Transforming Civil Society, Citizenship and Governance: The Third Sector in an Era of Global (Dis)Order – ISTR Fifth International Conference*, Cape Town, 7–10 July.

Guclu, A., J.G. Dees and B.B. Anderson (2002), *The Process of Social Entrepreneurship: Creating Opportunities Worthy of Serious Pursuit*, Durham, NC: Center for the Advancement of Social Entrepreneurship, Fuqua Business School, Duke University.

Guillet de Monthoux, P. (2004), *The art firm: Aesthetic management and metaphysical marketing*, Stanford, CA: Stanford University Press.

Gusfield, J. (1976), 'The literary rhetoric of science: Comedy and pathos in drinking driver research', *American Sociological Review*, **41**, 16–34.

Gustafsson, B.Å. (2004) *Närmiljö som lärmiljö. Betraktelser från Gnosjöregionen. Acta Vexionensia*, No. 52. Växjö: Växjö University Press.

Hall, P. (1985), 'Doing well by doing good: Business philanthropy and social investment, 1860–1984', in *Independent Sector, Giving and Volunteering: New Frontiers of Knowledge*, New York: Independent Sector, pp. 27–73.

Hall, P. (1992), *Inventing the Nonprofit Sector and Other Essays on Philanthropy, Voluntarism, and Nonprofit Organizations*, Baltimore, MD: Johns Hopkins University Press.

Hall, P. (1994), 'Historical perspectives on nonprofit organizations', in R. Herman and Associates (eds), *The Jossey-Bass Handbook of Nonprofit Leadership and Management*, San Francisco, CA: Jossey-Bass, pp. 3–43.

Hall, P. (2005), Personal communication, 12 September.

Hall, S. (2001), 'Foucault: Power, knowledge and discourse', in M. Wetherell, S. Taylor, S. Yates (eds), *Discourse Theory and Practice: A Reader*, London: Sage, pp. 72–81.

Hall, T. (1998), 'Introduction to part I: Selling the entrepreneurial city', in T. Hall and P. Hubbard (eds), *The Entrepreneurial City: Geographies of Politics, Regime and Representation*, West Sussex: John Wiley & Sons, pp. 27–31.

Hall, T. and P. Hubbard (1998), 'Afterword: Mappings of the entrepreneurial city', in T. Hall and P. Hubbard (eds), *The Entrepreneurial City: Geographies of Politics, Regime and Representation*, West Sussex: John Wiley & Sons, pp. 309–21.

Halliday, J. and M. Coombes (1995), 'In search of counterurbanisation: Some evidence from Devon on the relationship between patterns of migration and motivation', *Journal of Rural Studies*, **11**, 433–46.

Hamilton, C. (1990), 'Women, home and community: The struggle in an urban environment' in I. Diamond and G.F. Orenstein (eds), *Reweaving the World: The Emergence of Ecofeminism*, San Francisco, CA: Sierra Club Books, pp. 215–22.

Hancock, G. (1989), *Lords of Poverty: The Power, Prestige, and Corruption of the International Aid Business*, New York: Atlantic Monthly Press.

Handy, R. (1997), *The Social Gospel in America, 1870–1920*, New York: Oxford University Press.

Hannerz, U. (1987), 'The world in Creolisation', *Africa*, **57**, 546–59.

Harding, R. (2004), 'Social enterprise: The new economic engine', *Business Strategy Review*, Winter, 39–43.

Hardt, M. and A. Negri (2001), *Empire*, Cambridge, MA: Harvard University Press.

Hardy, D. and S. Clegg (1997), 'Relativity without relativism: Reflexivity in post-paradigm organization studies', *British Journal of Management*, **8**, 5–17.

Harmon, R. and L. Peterson (1990), *Reinventing the Factory*, New York: The Free Press.

Harris, M. (1997), 'Provisional panel: Perspectives on citizenship', *Contemporary Political Studies*, Conference Proceedings, pp. 1067–80, University of Ulster, Jordanstown, www.psa.ac.uk/cps/.

Harvey, D. (1985), *The Urbanization of Capital*, Oxford: Blackwell.

Harvey, S. (1996), 'Two models to sovereignty: A comparative history of the Nashantucket Pequot Tribal Nation and the Navajo Nation', *Native American Culture and Research Journal*, **20**, 147–95.

Hassard, J. and M. Parker (eds) (1994), *Towards a New Theory of Organizations*, London: Routledge.

Häußermann, H., M. Kronauer and W. Siebel (eds) (2004), *An den Rändern der Städte*, Frankfurt am Main: Suhrkamp.

Hawken, P. (1987), *Growing a Business*, Don Mills, ON: Collins Publishers.

Heald, M. (1970), *The Social Responsibilities of Business: Company and Community, 1900–1960*, Cleveland, OH: Case Western Reserve University Press.

Heilbrun, C.G. (1988), *Writing a Woman's Life*, New York: W.W. Norton & Company.

Henton, D., J. Melville and K. Walesh (1997), *Grassroots Leaders for a New Economy. How Civic Entrepreneurs Are Building Properous Communities*, San Francisco: Jossey-Bass.

Hernes, T. (2003) 'Organization as evolution of space', in B. Czarniawska and G. Sevon (eds), *Northern Lights – Organization Theory in Scandinavia*, Copenhagen: Liber/Abstract/Copenhagen Business School Press, pp. 267–90.

Hettne, B. (1982), *Development Theory and the Third World*, SAREC Report No. 2, SAREC, Stockholm.

Hindle, K., R. Kayseas, R.B. Anderson and R.G. Giberson (2005), 'Relating practice to theory in indigenous entrepreneurship: A pilot investigation of the Kitsaki partnership portfolio', *American Indian Quarterly*, **29** (1–2), 1–23.

Hirschman, A.O. (1977), *The Passions and the Interests : Political Arguments for Capitalism Before its Triumph*, Princeton, NJ: Princeton University Press.

Hirschman, A.O. (1980), *Getting Ahead Collectively. Grassroot Experiences in Latin America*, New York: Pergamon Press.

Hirschman, A.O. (1981), *Shifting Involvements. Private interest and Public Action*, Oxford: Martin Robertson.

Hirschman, A.O. (1982), *Shifting Involvements – Private Interest and Public Action*, Princeton, NJ: Princeton University Press.

Hirschman, A.O. (1984), *Getting Ahead Collectively*, Oxford: Pergamon Press.

Hirst, P. and J. Zeitlin (1992), 'Flexible specialization versus Post-Fordism', in M. Storper and A. Scott (eds), *Pathways to Industrialization and Regional Development*, London: Routledge, pp. 70–115.

Hjorth, D. (2001), *Rewriting Entrepreneurship: Enterprise Discourse and Entrepreneurship in the Case of Re-Organising ES*, Växjö: Växjö University Press.

Hjorth, D. (2003), *Rewriting Entrepreneurship – For a New Perspective on Organisational Creativity*, Copenhagen/Malmö/Oslo: CBS Press/Liber/Abstrakt.

Hjorth, D. (2004a), 'Creating space for play/invention – concepts of space and organizational entrepreneurship', *Entrepreneurship and Regional Development*, **16**, 413–32.

Hjorth, D. (2004b), 'Towards genealogic storytelling in entrepreneurship', in C. Steyaert and D. Hjorth (eds), *New Movements in Entrepreneurship*, Cheltenham, UK and Northampton, MA, USA: Edward Elgar, pp. 210–29.

Hjorth, D. (2005), 'Organizational entrepreneurship: With de Certeau on creating heterotopias (or spaces for play)', *Journal of Management Inquiry*, **14** (4), 386–98.

Hjorth, D. and B. Johannisson (2000), 'Entreprenörskap som skapelseprocess och ideologi', *Reprint Series 2000/2*, ESBRI – Entrepreneurship and small business research institute, Stockholm.

Hjorth, D. and B. Johannisson (2003), 'Conceptualising the opening phase of a regional development as the enactment of a collective identity', *Concepts and Transformation*, **8** (1), 69–92.

Hjorth, D. and C. Steyaert (2003), 'Entrepreneurship beyond (a new) economy: Creative swarms and pathological zones', in C. Steyaert and D. Hjorth (eds), *New Movements in Entrepreneurship*, Cheltenham, UK and Northampton, MA, USA: Edward Elgar, pp. 286–304.

Hjorth, D., B. Johannisson and C. Steyaert (2003), 'Entrepreneurship as discourse and life style', in B. Czarniawska and G. Sevón (eds), *The Northern Lights: Organization Theory in Scandinavia*, Malmö/Copenhagen/Oslo: Liber/Copenhagen Business School/Abstract, pp. 91–111.

Holmquist, C. (2003), 'Is the medium really the message? Moving perspective from the entrepreneurial actor to the entrepreneurial action', in C. Steyaert and D. Hjorth (eds), *New Movements in Entrepreneurship*, Cheltenham, UK and Northampton, MA, USA: Edward Elgar, pp. 73–86.

Holmquist, C. and E. Sundin (1988), 'Women as entrepreneurs in Sweden. Conclusions from a survey', *Frontiers of Entrepreneurship Research*, 625–37.

Homer-Dixon, T. (2001), *The Ingenuity Gap*, Toronto, ON: Vintage Canada.

Honig, B. (1998), 'Who gets the goodies? An examination of microenterprise credit in Jamaica', *Entrepreneurship and Regional Development*, **10**, 313–34.

Honig, B. (2000), 'Small business promotion and microlending: A comparative assessment of Jamaican and Israeli NGO's', *Journal of Microfinance*, **2** (1), 92–111.

Hopper, K. (1990), 'Public shelter as "a Hybrid Institution": Homeless men in historical perspective', *Journal of Social Issues*, **46** (4), 13–29.

Hopper, K. and J. Baumohl (1994), 'Held in abeyance: Rethinking homelessness and advocacy', *American Behavioral Scientist*, **37** (4), 522–52.

Hosking, D.M. and D. Hjorth (2004), 'Relational constructionism and entrepreneurship: Some key notes', in C. Steyaert and D. Hjorth (eds), *New Movements in Entrepreneurship*, Cheltenham, UK and Northampton, MA, USA: Edward Elgar, pp. 255–68.

Hubbard, P. and T. Hall (1998), 'The entrepreneurial city and the 'new urban politics', in T. Hall and P. Hubbard (eds), *The Entrepreneurial City: Geographies of Politics, Regime and Representation*, West Sussex: John Wiley & Sons, pp. 1–27.

Huyghe, F.B. (1993), 'Interview with Michel Serres', *Unesco Courier*, **46**, 4–7.

Hwang, H. and W. Powell (2005), 'Institutions and entrepreneurship', in S. Alvarez, R. Agarwal and O. Sorenson (eds), *Handbook of Entrepreneurship Research: Interdisciplinary Perspectives*, New York: Springer, pp. 201–27.

Indigenous Peoples' Human Rights Project (2003), *The Rights of Indigenous Peoples*, University of Minnesota Human Rights Center, www.hrusa.org/indig/studyguide.htm, viewed 9 June 2004.

Inkles, A. (1974), *Becoming Modern*, Cambridge, MA: Harvard University Press.

International Labour Organisation (1991), *Convention (No. 169) concerning Indigenous and Tribal Peoples in Independent Countries*, University of Minnesota Human Rights Library, www1.umn.edu/humanrts/instree/r1citp.htm, viewed 9 June 2004.

Jack, S.L. and A.R. Anderson (2002), 'The effects of embeddedness of the entrepreneurial process', *Journal of Business Venturing*, **17** (5), 467–87.

James, E. (1989), 'The private provision of social services: A comparison of

Sweden and Holland', in E. James (ed.), *The Nonprofit Sector in International Perspective*, Oxford: Oxford University Press.

Janis, I.L. (1972), *Victims of Groupthink: A Psychological Study of Foreign–policy Decisions and Fiascoes*, Boston, MA: Houghton Mifflin.

Janssens. M. and C. Steyaert (2002), 'Qualifying otherness', in S. Leijon, R. Lillhannus and G. Widell (eds), *Reflecting Diversity*, Gothenburg: BAS Publishers.

Jenkins, R. (1996), *Social Identity*, London: Routledge.

Jessop, B. (1989), 'Conservative regimes and the transition to Post-Fordism', in M. Gottdiener and M. Komninos (eds), *Capitalist Development and Crisis Theory*, New York: St. Martin's Press, pp. 261–99.

Jessop, B. (1998), 'The narrative of enterprise and the enterprise of narrative: Place marketing and the entrepreneurial city', in T. Hall and P. Hubbard (eds), *The Entrepreneurial City: Geographies of Politics, Regime and Representation*, West Sussex: John Wiley & Sons, pp. 77–103.

Johannisson, B. (1978), *Företag och närsamhälle – en studie i organisation*, Växjö: Växjö University Press.

Johannisson, B. (1983), 'Swedish evidence for the potential of local entrepreneurship in regional development', *European Small Business Journal*, **1** (2), 11–24.

Johannisson, B. (1984), 'A cultural perspective on small business – Local business climate', *International Small Business Journal*, **2** (2), 32–43.

Johannisson, B. (1988), 'Business formation – A network approach', *Scandinavian Journal of Management*, **4**, (3–4), 83–99.

Johannisson, B. (2000), 'Modernising the industrial district: Rejuvenation or managerial colonisation?', in E. Vatne and M. Taylor (eds), *The Networked Firm in a Global World: Small Firms in New Environments*, Aldershot: Ashgate, pp. 283–308.

Johannisson, B. (2002), 'Energising entrepreneurship. Ideological tensions in the medium-sized family business', in D.E. Fletcher (ed.), *Understanding the Small Family Business*, London: Routledge, pp. 46–57.

Johannisson, B. (2004), 'Entrepreneurship as the construction of individual and collective identity', paper presented at Entrepreneurship in New Territories: Towards New Groundings, *Third Movements of Entrepreneurship Publication-Workshop*, Dalhalla, Sweden, 6–8 June.

Johannisson, B. and A. Nilsson (1989), 'Community entrepreneurship – Networking for local development', *Journal of Entrepreneurship and Regional Development*, **1** (1), 1–19.

Johannisson, B. and C. Wigren (2006), 'Extreme entrepreneurs – Challenging the institutional framework', in P.R. Christensen and F. Poulfeldt (eds). *Managing Complexity and Change in SMEs*, Cheltenham, UK and Northampton, MA, USA: Edward Elgar.

Johannisson, B., O. Alexanderson, K. Nowicki and K. Senneseth (1994), 'Beyond anarchy and organization – Entrepreneurs in contextual networks', *Entrepreneurship and Regional Development*, **6** (4), 329–56.

Johansson, A.W. (1997), *Att förstå rådgivning till småföretagare*, Doctoral thesis, Academia Adacta A.B.: Bjärred.

Johansson, A.W. (2004), 'Narrating the entrepreneur', *International Small Business Journal*, **22** (3), 273–93.

Johnson Jr., J.H. (2002), 'A conceptual model for enhancing community competitiveness in the New Economy', *Urban Affairs Review*, **37** (6), 763–79.

Johnson, S. (2000), 'Literature review on social entrepreneurship', *Canadian Centre for Social Entrepreneurship.*

Johnson, S. (2001), 'Social entrepreneurship literature overview', www. bus.alberta.ca/csse/whats_news/review.htm.

Johnson, S. (2003), 'Young social entrepreneurs in Canada', *Canadian Centre for Social Entrepreneurship.*

Johnstone H. and D. Lionais (2004), 'Depleted communities and community business entrepreneurship: Revaluing space through place', *Entrepreneurship and Regional Development*, **16** (3), 217–33.

Jones, C. (2003a), 'Theory after the Postmodern Condition', *Organization*, **10**, 503–25.

Jones, C. (2003b), 'As if business ethics were possible, "within such limits" . . .', *Organization*, **10**, 223–48.

Jones, C. and A. Spicer (2005), 'Outline of a genealogy of the value of the entrepreneur', in G. Erreygers and G. Jacobs (eds), *Language, Communication and the Economy*, Amsterdam: Benjamins.

Kanter, R. (1999), 'From spare change to real change: The social sector as a beta site for business innovation', *Harvard Business Review*, May–June, 123–32.

Kao, R.W., K.R. Kao and R.R. Kao (2002), *Entrepreneurism for the Market Economy*, London: Imperial College Press.

Kärreman, D. (2003), 'Avhandlingsprojektet som identitetsarbete', in L. Strannegård (ed.), *Avhandlingen – Om att formas till forskare*, Lund: Studentlitteratur, pp. 125–45.

Kaufman, H. (1985), *Time, Chance, and Organizations*, Chatham, NJ: Chatham House.

Kay, N. (1997), *Patterns in Corporate Evolution*, Oxford: Oxford University Press.

Keeble, D. (1993), 'Small firm creation, innovation and growth in the urban–rural shift', in J. Curran and D.J. Storey (eds), *Small Firms in Urban and Rural Locations*, London: Routledge, pp. 54–78.

Keeble, D. (1996), 'North–south and urban–rural variations in SME performance, innovation and business characteristics', in A. Cosh and A. Hughes (eds), *The Changing State of British Enterprise: Growth, Innovation and Competitive Advantage in Small and Medium Sized Enterprises 1986–1995*, Cambridge: University of Cambridge, ESRC Centre for Business Research, pp. 83–93.

Keeble, D. and A. Gould (1985), 'Entrepreneurship and manufacturing firm formation in rural areas: The East Anglian case', in M.J. Healey and B.W. Ilbery (eds), *Industrialisation of the Countryside*, Norwich: Geobooks, pp. 197–219.

Keeble, D., P. Tylaer, G. Broom and J. Lewis (1992), Business Success in the Countryside: The Performance of Rural Enterprise, London: HMSO.

Keller, R. (1984), 'The Harvard "Pareto Circle" and the historical development of organization theory', *Journal of Management*, **10**, 193–203.

Kent, C.A., Sexton, D.L. and K.H. Vesper, (eds) (1982), *Encyclopedia of Entrepreneurship*, Englewood Cliffs, NJ: Prentice-Hall.

Klitgaard, R.E. (1990), *Tropical Gangsters*, New York: Basic Books.

Komninos, N. (1989), 'From national to local: The janus face of crisis', in M. Gottdiener and N. Komninos (eds), *Capitalist Development and Crisis Theory*, New York: St. Martin's Press, pp. 348–64.

Koppl. R. (ed.) (2003), 'Austrian economics and entrepreneurial studies', *Advances in Austrian Economics*, **6**, 1–298. This volume includes a translation of Schumpeter's article from the 1928 'Entrepreneur' as well as a symposium on this with contributions by Markus Becker, Thorbjørn Knudsen and others.

Kostera, M. (2005), *The Quest for the Self-Actualizing Organization*, Malmö/Copenhagen: Liber/Copenhagen Business School Press.

Kourilsky, M.L. and W.B. Walstad (2004), 'Introduction: New perspectives on social and educational entrepreneurs', *International Journal of Entrepreneurship Education*, **2** (1), special issue.

Kupferberg, F. (1998), 'Humanistic entrepreneurship and entrepreneurial career commitment', *Entrepreneurship and Regional Development*, **10**, 171–88.

Kumar, K. (1978), *Prophecy and Progress*, Harmondsworth: Penguin.

Kuhns, B.A. (2004), 'Developing communities, people, and businesses: In search of a model of community-based enterprises', in H.P. Welsch (ed.), *Entrepreneurship: The Way Ahead*, New York: Routledge, pp. 195–210.

Lacan, J. (1977), *Ecrits: A Selection*, trans. A. Sheridan, London: Tavistock.

Laclau , E. and C. Mouffe (1985), *Hegemony and Socialist Strategy: Towards a Radical Democratic Politics*, London: Verso.

Landström, H. (2000), *Entreprenörskapets rötter*, Lund: Studentlitteratur.

Lanz, S. and J. Becker (eds) (2003), *Space//Troubles. Jenseits des Guten*

Regierens: Schattenglobalisierung, Gewaltkonflikte und städtisches Leben, Berlin: b_books.

LaVere, D. (2004), *The Texas Indians*, College Station: Texas A&M Press.

Law, J. (1994), *Organizing Modernity*, Oxford: Blackwell.

Law, J. (2004), *After Method: Mess in Social Science Research*, London: Routledge.

Leadbeater, C. (1997), *The Rise of the Social Entrepreneur*, London: Demos.

Lefebvre, H. (1991), *The Production of Space*, Oxford: Blackwell.

Lefebvre, H. (2003), *Die Revolution der Städte*, Dresden and Berlin: DRESDEN Postplatz in Kooperation mit b_books.

Lehmann, H.T. (2005), *Postdramatisches Theater*, 3. veränd. Auflage, Frankfurt am Main: Verlag der Autoren.

Leiss, W. (1972/1994), *The Domination of Nature*, Montreal: McGill-Queen's University Press.

Lengers, B. (2004), 'Ein PS im Medienzeitalter. Mediale Mittel, Masken und Metaphern im Theater von René Pollesch', in H.L. Arnold (ed.), *Theater fürs 21. Jahrhundert. Sonderband Text + Kritik*, München: Richard Boorberg Verlag, pp. 143–56.

Lerner, G. (1986), *The Creation of Patriarchy*, New York: Oxford University Press.

Lerner, G. (1993), *The Creation of Feminist Consciousness From the Middle Ages to 1870*, New York: Oxford University Press.

Letts, C., W. Ryan, and A. Grossman (1997), 'Virtuous capital: What foundations can learn from venture capitalists', *Harvard Business Review*, March–April, 2–7.

Levin, M. (2005), 'Board composition of Swedish social enterprises: Governance theories vs co-operative philosophy', paper presented at the XXIst *ICA Conference*, Cork, 11–13 August.

Leyshon, A. (1992), 'The transformation of regulatory order', *Geoforum*, **23** (3), 347–63.

Liggett, H. (2003), *Urban Encounters*, Minneapolis: University of Minnesota Press.

Light, I. (2004), 'The ethnic ownership economy', in C. Stiles and C. Galbraith (eds), *Ethnic Entrepreneurship: Structure and Process*, Amsterdam: Elsevier Science, pp. 3–44.

Lindgren, M. (2000), *Kvinnor i friskolor: Om kön, entreprenörskap och profession i identitetsskapandet, FSF 2000:3*, Örebro: FSF.

Lindgren, M. and N. Wåhlin (2001), 'Identity construction among boundary-crossing individuals', *Scandinavian Journal of Management*, **17**, 357–77.

Lindgren, M. and J. Packendorff (2003), 'A project-based view of entrepreneurship: Towards action-orientation, seriality and collectivity', in

C. Steyaert and D. Hjorth (eds), *New Movements in Entrepreneurship*, Cheltenham, UK and Northampton, MA, USA: Edward Elgar, pp. 86–102.

Lindner, R. (2004), 'Die Großstädte und das Geistesleben. Hundert Jahre danach', in Walter Siebel (ed.), *Die europäische Stadt*, Frankfurt am Main: Suhrkamp, pp. 169–79.

Linstead, S. (2003), 'Question time: Notes on altecation', in R.I. Westwood and S. Clegg (eds), *Debating Organization: Point – Counterpoint in Organization Studies*, Malden, MA: Blackwell, pp. 368–79.

Lipsky, M. and S. Smith (1989), 'When social problems are treated as emergencies', *Social Science Review*, **63** (1), 5–25.

Lissak, R. (1989), *Pluralism and Progressives: Hull House and the New Immigrants*, Chicago, IL: University of Chicago Press.

Llewellyn, N., C. Edwards, A. Lawton and G. Jones (2000), 'Entrepreneurship and public service management: definitions, competencies, obstacles and examples', Research Report, Milton Keynes: Open University Business School, Public Interest and Non-Profit Managemeent Research Unit (PiN).

Lovins, A.B., L.H. Lovins and P. Hawken (1999), 'A road map for natural capitalism', *Harvard Business Review*, May–June, 145–58.

Low, M.B. (2001), 'The adolescence of entrepreneurship research: Specification of purpose', *Entrepreneurship Theory and Practice*, **25** (4), 17–25.

Löw, M. (2001), *Raumsoziologie*, Frankfurt am Main: Suhrkamp.

Luhmann, N. (1999), *Die Kunst der Gesellschaft*, Frankfurt am Main: Suhrkamp.

Lukes, S. (1990), *Power, A Radical View*, London: Macmillan.

Lundström, T. and F. Wijkström (1997), *The Swedish Non-profit Sector*, Manchester: Manchester University Press.

Lurie, N. (1986), 'Money, semantics and native American leadership', *Native American Quarterly Journal of Native American Studies*, **10**, 47–63.

Lyotard, J.F. (1984), *The Postmodern Condition: A Report on Knowledge*, Minneapolis: University of Minnesota Press.

Lyotard, J.F. (1988), *The Differend: Phrases in Dispute*, trans. G. van den Abbeele, Minneapolis: University of Minnesota Press.

Lyotard, J.F. and J.L. Thébaud (1985), *Just Gaming*, trans. W. Godzich, Minneapolis: University of Minnesota Press.

Macchiavelli, N. (1513/1992), *The Prince*, New York: Collier & Son.

Marcuse, P. (2001), 'The liberal/conservative divide in the history of housing policy in the United States', *Housing Studies*, **16** (6), 717–36.

Maresch, R. and N. Werber (2002), 'Permanenzen des raums', in R. Maresch and N. Werber (eds), *Raum Wissen Macht*, Frankfurt am Main: Suhrkamp, pp. 1–23.

Marshall, A. (1890/1922), *Principles of Economics*, 8th edition, London: Macmillan.

Martin, M.K. and B. Voorhies (1975), *Female of the Species*, New York: Columbia University Press.

Maskell, P. and A. Malmberg (1999), 'Localised learning and industrial competitiveness', *Cambridge Journal of Economics*, **23**, 167–85.

Massumi, B. (2002), *Parables for the Virtual. Movement, Affect, Sensation*, Durham, NC: Duke University Press.

Mayo, E. (1924), 'Civilization – the perilous adventure', *Harper's Magazine*, **149**, 590–97.

McAdam, D., J. McCarthy and M. Zald (1996), *Comparative Perspectives on Social Movements: Political Opportunities, Mobilizing Structures, and Cultural Framings*, New York: Cambridge University Press.

McAdams, D.P. (1993), *The Stories we Live by. Personal Myths and the Making of the Self*, New York: Guilford.

McDougall, P.P. and B.M. Oviatt, (2000), 'International entrepreneurship: The intersection of two research paths', *Academy of Management Journal*, **43** (5), 902–8.

McLeod, H. (1997), 'Cross over: The social entrepreneur', *Inc. Special Issue: State of Small*, **19** (7), 100–104.

Merchant, C. (1990), 'Ecofeminism and feminist theory', in I. Diamond and G.F. Orenstein (eds), *Reweaving the World: The Emergence of Ecofeminism*, San Francisco, CA: Sierra Club Books, pp. 100–105.

Mies, M. (1993a), 'Feminist research: Science, violence and responsibility', in M. Mies and V. Shiva (eds), *Ecofeminism*, New Dehli, India: Kali for Women, pp. 36–54.

Mies, M. (1993b), 'The need for a new vision: The subsistence perspective' in M. Mies and V. Shiva (eds), *Ecofeminism*, New Dehli, India: Kali for Women, pp. 297–324.

Mies, M. and V. Shiva (eds) (1993), *Ecofeminism*, New Delhi, India: Kali for Women.

Migdal, J.S. (1975), *Peasants, Politics, and Revolution: Pressures Toward Political and Social Change in the Third World*, Princeton, NJ: Princeton University Press.

Miller, D. (1990), *The Icarus Paradox. How Excellent Companies Can Bring About their Own Downfall*, New York: Harper & Row.

Mirchandani, K. (1999), 'Feminist insight on gendered work: New directions in research on women and entrepreneurship', *Gender, Work and Organization*, **6**, 224–35.

Mishler, E.G. (1986), *Research Interviewing: Context and Narrative*, Cambridge, MA: Harvard University Press.

Monroe, L. (2005), 'Prater's Arsch-Kicker. An Interview with René Pollesch', *Exberliner*, **29**, July 2005, 10–14.

Montagu, A. (1953/1999), *The Natural Superiority of Women*, Walnut Creek, CA: Altamira Press.

Moore, A. (2004), 'Milking the farm for alternative uses', *Estates Gazette*, Issue 423.

Moore, M. (1997), 'Societies, polities and capitalists in developing countries: A literature survey', *Journal of Development Studies*, **33** (3), 287–363.

Moran, P. and S. Ghoshal (1999), 'Markets, firms, and the process of economic development', *The Academy of Management Review*, **24** (3), 390–412.

Morgan, G. (1993), *Imaginization*, London: Sage.

Morgan, G. (1997), *Images of Organization*, 2nd edn, Thousand Oaks, CA: Sage.

Morris, M. (1998), *Entrepreneurial Intensity: Sustainable Advantages for Individuals, Organizations and Societies*, Westport, CT: Quorum Books.

Morris, M.H., L.F. Pitt and P. Berton (1996), 'Entrepreneurial activity in the Third World informal sector', *International Journal of Entrepreneurial Behaviour and Research*, **2** (1), 59–76.

Mort, G.S., J. Weerawardena and K. Carnegie (2003), 'Social entrepreneurship: Towards conceptualization', *International Journal of Nonprofit and Voluntary Sector Marketing* **8** (1), 76–88.

Muncy, R. (1991), *Creating a Feminine Dominion in American Reform*, New York: Oxford University Press.

Nationalencyclopedien (1992), *Gnosjöanda*, [Reference book], Höganäs: Bra Böcker.

Najafizadeh, M. and L.A. Mennerick (2003), 'Gender and social entrepreneurship in societies in transition: The case of Azerbaijan', *Journal of World Studies*, **20** (2), 31–48.

Nelson, J.A.(1996), *Feminism, Objectivity and Economics*, London: Routledge.

Nelson, L. (1990), 'The place of women in polluted places' in I. Diamond and G.F. Orenstein (eds), *Reweaving the World: The Emergence of Ecofeminism*, San Francisco, CA: Sierra Club Books, pp. 173–88.

Norberg-Hodge, H. (1996), 'Shifting direction from global dependence to local interdependence', in J. Mander and E. Goldsmith (eds), *The Case Against The Global Economy and For A Turn Toward The Local*, San Francisco, CA: Sierra Club Books, pp. 393–406.

Norcliffe, G. (1994), 'Regional labor market adjustments in a period of structural transformation: The Canadian case', *Canadian Geographer*, **38** (1), 2–17.

Norman, N. (2005), 'Urbanomics', in S. Sheikh (ed.), *In the Place of the Public Sphere? Critical Readers in Visual Cultures 5*, Berlin: b_books, pp. 34–52.

Normann, R. (2001), *Reframing Business. When the Map Changes the Landscape*, West Susex: John Wiley & Sons.

Normark, P., J.E. Pettersson and Y. Stryjan (1993), 'Kooperativ statistik', in P. Normark et al. (eds), *Kooperativ omprövning*, Stockholm: Kooperativa Studier, pp. 172–92.

NUTEK (2002), 'Sårbara industriregioner – sårbarhet i lokala arbetsmarknadsregioner och kommuner till följd av industriell omstrukturering', Rapport nr: B 2002:01.

Oakeshott, R. (1978), *The Case for Workers' Co-ops*, London: Routledge and Kegan Paul.

O'Connor, E. (1999), 'The politics of management thought: A case study of the Harvard Business School and the Human Relations School', *Academy of Management Review*, **24** (1), 117–31.

O'Connor, E. (2000), 'Plotting the organization: The embedded narrative as a construct for studying change', *Journal of Applied Behavioral Science*, **36** (2), 174–92.

O'Connor, E. (2001), 'Back on the way to empowerment: The example of Ordway Tead and industrial democracy', *Journal of Applied Behavioral Science*, **37** (1), 15–32.

O'Connor, E. (2002), 'Storied business: Typology, intertextuality, and traffic in entrepreneurial narrative', *Journal of Business Communication*, **39** (1), 36–54.

O'Connor, E. (2004), *Catching Up With Homelessness*, unpublished report, Los Altos, CA.

Ogbor, J.O. (2000), 'Mythicizing and reification in entrepreneurial discourse: Ideology-critique of entrepreneurial studies, *Journal of Management Studies*, **37**, 605–35.

Orenstein, G.F. (1990), 'Artists as healers: Envisioning life-giving culture', in I. Diamond and G.F. Orenstein (eds), *Reweaving the World: The Emergence of Ecofeminism*, San Francisco, CA: Sierra Club Books, pp. 279–87.

Organisation for Economic Co-operation and Development [OECD] (1998), *Fostering Entrepreneurship*, Paris: OECD.

Ortner, S.B. (1974), 'Is female to male as nature is to culture?', in M.Z. Rosaldo and L. Lamphere (eds), *Women, Culture, and Society*, Stanford, CA: Stanford University Press, pp. 67–87.

Osborne, D. and T. Gaebler (1992), *Reinventing Government: How the Entrepreneurial Spirit is Transforming the Public Sector*, Reading, MA: Addison-Wesley.

Ouchi, R. (1980), 'Markets, bureaucracies and clans', *Administrative Science Quarterly*, **25**, 129–41.

Painter, J. (1998), 'Entrepreneurs are made, not born: Learning and urban regimes in the production of entrepreneurial cities', in T. Hall and P. Hubbard (eds), *The Entrepreneurial City: Geographies of Politics, Regime and Representation*, West Sussex: John Wiley & Sons, pp. 259–75.

Parker, B. (2004), 'Globalization as process', in R.I. Westwood and S. Clegg (eds), *Debating Organization: Point – Counterpoint in Organization Studies*, Malden, MA: Blackwell, pp. 234–51.

Parker, I. (1992), *Discourse Dynamics: Critical Analysis for Social and Individual Psychology*, London: Routledge.

Parker, S. (2004), *Urban Theory and the Urban Experience*, London and New York: Routledge.

Parsons, T. and E.A. Shils (1951), *Towards a General Theory of Action*, Cambridge, MA: Harvard University Press.

Pastakia, A. (1998), 'Grassroots ecopreneurs: Change agents for a sustainable society', *Journal of Organizational Change Management*, **11** (2), 157–73.

Pattiniämi, P. (2001), 'Finland: Labour co-operatives as an innovative response to unemployment', in C. Borzaga. and J. Defourny (eds), *The Emergence of Social Enterprise*, London and New York: Routledge, pp. 82–99.

Pearce, J. (1994), 'Enterprise with social purpose', *Town and County Planning*, **63** (March), 84–5.

Peck, J. and A. Tickell (1992), 'Local modes of social regulation', *Geoforum*, **23** (3), 347–63.

Penrose, E. (1959/1995), *The Theory of the Growth of the Firm*, Oxford: Oxford University Press.

Peredo, A.M. (2001), 'Communal enterprises, sustainable development and the alleviation of poverty in rural Andean communities', Ph.D. thesis, University of Calgary.

Peredo, A.M. (2003), 'Emerging strategies against poverty: The road less traveled', *Journal of Management Inquiry*, **12** (2), 155–66.

Peredo, A.M. and J.J. Chrisman (2005), 'Toward a theory of community-based enterprise', *Academy of Management Review*, forthcoming.

Peredo, A.M., R.B. Anderson, C.S. Galbraith, B. Honig and L.P. Dana (2004), 'Towards a theory of indigenous entrepreneurship', *International Journal of Entrepreneurship and Small Business*, **1** (1–2), 1–20.

Pestoff, V.A. (1998), *Beyond the Market and State. Social enterprises and Civil Democracy in a Welfare Society*, Aldershot: Gower.

Pestoff, V.A. (2000), 'Enriching Swedish women's work environment: The case of social enterprises in day care', *Economic and Industrial Democracy*, **21**, 39–70.

Petersen, A., I. Barns, J. Dudley and P. Harris (1999), *Poststructuralism, Citizenship and Social Policy*, London: Routledge.

Peterson, R. (1977), *Small Business Building a Balanced Economy*, Erin, ON: Press Porcepic.

Peterson, R. (1988), 'Understanding and encouraging entrepreneurship internationally', *Journal of Small Business Management*, **26** (2), 1–8.

Pettersson, K. (2002), *Företagande män och osyngliggjorda kvinnor – Diskursen om Gnosjö ur ett könsperspektiv*, Ph.D. thesis, Geografiska Regionstudier, 49, Kulturgeografiska institutionen Uppsala University.

Pettersson, K. (2004), 'Masculine entrepreneurship – The Gnosjö discourse in a feminist perspective', in D. Hjorth and C. Steyaert (eds), *Narrative and Discursive Approaches in Entrepreneurship*, Cheltenham, UK and Northampton, MA, USA: Edward Elgar. pp. 177–193.

Pharoah, C. and D. Scott (2002), 'Social enterprise in the voluntary and community sector: Challenges for policy and practice', *Transforming Civil Society, Citizenship and Governance: The Third Sector in an Era of Global (Dis)Order – ISTR Fifth International Conference*, Cape Town, 7–10 July.

Philipose, P. (1989), 'Women act: Women and environmental protection in India', in J. Plant (ed.), *Healing the Wounds: The Promise of Ecofeminism*, Toronto, ON: Between the Lines, pp. 67–75.

Piore, M.J. and C.F. Sabel (1984), *The Second Industrial Divide. Possibilities for Prosperity*, New York: Basic Books.

Plant, J. (1990), 'Searching for common ground: Ecofeminism and bioregionalism', in I. Diamond and G.F. Orenstein (eds), *Reweaving the World: The Emergence of Ecofeminism*, San Francisco, CA: Sierra Club Books, pp. 155–61.

Plant, J. (1997), 'Learning to live with differences: The challenge of ecofeminist community', in K.J. Warren (ed.), *Ecofeminism: Women, Culture, Nature*, Bloomington, ID: Indiana University Press, pp. 120–39.

Polanyi, K. (1944/2001), *The Great Transformation: The Political and Economic Origins of Our Time*, Boston, MA: Beacon Press.

Polikoff, B. (1999), *With One Bold Act: The Story of Jane Addams*, Chicago: Boswell Books.

Pollesch, R. (2002a), 'Stadt als Beute', in B. Masuch (ed.), *WOHNFRONT 2001–2002*, Berlin: Alexander Verlag, pp. 5–42.

Pollesch, R. (2002b), 'Insourcing des Zuhause. Menschen in Scheiss-Hotels', in B. Masuch (ed.), *WOHNFRONT 2001–2002*, Berlin: Alexander Verlag, pp. 43–81.

Pollesch, R. (2003), 'Ich bin Heidi Hoh – René Pollesch im Gespräch mit Jürgen Berger', in R. Pollesch, *World Wide Web Slums*, Reinbek bei Hamburg: Rowohlt, pp. 341–9.

Pomerantz, M. (2003), 'The business of social entrepreneurship in a "down economy" ', *In Business*, **25**, 25–8.

Porter, M. and M. Kramer (1999), 'Philanthropy's new agenda: Creating value', *Harvard Business Review*, November–December, 121–130.

Portes, A. (1998), 'Social capital: Its origins and applications in modern sociology', *Annual Review of Sociology*, **24**, 1–24.

Portes, A. and R. Bach (1985), *Latin Journey: Cuban and Mexican*

Immigrants in the United States, Berkeley, CA: University of California Press.

Portes, A. and J. Sensenbrenner (1993), 'Embeddedness and immigration: Notes on the social determinants of economic action', *The American Journal of Sociology*, **98**, 1320–50.

Potter, J. (1996), *Representing Reality: Discourse, Rhetoric and Social Construction*, Thousand Oaks, CA: Sage Publications.

Potter, J. and M. Wetherell (1987), *Discourse and Social Psychology*, London: Sage.

Prabhu, G.N. (1999), 'Social entrepreneurial leadership', *Career Development International*, **4** (3), 140–45.

Prasad, A. (1997), 'Provincializing Europe: Towards a post-colonial reconstruction: A critique of Baconian science as the last stand of imperialism', *Studies in Cultures, Organisations And Societies*, **3**, 91–117.

Primavesi, A. (1994), 'A time in the affairs of women?', in D.G. Hallman (ed.), *Ecotheology: Voices From South and North*, Geneva, Switzerland: WCC Publications.

Putnam, R.D. (1993), 'The prosperous community: Social capital and public life', *American Prospect*, **13**, 35–42.

Putnam, R.D., R. Leonardi and R.Y. Nanetti (1993), *Making Democracy Work: Civic Traditions in Modern Italy*, Princeton, NJ: Princeton University Press.

Pyke, F., G. Becattini and W. Sengenberger (eds) (1990), *Industrial Districts and Inter-Firm Co-operation in Italy*, Geneva: ILO.

Quarsell, R. (1993), 'Välgörenhet, filantropi och frivilligt socialt arbete – en historisk översikt', in SOU 1993:82, *Frivilligt Socialt Arbete*, Stockholm: Allmänna förlaget.

Quarter, J., L. Mook and B.J. Richmond (2004), *What Counts. Social Accounting for Nonprofits and Cooperatives*, Upper Saddle River, NJ: Prentice Hall.

Quinby, L. (1990), 'Ecofeminism and the politics of resistance', in I. Diamond and G.F. Orenstein (eds), *Reweaving the World: The Emergence of Ecofeminism*, San Francisco, CA: Sierra Club Books, pp. 122–7.

Rabinow, P. (1984), *The Foucault Reader*, New York: Pantheon Books.

Regional Growth Programme (RDP) (2003), Regionalt tillväxtprogram för Sörmland 2004–2007, County administrative board in Södermanland.

Rehn, A. and S. Taalas (2004), 'Acquaintances and connections – *Blat*, the Soviet Union, and mundane entrepreneurship', *Entrepreneurship and Regional Development*, **16**, May, 235–50.

Reich, R. (1987), 'Entrepreneurship reconsidered: the team as a hero', *Harvard Business Review*, May/June, 77–83.

Reis, T.K. (1999), *Unleashing the New Resources and Entrepreneurship for the Common Good: a Scan, Synthesis and Scenario for Action*, Battle Creek, MI: W.K. Kellogg Foundation.

Reis, T.K. and S.J. Clohesy (2001), 'Unleashing new resources and entrepreneurship for the common good', *New Directions for Philanthropic Fundraising*, **32**, 109–44.

Rich, A. (1976/1986), *Of Woman Born: Motherhood as Experience and Institution*, New York: W.W. Norton & Company.

Richardson, L. (1994), 'Writing: A method of inquiry', in N.K. Denzin and Y.S. Lincoln (eds), *Handbook of Qualitative Research*, London: Sage, pp. 516–29.

Roberts, D. and C. Woods (2005), 'Changing the world on a shoestring: The concept of social entrepreneurship', *University of Auckland Business Review*, Autumn, 45–51.

Rockefeller, J. (1917), *The Personal Relation in Industry*, New York: Bonibooks.

Roethlisberger, F. (1977), *The Elusive Phenomena: An Autobiographical Account of My Work in the Field of Organizational Behavior at the Harvard Business School*, Cambridge, MA: Harvard University Press.

Ronneberger, K. (2001), 'Konsumfestungen und Raumpatrouillen. Der Ausbau der Städte zu Erlebnislandschaften', in J. Becker (ed.), *BIGNES? Size does matter. Image/Politik. Städtisches Handeln. Kritik der unternehmerischen Stadt*, Berlin: b_books, pp. 28–42.

Ronneberger, K., S. Lanz and W. Jahn (1999), *Die Stadt als Beute*, Bonn: Dietz.

Rorty, R. (1989), *Contingency, Irony and Solidarity*, Cambridge: Cambridge University Press.

Rorty, R. (1991), *Essays on Heidegger and Others*, Cambridge: Cambridge University Press.

Ross, D.P. and P.J. Usher (1986), *From the Roots Up: Economic Development as if Community Mattered*, Toronto, Canada: James Lorimer & Company.

Rostow, W.W. (1960), *The Stages of Economic Growth*, Cambridge: Cambridge University Press.

Ruether, R.R. (1992/1994), *Gaia & God: An Ecofeminist Theology of Earth Healing*, San Francisco, CA: Harper Collins.

Sagawa, S. and E. Segal (2000), 'Common interest, common good: Creating value through business and social sector partnership', *California Management Review*, **42** (2), 105–22.

Salomonsson, A. (1996), 'Regionaliteten som problem', in M. Idvall and A. Salomonsson (eds), *Att skapa en region – om identitet och territorium* (1996: 1), Stockholm: NordREFO.

Samverkan inom rehabiliteringsområdet interdepartmental work-team' (2000), in *Samhällsekonomiska effekter vid rehabilitering* (Report 2000:11), Stockholm: Socialstyrelsen.

Sarasvathy, S. (2001), 'Causation and effectuation: Toward a theoretical shift from economic inevitability to entrepreneurial contingency', *Academy of Management Review*, **26** (2), 243–63.

Sarasvathy, S. (2004), 'The questions we ask and the questions we care about: Reformulating some problems in entrepreneurship research', *Journal of Business Venturing*, forthcoming.

Saxenian, A. (2000), 'The origins and dynamics of production networks in Silicon Valley', in R. Swedberg (ed.), *Entrepreneurship: A Social Science View*, Oxford: Oxford University Press.

Schlesinger, M. (1998), 'Mismeasuring the consequences of ownership: External influences and the comparative performance of public, for-profit, and private nonprofit organizations', in W. Powell and E. Clemens (eds), *Private Action and the Public Good*, New Haven, CT: Yale University Press, pp. 85–113.

Schlögel, K. (2003), *Im Raume lesen wir die Zeit: Über Zivilisationsgeschichte und Geopolitik*, München and Wien: Carl Hanser.

Schumacher, E.F. (1973), *Small is Beautiful: Economics as if People Mattered*, New York: Harper & Row.

Schumpeter, J.A. (1911), *Theorie der Wirtschaftlichen Entwicklung*, Leipzig: Duncker & Humblot.

Schumpeter, J.A. (1934), *Theory of Economic Development*, Cambridge, MA: Harvard University Press.

Schumpeter, J.A. (1951/1989), *Essays on Entrepreneurs, Innovations, Business Cycles, and the Evolution of Capitalism*, ed. by R.V. Clemence, New Brunswick, NJ: Transaction Publishers.

Schumpeter, J.A. (1994), *Capitalism, Socialism and Democracy*, London: Routledge.

Schumpeter, J.A. (2000), 'Entrepreneurship as innovation', in R. Swedberg (ed.), *Entrepreneurship: The Social Science View*, Oxford: Oxford University Press, pp. 51–75.

Schumpeter, J.A. (2002), 'New translations: Theorie der wirtschaftlichen Entwicklung', *American Journal of Economics and Sociology*, **61** (2), pp. 405–37. Translations of parts of Chs 2 (pp. 103–107, 156–64) and 7 (pp. 525–48) by M. Becker and T. Knudsen.

Schumpeter, J.A. (2003), 'The theory of economic development', in J. Backhaus (ed.), *Joseph Alois Schumpeter*, Boston: Kluwer, pp. 61–116. This text constitutes Ch. 7 in *Theorie der Wirtschaftlichen Entwicklung* (1911) and has been translated by U. Backhaus.

Schuyler, G. (1998), 'Social entrepreneurship: Profit as a means, not an end', Kauffman Center for Entrepreneurial Leadership Clearinghouse on Entrepreneurial Education (CELCEE), www.celcee.edu/products/digest/ Dig98-7html.

Scott, A.J. (1988), *New Industrial Spaces: Flexible Production Organization and Regional Development in North America and Western Europe*, Studies in Society and Space, 3, London: Pion.

Scott, M.G. and A.R. Anderson (1993), 'The environment for rural entrepreneurship: The commodification of the countryside', in S. Birley and I. Macmillan (eds), *Entrepreneurship Research: Global Perspectives*, Amsterdam: North-Holland.

Sen, A. (1981), *Poverty and Famines. An Essay on Entitlement and Deprivation*, Oxford: Clarendon Press.

Serres, M. (1995), *Genesis*, trans. G. James and J. Nielson, Ann Arbor, MI: University of Michigan Press.

Serres, M. (1997), *The Troubadour of Knowledge*, trans. S.F. Glaser and W. Paulson, Ann Arbor, MI: University of Michigan Press.

Sexton, D.L. and J.D. Kasarda, (eds) (1992), *The State of the Art of Entrepreneurship*, Boston: PWS-Kent Publishing Company.

Sexton, D.L. and H. Landström (eds) (2000), *The Blackwell Handbook of Entrepreneurship*, Oxford: Blackwell.

Sexton, D.L. and R.W. Smilor, (eds) (1986), *The Art and Science of Entrepreneurship*, Cambridge, MA: Ballinger Publishing Company.

Sexton, D.L. and R.W. Smilor (eds) (1997), *Entrepreneurship 2000*, Chicago, IL: Upstart Publishing.

Shane, S. and S. Venkataraman (2000), 'The promise of entrepreneurship as a field of research', *Academy of Management Review*, **25** (1), 217–26.

Shionoya, Y. (1990), 'The origin of the Schumpeterian research program: A chapter omitted from Schumpeter's *Theory of Economic Development*', *Journal of Institutional and Theoretical Economics*, **146** (2), 314–27.

Shipek, F. (1982), 'Kumeyaay socio-political structure', *Journal of California and Great Basin Anthropology*, **4**, 293–303.

Shiva, V. (1990), 'Development as a new project of western patriarchy', in I. Diamond and G.F. Orenstein (eds), *Reweaving the World: The Emergence of Ecofeminism*, San Francisco, CA: Sierra Club Books, pp. 189–200.

Shiva, V. (1993), 'Reductionism and regeneration: A crisis in science', in M. Mies and V. Shiva (eds), *Ecofeminism*, New Dehli, India: Kali for Women, pp. 22–35.

Sievers, B. (2001), 'If pigs had wings: The appeals and limits of venture philanthropy', www.philanthropyuk.org/documents/BruceSievers.pdf.

Silverman, D. (1970), *The Theory of Organisations*, London: Heinemann.

Simmel, G. (2002), 'The Metropolis and Mental Life', in G. Bridge and S. Watson (eds), *The Blackwell City Reader*, Oxford: Blackwell, pp. 11–20.

Sipiora, P. and J. Atwill (1990), 'Rhetoric and cultural explanation: A discussion with Gayatri Chakravortry Spivak', **JAC**, 10.2., www.jac.gsu.edu/jac/10.2/Articles/5.htm.

Sköldberg, K. (2005), 'Management as romantic irony', in U. Johansson and
    J. Woodilla (eds), *Irony and Organizations*, Malmö: Liber-Copenhagen
    business School Press, pp. 126–50.
Sloterdijk, P. (2004), *Sphären III: Schäume*, Frankfurt am Main: Suhrkamp.
Smith, D. (1979), 'A sociology for women', in J. Sherman and E. Beck (eds),
    The Prism of Sex: Essays in the Sociology of Knowledge, Madison, WI:
    University of Wisconsin Press.
So, A.Y. (1990), *Social Change and Development: Modernization,
    Dependency, and World-System Theories*, Newbury Park, CA: Sage
    Library of Social Research 178.
Soja, E.W. (1996), *Thirdspace. Journeys to Los Angeles and Other Real-and-
    Imagined Places*, Oxford: Blackwell.
Soja, E.W. (2000), *Postmetropolis: critical studies of cities and regions*,
    Oxford: Blackwell.
de Soto, H. (2001), *The Mystery of Capital: Why Capitalism Triumphs in the
    West and Fails Everywhere Else*, London: Black Swan.
Spinosa, C., F. Flores and H.L. Dreyfus (1997), *Disclosing New Worlds:
    Entrepreneurship, Democratic Action, and the Cultivation of Solidarity*,
    Cambridge, MA and London: MIT Press.
Spivak, G.C. (1990), *The Postcolonial Critic: Interviews, Strategies,
    Dialogues*, New York: Routledge.
Starhawk (1990), 'Power, authority, and mystery: Ecofeminism and earth-
    based spirituality', in I. Diamond and G.F. Orenstein (eds), *Reweaving the
    World: The Emergence of Ecofeminism*, San Francisco, CA: Sierra Club
    Books, pp. 73–86.
Stern, M. (1984), 'The emergence of the homeless as a public problem', *Social
    Service Review*, **58**, 291–301.
Stevens, E. (2001), *Testimony before the U.S. Senate Committee on Indian
    Affairs*, Oversight Hearing of the National Gaming Commission, 25 July.
Stevenson, H.H. (2004), 'Intellectual foundations of entrepreneurship', in H.P.
    Welsch (ed.), *Entrepreneurship: The Way Ahead*, New York: Routledge, pp.
    3–14.
Steyaert, C. (1998), 'A qualitative methodology for process studies of entre-
    preneurship: Creating local knowledge through stories', *International
    Studies of Management and Organisation*, **27** (3), 13–33.
Steyaert, C. (2000), 'Creating worlds: Political agendas of entrepreneurship',
    paper presented at the 11th *Nordic Conference on Small Business Research*,
    Aarhus, Denmark, 18–20 June.
Steyaert, C. (2002), 'Imaginative geographies: On creative spaces in organi-
    zations', Inaugural Lecture of the Chair in Organisational Psychology, St
    Gallen, Switzerland.
Steyaert, C. (2004), 'The prosaics of entrepreneurship', in C. Steyaert and D.

Hjorth (eds), *New Movements in Entrepreneurship*, Cheltenham, UK and Northampton, MA, USA: Edward Elgar, pp. 8–21.

Steyaert, C. (2005), 'Entrepreneurship: In between what? On the "frontier" as a discourse of entrepreneurship research', *International Journal of Entrepreneurship and Small Business*, **2**, 2–16.

Steyaert, C. and R. Bouwen (1997), 'Telling stories of entrepreneurship: Towards a narrative-contextual epistemology for entrepreneurial studies', in R. Donckels and A. Miettinen (eds), *Entrepreneurship and SME research: On Its Way to the Next Millennium*, Aldershot: Ashgate.

Steyaert, C. and J. Katz (2004), 'Reclaiming the space of entrepreneurship in society: Geographical, discursive and social dimensions', *Entrepreneurship and Regional Development*, **16** (3), pp. 179–96.

Stinchcombe, A. (1965), 'Social structure and organizations', in J. March (ed.), *Handbook of Organizations*, Chicago, IL: Rand McNally.

Stone, M. (1976), *When God Was a Woman*, New York: Dorset Press.

Storper, M. (1995), 'The resurgence of regional economies, ten years later: The region as a nexus of untraded interdependencies', *European Urban and Regional Studies*, **3** (2), 191–221.

Storper, M. and R. Walker (1989), *The Capitalist Imperative: Territory, Technology, and Industrial Growth*, Oxford: Blackwell.

Strid, M. (2004), 'Looking at knowledge processes from a spatial aspect', paper presented at *Entrepreneurship in New Territories: Towards New Groundings*, Third Movements of Entrepreneurship Publication Workshop, Dalhalla, Sweden, 6–8 June.

Stridh, K. (2003), *Utvärdering av Mångfald i Företagsamhet – ett projekt inom gemenskapsinitiativet Equal*, Halmstad: Internationell Kompetens AB.

Stryjan, Y. (1989a), 'Hunting and gathering: The self-managed organization and its environment', in *Co-operative Development and Change*, Stockholm: The Society for Co-operative Studies.

Stryjan, Y. (1989b), *Impossible Organizations*, New York: Greenwood Press.

Stryjan, Y. (1994a), 'The formation of new cooperatives: Theory and the Swedish case', *Economic and Industrial Democracy*, **15**, 565–94.

Stryjan, Y. (1994b), 'Co-operatives in the welfare market', in G. Perri and I. Vidal (eds), *Delivering Welfare*, Barcelona: CIES.

Stryjan, Y. (2001), 'Sweden: The emergence of work-integration social enterprises', in C. Borzaga and J. Defourny (eds), *The Emergence of Social Enterprise*, London and New York: Routledge, pp. 220–35.

Stryjan, Y. (2002), 'Social cooperatives in Sweden: Etudes in entrepreneurship', Huddinge: Working Paper Södertörns Högskola.

Stryjan, Y. (2003/5), 'Social democracy, the labour market and the third sector: The Swedish case', paper presented at *The Progressive Scholars' Forum*,

Tokyo/Sapporo, 11–15 October (publication of Japanese version pending by Tokyo: Minerva Publishers).

Stryjan, Y. and F. Wijkström (1996), 'Co-operatives and non-profit organisations in Swedish social welfare', *Annals of Public and Co-operative Economics*, **67** (1), 5–27.

Sturgeon, N. (1997), 'The nature of race: Discourses of racial difference in ecofeminism', in K.J. Warren (ed.), *Ecofeminism: Women, Culture, Nature*, Bloomington, IN: Indiana University Press, pp. 260–78.

Suchman, M. (1995), 'Managing legitimacy: Strategic and institutional approaches', *Academy of Management Review*, **20** (3), 571–610.

Sveningsson, S. and M. Alvesson (2003), 'Managing managerial identities: Organizational fragmentation, discourse and identity struggle', *Human Relations*, **56**, 1163–93.

Swedberg, R. (1999), *Entrepreneurship: The Social Science View*, Oxford: Oxford University Press.

Swedberg, R. (1991), *Schumpeter – A Biography*, Princeton, NJ: Princeton University Press.

Symon, G. (2000), 'Everday rhetoric: Argument and persuasion in everyday life', *European Journal of Work and Organizational Psychology*, **9**, 477–88.

Szablowski, D. (2002), 'Mining, displacement of the World Bank: A case study of compania minera antamina's operations in Peru', *Journal of Business Ethics*, **39** (3), 247–73.

Taylor, F. (1911), *The Principles of Scientific Management*, New York: Harper & Row.

Taylor, N., R. Hobbs, F. Nilsson, K. O'Halloran and C. Preisser (2000), 'The rise of the term social entrepreneurship in print publications: Frontiers of entrepreneurship research', proceedings of the annual *Babson College Entrepreneurship Research Conference*, Babson, College, Wellesley, MA.

Teece, D. (1980), 'Economies of scope and the scope of the enterprise', *Journal of Economic Behavior and Organization*, **1**, 223–47.

Tetzschner, H. (1998), 'Collective entrepreneurship and waves of co-operative development', *Economic Analysis*, **1** (3), 257–75.

Thalbuder, J. (1998), 'How nonprofit and for-profit differ', www.socialentrepreneurs.org/entredef.html.

Thomas, G. (1987), 'Revivalism, nation-building, and institutional change' in G. Thomas, J. Meyher, F. Ramirez and J. Boli (eds), *Institutional Structure: Constituting State, Society, and the Individual*, Newbury Park, CA: Sage.

Thompson, J.L. (2002), 'The world of the social entrepreneur', *The International Journal of Public Sector Management*, **5** (5), 412–31.

Thompson, J., G. Alvy and A. Lees (2000), 'Social entrepreneurship – A new look at the people and the potential', *Management Decision*, **38** (5), 328–38.

Thornton, J. (2005), 'Corporate takeover: A conversation on Buddhism, corporate power, confrontational tactics, and the future of the world with Rainforest Action Network chairman Jim Gollin', *Tricycle*, **14** (4), 66–70.

Titmuss, R.M. (1977), *The Gift Relationship: From Human Blood to Social Policy*, ed. by A. Oakley and J. Ashton, London: LSE Books.

Toffler, A. (1980), *The Third Wave*, New York: The Free Press.

Tönnies F. (1887/1963), *Community and Society: Gemeinschaft und Gesellschaft*, trans. C.P. Loomis, New York: Harper & Row.

Trahair, R. (1984), *The Humanist Temper: The Life and Work of Elton Mayo*, New Brunswick, NJ: Transaction Books.

Traill, C.P. (1836/1966), *The Backwoods of Canada*, Toronto, ON: McCelland & Stewart.

Trolander, J. (1987), *Professionalism and Social Change: From the Settlement House Movement to Neighborhood Centers, 1886 to the Present*, New York: Columbia University Press.

Trost, J. (1993), *Familjen i Sverige*, Stockholm: Liber Utbildning.

Tucker, V. (1999), 'The myth of development: A critique of a Eurocentric discourse', in R. Munck and D. O'Hearn (eds), *Critical Development Theory: Contributions to a New Paradigm*, London: Zed Books.

United Nations Development Programme (2001, *Human Development Report 2001: Making New Technologies Work for Human Development*, Oxford: Oxford University Press.

Unruh, D. (1979), 'Characteristics and types of participation in social worlds', *Symbolic Interaction*, **2**, 115–30.

Uzzi, B. (1997), 'Social structure and competition in interfirm networks: The paradox of embeddedness', *Administrative Science Quarterly*, **42** (1), 35–67.

Vad varje svensk bör veta (1991), *Gnosjöand*a [Reference book, author Sune Örnberg], Stockholm: Bonnier Fakta Bokförlag AB.

van Maanen, J. (1995), 'Style as theory', *Organization Science*, **6**, 133–43.

Venkataraman, S. (1997), 'The distinctive domain of entrepreneurship research: An editor's perspective', in J. Katz and J. Brockhaus (eds), *Advances in Entrepreneurship, Firm Emergence, and Growth*, Greenwich, CYT: JSAI Press.

Vickers, J.M. (1989), 'Memoirs of an ontological exile: The methodological rebellions of feminist research', in A. Miles and G. Fine (eds), *Feminism: From Pressure to Politics*, Montreal, Canada: Black Rose Books, pp. 37–56.

Vinje, D. (1996), 'Native American economic development on selected reservations: A comparative study', *The American Journal of Economics and Sociology*, **55**, 427–43.

Vogl, J. (2002), *Kalkül und Leidenschaft: Poetik des ökonomischen Menschen*, München: Sequenzia.

Vyakarnam, S., R.C. Jacobs and J. Handelberg (1999), 'Formation and development of entrepreneurial teams in rapid-growth business', paper presented at the *Frontiers of Entrepreneurship Conference*, Babson College, Wellesley, MA.

Wallace, S.L. (1999) , 'Social entrepreneurship: The role of social purpose enterprises in facilitating community economic development', *Journal of Developmental Entrepreneurship*, **4**, 153–74.

Wåhlin, N. (1999), 'Reflexive identity creation through boundary spanning and boundary crossing', in B. Johannisson and H. Landström (eds), *Images of Entrepreneurship and Small Business*, Lund: Studentlitteratur, pp. 115–40.

Warring, M. (1990), *If Women Counted: A New Feminist Economics*, New York: HarperCollins.

Warren, L. (2004), 'Negotiating entrepreneurial identity – communities of practice and changing discourses', *The International Journal of Entrepreneurship and Innovation*, **5** (1), 25–35.

Watson, T.J. (1977), *The Personnel Managers: A Study in the Sociology of Work and Employment*, London: Routledge.

Watson, T.J. (2000), 'Ethnographic fiction science: Making sense of managerial work and organizational research: Processes with Caroline and Terry', *Organization*, **7**, 489–510.

Watson, T.J. (2001), *In Search of Management* (revised edn), London: Thomson Learning.

Watson, T.J. (2003), *Sociology, Work and Industry*, fourth edition, London: Routledge.

Weber, M. (1980), 'Die Stadt', in M. Weber, *Wirtschaft und Gesellschaft: Grundriß der verstehenden Soziologie*, Tübingen: Mohr Siebeck, pp. 727–814.

Wells, B. and D. Wirth (1997), 'Remediating development through an ecofeminist lens', in K.J. Warren (ed.), *Ecofeminism: Woman, Culture, Nature*, Bloomington, ID: Indiana University Press, pp. 300–313.

Welsch, H.P. (2004), *Entrepreneurship: The Way Ahead*, New York: Routledge.

Welsch, H.P. and B.A. Kuhns (2002), 'Community-based enterprises: Propositions and cases', paper presented at the *USASBE Annual National Conference*, 17–20 January, Reno, Nevada.

Welsch, H.P. and J. Liao (2003), 'Strategies for entrepreneurship development: Striking a balance between explorative and exploitative research', in C. Steyaert and D. Hjorth (eds), *New Movements in Entrepreneurship*, Cheltenham, UK and Northampton, MA, USA: Edward Elgar, pp. 20–34.

Welsch, H.P. and M.A. Maltarich (2004), 'Emerging patterns of entrepreneurship: Distinguishing attributes of an evolving discipline', in H.P. Welsch (ed.), *Entrepreneurship: The Way Ahead*, New York: Routledge, pp. 55–70.

Wendeberg, B. (1982), *Gnosjöandan – Myt eller verklighet*, Värnamo: U B Wendeberg Förlag HB.

Wenger, E. (1998), *Communities of Practice – Learning, Meaning, and Identity*, Cambridge: Cambridge University Press.

Westhead, P. and M. Wright (1999), 'Contributions of novice, portfolio and serial founders located in rural and urban areas', *Regional Studies*, **33** (2), 157–73.

Westlund, H. (2001), 'Social economy and employment. The case of Sweden', paper presented at the *Uddevalla Symposium* 2001, Regional Economies in Transition, 14–16 June, Vänersborg, Sweden.

Westwood, R.I. and S. Clegg (2003), *Debating Organization: Point–Counterpoint in Organization Studies*, Malden, MA: Blackwell, pp. 1–43.

Wetherell, M. and J. Potter (1992), *Mapping the Language of Racism. Discourse and the Legitimation of Exploitation*, London: Harvester Wheatsheaf.

White, M. and A. Hunt (2000), 'Citizenship: Care of the self, character and personality', *Citizenship Studies*, **4** (2), 93–116.

Whitsett, D. and L. Yorks (1983), *From Management Theory to Business Sense: The Myths and Realities of People at Work*, New York: Amacom.

Wigren, C. (2003), *The Spirit of Gnosjö: The Grand Narrative and Beyond*. Ph.D. thesis, JIBS Dissertation Series, No. 017. Jönköping.

Williams, A.S. and P.C. Jobes (1995), 'Economic and quality of life considerations in urban–rural migration', *Journal of Rural Studies*, **6**, 187–94.

Williamson, O. (1975), *Markets and Hierarchies: Analysis and Antitrust Implications*, New York: The Free Press.

Wirth, A. (2003), 'René Pollesch – Generationsagitproptheater für Stadtindianer', in A. Dürrschmidt and B. Engelhardt (eds), *Werk-Stück. Regisseure im Portrait. Arbeitsbuch 2003*, Berlin: Theater der Zeit, pp. 126–32.

Woodworth, W., G. Meyer and N. Smallwood (1982), 'Organization Development: A Closer Scrutiny', *Human Relations*, **35**, 307–19.

World Bank (2001), *Indigenous Peoples*, Draft Operational Policies (OP 4.10), The World Bank Group, viewed 9 June 2004.

Wrege, C. (1979), 'Antecedents of organizational behavior: Dr. E.E. Southard and Mary Jarrett, the "Mental Hygiene of Industry", 1913–1920', Proceedings of the *Academy of Management*, pp. 17–21.

Yaziji, M. (2004), 'Turning gadflies into allies', *Harvard Business Review*, **82** (2), 110–15.

Yin, R. (1994), *Case Study Research: Design and Methods*, 2nd edition, Thousand Oaks, CA: Sage.

Young, D. (1999), 'Nonprofit management studies in the United States: Current developments and future prospects', *Journal of Public Affairs Education*, **5** (1), 13–23.

Yunus, M. and A. Jolis (2003), *Banker to the Poor: The Autobiography of Muhammad Yunus, Founder of the Grameen Bank*, London: Aurum.

Index

Aboriginal peoples 56, 77, 186
  see also indigenous peoples
abundantia 99, 109, 115, 117, 118, 119
academic discourse 121–2, 137–8
  accountability and blame 125
  business-non-business binary 128–9
  deconstructive practices 136–7
  deconstructive reading 123–35
  demise of present 127
  economic activity 129–30
  entitlement 125–6
  external pressures 127–8
  globalization 128
  maleness 135
  medical treatment analogy 124–5,
    126, 129–30
  normalization of business practices
    131–2
  one-sidedness and dependence 124–5
  paralogy 138–40
  progressive development 126–7
  rhetoric 122–3
  science 130–131
  social–non-social divide 132–3
  supernatural talents 133–5
  technical rationality 130
academic entrepreneurship 89–91
accumulation regime 69, 70–71, 74
Ackroyd, S. 95
adaptation 24, 25, 27
Addams, Jane 86–9, 92, 94
Adorno, T.W. 255
aequitas 99, 109, 115, 117, 118, 119
affiliation, financing by 40
agricultural economy 147
agricultural properties 146–8
Ahl, H. 237, 239
Aldrich, H. 94
alliances 71, 77, 80
altruism 27, 180
Aluma project 98, 111, 114, 117, 118
Alvesson, M. 191, 234, 237, 243, 246

Alvord, S.H. 62
America *see* US
Amnesty International 72
Andean indigenous peoples 56, 77
Anderson, R.B. 57, 77
androcentric economic theory 168
Anne's Perennials 176–8, 181, 182,
    184–5
articulation 212, 228, 229
Ashoka 80, 104
Asian Development Bank 59–60
assimilation models 65–7
associations 51
Atkinson, R. 241

Barns, I. 120
barter 173, 175
Bauman, Z. 99
Becker, J. 258
becoming otherwise 151–3, 154, 156,
    157, 161
belonging, narratives on 221–3
Berlin 266
'Big' Bengt Erlandsson 203–5, 206, 208
bioregionalism 184–5
Blumer, H. 92
boosterism 260
Bornstein, D. 21, 105
Boschee, J. 105
Botswana 172–4 *see also* Thuli
    (subsistence farmer)
boundary work 210–212, 222–3,
    227–8
  re-construction of actor networks
    226–7
  re-construction of traditions 224–6
Bourdieu, P. 36–7
Brewery, The 98, 111–12, 117, 118
Brown, D. 62
Buller, H. 149
Burr, V. 236, 243
business entrepreneurs 64, 104–5, 113

business schools 79, 80, 90, 92
Butler, B.E. 120

Canada 60
  Aboriginal peoples 56, 77
  Traill, Catharine Parr 174–6, 180,
    181, 182, 184
capitalism 22, 81, 100, 108
Capitalism, Socialism and Democracy
  (Schumpeter) 22
careers of social problems 92, 93–4, 95
Castells, M. 256
Catford, J. 104, 105, 132–3
Catherine B. Reynolds Foundation
  79–80
Centers for Independent Living (CIL) 41
Champion, T. 146, 147
change *see* economic change; social
  change
charity 38, 39, 44
Chia, R. 150
Chicago 88
citizen 100–101, 109, 114–15
citizenship 107–9, 114–18
city 256
City as Prey (Stadt als Beute) (Pollesch)
  251–2, 253, 261, 266
city management 258
city marketing 258, 260
city of enterprise 259–60, 261
cityspace 254, 256, 266, 268
civic entrepreneurs 103
civil sector organizations 72, 74
cluster strategies 210–211
Coates, J. 171, 172
Coleman, J.S. 36, 37, 53
collective activity 57, 77
collective entrepreneurship 208
collective identity 192, 208
  construction 188, 190, 198, 203, 227
  reconstruction 192, 201
colonization 67
commercial entrepreneurs 104, 105
commodification 48
common good 77
community 107
community-based economic
  development 76
Community-Based Enterprise (CBE) 77
community-building 176–8, 181, 185

community development 210, 216, 229
community enterprises 39, 44–5, 52
  Medvind 44–5, 52, 54
  see also cooperative enterprises
community entrepreneurs 103, 230
community entrepreneurship 228–30
community identity 188
  see also collective identity
community-rebuilding 65, 67
consumer 100–101, 107–9
contingency models 65, 68–72
contribution strategies 51–2
control societies 257–8
conversion of entitlements 39–41, 46
conversion practices 53
cooperative enterprises 48–51, 62
  community development enterprises
    39, 44–5, 52
  parents' cooperatives 40, 49, 55
  social cooperatives 39, 41–4, 49, 50,
    55
  STIL 41, 55
  welfare service cooperatives 39–41, 51
Corbridge, S. 68, 70
corporate social responsibility 81, 186
counterspaces 269
counterurbanization 146–8, 149
Cownie, D. 173
creative citizenship 117
creative destruction 21–2
credit cooperatives 51
creolization 202
cross-appropriation 212, 228, 229
Cruikshank, J. 89, 90, 91
culture vs business 219–21
Czarniawska, B. 139

Daes, E.I. 59
Davies, B. 237
Davoudi, S. 241
de Certeau, M. 7
De Leeuw, E. 134
De Leonardis, O. 130
debt crises 66
deconstructive readings 136–7
Dees, J.G. 63, 64, 133
Deetz, S. 234
Defourny, J. 5
Deleuze, G. 8, 252, 257, 258, 264
Delillo, D. 256–7

dependence 125
dependency theory 65, 67
Derrida, J. 123, 137, 140–141, 142
developer entrepreneur 151, 153–6
developing people *see* indigenous people
development 24, 25, 27, 65–6
    assimilation models 65–7
    contingency models 68–72
    dependency models 67–8
    and indigenous people 58, 65–72
    modernization models 65–7
    regulation theory 69–72
deviation 25–6, 224, 226, 227
    rock culture as 216–21
Dicken, P. 71
DiE (Diversity in Entrepreneurship) 231–2, 234, 240
Diederichsen, D. 266
disabled people 40–41, 42, 206
    integration strategies 41–5
discourse 139–40
    of entrepreneurship 238–41
    and identity 236–7
    of managerial entrepreneurialism 258
    and rhetoric 122
    see also academic discourse
discourse theatre 252–3, 255
Diversity in Entrepreneurship (DiE) 231–2, 234, 240
Dobers, P. 260
Doerr, John 80, 82
donations 6, 39, 52–3, 80, 93
Donham, Wallace B. 89, 90, 91, 92
down-shifting 160
Drayton, W. 80, 104
Dreyfus, H.L. 115, 116
du Gay, P. 129, 240
Dunning, J.H. 71
dynamic theory 30–31

eco-businesswomen 170, 176–8
ecofeminism 183–4, 185
ecofeminists 175, 179
economic capital to social capital 52–3
economic change 24, 29, 30, 32–3
economic development 30, 31, 61, 65, 76, 77
    assimilation models 65–7
    community-based 76
    contingency models 68–72

dependency models 67–8
    and indigenous people 58, 65–72
    modernization models 65–7
    regulation theory 69–72
economic discourse 249
economic entrepreneurs 133
economic entrepreneurship 33, 34, 56
economic globalization 66
economic resources 52–3
economic self-sufficiency 77
economic stagnation 223
economic theory 23, 25, 30, 31–2, 108, 168
    see also Schumpeter, J.A.
education 82, 98
egoism 27
Eliott, Howard 90
Ellison, Larry 80, 82
embedded resources 46–8
    see also social capital
embourgeoisement 147, 149, 152, 161
Emerson, J. 80
enterprise development 49, 63, 76
enterprise discourse 107, 232, 240, 244–5, 247–8, 253
    apocalyptic reading 255–9
entitlement 125–6
entitlements 46, 48
    pooling and conversion 39–41, 46
entrepreneur–client relationality 152–3
entrepreneur-developer 148, 153–4, 161
entrepreneur-developer clients 159–62
entrepreneurial cities 258, 259–60, 261, 264, 269–70
entrepreneurial discourses 247–9
entrepreneurial governance 258–9, 260
entrepreneurial identity 237, 244–7
    see also identity construction
entrepreneurial processes 180, 212–13
entrepreneurial self-creation 170
entrepreneurial spaces 254, 255, 268, 269
entrepreneurial women 182–6
    see also female entrepreneurs
entrepreneurs 27–9, 99, 147, 151, 235, 239
entrepreneurship 61–2, 63–4, 119–20
    bioregional view 184–5
    as boundary work 210–212
    definition 34, 75

discourses of 238–41
ecofeminist view 183–4
and life orientations 151–3
social constructionist view 210–212
social sphere 92, 94
survival subsistence view 185–6
see also indigenous entrepreneurship;
    public entrepreneurship; social
    entrepreneurship
entrepreneurship research 253–5, 261–2
equality discourse 232, 240–241, 245,
    249–50
Erlandsson, 'Big' Bengt 203–5, 206, 208
ethics 99, 141–2
ethnic entrepreneurship 75–6
European Economic Union 72
experience economy 208
experiential learning 206
external pressures 127–8

Fair Play 98, 113–14, 117, 118
family as value source 198–200
female entrepreneurs 172, 182–6, 190,
    207–8
    Anne's Perennials 176–8, 181, 182,
        184–5
    Lena (keep-fit company) 232–3,
        242–3, 246–7, 249
    Sara (mushroom company) 232–3,
        241, 243, 244–5, 247–8
    Thuli (subsistence farmer) 172–4,
        176, 180, 181, 182
    Traill, Catharine Parr 174–6, 180,
        181, 182, 184
female support systems 181
feminist shared texts 178–81
Fielding, A. 146, 149
Fielding, T. 147
financing by affiliation 40
firstspace epistemologies 262–3, 269
Fletcher, D.E. 151
Flexner, Abraham 90
for-profit educational enterprises 80, 82
for-profit organizations 61, 62, 64
Ford family (urban shifters) 159–62
Fordist regime of accumulation 70, 71
Foscarinis, M. 84, 85
Foucault, M. 100, 255, 257, 264, 265,
    268
Fournier, V. 245

Galaskiewicz, J. 81
Game, A. 139
gap between rich and poor 67, 104
gardeners, women 176–8
gardening 112–13, 69, 179
gardens 117
Gates, Bill 80
gatherer-hunter societies 58, 166
gender 135, 239–40
Gentile, M.C. 3–4
geographic dislocation 56
geographic mobility 159
Giberson, R. 57
global economic system 70, 71, 72, 104
global economy 68, 69, 72
global entrepreneurship 62
global institutions 67, 72
globalization 128
Gnosjö 188–91, 207–9
    business community, social world
        194–8, 202, 203–7
    collective identity 192, 201, 208
    Erlandsson, 'Big' Bengt 203–5, 206,
        208
    family as value source 198–200
    master narrative 192–4, 196, 197,
        200, 207
    Mr. Gnosjö 196, 205–6
    outsider/insider relationship 203–7
    patriarchal society 199–200, 204
    Spirit of Gnosjö 191, 192–3, 196,
        197, 202, 207–8
    values and norms 198–200, 201–2,
        204, 205
Goldman, S. 71
Goldthorpe, J.H. 149–50
Gordon, C. 101, 107
governmental organizations 62
governmentality 100, 126
Gray, C. 174, 175
green capitalism movement 186
green revolution 66
Green Room project 98, 112–13, 117
grounded enterprise 179
grounded entrepreneurship 181, 186–7
group survival 181
Guattari, F. 264
Guclu, A. 131

habitual entrepreneurs 206

Hall, P. 95
Hall, T. 259, 263
handicapped people 40–41, 42, 206
    integration strategies 41–5
Hannerz, U. 202
Harré, R. 237
Harris, M. 109
Harvard 79–80, 92
Harvard Business School (HBS) 89–90,
    91
'Heidi Hoh' plays (Pollesch) 257
heterotopias 264, 265, 266, 267, 268
heterotopic space 265
heterotopology 265, 268
Hettne, B. 67
High Chaparral 204, 206
high-profile social entrepreneurship
    (HPSE) 79–83, 91
high-tech CEOs 80
high-tech entrepreneurship 81–2
Hindle, K. 63
Hirschman, A.O. 100, 108
Hirst, P. 69, 70
Hjorth, D. 137–8, 180, 253
Home Service project 98, 112, 115, 116,
    117, 118
Homeless Eligibility Clarification Act
    84
homeless people 98, 111, 114, 118
    see also Aluma project
homelessness 83–4
homelessness industry 83–6, 92
homelessness movement 84
Homer-Dixon, T. 170
Honig, B. 76
horticulture *see* gardening
Hosking, D.M. 169
*How to Change the World: Social
    Entrepreneurs and the Power of
    New Ideas* (Bornstein) 21
HPSE (high-profile social
    entrepreneurship) 79–83, 91
Hubbard, P. 259, 263
Hull House 86, 87–9, 94
    see also settlement houses
Hultsfred 214, 216, 223, 225
    boundary work 224–8
    community–RockCity relations
        228–30
    culture vs business 219–21

    deviation and belonging 216–19,
        221–3, 226, 227
    identity construction 224–7, 228
    RockCity 214, 215, 218–19, 224–6,
        227
    RockParty 214–15, 216–17
Hultsfred Festival 214, 216, 219–21,
    227
Hunt, A. 109, 118
hunter-gatherers 58, 166

ICS cooperative 42, 44
idealistic entrepreneurs 103
identity and discourse 236–7
identity construction 188, 224–6, 226–7,
    228, 232–3, 237
identity work 237, 243–4
immigrant populations 75
immigrants 42, 112, 189, 198
import substitution 67
independent living cooperatives 40–41,
    49
    Centers for Independent Living (CIL)
        41
    STIL (Stockholm Independent
        Living) 41, 55
indigenous enterprises 71
indigenous entrepreneurship 12, 57, 61,
    62–3, 64, 72
    from within communities 77
    and ethnic entrepreneurship 75–6
    and social entrepreneurship 75, 76–8
indigenous peoples 56, 58–61, 77
    of Andean countries 56, 77
    assimilation models 65–7
    of Canada 56, 77
    community rebuilding 65, 67
    contingency models 68–72
    definitions 58–60
    dependency models 67–8
    economic development 58, 65–72
    and global economy 72–5
    and institutional forces 72–5
    modernization models 65–7
    nation rebuilding 56, 62–3
    regulation theory 69–72
    UN Draft Declaration on the Rights
        of Indigenous Peoples 60
individualism 103
individualist discourse 135

industrialization 56, 145
innovation 36, 212
insiders in social worlds 194, 198, 202,
    205, 207
institutional forces and indigenous
    people 72–5
integration of disabled people 41–5
    high-profile strategy 44–5
    low-key strategy 41–4
intrinsic rewards 180
Inuit people 56, 77

Jahn, W. 258
Jante Law 201, 221, 275
jazz improvization analogy 171–2, 179
Jessop, B. 259
job-creation cooperatives 42
Johannisson, B. 167, 253
Johansson, A.W. 232, 244, 248
Johnstone, H. 168
joint ventures 77
justice 141–2

Kao, R.W. 75
Katrineholm 231–2
    see also Lena (keep-fit entrepreneur);
        Sara (mushroom entrepreneur)
Katz, J. 138, 238
Kaufman 94
keep-fit company see Lena (keep-fit
    entrepreneur)
Kerston 146, 148, 153–6
    see also property entrepreneurs;
        urban–rural migration
KFV region 233–4, 243
kinship 198
    see also family
knowledge 126, 131
    unequal distribution of 124
KnowledgeUniverse 82

labour-market integration strategy 41–4
Laclau, E. 240
languaging 111
Lanz, S. 258
Laura Spelman Rockefeller Fund
    (LSRM) 91
Leadbeater, C. 4
leaders 26
    see also entrepreneurs

Leapfrog Enterprises 82
Lefebvre, H. 262, 263, 265, 269
legitimacy building 93
Lena (keep-fit entrepreneur) 232–3,
    242–3, 246–7, 249
Letts, C.W. 62
life orientations 150–153, 155, 156, 159
life-style business 180
Liggett, H. 262, 269
Lindgren, M. 232, 233
Lindner, R. 256
Lionais, D. 168
lived spaces 254, 264–8
    of representation 269
localized enterprises 165
location marketing 258, 260
Lockwood, D. 149–50
Ludlow massacre 91
Lyotard, J.F. 139, 140

Making Democracy Work (Putnam) 37
male bias discourse 135, 239–40
Malmö 111–12, 117–18
Man of Action 26–7
    see also entrepreneurs
management knowledge 116
managerial entrepreneurship 252, 258
Maori, New Zealand 56, 77
marginalized people 42, 206
market mechanisms 256
marketing cities 260
Martinez, M. 94
master narrative 192–4, 253
Mauri, D. 130
Mayo, Elton 89, 90–91, 92–3, 94
McAdams, D.P. 243
McLeod, H. 103
meaningful work 179
medical treatment analogy 124–5, 126,
    129–30
Medvind 44–5, 52, 54
    see also community enterprises
mentally handicapped people 42, 44, 206
mentoring approach to social
    entrepreneurship 80
Metcalfe, A. 139
Metropolis and Mental Life (Simmel)
    256
Mies, M. 183, 185–6
Milken, Michael 82

mode of social regulation (MSR) 70,
    71–2, 74
modernization theory 65–7, 68
Monroe, L. 265, 267
Moore, M. 66
moral currency 93
moral poverty 93
Morris, C. 149
Morris, M. 75
Mort, G.S. 127–8, 135
Mother Earth 169, 179, 180, 184, 186
Mouffe, C. 240
multigenerational timeline 180
multinational corporation 67
mundane entrepreneurs 103
mushroom company *see* Sara
    (mushroom entrepreneur)
music industry as deviation 218–19
mutuality 39

NAFTA 66, 72
narratives 182, 192
    on deviating and belonging 216–24
nation rebuilding 56, 62–3
nation states 77
natural capitalism movement 186
negative growth 66
neoliberalism 107
networks 52, 76, 112, 118
    closure 54–5
new combinations 28, 29, 33, 94
new-Swedes 98, 117
New Zealand 56, 60, 77
Newhall, Eddie 148, 153–6, 157–8, 161
Newhall, Sylvie 156–9, 161–2
non-business practices 132
non-development 25–6
non-entrepreneurial organizations 129
non-entrepreneurial person 26–7
non-governmental organizations (NGOs)
    62, 72
non-market property-rights 48
non-market resources *see* social capital
non-monetary success 180
non-profit organizations 104
non-public initiatives 40
normalization 115, 116
    of business practices 131–2
not-for-profit organizations 64

Ogbor, J.O. 238, 239
old shipyard park 98, 111, 114, 117, 118
Open Gardens 112
opportunity enactment 151, 152, 154–5,
    163
Order of Things (Foucault) 265
Orenstein, G.F. 171, 184
organization theory 150
organizational behaviour 91
organizational development 91
organizing relationships 150
orientations 150
Österlen 112
otherness 245
outdoor skateboard arena 98, 111, 114,
    117, 118
outsiders in social worlds 203, 205, 207

Painter, J. 259–60
paralogy 138–9, 140
parents' cooperatives 40, 49, 55
patriarchal society 168, 199–200, 204
Peace Corps 83
Pearce, J. 132
Peredo, A.M. 77
Perot, Ross 80
personality traits 135
personnel policies and practices 91
Pettersson, K. 190, 196, 199, 207–8
philanthropists 80–81, 91
philanthropy 80–81, 82, 93
physical work, healing power of 179–80
physically handicapped people 40–41,
    206
place 168, 179, 184
Plant, J. 170, 184
Polanyi, K. 48, 70
Polikoff, B. 87, 88, 89
Pollesch, R. 252, 261, 264–5, 267
    City as Prey (Stadt als Beute) 251–2,
        253, 261, 266
    'Heidi Hoh' plays 257
pooling entitlements 39–41, 46
pooling resources 49
Portes, A. 36, 37
post-industrial society 68
Potter, J. 126
poverty 58, 66, 83, 84
power 238–9
    through female support systems 181

power structures 193
PR-entrepreneur 156–9
procurement strategies 51–2
profit 104–5, 132–3
property developers 148, 153–4
property entrepreneurs 151, 153–6
property rights 46, 48
property rights regimes 51
public 97, 99–101
public entrepreneurs 115, 117
public entrepreneurship 99, 117,
        119–20
    Brewery, The 98, 111–12, 117, 118
    and citizenship 114–18
    consumer to citizen 107–9
    Fair Play 98, 113, 117, 118
    Green Room 98, 112–13, 117
    Home Service 98, 112, 115, 116, 117,
        118
    old shipyard park 98, 111, 114, 117,
        118
    social to public 106–7
    sociality, creating 116–18
    workshops 110–11, 113–14
public space 108, 109, 114, 115, 118,
        119
punk rebels 214, 216–17
Putnam, R.D. 37

quilting analogy 171

Rabinow, P. 115, 116
rational choice 26, 27
Reagan, President Ronald 84, 85
reciprocated typification 93
reciprocity 48, 51, 52, 180
reconceptualized time 180
reconfiguration 212, 228, 229
regime of accumulation 69, 70–71, 74
regulars in social worlds 194, 197, 198,
        203
regulation theory 65, 69–72
rehabilitation services 43
relational choice 157
relational networks 75–6
relational thinking 151, 152
relationality 158–9, 163
relationship building 181
representational spaces 262, 263, 265,
        269

representations of space 262, 269
resources 12
    conversion 40
    embedded 46–8
    non-market, conversion of 46–52
    see also social capital
responsibility 107, 141–2
responsible entrepreneurship 186
rhetorical readings 136–7
Rich, A. 184
risk-taking 135
Robert, George R. 80
rock festivals *see* Hultsfred Festival
rock music culture as deviation 216–18
RockCity 214, 215, 218–19, 224–6, 227,
        228–30
    see also Hultsfred; Hultsfred Festival
Rockefeller, John D. 89, 91, 92
Rockefeller University 91
RockParty 214–15, 216–17
    see also Hultsfred
Ronneberger, K. 258
Rorty, R. 120
Ruether, R.R. 166, 167, 168, 172, 186
rural communities 145–6, 151
    embourgeoisement 147, 149, 152,
        161
rural economy 185
rural properties 146–8
rural social change 146, 152–3, 162–4
rural–urban shifters 159–62

Sara (mushroom entrepreneur) 232–3,
        241–3, 244–5, 247–8
Sarasvathy, S. 238, 247
Schumpeter, J.A. 11, 21, 24
    *Capitalism, Socialism and
        Democracy* 22
    creative destruction 21–2
    entrepreneurship and social change
        21–4, 32–4
    *Theorie der Wirtschaftlichen
        Entwicklung* 11, 22–3
    (Chapter 2) 23, 24–9
    (Chapter 7) 23, 30–32
    Theory of Economic Development 11,
        23
    younger, more radical 24–5
Schuyler, G. 105
Scott, A.J. 69

secondspace epistemologies 263, 269
self-creating women 182–6
    see also Anne's Perennials; Lena
        (keep-fit entrepreneur); Sara
        (mushroom entrepreneur);
        Thuli (subsistence farmer);
        Traill, Catharine Parr
self-employment 118
self-esteem 201
self-identity 236–7
self-regulating markets 61
Sensenbrenner, J. 36, 37
settlement house movement 86, 88
settlement houses 86, 89
    see also Hull House; Toynbee Hall
Shiva, V. 183, 185
Sierra Club 72
Silicon Valley 80, 81
Silverman, D. 150
Simmel, G. 256
skateboard park 98, 111, 114, 117, 118
Sköldberg, K. 191, 204, 205
Skoll Foundation 80
Skoll, Jeff 6, 80
Snyder, Mitch 83–4, 85
soccer team training 98, 113
social 99–101
social becoming 152–3
social benefits 62
social capital 36–8, 48–9
    and community enterprises 44–5
    conversion 39–41, 51–3
    to economic capital 51–2
    from economic capital 52–3
    entitlements 39–41
    to other social capital 52
    pooling of 40–41, 42–3, 49
    and social cooperatives 41–4
    and welfare cooperatives 39–41
social cauldron 94
social change 149–50, 163, 201
    opportunity enactment 151, 152,
        154–5, 163
    in rural communities 147–8, 151,
        152
social cohesion 56
social control 37
social cooperatives 39, 41–4, 49, 55
    see also cooperative enterprises
social creativity 119

social enterprises 105, 126–7, 129, 132
    community development enterprises
        44–5
    independent living cooperatives
        40–41, 49, 55
    medical treatment analogy 124,
        126–7
    parents' cooperatives 40, 49, 55
    social cooperatives 39, 41–4, 49, 55
    in Sweden 38–45
    welfare service cooperatives 39–41,
        51
social entrepreneurs 53–4, 64, 133, 134
    and business entrepreneurs,
        difference 104–5
    characteristics of 105
    gendered division 135
social entrepreneurship 3–6, 21, 33,
        61–4, 103–6
    academic discourse *see* academic
        discourse
    definitions of 62
    high-profile 79–83, 91
    opportunities for 91–6
    research funding 6, 79–80
    and social capital 36–8, 51
    see also entrepreneurship; indigenous
        entrepreneurship; public
        entrepreneurship
social exclusion 241
social investing 80–81
social learning 206
social mission 64
social mobility 159, 161
social problems 92, 119
    careers of 92, 93–4, 95
social protest 84, 92
social purpose entrepreneurs 124
social regulation 70, 71–2, 74
social science research narratives 192
social space 107, 109, 258
social sphere of entrepreneurship 92, 94
social to public 106–7
social value 64, 105
social venture portfolios 80–81
social welfare 112
social well-being 61
social worlds 190, 194–5, 198, 203, 207
sociality 101, 109, 114, 115
    creation of 9, 116–18, 119
    in a public space 110, 117

socially embedded resources 46
socially produced space 269
socially responsible businesses 64
Soja, E.W. 256, 262, 263
space 167–8, 179, 184
　cityspace 254, 256, 266, 268
　commodification of 256
　heterotopic space 265
　lived 254, 264–8, 269
　public 108, 109, 114, 115, 118
　representational 262, 263, 265,
　　269
　representations of 262, 269
　social 107, 109, 258
　thirdspace 263, 264, 267–8, 270
　urban 252, 253, 254, 268, 269
spaces 262, 269
spatial practice 262
spatial processes 262, 269
spatial thinking 262–4, 269, 270
special interest groups 72
species survival 166–8
Spinosa, C. 115, 116, 226, 228
Spirit of Gnosjö 191, 192–3, 196, 197,
　202, 207–8
　see also Gnosjö
sponsoring 52–3
sports 98, 113
Stadt als Beute (Pollesch) 251–2, 253,
　261, 266
stagflation recession 84
start-up services 112, 116
state 72, 74
static economic behaviour 25–6, 31
static person 26–7
static theory 30
statics 25–6
Steyaert, C. 137–8, 170, 180, 238, 253
STIL (Stockholm Independent Living)
　41, 55
Stone, M. 167
stories of place 170
strangers in social worlds 194, 196, 198,
　202, 203
strategic philanthropy 81, 82
Sturgeon, N. 183
subsistence economies 180, 185
subsistence farming 172–4, 182
subsistence gardening 166
subsistence in Botswana 172–4

success, non-monetary 180
supernatural talents 133–5
support systems 181
supranational bodies 72, 74
survival subsistence 185–6
sustainable development 186–7
Sveningsson, S. 237, 243, 246
sweat equity 43
Sweden
　community development enterprises
　　44–5
　new-Swedes 98, 117
　social cooperatives 41–4
　welfare service cooperatives 39–41
　welfare state 38–41
　workshops 110–114
　see also Gnosjö
Szablowski, D. 74

Taylor, F. 81
technical rationality 130
technological developments 68
tenant farmers 147, 148, 151
*Theorie der Wirtschaftlichen
　Entwicklung* (Schumpeter) 11,
　22–3
　(Chapter 2) 23, 24–9
　(Chapter 7) 23, 30–32
Theory of Economic Development
　(Schumpeter) 11, 23
thirdspace 263, 264, 267–8, 270
thirdspace epistemologies 263–4, 269,
　270
Thompson, J. 105, 125, 131–2, 134
Thuli (subsistence farmer) 172–4, 176,
　180, 181, 182
time, reconceptualized 180
TIME sector 225, 229
Toffler, A. 68
tourist industry 112
tourists in social worlds 194–5, 197,
　198, 203
Toynbee, Arnold 86
Toynbee Hall 86–7, 88
　see also Hull House; settlement
　　houses
traditional culture 66, 77
traditional lands 77
traditional values 77, 200
Trahair, R. 89, 90, 91

Traill, Catharine Parr 174–6, 180, 181,
    182, 184
trust 44, 45
Tucker, V. 68

UK
    farming community 147
    urban–rural migration 146, 148, 149,
        151
    see also Kerston
underdeveloped populations *see*
    indigenous peoples
underdevelopment 67
underprivileged people 124
unemployment 112, 117
United Nations (UN) 59, 72
    Draft Declaration on the Rights of
        Indigenous Peoples 60
University of Chicago 91
Unruh, D. 190, 194
urban discourses 259, 261
urban entrepreneurialism 259–60, 261,
    263, 269
urban life 256
urban–rural migration 146, 148, 149,
    151
urban–rural shifters 146–8, 156–9, 161
urban spaces 252, 253, 254, 268, 269
urbanization 145, 256, 258
US
    academic entrepreneurship 89–91
    Centers for Independent Living (CIL)
        41
    Great Society 83
    high-profile social entrepreneurship
        (HPSE) 79–83, 91
    homelessness industry 83–6
    Hull House 86, 87–9, 94
    settlement house movement 86, 88

value sources 99, 198

values and norms 77, 200, 203
venture capitalists 80, 82
venture philanthropy 80
voluntary work 51, 214, 215, 217

Wåhlin, N. 232, 233
Wal-Mart 82
Wallace, S.L. 123, 129
War on Poverty 83
Watson, T.J. 151
Weber, M. 256
welfare cooperatives 39–41, 51
welfare entitlements 39–40, 42–3
    see also social capital
welfare state 38–41, 104, 107
Wendeberg, B. 199, 201
White, M. 109, 118
women entrepreneurs 172, 182, 190,
    207–8
    Anne's Perennials 176–8, 181, 182,
        184–5
    Lena (keep-fit company) 232–3,
        242–3, 246–7, 249
    Sara (mushroom company) 232–3,
        241, 243, 244–5, 247–8
    Thuli (subsistence farmer) 172–4,
        176, 180, 181, 182
    Traill, Catharine Parr 174–6, 180,
        181, 182, 184
women's movement 183
work orientations 149–50
worker-cooperatives 41–2
World Bank 58, 59, 67, 72, 74
World Council of Indigenous People 72
World Trade Organization (WTO) 66,
    67, 72
Wright, E. 149

youth park *see* old shipyard park

Zeitlin, J. 69, 70